Handbook of Geriatric Oncology

Practical Guide to Caring for the Older Cancer Patient

Editors

Beatriz Korc-Grodzicki, MD, PhD
*Chief, Geriatrics Service, Department of Medicine, Memorial Sloan
  Kettering Cancer Center, and Professor of Clinical Medicine, Weill
  Cornell Medical College*
New York, New York

William P. Tew, MD
*Associate Attending Physician, Memorial Sloan Kettering Cancer Center,
  and Associate Professor of Medicine, Weill Cornell Medical College*
New York, New York

demosMEDICAL
New York

Visit our website at www.demosmedical.com

ISBN: 9781620701041
e-book ISBN: 9781617052828

Acquisitions Editor: David D'Addona
Compositor: diacriTech

Medicine is an ever-changing science. Research and clinical experience are continually expanding our knowledge, in particular our understanding of proper treatment and drug therapy. The authors, editors, and publisher have made every effort to ensure that all information in this book is in accordance with the state of knowledge at the time of production of the book. Nevertheless, the authors, editors, and publisher are not responsible for errors or omissions or for any consequences from application of the information in this book and make no warranty, expressed or implied, with respect to the contents of the publication. Every reader should examine carefully the package inserts accompanying each drug and should carefully check whether the dosage schedules mentioned therein or the contraindications stated by the manufacturer differ from the statements made in this book. Such examination is particularly important with drugs that are either rarely used or have been newly released on the market.

Library of Congress Cataloging-in-Publication Data
Names: Korc-Grodzicki, Beatriz, editor. | Tew, William P., editor.
Title: Handbook of geriatric oncology : practical guide to caring for the
    older cancer patient / editors, Beatriz Korc-Grodzicki, William P. Tew.
Description: New York : Demos Medical Publishing, [2017] | Includes
    bibliographical references and index.
Identifiers: LCCN 2017011329| ISBN 9781620701041 | ISBN 9781617052828 (e-book)
Subjects: | MESH: Neoplasms—therapy | Aged | Patient-Centered Care | Aging—physiology
Classification: LCC RC281.A34 | NLM QZ 266 | DDC 618.97/6994—dc23
LC record available at https://lccn.loc.gov/2017011329

Printed in the United States of America by McNaughton & Gunn.
16 17 18 19 20 / 5 4 3 2 1

Contents

Section III. Geriatric Assessment

Section IV. Select Cancers in the Elderly

Contributors

Theresa Affuso, LAc   Acupuncturist, Integrative Medicine, Memorial Sloan Kettering Cancer Center, New York, New York

Koshy Alexander, MD   Assistant Attending, Geriatrics, Memorial Sloan Kettering Cancer Center, Weill Cornell Medical Center, New York, New York

Mariam Alexander, MD, PhD   Resident, Department of Medicine, Upstate Medical University, Syracuse, New York

Shabbir M. H. Alibhai, MD, MSc   Associate Professor, Department of Medicine, University Health Network and University of Toronto, Toronto, Ontario, Canada

Yesne Alici, MD   Assistant Attending Psychiatrist, Memorial Sloan Kettering Cancer Center, New York, New York

Keith M. Bellizzi, PhD, MPH   Associate Professor, Human Development and Family Studies, University of Connecticut, Storrs, Connecticut

Marc Bonnefoy, MD, PhD   Professor, Oncogeriatric Unit, Geriatric Department Centre, Hospitalier Lyon Sud, Pierre-Bénite Cedex, Lyon University, Lyon, France

Manpreet K. Boparai, PharmD, BCACP, CGP   Geriatric Clinical Pharmacy Specialist, Department of Pharmacy, Memorial Sloan Kettering Cancer Center, New York, New York

Emily Chai, MD   Associate Professor, Brookdale Department of Geriatrics and Palliative Medicine, and Director, Lillian and Benjamin Hertzberg Palliative Care Institute, Icahn School of Medicine at Mount Sinai, New York, New York

Andrew Chapman, DO, FACP   Clinical Professor and Vice Chair for Clinical Operations, Department of Medical Oncology, Thomas Jefferson University Hospital, Philadelphia, Pennsylvania

Melissa Crawley, MD   Fellow, Division of Hematology/Oncology, University of Tennessee, Health Science University, Memphis, Tennessee

Gary Deng, MD, PhD   Medical Director, Integrative Medicine Service, Memorial Sloan Kettering Cancer Center, New York, New York

Anca Dinescu, MD   Physician, Geriatrics, Extended Care and Palliative Care Department, Washington VA Medical Center, Washington; Assistant Professor Internal Medicine, George Washington University, Washington, DC

Patrick Doggett, MD   Geriatric Fellow, Department of Family and Community Medicine, Geriatric and Palliative Care Division, Thomas Jefferson University Hospital, Philadelphia, Pennsylvania

Claire Falandry, MD, PhD   Professor, Gynecology Oncology, Geriatric Department Centre, Hospitalier Lyon Sud, Pierre-Bénite Cedex, Lyon University, Lyon, France

Carolyn Fulton, LCSW-R   Clinical Social Worker II, Memorial Sloan Kettering Cancer Center, New York, New York

Ajeet Gajra, MD, FACP   Physician and Professor of Medicine, Department of Medicine, Upstate Medical University, Syracuse, New York

Francesca Gany, MD, MS   Chief, Immigrant Health and Cancer Disparities Center, Department of Psychiatry and Behavioral Sciences, Memorial Sloan Kettering Cancer Center; Professor of Medicine and Professor of Healthcare Policy and Research, Weill Cornell Medical College, New York, New York

Suzanne D. Gerdes, MS, RD, CDN   Clinical Dietitian/Nutritionist, Department of Food and Nutrition, Memorial Sloan Kettering Cancer Center, New York, New York

Sergio Giralt, MD   Melvin Berlin Family Chair in Myeloma Research, Professor of Medicine, Weill Cornell Medical College; Chief Attending, Adult BMT Service, Memorial Sloan Kettering Cancer Center, New York, New York

Paul Glare, MBBS, FRACP, FFPMANZCA, FACP   Chair, Department of Pain Medicine, University of Sydney, Pain Management Research Institute, St. Leonards, Australia

Javier Gonzalez, MFA   Director of Linguistics and Cultural Responsiveness, Immigrant Health and Cancer Disparities Center, Department of Psychiatry and Behavioral Sciences, Memorial Sloan Kettering Cancer Center, New York, New York

Bonnie E. Gould Rothberg, MD, PhD, MPH   Assistant Professor of Medicine (Medical Oncology), Epidemiology and Pathology, Yale Cancer Center, Yale School of Medicine, New Haven, Connecticut

Paul A. Hamlin, MD   Chief Attending, Lymphoma Service, Department of Medicine, Memorial Sloan Kettering Cancer Center, New York, New York

Mahdi Harchaoui, MD   Physician, Oncogeriatric Unit, Geriatric Department Centre, Hospitalier Lyon Sud, Pierre-Bénite Cedex, Lyon University, Lyon, France

Marine Haution-Bitker, MD   Physician, Oncogeriatric Unit, Geriatric Department Centre, Hospitalier Lyon Sud, Pierre-Bénite Cedex, Lyon University, Lyon, France

Nikesha Haynes-Gilmore, PhD   Clinical Project Manager, James P. Wilmot Cancer Institute, University of Rochester School of Medicine and Dentistry, Rochester, New York

Holly M. Holmes, MD, MS   Associate Professor and Division Director, Division of Geriatric and Palliative Medicine, The University of Texas Houston Health Science Center; Associate Professor, McGovern Medical School, Houston, Texas

Li-Wen Huang, MD   Clinical Fellow, Division of Hematology-Oncology, University of California San Francisco, San Francisco, California

Xiaoxiao Huang, MA   Language Service Education/Training Coordinator, Immigrant Health and Cancer Disparities Service, Department of Psychiatry and Behavioral Sciences, Memorial Sloan Kettering Cancer Center, New York, New York

Reena Jaiswal, MD   Assistant Attending Psychiatrist, Memorial Sloan Kettering Cancer Center, New York, New York

Trevor A. Jolly, MBBS   Assistant Professor, Lineberger Comprehensive Cancer Center, Division of Geriatric Medicine & Center for Aging and Health Department of Medicine, University of North Carolina, Chapel Hill, North Carolina

Ravindran Kanesvaran, MD, MRCP (UK)   Consultant, Division of Medical Oncology, National Cancer Centre Singapore, Singapore

Cindy Kenis, RN, PhD   Geriatric Oncology Nurse and Chair of the SIOG Nursing & Allied Health Interest Group, Department of General Medical Oncology and Geriatric Medicine, University Hospitals Leuven, Leuven, Belgium

Soo Jung Kim, MSN, ANP, AGPCNP-BC   Memorial Sloan Kettering Cancer Center, New York, New York.

Beatriz Korc-Grodzicki, MD, PhD   Chief, Geriatrics Service, Department of Medicine, Memorial Sloan Kettering Cancer Center; Professor of Clinical Medicine, Weill Cornell Medical College, New York, New York

Olivia Le Saux, MSc   Resident, Oncogeriatric Unit, Geriatric Department, Centre, Hospitalier Lyon Sud, Pierre-Bénite Cedex, Lyon University, Lyon, France

Clémence Lecardonnel, MD   Physician, Oncogeriatric Unit, Geriatric Department Centre, Hospitalier Lyon Sud, Pierre-Bénite Cedex, Lyon University, Lyon, France

Chung-Han Lee, MD, PhD   Assistant Attending, Department of Medicine, Memorial Sloan Kettering Cancer Center, Weill Cornell Medical Center, New York, New York

Jessica Lee, MD, MS   Assistant Professor, The University of Texas Houston Health Science Center; Associate Professor, McGovern Medical School, Houston, Texas

Stuart M. Lichtman, MD   Attending, Medical Oncology, Department of Medicine, Memorial Sloan Kettering Cancer Center, New York, New York

Kah Poh Loh, MBBCh BAO   Geriatric Oncology/Hematology Fellow, James P. Wilmot Cancer Institute, University of Rochester School of Medicine and Dentistry, Rochester, New York

Sincere McMillan, MS, RN, ANP-BC   Nurse Practitioner, Geriatrics, Department of Medicine, Memorial Sloan Kettering Cancer Center, New York, New York

Ronald J. Maggiore, MD   Assistant Professor of Medicine, James P. Wilmot Cancer Institute, University of Rochester, Rochester, New York

Allison Magnuson, DO   Assistant Professor, James P. Wilmot Cancer Institute, University of Rochester School of Medicine and Dentistry, Rochester, New York

Linda Mathew, LCSW, OSW-C Clinical Social Worker II, Memorial Sloan Kettering Cancer Center, New York, New York

Supriya G. Mohile, MD, MS Associate Professor, James P. Wilmot Cancer Institute, University of Rochester School of Medicine and Dentistry, Rochester, New York

Florence Murard-Reeman, MD Physician, Oncogeriatric Unit, Geriatric Department Centre, Hospitalier Lyon Sud, Pierre-Bénite Cedex, Lyon University, Lyon, France

Hyman B. Muss, MD Mary Jones Hudson Distinguished Professor of Geriatric Oncology, Professor of Medicine, University of North Carolina; Director of Geriatric Oncology, Lineberger Comprehensive Cancer Center, Chapel Hill, North Carolina

Christian J. Nelson, PhD Associate Attending, Department of Psychiatry and Behavioral Sciences, Memorial Sloan Kettering Cancer Center, Weill Cornell Medical Center, New York, New York

Ginah Nightingale, PharmD, BCOP, CGP Assistant Professor, Department of Pharmacy Practice, Jefferson College of Pharmacy, Thomas Jefferson University, Philadelphia, Pennsylvania

Colette Owens, MD Instructor, Medical Oncology Service, Division of Network Medicine Services, Memorial Sloan Kettering Cancer Center, New York, New York

Martine T. E. Puts, RN, PhD Assistant Professor, Canadian Institutes of Health; New Investigator, Lawrence S. Bloomberg Faculty of Nursing, University of Toronto, Toronto, Ontario, Canada

Arati V. Rao, MD Director, Clinical Research, Hematology-Oncology, Gilead Sciences, Inc., Foster City, California

Dana E. Rathkopf, MD Assistant Attending, Department of Medicine, Memorial Sloan Kettering Cancer Center, New York, New York

Pedro Recabal, MD Fellow, Urology Service, Department of Surgery, Memorial Sloan Kettering Cancer Center, New York, New York; Department of Urology, Fundacion Arturo Lopez Perez, Santiago, Chile

Miriam B. Rodin, MD, PhD, CMD Professor of Geriatric Medicine, Department of Internal Medicine, Division of Geriatric Medicine, St. Louis University Medical School, St. Louis, Missouri

Benedicte Rønning, MD Department of Geriatric Medicine, Oslo University Hospital; Institute of Clinical Medicine, University of Oslo, Oslo, Norway

Siri Rostoft, MD, PhD Assistant professor, Department of Geriatric Medicine, Oslo University Hospital; Institute of Clinical Medicine, University of Oslo, Oslo, Norway

Andrew J. Roth, MD Attending, Department of Psychiatry and Behavioral Sciences, Memorial Sloan Kettering Cancer Center; Clinical Professor of Psychiatry, Weill Cornell Medical Center, New York, New York

Rebecca Saracino, MA   Pre-doctoral Research Fellow, Fordham University, New York, New York

Shlomit Strulov Shachar, MD   Attending, Lineberger Comprehensive Cancer Center, Division of Oncology, Department of Medicine, University of North Carolina, Chapel Hill, North Carolina

Armin Shahrokni, MD, MPH   Assistant Attending, Department of Medicine/ Geriatrics & Gastrointestinal Oncology Services, Memorial Sloan Kettering Cancer Center, New York, New York

Kevin J. Shih, MD   Internal Medicine Resident, PGY2, The University of Texas Houston Health Science Center; Associate Professor, McGovern Medical School, Houston, Texas

Jonathan Siman, LAc   Acupuncturist, Integrative Medicine, Memorial Sloan Kettering Cancer Center, New York, New York

Shreya Sinha, MD   Fellow, Hematology, Department of Medicine, Upstate Medical University, Syracuse, New York

Kristine Swartz, MD   Assistant Professor, Department of Family and Community Medicine, Geriatric and Palliative Care Division, Thomas Jefferson University Hospital, Philadelphia, Pennsylvania

William P. Tew, MD   Associate Attending Physician, Memorial Sloan Kettering Cancer Center; Associate Professor of Medicine, Weill Cornell Medical College, New York, New York

Noam VanderWalde, MD   Director of Clinical Research, Department of Radiation Oncology, West Cancer Center; Assistant Professor, University of Tennessee Health Science Center, Memphis, Tennessee

Katherine Wang, MD   Assistant Professor, Brookdale Department of Geriatrics and Palliative Medicine, Icahn School of Medicine at Mount Sinai, New York, New York

Sophie Watelet, MD   Physician, Oncogeriatric Unit, Geriatric Department Centre, Hospitalier Lyon Sud, Pierre-Bénite Cedex, Lyon University, Lyon, France

Grant R. Williams, MD   Assistant Professor, Divisions of Hematology/Oncology & Gerontology, Geriatrics, and Palliative Care, Institute for Cancer Outcomes and Survivorship, University of Alabama at Birmingham, Birmingham, Alabama

Donna J. Wilson, RN, MSN, RRT   Clinical Fitness Specialist/Personal Trainer, Integrative Medicine Center, Memorial Sloan Kettering Cancer Center, New York, New York

Elizabeth Won, MD   Assistant Attending, Department of Medicine, Gastrointestinal Medical Oncology, Memorial Sloan Kettering Cancer Center, New York, New York

Daniel W. Yokom, MD   Clinical Research Fellow, Medical Oncology, Princess Margaret Cancer Centre, University Health Network, Toronto, Ontario, Canada

Foreword

The *Handbook of Geriatric Oncology* arrives at an optimal time for the practicing physician, as the number of older adults with cancer is on a steep rise globally. This growth in the number of older adults with cancer, which is a result of aging of the worldwide population and the association of cancer with aging, coincides with an anticipated workforce shortage in both oncology and geriatrics. Hence, care of the older patient with cancer is now the "bread and butter" of not only oncologists and geriatricians, but also primary care providers, subspecialists, and members of the multidisciplinary team. However, training in geriatric oncology is often not a standard component of medical education. Nevertheless, health care providers need to be armed with the latest data on how to optimize and embrace the complexity of care in the older cancer patient. Dr Beatriz Korc-Grodzicki (geriatrician) and Dr William Tew (medical oncologist), leading experts in the field of geriatric oncology, join forces to address this need by providing a *Handbook of Geriatric Oncology* that serves as a key reference for oncologists, geriatricians, and other health care providers caring for an aging population with cancer.

One might ask, "What makes care of older adults with cancer different from any other patient?" The answers to that question are clearly elucidated in this book, which weaves together the best practices from geriatrics and oncology in order to optimize the care of older adults with cancer. First, this *Handbook* describes how to assess the older adult and gain a better understanding of the patient's "functional age" rather than just the chronological age. Second, it provides insight into these patients' unique areas of physiologic, functional, and social vulnerability, and suggests interventions to help the patient. Third, this *Handbook* summarizes cutting-edge data that inform best practices in the care of older adults with cancer. Last, and most important, this *Handbook* suggests how to communicate these findings to a patient. In addition, this integration of knowledge and skill sets results in a collaborative informed decision that is in line with the patient's goals and preferences, maximizing the benefits and minimizing the risks of cancer therapy.

The critical need for education and training in geriatric oncology has been recognized by the Institute of Medicine and the American Society of Clinical Oncology. Drs Tew and Korc-Grodzicki have brought together world experts who address this need by providing a concise reference that can be used in daily practice, covering topics ranging from how to assess the older adult with cancer, to treatment of specific cancers in older adults, to key issues regarding survivorship, palliative care, and integrative medicine. Caring for older adults with cancer is a gratifying, personally rewarding experience that brings together the complexity of medicine with the most touching and meaningful aspects of the human condition.

George J. Bosl, MD
Patrick M. Byrne Chair in Clinical Oncology
Memorial Sloan Kettering Cancer Center
New York, New York

Arti Hurria, MD
Professor and Director, Cancer and Aging Research Program
City of Hope Comprehensive Cancer Center
Duarte, California

Acknowledgments

We would like to acknowledge Ms. Casida Caines and Lillian Saillant for their superb administrative support; the Beatrice and Samuel A. Seaver Foundation and the Joachim Silbermann Family Program in Aging and Cancer for their financial support; and the outstanding members of the interprofessional MSKCC "65+ team" for their commitment to bettering the lives of older adults with cancer.

Geriatric Oncology: Overview

1 Introduction to Geriatric Oncology

Stuart M. Lichtman

INTRODUCTION

Age is the single most important risk factor for developing cancer, with 60% of all newly diagnosed malignant tumors and 70% of all cancer deaths occurring in persons 65 years or older. It has been estimated that by the year 2030, 20% of the U.S. population (70 million people) will be older than age 65 years. The median age range for diagnosis for most major tumors is 68 to 74 years, and the median age range at death is 70 to 79 years. The mortality rate is disproportionately higher for the elderly population. There are several potential reasons for this, including more aggressive biology, competing comorbidity, decreased physiologic reserve compromising the ability to tolerate therapy, physicians' reluctance to provide aggressive therapy, and barriers in the elderly person's access to care (1). The elderly patient with cancer often has an elderly caregiver, or is socially isolated. The older patients have not been participants in clinical trials and the data necessary to help clinicians care for these patients is lacking. All of these factors contribute to the difficulty of caring for these complex, heterogeneous, and vulnerable patients (2). The field of geriatric oncology has become increasingly recognized as an important component of cancer care and cancer research. This introductory chapter explores the major issues confronting clinicians, which are assessment and aging physiology.

GERIATRIC ASSESSMENT (GA) IN ONCOLOGY

The identification of problems in older patients is critical in prognostication and decision making. Researchers in geriatric oncology have demonstrated that the traditional method of routine history and physical is inadequate in determining elder-specific issues (3,4). Clinicians have not been trained to ask the appropriate questions and interpret the available data. Medical oncologists have used performance status scales such as the Karnofsky and Eastern Cooperative Oncology Group (ECOG) scales to help stratify patients for treatment and as part of clinical trial eligibility. This has been a valuable tool and, for the general oncology population, has been helpful and has withstood the test of time. However, this simple approach is not adequate in the complex, heterogeneous older population. These performance status scales often do not reflect the functional status of older patients (4). Clinicians will appropriately refer to published clinical trials and established national and international guidelines to assist in decision making and evaluating treatment options.

Unfortunately, older patients have been grossly under represented in clinical trials, and data reporting has been inadequate (5,6). This includes registration trials for new drugs (7,8). When they do participate, they are an exceptional group of elders who have passed the often stringent eligibility requirements and usually have minimal to no comorbidity and an excellent performance and functional status. Therefore, the available data usually do not reflect the average patient seen in practice. The result is that there is a paucity of data with which to make true evidence-based decisions.

To obtain this important information, researchers in geriatric oncology have been developing GA scales appropriate for the oncology patient. There is a need to assess basic information. Functional assessments (see Chapter 13) include activities of daily living (toileting, feeding, dressing, grooming, ambulation, bathing) and instrumental activities of daily living (using the telephone, shopping, food preparation, housekeeping, laundry, transportation, and ability to take medication accurately). Dependence in these areas has shown to be a prognostic factor for poor outcomes and treatment-related toxicity (9–11). The presence of geriatric syndromes (delirium, dementia, incontinence, falls, pressure ulcers, malnutrition, osteoporosis, hearing and vision difficulties, and sleep disorders) also has a negative impact (12). The study of the overall evaluation of the older patient has been an extrapolation of the established comprehensive geriatric assessment (CGA), an interdisciplinary diagnostic process focusing on the medical, psychosocial, and functional capabilities of the patient, in order to develop a coordinated and integrated plan for treatment and follow-up (13). It is recognized that a CGA as performed by geriatricians is not practical in the usual outpatient oncology setting. Researchers are trying to streamline the approach by determining the most important questions in terms of oncologic care and then validating this approach in various settings. A position paper published by the International Society of Geriatric Oncology (SIOG) highlighted the issues in this field and discussed the domains that needed to be evaluated and the important questions to be addressed (13).

There is a significant clinical rationale for performing GAs. A GA can provide relevant clinical information beyond that captured in a standard history and physical examination. It can help predict oncology treatment-related complications and overall survival. Data is emerging that it is helpful in making oncology treatment decisions. There are questions concerning what components of the GA should be incorporated in oncology-related assessments and how the problems which are detected can be addressed.

In terms of predictive models, one area that has developed a significant amount of important data is the risk of therapy-related toxicity. Two models have been developed and are described in detail in Chapter 13. The Cancer and Aging Research Group (CARG) score has been shown to be predictive for significant (grade 3+) hematologic toxicity (10). The power of this model is that it has been shown to be better than clinical judgment in predictive value. The study also demonstrated that those older patients with the lowest scores (0–3) still had a 25% risk of ≥ grade 3 toxicity. The Chemotherapy Risk Assessment Scale for High-Age Patients (CRASH) score is able to distinguish several risk levels of severe toxicity. It predicts separately hematologic and nonhematologic toxicity (14). Oncology-specific geriatric screening tools are also being developed to predict other outcomes (15,16) and are discussed in Chapter 14.

Another important consideration is recognizing frailty (see Chapter 14). The frail patient can be thought of an individual who has a higher susceptibility to adverse outcomes, such as mortality and institutionalization. From an oncology perspective, the "frail" label often indicates a patient who is dependent on others for basic activities and if given standard therapies will often not complete the treatment, have excessive toxicity, and therefore will not benefit. Clinicians need to recognize this group to avoid excessive toxicity and suffering (17,18). Predictors of mortality can be helpful to clinicians to weigh the risk versus benefits of therapy, particularly adjuvant treatment. The website e-prognosis (www.eprognosis.com) is one such example. Gait speed has been shown to be a powerful predictor of survival (19) and is clearly simple to evaluate. GA can also be helpful in predictions of delirium (11). These scales and predictive models have been shown not to be time-consuming to the medical staff, are often self-administered by the patient or can be done by nursing. Newer technologies are beginning to be utilized to capture and evaluate this information (20).

PHYSIOLOGY OF AGING AND DRUG THERAPY

A number of physiological changes accompany aging (21,22). Drug compliance is an important issue, particularly with the marked increase in oral anticancer therapies which compound the problem of polypharmacy (23–25). Studies have emphasized that obesity is a significant problem in the elderly population and should be considered in trials (26–28). Other variables to be considered are the effect of age and diet, and genetic polymorphisms (29). Polypharmacy can also affect metabolism due to the potential of drug–drug interactions. There is an age-related reduction in glomerular filtration rate which is not reflected by an increase in serum creatinine levels, because of the simultaneous loss of muscle mass that occurs with age. It should be noted that many older patients who have a serum creatinine in the normal range for a particular laboratory have renal insufficiency (30). Dosing recommendations for older patients and those with renal insufficiency have been published (22,31–35). Appropriate dose modifications can foster safe and effective outcomes (36). The study of the pharmacokinetics of chemotherapy in older patients has truly been lacking. Future study is required.

RESEARCH

Research in geriatric oncology is being performed by a growing number of investigators. The SIOG, founded in the year 2000, fosters the mission of developing health professionals in the field of geriatric oncology, in order to optimize treatment of older adults with cancer, through education, clinical practice, and research. The Society's publication, the *Journal of Geriatric Oncology*, is the first journal devoted solely to the field. The Cancer and Leukemia Group B (now the Alliance for Clinical Trials in Oncology) Cancer in the Elderly Committee has supported furthering research in geriatric oncology through clinical trials and secondary data analyses (37,38). The CARG initiated and supported trials in different clinical settings and, most importantly, mentors junior investigators in geriatric oncology and studies novel clinical trial designs (39). The Gynecologic Oncology Group Elderly (now NRG Oncology) task force is supporting the first prospective trial in older women with ovarian cancer and planning further studies in other diseases and modalities. The American Society of Clinical Oncology (ASCO) also fosters a number of initiatives in geriatric oncology. These include a Geriatric Oncology Issue Exploration Team, educational materials including ASCO University, sessions at the annual meeting including a geriatric oncology track, the B. J. Kennedy Award for Excellence in Geriatric Oncology, articles in the ASCO Post, and a geriatric oncology component of the Cancer Education Committee. ASCO has also published a position paper encouraging research in older patients to increase the available evidence-based data (1). One area of great interest is rethinking clinical trial design. It is important that clinical trials prospectively obtain important patient data such as baseline functional status. Eligibility, appropriate endpoints, and toxicity evaluation should be reconsidered for older patients (40,41). Data analysis and clinical trial reporting also have to be adapted for appropriate evaluation and interpretation. These issues are imperative to obtain quality data so clinicians have the ability to make meaningful decisions.

The care of the older cancer patient is a complex endeavor. It requires careful thought and evaluation. Goals of therapy must be carefully considered. A multidisciplinary approach is preferred. Geriatric oncology ought to move to the forefront of oncology care. These vulnerable patients should be the focus of our endeavors.

TAKE HOME POINTS

1. Older patients comprise the majority of cancer patients in both incidence and mortality.
2. Geriatric-specific assessment is required to evaluate these patients.
3. GA adds to the routine history and physical exam, uncovering problems not previously recognized.
4. Oncology-specific prediction tools are available to help in this geriatric evaluation.
5. Aging physiology must be considered before deciding upon and dosing anticancer therapy.

REFERENCES

1. Williams GR, Mackenzie A, Magnuson A, et al. Comorbidity in older adults with cancer. *J Geriatr Oncol.* 2015. doi:10.1016/j.jgo.2015.1012.1002.
2. Rao AV, Cohen HJ. Preface. *Clin Geriatr Med.* 2016;32(1):xiii-xiv.
3. Extermann M, Balducci L, Lyman GH. What threshold for adjuvant therapy in older breast cancer patients? *J Clin Oncol.* 2000;18(8):1709-1717.

4. Extermann M, Overcash J, Lyman GH, et al. Comorbidity and functional status are independent in older cancer patients. *J Clin Oncol.* 1998;16(4):1582-1587.
5. Lichtman SM. Call for changes in clinical trial reporting of older patients with cancer. *J Clin Oncol.* 2012;30(8):893-894.
6. Hutchins LF, Unger JM, Crowaley JJ, et al. Underrepresentation of patients 65 years of age or older in cancer-treatment trials. *N Engl J Med.* 1999;341(27):2061-2067.
7. Scher KS, Hurria A. Under-representation of older adults in cancer registration trials: known problem, little progress. *J Clin Oncol.* 2012;30(17):2036-2038.
8. Talarico L, Chen G, Pazdur R. Enrollment of elderly patients in clinical trials for cancer drug registration: a 7-year experience by the US Food and Drug Administration. *J Clin Oncol.* 2004;22(22):4626-4631.
9. Audisio RA, Pope D, Ramesh HS, et al. Shall we operate? Preoperative assessment in elderly cancer patients (PACE) can help. A SIOG surgical task force prospective study. *Crit Rev Oncol Hematol.* 2008;65(2):156-163.
10. Hurria A, Togawa K, Mohile SG, et al. Predicting chemotherapy toxicity in older adults with cancer: a prospective multicenter study. *J Clin Oncol.* 2011;29(25):3457-3465.
11. Korc-Grodzicki B, Sun SW, Zhou Q, et al. Geriatric assessment as a predictor of delirium and other outcomes in elderly patients with cancer. *Ann Surg.* 2015;261(6):1085-1090.
12. Reuben DB, Rubenstein LV, Hirsch SH, et al. Value of functional status as a predictor of mortality: results of a prospective study. *Am J Med.* 1992;93(6):663-669.
13. Wildiers H, Heeren P, Puts M, et al. International Society of Geriatric Oncology consensus on geriatric assessment in older patients with cancer. *J Clin Oncol.* 2014;32(24):2595-2603.
14. Extermann M, Boler I, Reich RR, et al. Predicting the risk of chemotherapy toxicity in older patients: the Chemotherapy Risk Assessment Scale for High-Age Patients (CRASH) score. *Cancer.* 2012;118(13):3377-3386.
15. Kenis C, Decoster L, Van Puyvelde K, et al. Performance of two geriatric screening tools in older patients with cancer. *J Clin Oncol.* 2014;32(1):19-26.
16. Bellera CA, Rainfray M, Mathoulin-Pelissier S, et al. Screening older cancer patients: first evaluation of the G-8 geriatric screening tool. *Ann Oncol.* 2012;23(8):2166-2172.
17. Fried LP, Tangen CM, Walston J, et al. Frailty in older adults: evidence for a phenotype. *J Gerontol A Biol Sci Med Sci.* 2001;56(3):M146-M156.
18. Rockwood K, Song X, MacKnight C, et al. A global clinical measure of fitness and frailty in elderly people. *CMAJ.* 2005;173(5):489-495.
19. Studenski S, Perera S, Patel K, et al. Gait speed and survival in older adults. *JAMA.* 2011;305(1):50-58.
20. Kelly CM, Shahrokni A. Moving beyond Karnofsky and ECOG performance status assessments with new technologies. *J Oncol.* 2016;2016:6186543.
21. Lichtman SM. Therapy insight: therapeutic challenges in the treatment of elderly cancer patients. *Nat Clin Pract Oncol.* 2006;3(2):86-93.
22. Lichtman SM, Wildiers H, Chatelut E, et al. International Society of Geriatric Oncology Chemotherapy Taskforce: evaluation of chemotherapy in older patients—an analysis of the medical literature. *J Clin Oncol.* 2007;25(14):1832-1843.
23. Lichtman SM. Polypharmacy: geriatric oncology evaluation should become mainstream. *J Clin Oncol.* 2015;33(13):1422-1423.
24. Nightingale G, Hajjar E, Swartz K, et al. Evaluation of a pharmacist-led medication assessment used to identify prevalence of and associations with polypharmacy and potentially inappropriate medication use among ambulatory senior adults with cancer. *J Clin Oncol.* 2015;33(13):1453-1459.

25. Partridge AH, Archer L, Kornblith AB, et al. Adherence and persistence with oral adjuvant chemotherapy in older women with early-stage breast cancer in CALGB 49907: adherence companion study 60104. *J Clin Oncol.* 2010;28(14):2418-2422.

26. Campbell PT, Newton CC, Dehal AN, et al. Impact of body mass index on survival after colorectal cancer diagnosis: the Cancer Prevention Study-II Nutrition Cohort. *J Clin Oncol.* 2012;30(1):42-52.

27. Gibson TM, Park Y, Robien K, et al. Body mass index and risk of second obesity-associated cancers after colorectal cancer: a pooled analysis of prospective cohort studies. *J Clin Oncol.* 2014;32(35):4004-4011.

28. Renfro LA, Loupakis F, Adams RA, et al. Body mass index is prognostic in metastatic colorectal cancer: pooled analysis of patients from first-line clinical trials in the ARCAD database. *J Clin Oncol.* 2016;34(2):144-150.

29. Walko CM, McLeod HL. Personalizing medicine in geriatric oncology. *J Clin Oncol.* 2014;32(24):2581-2586.

30. Launay-Vacher V, Oudard S, Janus N, et al. Prevalence of renal insufficiency in cancer patients and implications for anticancer drug management: the renal insufficiency and anticancer medications (IRMA) study. *Cancer.* 2007;110(6):1376-1384.

31. Launay-Vacher V, Chatelut E, Lichtman SM, et al. Renal insufficiency in elderly cancer patients: International Society of Geriatric Oncology clinical practice recommendations. *Ann Oncol.* 2007;18(8):1314-1321.

32. Lichtman SM, Wildiers H, Launay-Vacher V, et al. International Society of Geriatric Oncology (SIOG) recommendations for the adjustment of dosing in elderly cancer patients with renal insufficiency. *Eur J Cancer.* 2007;43(1):14-34.

33. Launay-Vacher V, Aapro M, De Castro G Jr., et al. Renal effects of molecular targeted therapies in oncology: a review by the Cancer and the Kidney International Network (C-KIN). *Ann Oncol.* 2015;26(8):1677-1684.

34. Hurria A, Lichtman SM. Clinical pharmacology of cancer therapies in older adults. *Br J Cancer.* 2008;98(3):517-522.

35. Wildiers H. Mastering chemotherapy dose reduction in elderly cancer patients. *Eur J Cancer.* 2007;43(15):2235-2241.

36. Lichtman SM, Cirrincione CT, Hurria A, et al. Effect of pretreatment renal function on treatment and clinical outcomes in the adjuvant treatment of older women with breast cancer: alliance A171201, an ancillary study of CALGB/CTSU 49907. *J Clin Oncol.* 2016;34(7):699-705.

37. Hurria A, Cirrincione CT, Muss HB, et al. Implementing a geriatric assessment in cooperative group clinical cancer trials: CALGB 360401. *J Clin Oncol.* 2011;29(10):1290-1296.

38. Hurria A, Cohen HJ, Extermann M. Geriatric oncology research in the cooperative groups: a report of a SIOG special meeting. *J Geriatr Oncol.* 2010;1(1):40-44.

39. Hurria A, Dale W, Mooney M, et al. Designing therapeutic clinical trials for older and frail adults with cancer: U13 conference recommendations. *J Clin Oncol.* 2014;32(24):2587-2594.

40. Wildiers H, Mauer M, Pallis A, et al. End points and trial design in geriatric oncology research: a joint European Organisation for Research and Treatment of Cancer—Alliance for Clinical Trials in Oncology—International Society of Geriatric Oncology position article. *J Clin Oncol.* 2013;31(29):3711-3718.

41. Lichtman SM. Clinical trial design in older adults with cancer—the need for new paradigms. *J Geriatr Oncol.* 2012;3:368-375.

2   Physiologic Changes of Aging

Olivia Le Saux, Sophie Watelet, Marine Haution-Bitker,
Florence Murard-Reeman, Clémence Lecardonnel,
Mahdi Harchaoui, Marc Bonnefoy, and
Claire Falandry

INTRODUCTION

Aging is an inevitable, irreversible, and complex biological process that negatively impacts multiple organ systems and their ability to function (1). Over time, it leads to a decrease in physiologic reserve and an increased risk of many diseases. Ultimately, it will result in death. The development of these changes is not homogeneous and, therefore, will not happen at the same rate in every person (individual variability) nor at the same rate for every organ (intra individual variability). These changes are responsible for the vulnerability of elderly patients in critical situations. For example, the aging of the central nervous system makes the patient more prone to confusion, the aging of the renal system to dehydration or drug-related toxicity. Genetic, epigenetic, and environmental factors affect this process (2). Beyond these biological processes, aging is also associated with a significant shift in social role, which is not discussed in this chapter.

Bouchon conceptualized the loss of function of any organ during aging as being explained by three conditions (3):

1. Physiologic aging leads to a progressive loss of function, without reaching the threshold of insufficiency.
2. The function can be worsened by a chronic disease.
3. The function can be worsened by acute disease leading to insufficiency.

These last two conditions are modifiable, leading to the necessity to adapt care in the elderly.

We will review age-associated physiologic changes according to different systems. The main strategies to prevent organ insufficiency or geriatric deconditioning are summarized in Table 2.1.

(*text continues on page 16*)

TABLE 2.1 Summary of Age-Related Changes, Their Consequences, and Preventive Measures

Age-Related Changes	Increased Incidence of	Medical Conditions Exposed Under Acute Stress	Preventive Measures
Cardiovascular system			
- Decrease in elasticity	- Isolated systolic hypertension	- Heart failure	- Primary prevention of cardiovascular risk factors: smoking cessation, arterial hypertension control, glycemic control
- Increase in stiffness of the arterial system	- Diastolic dysfunction	- Congestive cardiac dysfunction	
- Increased afterload on the left ventricle	- Atrioventricular conduction defects	- Atrial fibrillation	
- Increase in systolic blood pressure	- Aortic valve calcification	- Acute coronary syndrome	
- Left ventricular hypertrophy	- Orthostatic hypotension	- Cerebrovascular accidents	- Physical activity
- Increased duration of relaxation of the left ventricle in diastole	- Atherosclerosis	- Falls	- Mediterranean diet
- Dropout of atrial pacemaker cells	- Dementia		- Avoid fluid overload
- Decrease in intrinsic heart rate			- Routine evaluation for orthostatic hypotension
- Fibrosis of the cardiac skeleton			± prescription of support stockings
- Calcification at the base of the aortic valve			
- Damage to the His bundle			
- Decreased responsiveness to beta adrenergic receptor stimulation			
- Decreased reactivity to baroreceptors and chemoreceptors			
- Increase in circulating catecholamines			

(continued)

TABLE 2.1 Summary of Age-Related Changes, Their Consequences, and Preventive Measures *(continued)*

Age-Related Changes	Increased Incidence of	Medical Conditions Exposed Under Acute Stress	Preventive Measures
Respiratory system			
- Loss of one-third of surface area per volume - Decrease of carbon monoxide transfer with age - **Normal increase in airspace size without wall destruction** - Increase in anatomic dead space - Decrease in functional reserves - Increase of the alveolar-arterial oxygen gradient **with a slight decrease in arterial oxygen tension** - Less vigorous cough - Slower mucociliary clearance	- Emphysema	- Bronchopulmonary infection - Hypoxia - Diminished ventilatory response in cases of heart failure, infection, or airway obstruction - Delayed diagnosis due to decreased perception of bronchoconstriction	- Physical activity and exercise training - Influenza vaccine - Mobilization of the patient ("don't put them in a bed, give them a chair") when hospitalized
Central nervous system			
- Loss of cortical neurons - Rarefaction of white matter - Decrease of neurotransmitters such as acetylcholine - Increased time response - Moderate decrease in memory skills (acquisition of new information) - Disrupted and decreased sleep - Decreased sensation of thirst	- Degenerative diseases - Dementia - Depression	- Confusion - Regressive psychomotor syndrome - Dehydration - Chemo brain	- Mediterranean diet - Maintain social network/ social activities - Psychotherapy - Decrease number of comedications - Correction of sensorial deficiencies - Cognitive stimulation activities/cognitive training

(continued)

TABLE 2.1 Summary of Age-Related Changes, Their Consequences, and Preventive Measures (*continued*)

Age-Related Changes	Increased Incidence of	Medical Conditions Exposed Under Acute Stress	Preventive Measures
Renal system			
- Decreased renal mass and function - Decrease in glomerular filtration rate and creatinine clearance - Decreased ability to dilute urine or excrete an acid load	- Chronic renal insufficiency	- Acute renal insufficiency - Drug-related toxicity - Dehydration - Nephrotoxicity due to intravenous contrast	- Primary prevention of cardiovascular risk factors - Therapeutic drug monitoring, dose adjustments - Avoid medications with nephrotoxic potential (e.g., NSAIDs) - Encourage oral hydration - Decrease the number of prescription and nonprescription medications (use of STOPP/START (4) or Beers Criteria (5)
Hematopoietic and Immune systems			
- Reduced functional bone marrow reserves - Impaired white blood cell function - Procoagulant state	- Anemia - Infections - Cancer - Autoimmune disorders	- Delayed responses to blood loss or hypoxia - Increased myelotoxicity from chemotherapy	- Routine evaluation and treatment of reversible anemia (e.g., vitamin B_{12} deficiency) - Stress management therapies, including psychosocial support and coping skills - Attention to vaccinations - Long-term moderate exercise - Nutritional supplementation (vitamins B_{12} and D) and healthy diet

(continued)

TABLE 2.1 Summary of Age-Related Changes, Their Consequences, and Preventive Measures (*continued*)

Age-Related Changes	Increased Incidence of	Medical Conditions Exposed Under Acute Stress	Preventive Measures
Gastrointestinal system			
- Xerostomia and thinner gums - Gastric hypochlorhydria - Increased intestinal transit time - Decreased hepatic mass and blood flow	- Colon cancer - Diverticula - Constipation - Atrophic gastritis - Incontinence	- Malnutrition - Fecal impaction and confusion	- Evaluation for drug-related side effects - Decrease alcohol intake - Improve nutrition - Encourage oral hydration - Physical activity
Genitourinary system			
- Decrease in bladder capacity - Decrease of sensation of needing to void the bladder - BPH - Menopause and andropause	- Urinary incontinence - Erectile dysfunction - Dyspareunia - Symptomatic BPH	- Urinary tract infection - Acute retention of urine	- Sphincter reeducation - Hormone replacement therapy is controversial - Avoiding anticholinergic therapies

(*continued*)

TABLE 2.1 Summary of Age-Related Changes, Their Consequences, and Preventive Measures (*continued*)

Age-Related Changes	Increased Incidence of	Medical Conditions Exposed Under Acute Stress	Preventive Measures
		Musculoskeletal system	
- Decrease of muscle mass relative to body weight - Impaired motility and balance - Increased insulin resistance - Changes in the volume of distribution for drugs - Bone loss	- Osteoarthritis - Osteoporosis - Sarcopenia - Cachexia	- Dehydration - Malnutrition - Falls - Fractures - Drug-related toxicity	- Dose adjustments of hydrophilic drugs - Encourage motility and physical activity (strength and endurance), stabilometry (postural sway), and body balance - Nutrition (protein and energy intakes) - Encourage oral hydration - Mobilization of the patient ("don't put them in a bed, give them a chair") when hospitalized - Activities led by a physical therapist - Calcium and vitamin D supplementation

(*continued*)

TABLE 2.1 Summary of Age-Related Changes, Their Consequences, and Preventive Measures (continued)

Age-Related Changes	Increased Incidence of	Medical Conditions Exposed Under Acute Stress	Preventive Measures
Skin system			
- Atrophy - Decreased elasticity - Xerosis - Impaired metabolic and reparative responses	- Decreased vitamin D synthesis - Cutaneous cancers - Decubitus ulcers	- Delayed wound healing	- Vitamin D supplementation - Mobilization of patients
Sensory system			
- Hypogeusia - Hypoosmia - Lachrymal insufficiency - Presbyopia - Presbycusis	- Nutritional deficiencies - Cataract - Age-related macular degeneration - Dementia - Social withdrawal	- "Phantom visions" (Charles Bonnet hallucinations) - Confusion	- Screening and treatment of any deficiency - Encourage "food-pleasure" - No restrictive diets

BPH, benign prostatic hyperplasia; NSAIDs, nonsteroidal anti-inflammatory drugs; START, screening tool to alert to right treatment; STOPP, screening tool of older people's prescriptions.

AGE-ASSOCIATED PHYSIOLOGIC AGING

Cardiovascular System

Changes in the cardiovascular system are very prevalent in the aging process. Age-related changes are listed in Table 2.1. The most important changes and their consequences are (6):

- Decreased aortic compliance, which results in an increased left ventricular afterload, increased systolic blood pressure, decreased diastolic blood pressure, and an increase in pulse pressure.
- Modest left ventricular hypertrophy in response to a dropout of myocytes, along with increased left ventricular afterload and prolonged relaxation of the left ventricle during diastole.
- Dropout of atrial pacemaker cells, resulting in a decrease in intrinsic heart rate.
- Thickening of the annulus of both the aortic and mitral valves, with development of valvular calcification.
- Apoptosis of sinoatrial pacemaker cells, fibrosis, and loss of His bundle cells, as well as fibrosis and calcification of the fibrous skeleton of the heart that can lead to various auriculoventricular blocks.
- Decreased responsiveness to beta adrenergic receptor stimulation, decreased reactivity to baroreceptors and chemoreceptors, and increased circulating catecholamines, resulting in a marked decrease in the maximum heart rate in response to exercise or other stressors.

Respiratory System

There are multiple physiologic changes of the respiratory system associated with aging (7). The most important changes and their consequences are:

> Decrease in static elastic recoil of the lung, in respiratory muscle performance, and in compliance of the chest wall, resulting in increased work of breathing compared with younger subjects and a diminished respiratory reserve in cases of acute illness (8).
> Decrease in expiratory flow rates (small airway disease).
> Less vigorous cough and slower mucociliary clearance, leading to increased frequency of infections.

Central Nervous System

Structural changes associated with aging include decrease of brain volume (predominant in the frontal and temporal lobes and in the white matter), neuronal loss, decrease in neuronal size, and synaptic density (9). There is less available acetylcholine due to decrease in the number of cholinergic neurons, with less synthesis and release of acetylcholine (10). Dopamine and corresponding receptors in the striatum and substantia nigra may also be decreased in normal aging (11).

Neurocognitive changes are neither uniform nor inevitable. Some functions, such as language ability and vocabulary or visuospatial abilities, are resilient to brain aging. Other abilities, such as visual confrontation naming, verbal fluency, visual construction skills, conceptual reasoning, memory, selective attention, and processing speed, decline gradually over time (12). Episodic memory shows lifelong decline, whereas semantic memory shows late-life decline (13). Nondeclarative memory remains unchanged across the lifespan. Retention of information is preserved in cognitively healthy older adults; however, rate of acquisition and memory retrieval decline with aging (14). **Executive function changes** include a decline with age in concept formation, abstraction, mental flexibility, response inhibition, and inductive reasoning. In contrast, ability to appreciate similarities, describe the meaning of proverbs, and reason about familiar material remains stable throughout life.

Renal System

Structural and functional changes are summarized in Table 2.2 (15,16). The consequences of these age-related changes include decreased renal function overall, leading to a decrease in glomerular filtration rate and creatinine clearance and a decreased ability to dilute urine or excrete an acid load. It is important to emphasize the role of calculating glomerular filtration rate in all older adults as part of their overall physical evaluation. Due to decrease in overall muscle mass with age, serum creatinine level is not an accurate representation of renal function.

Hematopoietic and Immune Systems

Bone marrow is considered a self-renewing tissue. However, hematopoietic stem cells (HSC) experience phenotypic and functional changes with aging: expansion of the HSC compartment, skewing of differentiation toward myeloid progenitors, and decreased regenerative capacity (17,18). These changes lead to:

a. **Immunosenescence**: decreased efficiency of adaptive immune responses. Naive T and B cells decline, although the functions of memory cells are relatively preserved.
b. **Inflammation ("inflammaging")**: dysfunction in innate immunity associated with a pro-inflammatory profile. The increase in functional CD8+ lymphocytes T with aging also contributes to inflammation, due to their production of pro-inflammatory cytokines.

Immunosenescence has clinical consequences such as increased risk of infections, cancer, and autoimmune disorders, and less effective responses upon exposure to new antigens (e.g., through vaccinations) (19). Inflammaging and in particular elevations in levels of tumor necrosis factor (TNF), interleukin-6 (IL-6), IL-1, and C-reactive protein (CRP) are strong independent risk factors for morbidity and mortality in older people (20).

Aging is associated with myeloid-biased blood cell composition and increased prevalence of myeloid malignancies such as myelodysplasia and myeloproliferative neoplasms. There is increased incidence of anemia, and also increased incidence of chemotherapy-induced short-term and long-term toxicities with increased and

TABLE 2.2 Summary of Structural and Functional Changes With Aging

Structural changes

Macroanatomical changes

Decrease in kidney mass more pronounced in the renal cortex

Larger and more numerous kidney cysts

Microanatomical changes

Decreased number of functional glomeruli

Increased prevalence of nephrosclerosis (arteriosclerosis, glomerulosclerosis, and tubular atrophy with interstitial fibrosis)

Glomerular basement membrane thickening

Age-related vasculopathy: fibrointimal hyperplasia, hyaline arteriolosclerosis, increased renal vasoconstriction, and mural resistance

Functional changes

Glomerular

Creatinine clearance and glomerular filtration rates decrease

Tubular

Impaired sodium balance

Loss of the ability to concentrate or dilute the urine

Increased potassium retention

Impaired excretion of acid loads

Vascular

Renal blood flow decreases

Endocrine

Decreased serum renin and aldosterone

Decreased vitamin D activation

Reversal of day-night urine production

cumulative risk of chemotherapy-induced neutropenia, secondary myelodysplasias, and acute leukemias (21).

Gastrointestinal System

Concerning the oropharynx, decreased salivary flow and thinner gums with increased likelihood of cavities have been observed.

Age-related changes of esophageal function (presbyesophagus) (22) are impaired motility with decreased peristaltic response, increased nonperistaltic response, delayed transit time, and/or decreased relaxation of the lower sphincter tone on swallowing. These changes may lead to dysphagia and reduction of calorie intake.

Atrophic gastritis is common in healthy elderly people, as shown in a Scandinavian study (approximately 40% of elderly people over 65) (23). Atrophic gastritis results in achlorhydria (which may be enhanced by use of proton pump inhibitors), deficient intrinsic factor secretion, and decreased pepsinogen production. Vitamin B_{12} deficiency is common among the elderly. Elderly people are particularly at risk of vitamin B_{12} deficiency because of the high prevalence of atrophic gastritis–associated food-cobalamin (vitamin B_{12}) malabsorption, and the increasing prevalence of pernicious anemia with advancing age.

Decreased liver weight and a decreased blood flow have a significant impact on drug metabolism and increased incidence of adverse drug reactions and drug–drug interactions.

With age, the colon becomes hypotonic, which leads to increased storage capacity, longer stool transit time, and greater stool dehydration with increased risk of chronic constipation. Diverticular disease is common (prevalence close to 50% of those older than 80), but symptoms are less frequent (only about 25% of people affected) (24). Loss of control of the external anal sphincters in the elderly may lead to fecal incontinence.

Genitourinary System

Bladder capacity decreases from 500 to 600 mL in younger adults to 250 to 600 mL in the older population. More importantly, the sensation of needing to void occurs in younger persons when the bladder is little more than half full; in many who are older, the sensation occurs much later or sometimes not at all, leading to overflow incontinence. Studies of sensation of bladder filling in association with cerebral perfusion have demonstrated decreased perfusion of right insula (25). The delayed voiding sensation and decreased bladder capacity may conspire to give an elderly person less time to reach the lavatory. Moreover, both sexes void less successfully later in life, which leads to larger residual volumes (50–150 mL) and increased frequency of urinary tract infections.

Enlargement of the **prostate** occurs in most older men; by age 80, more than 90% of men have symptomatic BPH. Furthermore, the risk of developing histological prostate cancer increases with age (50% between 70 and 80). However, the probability of developing clinically significant cancer or prostate cancer-related death is significantly lower (9.5% and 2.9%, respectively) (26).

Musculoskeletal System

Muscle mass and strength decrease with age, leading to **sarcopenia** (27). In addition, muscle quality decreases due to infiltration of fat and connective tissue. These changes have been associated with decreased strength, impaired motility, age-related increased insulin resistance, changes in the volume of distribution for water-soluble drugs, slower gait speed, and decreased survival (28).

The process of **bone** turnover is usually in equilibrium. However, as we age, chronic inflammation and alteration of the growth hormone and insulin-like factor axis lead to a decrease in the number and function of osteoblasts and decreased bone formation. By age 80, it is estimated that the body's total bone mass will be about 50% of its peak value (29). Due to age-related effects on angiogenesis and on the number and activity of mesenchymal progenitor cells, the rate of fracture repair may be delayed (30). Decrease in the number of functional chondrocytes, reduced water content, decreased proteoglycans synthesis, loss of chondroitin sulfate, and cross-linking of glycated collagen contribute to stiffening of the **cartilage** and increased incidence of degenerative joint disease (31).

Skin System

Normal aging must be distinguished from solar-induced cutaneous changes, even though these changes are more common in the elderly. The aging of the skin leads to atrophy of the epidermis and flattening of the dermal epidermal junction, which decreases the area available for nutrient transfer, including protective lipids in the stratum corneum. This results in dry skin (xerosis) and a compromise in the barrier function of the skin (32). The turnover rate of cells in the stratum corneum decreases with age, so reepithelialization takes longer than in younger adults. The number of Langerhans cells and melanocytes is decreased, leading to reduced pigmentation.

Dermal collagen becomes stiffer; elastin is more cross-linked and has a higher degree of calcification. These changes cause the skin to lose its tone and elasticity, resulting in wrinkling. The number of hair follicles declines with age, but their structure remains unchanged. Aging does not affect the sebaceous glands, but some changes occur in the exocrine sweat glands.

Sensory System

The structure of the **eye** changes with age. Atrophy of periorbital tissues may lead to ectropion or entropion and watering eyes due to displacement of the lacrimal puntum (less effective drainage). There is atrophy and yellowing of the conjunctiva and loss of accommodation or presbyopia (decreased lens elasticity) (33).

Presbycusis is characterized by reduced hearing sensitivity and speech understanding in noisy environments, slowed central processing of acoustic information, and impaired localization of sound sources (34). The first sign of presbycusis is characterized by loss of threshold sensitivity in the high-frequency region of the hearing spectrum. Moreover, with age, the walls of the external auditory canal thin and the cerumen becomes drier and more tenacious, increasing the risk of cerumen impaction.

Taste may also be affected by the aging process. Although the number of papillae on the tongue decreases with aging, neurophysiologic responses of individual papillae are minimally altered. There is no relation between gustatory acuity and number of taste buds. Loss of **taste** in older patients is in large part due to decreased olfaction rather than taste itself (35).

CONCLUSION

Study of aging is difficult, primarily because it is a highly heterogeneous phenomenon with inter- and intra individual variability. Comprehensive assessment of elderly patients is of the highest importance, as some elderly patients may be vulnerable and cancer or the therapy we use to treat this disease (whether chemotherapy, radiotherapy, or surgery) may decompensate an underlying frailty.

TAKE HOME POINTS

1. Aging is characterized by progressive changes that are associated with increased susceptibility to many diseases.
2. Aging is influenced by genetic, epigenetic, and environmental factors.
3. With aging, organ functions decrease and the capacity of the patient to adapt to stress factors is decreased.
4. "Inflammaging" and elevations in levels of TNF, IL-6, IL-1, and CRP are strong independent risk factors for morbidity and mortality in older people.
5. Evaluation of the elderly patient's global health status using comprehensive geriatric assessment is therefore very important in the therapeutic decision.

REFERENCES

1. Harman D. Aging: overview. *Ann N Y Acad Sci.* 2001;928:1-21.
2. Steves CJ, Spector TD, Jackson SH. Ageing, genes, environment and epigenetics: what twin studies tell us now, and in the future. *Age Ageing.* 2012;41(5):581-586.
3. Bouchon JP. 1+2+3 ou comment tenter d'être efficace en gériatrie. *La Revue du Praticien.* 1984;34:888-892.
4. O'Mahony D, O'Sullivan D, Byrne S, et al. STOPP/START criteria for potentially inappropriate prescribing in older people: version 2. *Age Ageing.* 2015;44(2): 213-218.
5. American Geriatrics Society Beers Criteria Update Expert Panel. American Geriatrics Society 2015 updated Beers criteria for potentially inappropriate medication use in older adults. *J Am Geriatr Soc.* 2015;63(11):2227-2246.
6. Cheitlin MD. Cardiovascular physiology—changes with aging. *Am J Geriatr Cardiol.* 2003;12(1):9-13.
7. Janssens JP, Pache JC, Nicod LP. Physiological changes in respiratory function associated with ageing. *Eur Respir J.* 1999;13(1):197-205.
8. Janssens JP. Aging of the respiratory system: impact on pulmonary function tests and adaptation to exertion. *Clin Chest Med.* 2005;26(3):469-484, vi-vii.
9. Terry RD, Katzman R. Life span and synapses: will there be a primary senile dementia? *Neurobiol Aging.* 2001;22(3):347-348; discussion 353-354.
10. Schliebs R, Arendt T. The cholinergic system in aging and neuronal degeneration. *Behav Brain Res.* 2011;221(2):555-563.
11. Anglade P, Vyas S, Javoy-Agid F, et al. Apoptosis and autophagy in nigral neurons of patients with Parkinson's disease. *Histol Histopathol.* 1997;12(1):25-31.
12. Harada CN, Natelson Love MC, Triebel KL. Normal cognitive aging. *Clin Geriatr Med.* 2013;29(4):737-752.
13. Ronnlund M, Nyberg L, Backman L, Nilsson LG. Stability, growth, and decline in adult life span development of declarative memory: cross-sectional and longitudinal data from a population-based study. *Psychol Aging.* 2005;20(1):3-18.
14. Haaland KY, Price L, Larue A. What does the WMS-III tell us about memory changes with normal aging? *J Int Neuropsychol Soc.* 2003;9(1):89-96.
15. Bolignano D, Mattace-Raso F, Sijbrands EJ, Zoccali C. The aging kidney revisited: a systematic review. *Ageing Res Rev.* 2014;14:65-80.

16. Martin JE, Sheaff MT. Renal ageing. *J Pathol.* 2007;211(2):198-205.
17. Wahlestedt M, Pronk CJ, Bryder D. Concise review: hematopoietic stem cell aging and the prospects for rejuvenation. *Stem Cells Transl Med.* 2015;4(2):186-194.
18. Geiger H, de Haan G, Florian MC. The ageing haematopoietic stem cell compartment. *Nat Rev Immunol.* 2013;13(5):376-389.
19. Franceschi C. Inflammaging as a major characteristic of old people: can it be prevented or cured? *Nutr Rev.* 2007;65(12 pt 2):S173-S176.
20. Baylis D, Bartlett DB, Syddall HE, et al. Immune-endocrine biomarkers as predictors of frailty and mortality: a 10-year longitudinal study in community-dwelling older people. *Age (Dordr).* 2013;35(3):963-971.
21. Muss HB, Berry DA, Cirrincione C, et al. Toxicity of older and younger patients treated with adjuvant chemotherapy for node-positive breast cancer: the Cancer and Leukemia Group B Experience. *J Clin Oncol.* 2007;25(24):3699-3704.
22. Boss GR, Seegmiller JE. Age-related physiological changes and their clinical significance. *West J Med.* 1981;135(6):434-440.
23. Christiansen PM. The incidence of achlorhydria and hypochlorhydria in healthy subjects and patients with gastrointestinal diseases. *Scand J Gastroenterol.* 1968;3(5):497-508.
24. Almy TP, Howell DA. Medical progress. Diverticular disease of the colon. *N Engl J Med.* 1980;302(6):324-331.
25. Griffiths D. Imaging bladder sensations. *Neurourol Urodyn.* 2007;26(suppl 6): 899-903.
26. Carter HB, Piantadosi S, Isaacs JT. Clinical evidence for and implications of the multistep development of prostate cancer. *J Urol.* 1990;143(4):742-746.
27. Rosenberg IH. Sarcopenia: origins and clinical relevance. *J Nutr.* 1997;127(suppl 5): 990S-991S.
28. Reinders I, Murphy RA, Brouwer IA, et al. Muscle quality and myosteatosis: novel associations with mortality risk: the age, gene/environment susceptibility (AGES)-Reykjavik Study. *Am J Epidemiol.* 2016;183(1):53-60.
29. Kloss FR, Gassner R. Bone and aging: effects on the maxillofacial skeleton. *Exp Gerontol.* 2006;41(2):123-129.
30. Brandes RP, Fleming I, Busse R. Endothelial aging. *Cardiovasc Res.* 2005;66(2):286-294.
31. Verzijl N, DeGroot J, Ben ZC, et al. Crosslinking by advanced glycation end products increases the stiffness of the collagen network in human articular cartilage: a possible mechanism through which age is a risk factor for osteoarthritis. *Arthritis Rheum.* 2002;46(1):114-123.
32. Montagna W, Carlisle K. Structural changes in ageing skin. *Br J Dermatol.* 1990;122(suppl 35):61-70.
33. Strenk SA, Strenk LM, Koretz JF. The mechanism of presbyopia. *Prog Retin Eye Res.* 2005;24(3):379-393.
34. Gates GA, Mills JH. Presbycusis. *Lancet.* 2005;366(9491):1111-1120.
35. Hall KE, Proctor DD, Fisher L, Rose S. American Gastroenterological Association Future Trends Committee report: effects of aging of the population on gastroenterology practice, education, and research. *Gastroenterology.* 2005;129(4):1305-1338.

3 Frailty

Kevin J. Shih, Jessica Lee, and Holly M. Holmes

INTRODUCTION

Rapid changes in the aging of the population serve as a reminder of the shifts in priorities that will occur in medical care within the next several decades. With the heterogeneity in the health and functional age of older patients comes significant uncertainty about the optimal screening, diagnostic, and treatment strategies tailored to the individual patient (1). Already, the impact has been felt as the geriatric population in the United States—persons 65 years of age and older—increased 24.7% from 2003 to 2013, with more hospitalizations and the increasing cost of maintaining programs that many rely on for medical coverage (2). The geriatric population is expected to constitute 21.7% of the U.S. population by 2040 (3). Another implication of this trend is the increased incidence of cancer due to the higher risk of cancer diagnoses as people age. By 2020, more than 63% of patients diagnosed with cancer are expected to be over 65 years old (4). Despite this trend, there still remains an inadequate number of cancer trials that are sufficiently powered and designed to study treatment outcomes for older patients with cancer (5). The lack of enrollment of older patients in part stems from reluctance to aggressively treat overly "frail" patients without a standardized outcome-based risk stratification algorithm (6,7).

Once a nebulous descriptor for disability among hospitalized patients and those of highly advanced age, the concept of *frailty* has emerged as a clinical syndrome defined by decreased physiologic reserves to maintain homeostasis after a stressor (8). The predominant model for considering frailty in older adults uses a defined frailty phenotype, which posits that any underlying pathophysiologic processes manifest themselves through clinically measurable physical traits (8). Screening tools for frailty have been developed and validated for their association with adverse outcomes in general older patients, and to varying degrees, some of these tools have been applied in geriatric oncology settings (9). More frequently, the detection of frailty in older adults with cancer has been based on the use of geriatric assessment (GA) to assess deficiencies in multiple domains such as functional status, cognition, nutrition, comorbid conditions, and others, to determine a patient's status as fit or frail and to risk-stratify patients to treatment regimens (9,10). While there are other models to define frailty in older patients, the goal of this chapter is to discuss the current models based on the frailty phenotype and GA and provide concise recommendations regarding their use in clinical practice.

DEVELOPMENT OF FRAILTY CRITERIA

There are two main pathways that contribute to the development of frailty. The first is a consequence of aging in which an individual's physiologic reserves gradually decrease, leading to a decline in the ability to return to homeostasis after an insult (11). For example, the decrease of estrogens during menopause may lead to increased bone resorption, which over time can cause osteoporosis. Alterations in adipose tissue distribution that affect pharmacokinetics can cause changes in the way older adults react to medications. Increased fat cells may also lead to chronic elevation of inflammatory markers (including Interleukin-6 [IL-6] and tumor necrosis factor-α [TNF-α]) that potentiates the catabolism of muscle mass. Furthermore, progenitor cells become senescent, leading to reduced replication and tissue repair, which results in sarcopenia (8). The second pathway is a result of an accumulation of chronic conditions and deficits that can result in reduced functional status and frequent hospitalizations (12). There is further interplay between factors such as malnutrition, alterations in metabolism, and decreased activity level as demonstrated in Figure 3.1 (8).

Figure 3.1 expresses the theoretical basis for the mechanisms of frailty. For a clinically useful, operational definition, Fried et al. identified a set of clinical frailty

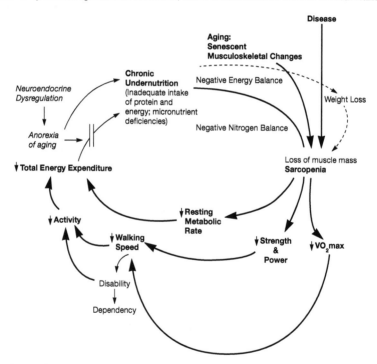

FIGURE 3.1 Cycle of frailty.

Source: From Ref. (8). Fried LP, Tangen CM, Walston J, et al. Frailty in older adults: evidence for a phenotype. *J Gerontol A Biol Sci Med Sci.* 2001;56(3):M146-M157.

traits shown in Table 3.1. The criteria are simple clinical measures and questions that can be completed quickly in an outpatient setting.

The Fried criteria were developed and validated using data from the Cardiovascular Health Study (CHS), a 7-year, prospective, observational study of older persons. Exclusion criteria included those with active cancer treatment (although it did include a prior cancer diagnosis), depression, or dementia. Using the CHS, Fried et al. examined the correlation between the frailty phenotype and adverse geriatric outcomes such as falls, worsening functional status, hospitalizations, and death. Covariate-adjusted hazard ratios (HRs) for death and hospitalization at 7 years for frail individuals were 1.27 (confidence interval [CI] 1.11–1.46, $P = .0008$) and 1.63 (CI 1.27–2.08, $P = .0001$), respectively. Frail patients tended to be female, African American, and from lower socioeconomic areas (8). Furthermore, other factors associated with frailty, such as those used in the multi-domain GA (physical performance, disability, social support, comorbidities, and decreased cognition), showed a positive correlation to the frailty phenotype. Interestingly, the results showed that within the frail group, about 26% had disability (≥ 1 activities of daily living [ADL] deficit) and 68% had cormorbities (≥ 2). Although there was overlap, frailty remained a distinct clinical syndrome, as shown in Figure 3.2 (8).

Persons who were prefrail/intermediate (1 or 2 criteria) also had increased adverse outcomes and were at increased risk for developing frailty (odds ratio [OR] 2.63, 95% CI 1.94–3.56) compared to nonfrail individuals at 3 years. In terms of the applicability of these findings to geriatric oncology patients, shortcomings from the Fried validation studies included the exclusion of patients undergoing active cancer treatment and the lack of assessment of outcomes potentially related to cancer (8).

TABLE 3.1 Fried Frailty Criteria From the Cardiovascular Health Study

Frailty Criterion	Definition
Weight loss	Unintentional weight loss ≥10 lb in the last year
Weakness	Grip strength in the lowest 25% (by gender and BMI)
Exhaustion	Self-reported exhaustion from the CES-D Scale: "Everything I did was an effort" "Could not get going"
Low activity	Lowest 20% on the short version of the Minnesota Leisure Time Assessment: men <383 kcal/wk women <270 kcal/wk
Slow gait speed	Slowest 20% for walking 15 ft (by gender and height): ≥7 sec for <160 cm ≥6 sec for ≥160 cm

BMI, body mass index; CES-D, Center for Epidemiologic Studies Depression.

Source: Adapted from Ref. (8). Fried LP, Tangen CM, Walston J, et al. Frailty in older adults: evidence for a phenotype. *J Gerontol A Biol Sci Med Sci.* 2001;56(3):M146-M157.

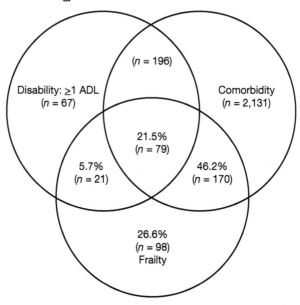

FIGURE 3.2 The prevalence of frailty, disability, and comorbidity in the Cardiovascular Health Study.

ADL, activities of daily living.

Source: From Ref. (8). Fried LP, Tangen CM, Walston J, et al. Frailty in older adults: evidence for a phenotype. *J Gerontol A: Biol Sci Med Sci.* 2001;56(3):M146-M157.

The Fried criteria were also validated using data from the Women's Health and Aging Study (WHAS), in which a modified set of Fried criteria was applied to tertiles of geriatric women based on disability. A probability model was fitted to these classes, which showed that predicted and observed frequencies of frailty in the WHAS populations fit well with the Fried criteria and that they did not aggregate randomly. The percentage of frail individuals in WHAS was quite similar to the CHS (11.6%–11.3%, respectively), and those who were frail had increased risk for disability (HR 15.79, 95% CI 5.83–42.78) and death (HR 6.03, 95% CI 3–12.08) as well (13).

FRAILTY DEFINED BY GA

While a model of frailty based on phenotype and frailty based on GA are well established in geriatric oncology and share the same fundamental tenets, operationally they are different. An advantage to using a GA is the ability to have a complete, multidimensional assessment of an individual's deficits, and to identify factors that have potential interventions. *Frailty* has been variably defined based on the number of GA deficits, ranging from two or more to four or more abnormal domains on GA (9). In this sense, the definition of frailty based on GA is similar to that in the model of the frailty index developed by Rockwood et al. (14). The frailty index is a count of

70 deficits developed using data from the Canadian Study of Health and Aging. Frailty is determined from a calculated index score based on the percentage difference from the average score on each item for other people of the same age (14). This model was later compressed to a seven-item Clinical Frailty Scale to create a tool that still operationalized frailty, was predictive of adverse outcomes, and was easier to use (12). The frailty index is similar to GA in that the frailty index is based on the accumulation of multiple diseases or conditions, loss of function or development of disability, and requires a comprehensive evaluation in order to be assessed (15).

Because a GA can be time-consuming to perform, multiple screening tools have been used to determine patients likely to be frail based on an abnormal GA, such as the Vulnerable Elders Survey (VES-13) and the G8—two tools that have the most predictive ability (10). However, screening with the VES-13 or G8 may miss frail and prefrail patients who have not yet attained disability or poor performance status, and does not capture the trajectory of deficit accumulation; therefore, these individuals may also have unforeseen detrimental treatment outcomes.

FRAILTY AND OUTCOMES IN PRACTICE

Overall, no single screening test has been recommended that can consistently identify frailty in older cancer patients, but some have been associated with GA and with outcomes. A study of patients with cancer undergoing abdominal surgery showed that the G8 had 97% sensitivity and 50% specificity for frailty (16). Another study found that the VES-13 had 68% sensitivity and 78% specificity (17). Both of these studies compared the screening tools to frailty as defined by the GA and regarded the Fried criteria as poorly predictive. However, studies of screening tools and GA have not taken into account that the Fried criteria cannot be compared to GA because they are *operationally different*. The latter evaluates performance status and disability through multi-domain deficits, whereas the former evaluates underlying pathologic processes through physical and clinical measures. If the purpose of frailty assessment is risk stratification, then frailty assessment must be primarily evaluated for the ability to predict adverse outcomes.

GA has been shown to predict treatment outcomes for geriatric cancer patients (18–20). There are few studies comparing the Fried criteria directly to GA. In a study of surgical oncology patients, Kristjansson et al. found discrepancies between the number of frail patients identified by a GA (43%) versus modified Fried criteria (13%) (21). Furthermore, the latter did not accurately predict short-term postoperative complications such as anastomotic leakages or cardiopulmonary issues. In spite of this, the study did conclude that both models predicted overall survival. Superficially, it appeared that the Fried criteria failed to properly risk-stratify the patients, but the lower frailty prevalence likely resulted from the modifications to the Fried criteria that were used.

Another common critique is that the Fried criteria lack generalizability to oncology patients, as the work excluded active cancer patients from its initial CHS study. This selection was undertaken to prevent confounding from cancer cachexia (8). Applying the frailty phenotype to newly diagnosed early-stage geriatric cancer patients is still valid. Terminal and recurrent cancer patients are a subset in which it may not hold and clinical judgment should prevail. Some studies state that the Fried criteria are inferior because they do not incorporate comorbidity and psychological assessments. As described earlier, two pathways contribute to the frailty phenotype: comorbidities and physiologic aging. Thus, comorbidity commonly overlaps with frailty, but it is not a requisite trait. Frailty itself is an independent predictor of adverse outcomes, as shown by numerous population studies. In terms of psychological assessments, depression can result in psychomotor retardation and pseudo-dementia, which can confound low activity assessments (22). It should be ruled out and/or treated before assessing for frailty.

Despite some early resistance, the frailty phenotype has been slowly gaining traction in the surgical and medical oncology communities now that there are more available studies evaluating prevalence, generalizability, and outcomes. A large ($n =$ 594) single-center trial showed that the Fried criteria were a valid and strong independent predictor of short-term surgical outcomes in the elderly and were able to augment the predictive power of current surgical risk models (23). In addition, a two-item assessment consisting of grip strength and weight loss (area under the receiver operating characteristic [ROC] curve: 0.589, $P = .001$) performed equally well as the full five criteria (area under the ROC curve: 0.597, $P = .001$) in predicting surgical outcomes, which can provide fast and accurate risk evaluation in a few minutes (24).

A small pilot study of short-term outcomes in gynecologic cancer patients ($n = 37$) undergoing surgery showed increased postoperative complications in frail (67%) versus nonfrail (24%) patients ($P = .04$). Another case-control study of prostate cancer patients undergoing androgen deprivation therapy (ADT) ($n = 134$) found that the ADT group was more frail and had a higher incidence of falls (14.3% vs. 2.8%, $P = .02$) compared to the control. Surprisingly, these trials noted that although frail patients met the weight loss threshold, they also tended to be more obese (body mass index [BMI] >30) (25,26).

CONCLUSION

Frailty is recognized as a vulnerable state of reduced physiologic reserves that puts an individual at increased risk of poor outcomes after a stressor. Frailty risk stratification can assist in identifying older patients with cancer who may have complications after treatment or even be unsuitable for more intense treatment modalities. Two predominant operational definitions exist: a multi-domain model based on GA and the frailty phenotype as defined by Fried's criteria.

The International Society of Geriatric Oncology (SIOG) recommends the use of GA but lacks specific guidelines for screening for frailty. Although studies have shown that GA is predictive of outcomes, GA is more time-consuming and may miss prefrail or nondisabled frail individuals. The Fried criteria have been shown to have good internal validity and predictive value in numerous geriatric epidemiologic studies. There are few direct studies comparing outcomes from the GA and the Fried criteria, but several other studies have shown that the Fried criteria are predictive of short-term complications in surgical and certain solid cancer populations.

TAKE HOME POINTS

1. As defined by Fried et al. (8), frailty is a syndrome of increased vulnerability to stressors due to multiple underlying pathophysiologic mechanisms (e.g., inflammatory and immune system dysregulation and sarcopenia) and can be defined based on the presence of at least 3 of 5 deficits among measures of gait speed, grip strength, weight loss, exhaustion, and physical activity.
2. A second common model of frailty is based on the accumulation of multiple conditions and accumulation of physiologic and functional deficits that predispose an individual to adverse outcomes, and has been operationalized by the frailty index.
3. In geriatric oncology, GA has been used to identify individuals who are frail; this definition is similar to the concept of deficit accumulation based on the frailty index. No consistent cut point for abnormalities in GA has been used to define "frailty" per se.
4. While the GA and frailty index are operationally different entities, the advantage of using GA to identify frail individuals is the ability to provide a multi-domain assessment with potentially intervenable issues, the results of which have been associated with cancer-specific outcomes in older patients.

REFERENCES

1. Walter LC, Covinsky KE. Cancer screening in elderly patients: a framework for individualized decision making. *JAMA*. 2001;285(21):2750-2756.
2. CMS.gov. Centers for Medicare & Medicaid Services. NHE fact sheet. December 3, 2015. Available at: https://www.cms.gov/research-statistics-data-and-systems/statistics-trends-and-reports/nationalhealthexpenddata/nhe-fact-sheet.html Accessed March 23, 2016.
3. Administration on Aging (AoA). *Aging Statistics—Administration for Community Living*. US Department of Health and Human Services, December 31, 2015. Available at: http://www.aoa.acl.gov/aging_statistics/index.aspx. Accessed March 23, 2016.
4. Parry C, Kent EE, Mariotto AB, et al. Cancer survivors: a booming population. *Cancer Epidemiol Biomarkers Prev*. 2011;20(10):1996-2005.
5. Wildiers H, Mauer M, Pallis A, et al. End points and trial design in geriatric oncology research: a joint European Organisation for Research and Treatment of Cancer—Alliance for Clinical Trials in Oncology—International Society of Geriatric Oncology position article. *J Clin Oncol*. 2013;31(29):3711-3718.
6. Herrera AP, Snipes SA, King DW, et al. Disparate inclusion of older adults in clinical trials: priorities and opportunities for policy and practice change. *Am J Public Health*. 2010;100(suppl 1):S105-S112.
7. Denson AC, Mahipal A. Participation of the elderly population in clinical trials: barriers and solutions. *Cancer Control*. 2014;21(3):209-214.
8. Fried LP, Tangen CM, Walston J, et al. Frailty in older adults: evidence for a phenotype. *J Gerontol A Biol Sci Med Sci*. 2001;56(3):M146-M157.

9. Handforth C, Clegg A, Young C, et al. The prevalence and outcomes of frailty in older cancer patients: a systematic review. *Ann Oncol.* 2015;26(6): 1091-1101.

10. Wildiers H, Heeren P, Puts M, et al. International Society of Geriatric Oncology consensus on geriatric assessment in older patients with cancer. *J Clin Oncol.* 2014;32(24):2595-2603.

11. Walston J, McBurnie MA, Newman A, et al. Frailty and activation of the inflammation and coagulation systems with and without clinical comorbidities: results from the cardiovascular health study. *Arch Intern Med.* 2002;162(20):2333.

12. Rockwood K. A global clinical measure of fitness and frailty in elderly people. *CMAJ.* 2005;173(5):489-495.

13. Xue QL, Bandeen-Roche K, Varadhan R, et al. Initial manifestations of frailty criteria and the development of frailty phenotype in the Women's Health and Aging Study II. *J Gerontol A Biol Sci Med Sci.* 2008;63(9):984-990.

14. Rockwood K, Stadnyk K, MacKnight C, et al. A brief clinical instrument to classify frailty in elderly people. *Lancet.* 1999;353(9148):205-206.

15. Cesari M, Gambassi G, Abellan van Kan G, Vellas B. The frailty phenotype and the frailty index: different instruments for different purposes. *Age Ageing.* 2013;43(1):10-12.

16. Kenig J, Zychiewicz B, Olszewska U, Richter P. Screening for frailty among older patients with cancer that qualify for abdominal surgery. *J Geriatr Oncol.* 2015;6(1):52-59.

17. Hamaker ME, Jonker JM, de Rooij SE, et al. Frailty screening methods for predicting outcome of a comprehensive geriatric assessment in elderly patients with cancer: a systematic review. *Lancet Oncol.* 2012;13(10):e437-e444.

18. Kristjansson SR, Nesbakken A, Jordhøy MS, et al. Comprehensive geriatric assessment can predict complications in elderly patients after elective surgery for colorectal cancer: a prospective observational cohort study. *Crit Rev Oncol Hematol.* 2010;76(3):208-217.

19. Hurria A, Togawa K, Mohile SG, et al. Predicting chemotherapy toxicity in older adults with cancer: a prospective multicenter study. *J Clin Oncol.* 2011;29(25):3457-3465.

20. Extermann M, Boler I, Reich RR, et al. Predicting the risk of chemotherapy toxicity in older patients: the Chemotherapy Risk Assessment Scale for High-Age Patients (CRASH) score. *Cancer.* 2012;118(13):3377-3386.

21. Kristjansson SR, Rønning B, Hurria A, et al. A comparison of two preoperative frailty measures in older surgical cancer patients. *J Geriatr Oncol.* 2012;3(1):1-7.

22. Drey M, Pfeifer K, Sieber CC, Bauer JM. The Fried frailty criteria as inclusion criteria for a randomized controlled trial: personal experience and literature review. *Gerontology.* 2011;57(1):11-18.

23. Makary MA, Segev DL, Pronovost PJ, et al. Frailty as a predictor of surgical outcomes in older patients. *J Am Coll Surg.* 2010;210(6):901-908.

24. Revenig LM, Canter DJ, Kim S, et al. Report of a simplified frailty score predictive of short-term postoperative morbidity and mortality. *J Am Coll Surg.* 2015;220(5): 904-911.e1.

25. Bylow K, Hemmerich J, Mohile SG, et al. Obese frailty, physical performance deficits, and falls in older men with biochemical recurrence of prostate cancer on androgen deprivation therapy: a case-control study. *Urology.* 2011;77(4):934-940.

26. Courtney-Brooks M, Tellawi AR, Scalici J, et al. Frailty: an outcome predictor for elderly gynecologic oncology patients. *Gynecol Oncol.* 2012;126(1):20-24.

4   Biologic Markers of Frailty

Kah Poh Loh, Nikesha Haynes-Gilmore, Allison Magnuson,
and Supriya G. Mohile

BIOLOGIC MARKERS OF FRAILTY

Older adults with cancer are a heterogeneous population, and their chronologic ages may not be reflective of their physiologic ages. Geriatric assessment (GA) to evaluate the overall health status of an older adult with cancer influences treatment decision making by providing a more accurate assessment of physiologic age (1,2). Several biologic markers correlate with aging and frailty and may offer a better assessment of physiologic age. In combination with GA, the use of biologic markers may better be able to personalize oncologic treatments in older adults in the future (Table 4.1).

Inflammation plays a vital role in the process of aging. Older adults often have low-grade, chronic systemic inflammation characterized by elevated circulating serum levels of white blood cells (WBCs), C-reactive protein (CRP), CXC chemokine ligand 10 (CXCL10), interleukin-6 (IL-6), and tumor necrosis factor-α (TNF-α) along with their cognate receptors (3). This heightened inflammatory state with aging is associated with an increased risk of morbidity and frailty. In a cross-sectional study of 558 women (aged 65–101), odds of frailty were four times higher in patients in the top tertile of WBC count and IL-6 than those with levels in the bottom tertile (4). Elevated circulating serum levels of IL-6 have also been shown to cause atherosclerosis, osteoporosis, sarcopenia, functional decline, and disability which ultimately may lead to mortality in this population (5). Additionally, patients with a cancer diagnosis and higher levels of IL-6 and CRP had higher odds of death compared to those without elevation of the markers, with hazard ratios of 1.64 and 1.63, respectively (5). Similarly, a high WBC count was also associated with frailty and mortality from cancer. The individual immune cell components may contribute differently to the frailty phenotype. In one study, increased levels of neutrophils and monocytes, but not lymphocytes, were positively associated with frailty, disability, and mortality (6). The direct correlation between WBC count and its subpopulations and frailty remains to be further elucidated.

Prothrombotic factors (fibrinogen, factor VIII, and d-dimers) and soluble vascular cell adhesion molecule (s-VCAM) are noted to be increased in parallel with chronic inflammatory markers due to the costimulatory and downstream effects between these pathways. In a large population cohort study involving 4,735 community-dwelling

TABLE 4.1 A Summary of Biomarkers of Frailty

Markers	Examples
Inflammation (including acute phase reactants) and coagulation system	High levels of CRP, IL-6, WBC, CXCL10, TNF-α, fibrinogen, factor VIII, d-dimers, s-VCAM
Endocrine markers	Impaired glucose tolerance, high cortisol level, and low levels of IGF-1 and DHEA-S
Cellular senescence	Telomere shortening, high levels of P16[ink4a]
Imaging	Sarcopenia (measurement of skeletal mass using whole-body DEXA or CT scan cross-sectional imaging)

CRP, C-reactive protein; CXCL10, CXC chemokine ligand 10; DEXA, dual-energy x-ray absorptiometry; DHEA-S, dehydroepiandrosterone sulfate; IGF-1, insulin-like growth factor-1; IL-6, interleukin-6; P16[ink4a], cyclin-dependent kinases 4 and 6 (CDK4/CDK6) inhibitor p16; s-VCAM, soluble vascular cell adhesion molecule; TNF-α, tumor necrosis factor-α; WBC, white blood cell.

adults 65 years and older (15% had cancer), those who were frail had higher levels of fibrinogen and factor VIII, independent of cardiovascular disease and diabetes (7). High d-dimers, s-VCAM, and IL-6 levels were also independently associated with 4-year mortality (3).

Endocrine biomarkers also correlate with aging and frailty. In a group of 102 women, older age was inversely associated with the levels of dehydroepiandrosterone sulfate (DHEA-S) and insulin-like growth factor-1 (IGF-1), and DHEA-S deficiency was also a predictor of bone loss (8). When compared to nonfrail community-dwelling older adults, serum levels of IGF-1 and DHEA-S in the frail population were significantly lower (9). The association was supported by a 10-year longitudinal study in which lower levels of DHEA-S (odds ratio [OR], 0.50) and higher cortisol-to-DHEA-S ratio (OR, 1.79) were predictive of frailty (10).

Telomeres are structures that cap the ends of DNA to avoid chromosomal damage. Telomere length shortens with aging, and correlates with senescence, apoptosis, and oncogenic transformation of somatic cells (11). Multiple studies have demonstrated that telomere length correlates with disability as well as with cancer and all-cause mortality (11). Cyclin-dependent kinases 4 and 6 (CDK4/CDK6) inhibitor pI6 (P16[ink4a]) is a tumor-suppressor protein which inhibits cyclin-dependent kinase (CDK) activity in the cell cycle (12). Prolonged expression of p16[INK4a] can induce irreversible cell cycle arrest and promote senescence (12). In animal and human models, this expression was found to be elevated with aging. Although in theory telomere length and *P16[ink4a]* could serve as biomarkers of aging, associations between frailty and mortality must be investigated further.

Sarcopenia is the loss of muscle mass associated with aging, and is defined as muscle mass that is two standard deviations below that of a healthy adult. Methods to assess muscle mass include whole-body dual-energy x-ray absorptiometry (four limbs) and CT cross-sectional imaging (lumbar muscles). Sarcopenia may contribute to frailty and thus these entities can be difficult to separate from one another (13). A meta-analysis demonstrated that low muscle mass was associated with decreased survival in patients with nonhematological cancers (14). Sarcopenia was also found to be predictive of postoperative complications in patients undergoing oncologic surgeries (15,16).

In conclusion, the interplay between frailty and biomarkers is complex, and is often affected by comorbidities and underlying diseases. Further studies are needed to validate the feasibility and utility of biomarkers in the geriatric oncology setting to help predict frailty, disability, treatment toxicities, and prognosis. More studies are needed to evaluate if biomarkers of aging can be modified by interventions and if these changes are correlated with outcomes. Of the various biologic markers, serum IL-6 has been studied most extensively. However, the exact mechanism by which IL-6 influences the pathophysiology of frailty, including how it interacts with other up- and downstream molecular and cellular immune factors, has yet to be elucidated.

TAKE HOME POINTS

1. Several biologic markers correlate with frailty, disability, and mortality in the general population and in patients with cancer, although none have enough data to support regular use in clinics.
2. Examples of biomarkers include markers of inflammation, endocrine pathways, and cellular senescence.
3. IL-6 has been more extensively studied than other markers and is associated with aging, frailty, and mortality in older adults.
4. Sarcopenia may serve as a biomarker for frailty and may be of particular interest in patients with cancer as a predictor of outcomes.
5. Studies are needed to evaluate how biomarkers can complement existing clinical parameters for the management of cancer in older adults.

REFERENCES

1. Kalsi T, Babic-Illman G, Ross PJ, et al. The impact of comprehensive geriatric assessment interventions on tolerance to chemotherapy in older people. *Br J Cancer.* April 2015;112(9):1435.
2. The National Comprehensive Cancer Network®. Older adult oncology: NCCN Guidelines. 2015. Available at: http://www.nccn.org/professionals/physician_gls/pdf/senior.pdf. Accessed January 9, 2016.
3. Hubbard JM, Cohen HJ, Muss HB. Incorporating biomarkers into cancer and aging research. *J Clin Oncol.* August 2014;32(24):2611-2616.
4. Leng SX, Xue Q-L, Tian J, et al. Inflammation and frailty in older women. *J Am Geriatr Soc.* June 2007;55(6):864-871.
5. Singh T, Newman AB. Inflammatory markers in population studies of aging. *Ageing Res Rev.* July 2011;10(3):319-329.
6. Leng SX, Xue Q-L, Huang Y, Ferrucci L, et al. Baseline total and specific differential white blood cell counts and 5-year all-cause mortality in community-dwelling older women. *Exp Gerontol.* December 2005;40(12):982-987.

7. Walston J, McBurnie MA, Newman A, et al. Frailty and activation of the inflammation and coagulation systems with and without clinical comorbidities: results from the Cardiovascular Health Study. *Arch Intern Med.* November 2002;162(20):2333-2341.

8. Haden ST, Glowacki J, Hurwitz S, et al. Effects of age on serum dehydroepiandrosterone sulfate, IGF-I, and IL-6 levels in women. *Calcif Tissue Int.* June 2000;66(6):414-418.

9. Leng SX, Cappola AR, Andersen RE, et al. Serum levels of insulin-like growth factor-I (IGF-I) and dehydroepiandrosterone sulfate (DHEA-S), and their relationships with serum interleukin-6, in the geriatric syndrome of frailty. *Aging Clin Exp Res.* April 2004;16(2):153-157.

10. Baylis D, Bartlett DB, Syddall HE, et al. Immune-endocrine biomarkers as predictors of frailty and mortality: a 10-year longitudinal study in community-dwelling older people. *Age (Dordr).* June 2013;35(3):963-971.

11. Bekaert S, De Meyer T, Van Oostveldt P. Telomere attrition as ageing biomarker. *Anticancer Res.* August 2005;25(4):3011-3021.

12. LaPak KM, Burd CE. The molecular balancing act of p16(INK4a) in cancer and aging. *Mol Cancer Res.* February 2014;12(2):167-183.

13. Mijnarends DM, Schols JM, Meijers JM, et al. Instruments to assess sarcopenia and physical frailty in older people living in a community (care) setting: similarities and discrepancies. *J Am Med Dir Assoc.* April 2015;16(4):301-308.

14. Shachar SS, Williams GR, Muss HB, Nishijima TF. Prognostic value of sarcopenia in adults with solid tumours: a meta-analysis and systematic review. *Eur J Cancer.* February 2016;57:58-67.

15. Boer BC, de Graaff F, Brusse-Keizer M, et al. Skeletal muscle mass and quality as risk factors for postoperative outcome after open colon resection for cancer. *Int J Colorectal Dis.* February 2016;31(6):1117-1124.

16. Kuroki LM, Mangano M, Allsworth JE, et al. Pre-operative assessment of muscle mass to predict surgical complications and prognosis in patients with endometrial cancer. *Ann Surg Oncol.* March 2015;22(3):972-979.

Geriatric Syndromes

5   Functional Dependency

Siri Rostoft and Benedicte Rønning

INTRODUCTION

Functional dependency is a geriatric syndrome where a person is not able to live independently and perform basic activities of daily living (ADLs). In older cancer patients, there are several reasons to evaluate functional status. First, functional status declines with aging, as all organ functions deteriorate with increasing age. As functional status provides an integrated picture of the person, it may be an overall indicator of a person's health—determined both by age-related changes and by comorbidities. Second, being able to live independently seems to be more important than survival for older patients with severe illness (1), making functional status an important outcome. Third, functional status is frequently underrated and underreported by medical doctors (2). Even though it has been shown that functional status is an important predictor of 1-year mortality in older hospitalized patients (3), it is seldom reported in the admission evaluation. In a large cohort of several thousand older surgical patients, ADL impairment was a consistent independent predictor of postoperative mortality (4). Nevertheless, surgical publications rarely report preoperative functional status. In addition, gait speed, which is an objective physical performance measure of functional status, is highly correlated with mortality (5). In a recent Delphi study on geriatric assessment in oncology, functional status was rated the most important domain to consider in older cancer patients (6).

DEFINITION

Functional dependency is usually defined as needing help in one of the basic ADLs such as bathing, dressing, using the toilet, eating, or rising from a chair. When a patient is functionally dependent, he or she cannot live without assistance. Instrumental activities of daily living (IADLs) describe more advanced activities necessary to live a fully independent life, like shopping, cooking, paying bills, and transportation. Of note, readers may come across a variety of definitions of functional dependency both in clinical practice and in scientific publications. It is important to emphasize that functional dependency may be the result of cognitive impairment. In fact, being functionally dependent is one of the diagnostic criteria for the syndrome of dementia. Thus, a complete evaluation of a patient's functional status should include an assessment of cognitive function in addition to an assessment of physical function.

DEVELOPMENT OF FUNCTIONAL DEPENDENCY

Functional dependency is considered a geriatric syndrome. It is usually caused by more than one single factor; it may develop slowly and may be the end result of chronic diseases and aging causing multiple impairments in an older person. However, functional dependency may also present more acutely in the setting of an acute medical illness or after cancer treatment such as extensive surgery or chemotherapy/radiation therapy. When the patient is vulnerable and has functional limitations before an acute illness or cancer treatment is initiated, the likelihood of developing functional dependency increases.

PREVALENCE

The prevalence of functional dependency in older patients varies considerably depending on the population assessed. In the nursing home population, the majority of patients are functionally dependent. In comparison, in the general population, data from Sweden show that about 75% of people at the age of 80 are functionally independent, and disability becomes common only after the age of 90 (7).

ASSESSMENT OF FUNCTIONAL STATUS

Information about functional status may be retrieved through a general clinical impression. Is the patient alert and orientated? Does she walk unaided to the consultation? Is she effortless in removing outerwear and sitting down? While such observations are helpful, the use of assessment tools provides more details, establishes a baseline, makes it easier to follow changes over time, and is helpful when communicating and documenting findings.

ACTIVITIES OF DAILY LIVING

1. Basic ADLs
    -The Katz index (8) (Figure 5.1)
    -The Barthel index (9)
2. IADLs
    -The Lawton–Brody scale (10) (Figure 5.2)

The term *ADLs* was first introduced by geriatrician Dr. Sidney Katz and colleagues from the Benjamin Rose Hospital in 1959. The purpose of their work was to create a tool for measuring changes in physical function in patients with disabling conditions such as stroke and hip fracture. A tool for measuring ADLs was also valuable in determining effects of treatment and for prognostic purposes. Several validated questionnaires for assessing dependency in ADLs and IADLs have been created. These questionnaires may be administered to the patient or a caregiver, or rated by observation (e.g., in a nursing home). The additional assessment of IADLs gives a

ACTIVITIES POINTS (1 OR 0)	INDEPENDENCE: (1 POINT) **NO** supervision, direction, or personal assistance	DEPENDENCE: (0 POINTS) **WITH** supervision, direction, personal assistance, or total care
BATHING POINTS: _____	**(1 POINT)** Bathes self completely or needs help in bathing only a single part of the body, such as the back, genital area, or disabled extremity.	**(0 POINTS)** Needs help with bathing more than one part of the body, getting in or out of the tub or shower. Requires total bathing.
DRESSING POINTS: _____	**(1 POINT)** Gets clothes from closets and drawers and puts on clothes and outer garments complete with fasteners. May have help tying shoes.	**(0 POINTS)** Needs help with dressing self or needs to be completely dressed.
TOILETING POINTS: _____	**(1 POINT)** Goes to toilet, gets on and off, arranges clothes, cleans genital area without help.	**(0 POINTS)** Needs help transferring to the toilet, cleaning self, or uses bedpan or commode.
TRANSFERRING POINTS: _____	**(1 POINT)** Moves in and out of bed or chair unassisted. Mechanical transferring aids are acceptable.	**(0 POINTS)** Needs help in moving from bed to chair or requires a complete transfer.
CONTINENCE POINTS: _____	**(1 POINT)** Exercises complete self-control over urination and defecation.	**(0 POINTS)** Is partially or totally incontinent of bowel or bladder.
FEEDING POINTS: _____	**(1 POINT)** Gets food from plate into mouth without help. Preparation of food may be done by another person.	**(0 POINTS)** Needs partial or total help with feeding or requires parenteral feeding.

FIGURE 5.1 Katz index.

more comprehensive impression of the patients' degree of dependency in everyday life. To be fully independent in feeding, for example, one also has to be able to go to the store, shop, and prepare a meal—the latter activities are included in IADL scales, such as the Lawton–Brody IADL scale. In clinical practice, it is critical to determine in which activities the patient needs assistance. This knowledge is important to plan for the appropriate level of care. The numerical properties of these scales make them useful in clinical research: both as prognostic factors and outcomes, and as repeated measures to evaluate changes in physical function over time.

Instrumental Activities of Daily Living (IADL)

Instructions: Circle the scoring point for the statement that most closely corresponds to the patient's current functional ability for each task. The examiner should complete the scale based on information about the patient from the patient him-/herself, informants (such as the patient's family member or other caregiver), and recent records.

A. Ability to use telephone	Score
1. Operates telephone on own initiative; looks up and dials numbers, etc.	1
2. Dials a few well-known numbers	1
3. Answers telephone but does not dial	1
4. Does not use telephone at all	0

B. Shopping	
1. Takes care of all shopping needs independently	1
2. Shops independently for small purchases	0
3. Needs to be accompanied on any shopping trip	0
4. Completely unable to shop	0

C. Food preparation	
1. Plans, prepares, and serves adequate meals independently	1
2. Prepares adequate meals if supplied with ingredients	0
3. Heats and serves prepared meals, or prepares meals but does not maintain adequate diet	0
4. Needs to have meals prepared and served	0

D. Housekeeping	
1. Maintains house alone or with occasional assistance (e.g., "heavy work domestic help")	1
2. Performs light daily tasks such as dishwashing, bed making	1
3. Performs light daily tasks but cannot maintain acceptable level of cleanliness	1
4. Needs help with all home maintenance tasks	1
5. Does not participate in any housekeeping tasks	0

E. Laundry	Score
1. Does personal laundry completely	1
2. Launders small items; rinses stockings, etc.	1
3. All laundry must be done by others	0

F. Mode of transportation	
1. Travels independently on public transportation or drives own car	1
2. Arranges own travel via taxi, but does not otherwise use public transportation	1
3. Travels on public transportation when assisted or accompanied by another	1

FIGURE 5.2 Lawton–Brody scale.

(*continued*)

4. Travel limited to taxi or automobile with assistance of another	0
5. Does not travel at all	0
G. Responsibility for own medications	
1. Is responsible for taking medication in correct dosages at correct time	1
2. Takes responsibility if medication is prepared in advance in separate dosages	0
3. Is not capable of dispensing own medication	0
H. Ability to handle finances	
1. Manages financial matters independently (budgets, writes checks, pays rent and bills, goes to bank), collects and keeps track of income	1
2. Manages day-to-day purchases, but needs help with banking, major purchases, etc.	1
3. Incapable of handling money	0

FIGURE 5.2 Lawton–Brody scale (*continued*).

Source: Adapted from Ref. (10). Lawton MP, Brody EM. Assessment of older people: self-maintaining and instrumental activities of daily living. *Gerontologist.* 1969;9(3):179-186.

PHYSICAL PERFORMANCE MEASURES

Examples of common tools for assessing physical performance:

1. Gait speed (11)
2. Timed up and go test (12)
3. Short Physical Performance Battery (13)

Physical performance measures are objective tests of physical function in which the patients perform one or more standardized tasks, such as walking (gait speed). Gait speed is easily measured by having the patient walk 5 m at a comfortable pace. Number of meters walked is divided by the seconds needed to complete the task, and gait speed is reported in meters per second. Normal gait speeds for healthy women between 70 to 79 and ≥80 years are 1.13 m/sec and 0.94 m/sec, respectively. For healthy men in corresponding age groups, the numbers are 1.26 m/sec and 0.97 m/sec. A gait speed of less than 0.8 m/sec is generally considered slow, and is predictive of poor clinical outcomes such as disability, falls, and institutionalization (5). The timed up and go test is a physical performance test that includes gait, balance, and mobility. The patient sits in an armchair, gets up from the chair, walks 3 m (10 ft) at usual pace, turns 180°, walks back, and sits down again. The result is measured in seconds needed to complete this task. The Short Physical Performance Battery consists of three elements: a balance test, gait speed, and a chair stand test.

ASSESSING FUNCTIONAL STATUS IN GERIATRIC ONCOLOGY

With the large number of tools available to assess physical function, the question remains: Which tools are best suited for onco-geriatric patients? Oncologists have traditionally assessed performance status (PS) in cancer patients using indexes such as the Eastern Cooperative Oncology Group performance status (ECOG PS) or the Karnofsky index of PS. The measurement of PS by these indexes and well-established measures is simple and also feasible in geriatric patients. However, in a clinical study of 363 cancer patients with mean age 72 years, the authors identified impairments in ADLs and/or IADLs in a considerable number of patients with ECOG PS less than two (14), indicating that evaluation of dependency in ADLs should be part of the routine patient assessment. The role of objective physical performance measures is well established and will perhaps be determined through future research. To date, no guidelines on how to best assess physical function in geriatric oncology exist, but we recommend, as a minimum, to evaluate PS and use a validated questionnaire on dependency in ADLs and IADLs.

FUNCTIONAL TRAJECTORIES AFTER CANCER TREATMENT

Few studies have looked at functional trajectories after treatment for cancer. In older patients with colorectal cancer undergoing surgery, it was found that approximately one-third of patients had lost ADL function after a median of 22 months follow-up (15). Amemiya et al. found that only a small number of patients over 75 years of age exhibited decline in ADLs 6 months after cancer surgery (16). More studies are needed in this area.

CONCLUSION

Functional dependency is an important factor to consider in older patients with cancer, before treatment, throughout the treatment trajectory, and after completion of treatment. Assessing functional dependency provides the treating physician with a baseline, and serves as a predictor of remaining life expectancy and treatment tolerance. The maintenance of functional independence is a major outcome for older patients treated for cancer, and should be assessed in addition to standard outcomes such as survival and disease progression.

TAKE HOME POINTS

1. Assessment of functional status is mandatory in older cancer patients.
2. An assessment of functional status includes basic and IADLs, PS, mobility, and cognition.
3. Functional dependency increases the risk of mortality, treatment toxicity, and institutionalization.
4. Functional dependency is an important treatment outcome.

REFERENCES

1. Fried T, Bradley E, Towle V, Allore H. Understanding the treatment preferences of seriously ill patients. *N Engl J Med.* 2002;346(14):1061-1066.
2. Covinsky K, Pierluissi E, Johnston C. Hospitalization-associated disability: "She was probably able to ambulate, but I'm not sure." *JAMA.* 2011;306(16):1782-1793.
3. Walter L, Brand R, Counsell S, et al. Development and validation of a prognostic index for 1-year mortality in older adults after hospitalization. *JAMA.* 2001;285(23):2987-2994.
4. Turrentine F, Wang H, Simpson V, Jones R. Surgical risk factors, morbidity, and mortality in elderly patients. *J Am Coll Surg.* 2006;203(6):865-877.
5. Studenski S, Perera S, Patel K, et al. Gait speed and survival in older adults. *JAMA.* 2011;305(1):50-58.
6. O'Donovan A, Mohile S, Leech M. Expert consensus panel guidelines on geriatric assessment in oncology. *Eur J Cancer Care.* 2015;24(4):574-589.
7. Santoni G, Angleman S, Welmer A-K, et al. Age-related variation in health status after age 60. *PLoS One.* 2015;10(3):e0120077.
8. Katz S, Downs T, Cash H, Grotz R. Progress in development of the index of ADL1. *Gerontologist.* 1970;10(1 pt 1):20-30.
9. Mahoney F, Barthel D. Functional evaluation: the Barthel index. *Md State Med J.* 1965;14:61-65.
10. Lawton MP, Brody EM. Assessment of older people: self-maintaining and instrumental activities of daily living. *Gerontologist.* 1969;9(3):179-186.
11. Cesari M, Kritchevsky SB, Penninx BW, et al. Prognostic value of usual gait speed in well-functioning older people. *J Am Geriatr Soc.* 2005;53(10):1675-1680.
12. Podsiadlo D, Richardson S. The timed "Up & Go": a test of basic functional mobility for frail elderly persons. *J Am Geriatr Soc.* 1991;39:142-148.
13. Guralnik J, Simonsick E, Ferrucci L, et al. A short physical performance battery assessing lower extremity function: association with self-reported disability and prediction of mortality and nursing home admission. *J Gerontol.* 1994; 49(2):M85-M94.
14. Repetto L, Fratino L, Audisio R, et al. Comprehensive geriatric assessment adds information to Eastern Cooperative Oncology Group performance status in elderly cancer patients: an Italian Group for Geriatric Oncology study. *J Clin Oncol.* 2002;20(2):494-502.
15. Rønning B, Wyller T, Jordhøy M, et al. Frailty indicators and functional status in older patients after colorectal cancer surgery. *J Geriatr Oncol.* 2014;5(1):26-32.
16. Amemiya T, Oda K, Ando M, et al. Activities of daily living and quality of life of elderly patients after elective surgery for gastric and colorectal cancers. *Ann Surg.* 2007;246(2):222-228.

6 Falls in the Older Cancer Patient

Soo Jung Kim and Beatriz Korc-Grodzicki

A *fall* is defined as unintentionally coming to rest on the ground or other lower level not due to an overwhelming intrinsic or environmental cause and without the loss of consciousness. Falling is a common, serious, and costly problem faced by older adults. It occurs more frequently in the older adult with cancer than in noncancer patients (1). Studies show that about 20% of older adults starting a course of chemotherapy fell in the prior 6 months (1,2). Approximately 26% of patients older than 75, who were evaluated prior to cancer surgery, experienced a fall over the last year and 37% of those who fell presented to the medical care provider using a cane, walker, or wheelchair (3). Falls in this vulnerable population are likely to be underestimated due to recall bias, among other factors (1). Depression, cognitive impairment, history of prior falls, and impairment of functional status are all significant predictors of falls in the cancer patient as well as the general geriatric population. Therefore, there is a particular need for falls screening among older patients with cancer (4).

This group of patients has added risk factors for falls, such as toxicity from cancer treatments or metastatic disease to the brain (1,5). Chemotherapy-induced peripheral neuropathy has been shown to be associated with falls (11.9%), as has functional impairment (26.6%), in a cohort of 421 patients (6). Another study showed that patients receiving neurotoxic doublet therapy had higher rates of fall-related injuries compared to those receiving a single neurotoxic agent and those receiving nonneurotoxic chemotherapy (7). Cancer patients are more likely to experience complications related to traumatic injury from falls, including cardiac arrest, respiratory failure, hypotensive shock, and anoxic encephalopathy, than are noncancer patients. In addition, the presence of falls was shown to be associated with an increased risk for serious chemotherapy toxicity in older cancer patients (8).

Despite the high frequency and seriousness of this problem, only 10% of older patients with cancer who self-reported a recent fall to their oncologists had appropriate medical record documentation (9). Oncologists are largely unfamiliar with the frequency and impact of falls and do not routinely document the presence of falls in their older patients. Therefore, it is likely that older cancer patients who fall go unrecognized by the oncologist provider. It is imperative to increase awareness of falls prevalence and its consequences among oncology providers in order to implement timely interventions and reduce risks associated with falls (9).

CAUSES AND RISK FACTORS FOR FALLS

There are numerous causes of falls in older adults. They can occur as a result of intrinsic factors, such as age-related physiologic changes, and/or the individual's medical conditions, environmental factors, or a combination of these (Table 6.1). "Accidental" or environment-related falls are the most frequently cited, accounting for 30% to 50% in most series. However, many falls attributed to accidents are the result of a combination of an individual's increased susceptibility with identifiable environmental hazards (10,11). Assessing intrinsic predisposing risk factors and situational risk factors are critical in determining the cause of a fall.

Vision, hearing, and proprioceptive system: Visual acuity, contrast sensitivity, and depth perception are extremely important to maintaining postural stability and avoiding a fall. Bifocal glasses are problematic for those at risk of falls because when

TABLE 6.1 Risk Factors for Falls and Potential Interventions

Risk Factors for Falls	Potential Interventions
Intrinsic risk factors	
Vision: Cataracts, impairment in visual perception, glare tolerance, dark adaption	Appropriate refraction, cataract surgery, medications, good lighting
Hearing	Cerumen removal, hearing aids
Vestibular changes: BPV, previous ear infections, drugs	Avoidance of toxic drugs, balance exercises, good lighting
Propioceptive disfunction: Peripheral neuropathy, cervical DJD	Treatment of underlying disease, appropriate walking aid, good footwear, balance exercises
Central neurologic: Impairment of mobilization, problem solving or judgment, dementia	Treatment of underlying disease, supervision, safe environment
Musculoskeletal: Arthritis, muscle weakness, contractures, foot disorders, bunions, calluses, deformities	Medical/surgical treatment of disease, strengthening exercises, gait training, walking aids, podiatry care, good shoes
Systemic diseases: Postural hypotension, cardiac, respiratory, metabolic diseases	Hydration, medication review, stockings, treatment of underlying disease
Depression, post-fall anxiety syndrome	Risk/benefit of antidepressant medications
Extrinsic risk factors	
Environment: Stairs, cords, furniture, rugs, poor lighting, surfaces with glare, inappropriate shoes, optical patterns of the floor	Environmental hazard checklist, home evaluation, appropriate adaptations, bathroom safety equipment
Medications: Sedatives, antidepressants, antihypertensives, diuretics, polypharmacy (five or more prescription medications)	Lowest effective dosage of essential medications; start low and go slow

BPV, benign positional vertigo; DJD, degenerative joint disease.

something happens that might cause a fall, these people are unable to focus on their feet or on the ground to stabilize themselves, as they look down through the reading portion of the bifocals. Similarly, cataracts are a significant risk factor and surgery on the first eye should be expedited in older persons when surgery is indicated (12). Hearing directly affects stability by the detection and interpretation of auditory stimuli that help orient a person in space. Greater than 50% of older people have some degree of hearing loss. The vestibular system assists with spatial orientation at rest and with acceleration, whereas the proprioceptive system provides for spatial orientation during position changes and while walking on uneven surfaces. Patients with impairment in any of these systems will have worsened stability (13).

Postural hypotension: Postural hypotension may result in a fall by compromising the cerebral blood flow (14). This condition affects 10% to 30% of older patients living in the community. It is often multifactorial in origin and the result of age-related physiologic changes present in the older patient (e.g., autonomic changes, decreased baroreceptor sensitivity), comorbidities, and medications used to treat them.

Medications such as antipsychotics, corticosteroids, anticholinergics, antidepressants, benzodiazepines, opiates, anxiolytics, antiarrhythmic, and diuretics have been found to increase risk for falls. Medications frequently used to treat diseases such as depression, heart failure, or hypertension may also increase falls risk. The use of four or more medications and changes in dosage have been shown to be associated with falling. Reduced falls risk was seen in interventions coupled with reduced polypharmacy. Medication review and avoidance/reduction of medications that may be inappropriate for older adults are mandatory in the care of older adults. Behavioral risk factors such as alcohol consumption have also been found to be associated with falls.

Gait instability is a common geriatric syndrome. Any impairment of the musculoskeletal system, including bones, joints, or muscles/tendons, may have an adverse effect on stability. Any of the arthritides may increase the likelihood of a fall through multiple mechanisms, including pain, muscle weakness, or decreased proprioception. Abnormalities of the foot should also be mentioned, as calluses, bunions, or toe and nail deformities can lead to poor gait (11).

Disorders affecting the **central nervous system**, such as cerebrovascular disease or Parkinson's disease, may predispose an older patient to falls. Similarly, dementia and other diseases that have a negative effect on cognition (by adversely affecting problem solving and judgment) increase the risk of falls (10,11).

In **cancer patients**, fatigue, anemia, neuropathy, generalized weakness, and bone metastasis can contribute to falls. Pain and neurotoxic chemotherapy increase falls risk. In the outpatient setting, fall predictors in the older cancer patient include dependency in activities of daily living (ADLs) and independent activities of daily living (IADLs), prior history of falls, malnutrition, comorbidities, depression, and low Eastern Cooperative Oncology Group (ECOG) performance status. In the inpatient setting, risk factors include metastatic disease to the brain and cognitive impairment (1,15). It is important to note that about 20% of patients receiving chemotherapy newly develop dependence in ADLs between the first and second chemotherapy cycle (16).

EVALUATING THE FALL PATIENT

Oncology providers need to routinely screen for falls. A positive screening should prompt further evaluation of the patient or referral for further evaluation of the cause of the fall(s). The 2010 AGS/BGS Guideline on Prevention of Falls in Older Persons (12) recommended three simple questions for falls screening that should be asked at least once a year (Figure 6.1):

1. Did you have two or more falls in last 12 months?
2. Did you present to an emergency department (ED) or clinic with an acute fall?
3. Do you have difficulty with walking or balance?

The American Geriatrics Society (AGS) also recommends that clinicians caring for older adults ask screening questions about **fear of falling** each year. Any positive answer to the screening questions puts the person screened in a high-risk group that warrants further evaluation. A multifactorial assessment should be performed, including obtaining complete history and physical exam, details of the fall (including symptoms prior to/at the time of the fall, and circumstances of the fall), frequency of falls, review of medications (prescription and over-the-counter medications), environmental risks, and contributing factors. Physical examination should begin with orthostatic blood pressure measurement, followed by assessment of gait, strength, and balance along with looking for the presence of carotid bruits, arrhythmias, focal neurological signs, nystagmus, weakness, tremor, visual disturbances, arthritis of joints, and cognitive impairment. A foot exam, assessment for proper footwear, and functional assessment (ability to perform ADLs) should also be included.

For the practicing oncologist, the Timed Up and Go (TUG) test may be a simple, effective, and brief screening tool for gait and balance (17,18) (Table 6.2). If the patient has deficits noted on the TUG test, further evaluation and referral for physical therapy should be considered.

Generally, laboratory tests have not been found to be useful in fall evaluations. If the patient's history or physical examination points to an underlying cause, appropriate tests should be performed. For example, a complete blood count, metabolic panel, and ECG can be ordered to rule out contributing factors such as anemia, electrolyte disturbances, and arrhythmias.

CONSEQUENCES OF FALLS

Falls are a cause of significant morbidity and mortality in older adults and contribute to immobility and institutionalization. In adults 65 and older, fall-related injuries account for more than 6% of all medical expenditures (10). Fractures, contusions, head trauma, internal injuries, and dislocations are some of the injuries associated with falls. Recovery after a fall is frequently slower in older adults and increases risk for deconditioning and subsequent falls. A fear of falling or **post-fall anxiety syndrome** may also develop, causing further weakness, deconditioning, and gait abnormalities from inactivity.

Older Cancer Patient Encounter
with Health Care Provider

Screening Questions
Did you have two or more falls in last 12 months?
Did the patient present to emergency department or clinic with an acute fall?
Do you have difficulty with walking or balance?
Do you have fear of falling?

NO

YES

Reassess Periodically

Evaluate Gait and Balance

Multifactorial Assessment
1. Obtain relevant medical
   history, physical examination,
   cognitive and functional
   assessment
2. Determine multifactorial risk:
   a. History of falls
   b. Medications
   c. Gait balance and mobility
   d. Visual acuity
   e. Other neurological
      impairments
   f. Muscle strength
   g. Heart rate and rhythm
   h. Postural hypotension
   i. Feet and footwear
   j. Environmental hazards
   k. Alcohol consumption

**Initiate Multifactorial/
Multicomponent Intervention**
1. Minimize medications
2. Provide individually tailored
   exercise program
3. Treat vision impairment
4. Manage postural
   hypotension
5. Manage heart rate and
   rhythm abnormalities
6. Supplement vitamin D
7. Manage foot problems and
   recommend appropriate
   footwear
8. Modify the home
   environment
9. Provide education and
   information

FIGURE 6.1 Evaluation/prevention of falls in older persons.

Source: Adapted from Ref. (12). Summary of the updated American Geriatrics Society/British Geriatrics Society clinical practice guideline for prevention of falls in older persons. *J Am Geriatr Soc.* 2011;59(1):148–157. doi:10.1111/j.1532–5415.2010.03234.x.

TABLE 6.2 Timed Up and Go Instructions

1. The patient should sit on a standard chair.
2. Ask the patient stand up from the chair without using the arms, walk 10 ft, turn, return to the chair, and sit down. Regular footwear and customary walking aids should be used.
3. Patients should be instructed to use a comfortable and safe walking speed.
4. A stopwatch should be used to time the test (in seconds).
5. Normal healthy elderly usually complete the task in 10 sec or less.
6. Results correlate with gait speed, balance, functional level, and the ability to go out, and can change over time.

In cancer patients, history of falls is correlated with heightened risk for chemotherapy toxicity and death (1). A study showed that age, gender, comorbidities, chemotherapy, cancer stage, and osteoporosis were significant predictors for fall-related injuries in elderly cancer patients treated with neurotoxic chemotherapy (7). Types and severity of injury in these patients included contusions, dislocations, fractures, and hematomas, with fracture rates reported up to 78% (7,15).

Research suggests that cancer patients are more likely to experience complications related to traumatic injuries from falls. However, there are almost no articles related to the implications of falls on cancer treatment, disease trajectory, and mortality (15).

PREVENTION OF FALLS

It is estimated that two-thirds of falls are potentially preventable through addressing environmental risks and obtaining adequate medical evaluation. After determining the cause of falls, several interventions can be implemented, including treatment of underlying medical conditions and making changes to medications that may increase falls risk (Table 6.1) (19). A referral can be made for physical therapy and occupational therapy for improved gait, balance, and coordination. Assist devices can also be helpful for patients with gait and balance impairments. In some cases, short-term rehabilitation may be necessary to provide safe care with diminished long-term disability.

A referral for home services and safety evaluation may be indicated to assist patients with environmental hazards and for home improvements such as grab bars in bathroom, elevated toilet seats, rubber mats, and adequate lighting. Exercise has been shown to reduce the number of falls through improvement in endurance, strength, and body mechanics. However, the patient's physical capacities and health status should be taken into account when selecting an exercise program. A referral to health care providers such as social workers, podiatrists, optometrists, and/or ophthalmologists may also be indicated to address care needs. The AGS also recommends daily vitamin D (VD) supplementation (800 IU) in all older adults who are at risk for falls and have VD deficiency (12).

VD DEFICIENCY

VD deficiency is common in older adults and its prevalence rises along with latitude, obesity, sedentary lifestyle, limited sunlight exposure, and aging. Furthermore, an increasing epidemic of obesity, which results in sequestration of VD in adipose tissue, also contributes to an increased risk of VD deficiency. Hypovitaminosis D is consistently associated with decrease in muscle function and performance and increase in disability. VD supplementation has been shown to improve muscle strength and gait in different settings, especially in elderly patients. Despite some controversies in the interpretation of a meta-analysis, a reduced risk of falls has been attributed to VD supplementation due to direct effects on muscle cells (20). Checking levels of VD and recommending supplementation should be considered in all older adults with cancer (9).

TAKE HOME POINTS

1. Oncology providers need to screen for falls as part of a routine evaluation and provide interventions and/or referrals as needed.
2. Assess for at least five frequent modifiable risk factors: polypharmacy, vision/hearing impairment, orthostatic hypotension, gait and balance instability, and environmental hazards.
3. A gait assessment using the TUG test is a simple evaluation that all clinicians can perform in clinic to assist in determining the need for further interventions.
4. The need for VD supplementation should be evaluated in all older adults with cancer.
5. In the older adult with cancer, injuries as a result of a fall can not only impair the patient's quality of life, but also complicate cancer treatment.

REFERENCES

1. Wildes TM, Dua P, Fowler SA, et al. Systematic review of falls in older adults with cancer. *J Geriatr Oncol.* 2015;6(1):70-83. doi:10.1016/j.jgo.2014.10.003.
2. Hurria A, Mohile S, Gajra A, et al. Validation of a prediction tool for chemotherapy toxicity in older adults with cancer. *J Clin Oncol.* 2016;34(20):2366-2371. doi:10.1200/jco.2015.65.4327.
3. Shahrokni A, Downey R, Strong V, et al. Electronic rapid fitness assessment: a novel tool for preoperative evaluation of the geriatric oncology patient. *J NCCN.* In press.
4. Vande Walle N, Kenis C, Heeren P, et al. Fall predictors in older cancer patients: a multi-center prospective study. *BMC Geriatr.* 2014;14:135. doi:10.1186/1471-2318-14-135.
5. Bylow K, Dale W, Mustian K, et al. Falls and physical performance deficits in older patients with prostate cancer undergoing androgen deprivation therapy. *Urology.* 2008;72(2):422-427. doi:10.1016/j.urology.2008.03.032.
6. Gewandter JS, Fan L, Magnuson A, et al. Falls and functional impairments in cancer survivors with chemotherapy-induced peripheral neuropathy (CIPN): a University of Rochester CCOP study. *Support Care Cancer.* 2013;21(7):2059-2066. doi:10.1007/s00520-013-1766-y.
7. Ward PR, Wong MD, Moore R, Naeim A. Fall-related injuries in elderly cancer patients treated with neurotoxic chemotherapy: a retrospective cohort study. *J Geriatr Oncol.* 2014;5(1):57-64. doi:10.1016/j.jgo.2013.10.002.

8. Hurria A, Togawa K, Mohile SG, et al. Predicting chemotherapy toxicity in older adults with cancer: a prospective multicenter study. *J Clin Oncol.* 2011;29(25): 3457-3465. doi:10.1200/jco.2011.34.7625.

9. Guerard EJ, Deal AM, Williams GR, et al. Falls in older adults with cancer: evaluation by oncology providers. *J Oncol Pract.* 2015;11(6):470-474. doi:10.1200/jop.2014.003517.

10. Rubenstein LZ. Falls in older people: epidemiology, risk factors and strategies for prevention. *Age Ageing.* 2006;35(suppl 2):ii37-ii41. doi:10.1093/ageing/afl084.

11. Soriano TA, DeCherrie LV, Thomas DC. Falls in the community-dwelling older adult: a review for primary-care providers. *Clin Interv Aging.* 2007;2(4):545-554.

12. Summary of the Updated American Geriatrics Society/British Geriatrics Society clinical practice guideline for prevention of falls in older persons. *J Am Geriatr Soc.* 2011;59(1):148-157. doi:10.1111/j.1532-5415.2010.03234.x.

13. Tinetti ME, Speechley M. Prevention of falls among the elderly. *N Engl J Med.* 1989;320(16):1055-1059. doi:10.1056/nejm198904203201606.

14. Lipsitz LA. Orthostatic hypotension in the elderly. *N Engl J Med.* 1989;321(14): 952-957. doi:10.1056/nejm198910053211407.

15. Sattar S, Alibhai SM, Spoelstra SL, et al. Falls in older adults with cancer: a systematic review of prevalence, injurious falls, and impact on cancer treatment. *Support Care Cancer.* 2016;24(10):4459-4469. doi:10.1007/s00520-016-3342-8.

16. Wildes TM, Depp B, Colditz G, Stark S. Fall-risk prediction in older adults with cancer: an unmet need. *Support Care Cancer.* 2016;24(9):3681-3684. doi:10.1007/s00520-016-3312-1.

17. Podsiadlo D, Richardson S. The timed "Up & Go": a test of basic functional mobility for frail elderly persons. *J Am Geriatr Soc.* 1991;39(2):142-148.

18. Barry E, Galvin R, Keogh C, et al. Is the Time Up and Go test a useful predictor of risk of falls in community dwelling older adults: a systematic review and meta-analysis. *BMC Geriatr.* 2014;14:14. doi:10.1186/1471-2318-14-14.

19. Moyer VA. Prevention of falls in community-dwelling older adults: U.S. Preventive Services Task Force recommendation statement. *Ann Intern Med.* 2012;157(3): 197-204. doi:10.7326/0003-4819-157-3-201208070-00462.

20. Halfon M, Phan O, Teta D. Vitamin D: a review on its effects on muscle strength, the risk of fall, and frailty. *BioMed Res Int.* 2015;2015:953241. doi:10.1155/2015/953241.

7   Nutrition

Suzanne D. Gerdes

INTRODUCTION

Nutrition is important at any age to maintain health. Aging brings on lifestyle changes and physiological changes as well as an increase in chronic diseases such as heart disease, kidney disease, diabetes, and cancer. Maintaining nutritional status can become challenging when symptoms of diseases, side effects of treatments, or difficulty purchasing and preparing foods arise. Poor nutrition is associated with increased morbidity and mortality, decreased functional capacity, and a loss of independence. Therefore, identifying patients at nutritional risk is essential, as early intervention in the geriatric population can help to minimize unintended weight loss, malnutrition, sarcopenia, and cachexia associated with many chronic diseases.

UNINTENDED WEIGHT LOSS

Older adults often find it difficult to regain lost weight due to loss of appetite as well as illness, use of medications, chronic diseases, social changes, and physiological changes of aging.

Chemosensory changes in aging impair patients' desire to eat (1). Older adults are more likely to incorrectly identify tastes than young adults (2) and poor vision lessens their sensory experience of eating, impacting their appetites (3). Poor dentition or use of dentures may also decrease sense of taste or make it more difficult to chew foods. Many medications decrease saliva production, impacting the sense of taste and smell of foods and leading to a loss of appetite (4).

Anorexia, present in 50% of patients with cancer, leads to unintentional weight loss. Hypercatabolism via proinflammatory cytokines plays a role in increasing muscle protein degradation, decreasing protein synthesis, and altering hunger hormones—leptin and ghrelin (4,5). As a result, not only is appetite lessened, but metabolic rate is also increased, thus increasing patients' nutrient needs.

The gastrointestinal (GI) tract changes during the aging process, long-term use of medications, and surgery. The sensation of hunger lessens with aging. The slower rate of peristaltic action of the GI tract also contributes to satiety as a result of delayed gastric emptying (6). Medication-related constipation impacts older adults' appetites as well (5). Cancer treatments such as radiation therapy, surgery, or complications may lead to esophagitis, reflux, or diarrhea. Adapted diets, including limiting patients' food selections, are required in these situations either temporarily or permanently to minimize side effects and improve nutritional status.

MALNUTRITION

Malnutrition is defined as a lack of adequate energy intake or inadequate protein or other nutrient intake that is required for maintaining and repairing healthy tissues. The prevalence of malnutrition varies from 2% to 10% among older community-dwelling adults and from 30% to 60% in hospitalized older adults (7,8). It is expected that the prevalence is actually even higher, as malnutrition continues to be underreported. It is associated with increased morbidity and mortality, decreased function and quality of life, increased frequency of hospital admissions, and longer length of hospital stay (LOS) (7,9).

Nutrition Screening

Timely nutrition screening is essential in identifying patients at risk for malnutrition. In the inpatient setting, the nutrition screen should be completed within 24 hours of admission. In the outpatient setting, the Joint Commission mandates that "nutritional screening may be performed at the first visit"; however, reassessment is done on an as-needed basis and when it is appropriate to the particular patient's visit (10). Further assessment is required to diagnose malnutrition, but utilizing the past medical history and physical examinations help to raise suspicion of malnutrition. Several screening tools have been developed to help identify patients at risk of malnutrition. Studies find that the Mini Nutrition Assessment (MNA) (see Figure 7.1) is the best predictor of malnutrition in the older adult, in both inpatient and community-dwelling settings (14). The MNA is not a diagnostic tool, and further assessment should be completed soon after patients are screened.

Diagnosis of Malnutrition

The Academy of Nutrition and Dietetics (AND) and the American Society for Parenteral and Enteral Nutrition (ASPEN) have worked together to create a standardized approach to the diagnosis of adult malnutrition (7). They identified several standardized characteristics as a means to identify malnutrition in adult patients. These characteristics are outlined in Table 7.1.

Laboratory data such as serum albumin (ALB) are poor indicators of nutritional status. ALB has a large body pool size with only 5% from daily hepatic synthesis (15). ALB also experiences frequent extravascular and intravascular space redistribution and is influenced by changes in plasma volume, as seen in dehydration or blood transfusions, and may be decreased due to the inflammatory response often seen in acute and chronic illness. Visceral proteins, including prealbumin (PAB), transferrin, retinol-binding protein, and C-reactive protein (CRP), while more sensitive than ALB, are also influenced by the inflammatory response and also fail to show consistent improvement with increasing nutrition. Therefore, serum proteins are of little benefit when assessing nutritional status. To ensure that patients are meeting their nutrient needs, patients should be reassessed at frequent intervals throughout their hospital stay.

Mini Nutritional Assessment

MNA®

Nestlé
NutritionInstitute

| Last name: | | | First name: | | |
| Sex: | Age: | Weight, kg: | Height, cm: | Date: |

Complete the screen by filling in the boxes with the appropriate numbers. Total the numbers for the final screening score.

Screening

A Has food intake declined over the past 3 months due to loss of appetite, digestive problems, chewing or swallowing difficulties?
0 = severe decrease in food intake
1 = moderate decrease in food intake
2 = no decrease in food intake ☐

B Weight loss during the last 3 months
0 = weight loss greater than 3 kg (6.6 lbs)
1 = does not know
2 = weight loss between 1 and 3 kg (2.2 and 6.6 lbs)
3 = no weight loss ☐

C Mobility
0 = bed or chair bound
1 = able to get out of bed / chair but does not go out
2 = goes out ☐

D Has suffered psychological stress or acute disease in the past 3 months?
0 = yes   2 = no ☐

E Neuropsychological problems
0 = severe dementia or depression
1 = mild dementia
2 = no psychological problems ☐

F1 Body Mass Index (BMI) (weight in kg) / (height in m)^2 ☐
0 = BMI less than 19
1 = BMI 19 to less than 21
2 = BMI 21 to less than 23
3 = BMI 23 or greater ☐

IF BMI IS NOT AVAILABLE, REPLACE QUESTION F1 WITH QUESTION F2.
DO NOT ANSWER QUESTION F2 IF QUESTION F1 IS ALREADY COMPLETED.

F2 Calf circumference (CC) in cm
0 = CC less than 31
3 = CC 31 or greater ☐

Screening score ☐☐
(max. 14 points)

12-14 points: ☐ Normal nutritional status
8-11 points: ☐ At risk of malnutrition
0-7 points: ☐ Malnourished

Save
Print
Reset

Ref. Vellas B, Villars H, Abellan G, et al. Overview of the MNA®—Its History and Challenges. J Nutr Health Aging 2006;10:456–465.
Rubenstein LZ, Harker JO, Salva A, Guigoz Y, Vellas B. Screening for Undernutrition in Geriatric Practice: Developing the short-Form Mini Nutritional Assessment (MNA-SF). J. Geront 2001;56A:M366–377.
Guigoz Y. The Mini-Nutritional Assessment (MNA®) Review of the Literature - What does it tell us? J Nutr Health Aging 2006;10:466–487.
Kauser MJ, Bauer JM, Ramsch C, et al. Validation of the Mini Nutritional Assessment Short-Form (MNA®-SF): A practical tool for identification of nutritional status. J Nutr Health Aging 2009;13:782-788.
®Société des Produits Nestlé, S.A., Vevey, Switzerland, Trademark Owners
© Nestlé, 1994, Revision 2009. N67200 12/99 10M
For more information: www.mna-elderly.com

FIGURE 7.1 Mini Nutrition Assessment—a screening tool for malnutrition.

Sources: Refs. (11–14).

Sarcopenia

Sarcopenia is defined as the age-related loss of muscle mass, combined with loss of strength, functionality, or both (16). Young adults' body weight is 37% to 46% skeletal muscle. Toward the fourth decade of life, muscle mass begins to decline at the rate of about 1% muscle loss every year (9). Meanwhile, fat mass continues to accumulate and infiltrate muscle tissue. Sarcopenia increases the risk of disability by an estimated 27% due to a high rate of falls and fractures (17). Sarcopenia and malnutrition often occur together due to common causes such as cytokine production

TABLE 7.1 AND/ASPEN Clinical Characteristics That the Clinician Can Obtain and Document to Support a Diagnosis of Malnutrition

Clinical Characteristics	Acute Illness or Injury Nonsevere		Severe		Chronic Illness Nonsevere		Severe		Social/Environmental Circumstances Nonsevere		Severe	
Energy intake	<75% of estimated energy requirement for >7 d		≤50% of estimated energy requirement for ≥5 d		<75% of estimated energy requirement for ≥1 mo		<75% of estimated energy requirement for ≥1 mo		<75% of estimated energy requirement for ≥3 mo		<50% of estimated energy requirement for ≥1 mo	
Interpretation of weight loss	%	Time	%	Time	%	Time	%	Time	%	Time	%	Time
	1–2	1 wk	>2	1 wk	5	1 mo	>5	1 mo	5	1 mo	>5	1 mo
	5	1 mo	>5	1 mo	7.5	3 mo	>7.5	3 mo	7.5	3 mo	>7.5	3 mo
	7.5	3 mo	>7.5	3 mo	10	6 mo	>10	6 mo	10	6 mo	>10	6 mo
					20	1 y	>20	1 y	20	1 y	>20	1 y
Body fat	Mild		Moderate		Mild		Severe		Mild		Severe	
Muscle mass	Mild		Moderate		Mild		Severe		Mild		Severe	
Fluid accumulation	Mild		Moderate to severe		Mild		Severe		Mild		Severe	
Reduced grip strength	N/A		Measurably reduced		N/A		Measurably reduced		N/A		Measurably reduced	

Source: Adapted from Ref. (7). White JV, Guenter P, Jensen G, et al. Consensus statement of the Academy of Nutrition and Dietetics/American Society for Parenteral and Enteral Nutrition: characteristics recommended for the identification and documentation of adult malnutrition (undernutrition). J Acad Nutr Diet. 2012;112:730-738.

and poor nutrient intake (18). If assessments such as hand-grip dynamometry or the 4-m walking speed indicate sarcopenia, nutritional and physical activity interventions should be considered (9,17,18).

Cachexia

Cachexia differs from sarcopenia in that fat mass is also lost in addition to an accelerated loss of skeletal muscle mass and anorexia (19). Proinflammatory cytokines, in addition to other agents produced by tumors, are also implicated in cachexia (19,20). Nutritional interventions may improve the precachexia and cachexia stages. However, individuals in the refractory cachexia stage, characterized by active catabolism, low-performance status, and life expectancy of less than 3 months, are unlikely to benefit from nutritional interventions (21).

OPTIMIZING NUTRITION

Critically ill patients are at increased risk of malnutrition throughout their hospital stay, if there are extended periods of time spent nil per os (NPO), frequent disruptions in oral or enteral nutrition, or if patients had difficulty eating prior to hospitalization.

Oral Nutrition

In all cases possible, NPO orders should be minimized. Older adults find that health and following a special diet are major barriers to eating adequate calories and protein (22). Diets should be liberalized and modified-texture diets should be provided when applicable. Additionally, losing the ability to shop for food greatly impacts older adults' food selections. Community resources such as Meals on Wheels or programs through United States Department of Agriculture (USDA) can help to fill the gaps for older adults living in the community. Oral nutrition supplements may be helpful in increasing caloric and protein intake; examples are provided in Table 7.2.

Appetite Stimulants

In patients who are unable to meet their nutrition needs with nutritional intervention, appetite stimulants may aid in reducing anorexia and improving caloric intake. Medications that stimulate appetite include corticosteroids, progesterone analogs, cannabinoids, and serotonin antagonists. These agents work on various neuropeptides, neurotransmitters, and receptors in the hypothalamus, which help to improve appetite (23). Corticosteroids, such as dexamethasone, have been shown to be beneficial in improving appetite and managing symptoms such as nausea, vomiting, and drowsiness (24). They are also associated with toxicities such as immunosuppression, glucose intolerance, decrease in muscle mass, and adrenal suppression (23). Progesterone analogs, like megestrol acetate, were developed as an appetite stimulant after finding that the medication had the side effect of weight gain (25). In comparison studies, megestrol acetate was superior to dexamethasone and the anabolic corticosteroid fluoxymesterone in measures of appetite (26). However, potentially serious side effects of

TABLE 7.2 Oral Nutrition Supplements Comparison

Nutrition Supplement	Nutrition Content per 237 mL		Description	Features
	Calories	**Protein (g)**		
Ensure® (Abbott) Boost® (Nestle)	255	9	Standard formula	Lactose-free Gluten-free Kosher
Ensure® Plus (Abbott) Boost® Plus (Nestle)	355	13	Concentrated formula for weight gain	Lactose-free Gluten-free Kosher
Glucerna®	190	10	Low-sugar formula for diabetics	Lactose-free Gluten-free Kosher
Nepro® (Abbott) Suplena® (Abbott) Novasource® (Nestle) Renalcal® (Nestle)	425	11	Low-potassium, low-phosphorus formula	Lactose-free Gluten-free Kosher
Ensure® Clear Boost® Breeze	180	8	Fruit-flavored	Fat-free Lactose-free Gluten-free Kosher
Carnation® Breakfast Essentials (Carnation) *with whole milk	280	12	Milk-based, can be mixed with milk or water. May be available in sugar-free versions.	Contains lactose

*Calorie content calculated using whole milk with Carnation Breakfast Essentials powder.

progesterone analogs include edema, hot flashes, euphoria, glucose intolerance, exacerbation of arterial hypertension, and thromboembolism (25). The anabolic corticosteroid fluoxymesterone is used to stimulate muscle anabolism in athletes; however, there is a lack of research examining the role of progesterone analogs in older cancer patients (24). The mechanism of cannabinoids such as dronabinol, while poorly understood, is thought to suppress nausea and increase appetite. In studies of cancer patients, dronabinol did not significantly improve appetite or quality of life and was found to be inferior to megestrol acetate (27). Additionally, cannabinoids may cause delirium, dizziness, and ataxia. Cyproheptadine, a histamine and serotonin antagonist, is believed to counteract increased serotonin activity, thereby stimulating appetite. Its effects increased weight in patients with carcinoid syndrome. However, it may also lead to sedation (24). Other appetite stimulants, including mirtazapine, hydrazine sulfate, and olanzapine, lack evidence to support their routine use in cancer patients. Overall, in older cancer patients the risks and benefits of appetite stimulants must be weighed. Although these medications can enhance many patients' perceived hunger sensations, appetite stimulants may be inappropriate in a population that is sensitive to change in mental status, immunosuppression, and declining muscle mass.

Artificial Nutrition Therapy

Artificial nutrition therapy should be considered for patients who are unable to meet their needs via an oral diet. Indications for **enteral nutrition** include inability to swallow, inadequate oral intake, acute pancreatitis, and high output proximal fistula. If malnourished patients are expected to have compromised ability to eat for a prolonged period of time, enteral nutrition is recommended (24). However, patients who present with terminal disease, including terminal dementia, are not recommended for feeding tube placement (28). The ethical implications, such as patient preference and religious positions, as well as benefits versus risks of placing feeding tubes, should be weighed prior to placement.

   Parenteral nutrition should be considered in patients who are unable to absorb or ingest adequate nutrition when enteral nutrition is not feasible (24,29). It is recommended that severely malnourished patients receiving anticancer therapies and malnourished patients in the perioperative setting receive parenteral nutrition to treat and prevent nutrient deficiencies, limit adverse effects of anticancer therapies, or enhance compliance to therapies (24,29). Additionally, parenteral nutrition is appropriate in patients with severely compromised GI function, such as radiation enteritis, in which the cancer is well controlled. However, parenteral nutrition is not recommended in terminally ill patients. Studies suggest that if terminally ill patients experience hunger or thirst, it may be alleviated by feeding patients small amounts (24).

TAKE HOME POINTS

1. Nutritional status should be screened upon admission and at frequent intervals when in inpatient hospital settings, as well as at the first visit and when applicable to outpatient visits.
2. ALB is a poor marker of nutrition status.
3. Obese patients are also at risk of malnutrition, sarcopenia, and cachexia despite high body mass index (BMI).
4. Liberalize diets to improve patients' dietary intake.
5. Artificial nutrition therapy can help to correct nutrient deficiencies but is not indicated in terminally ill patients.

REFERENCES

1. Correia C, Lopez KJ, Wroblewski KE, et al. Global sensory impairment in older adults in the United States. *J Am Geriatr Soc.* 2016;64(2):306-313.
2. Kennedy O, Law C, Methven L, et al. Investigating age-related changes in taste and effects on sensory perceptions of oral nutritional supplements. *Age Ageing.* 2010;39:738-745.

3. Lee CG, Boyko EJ, Nielson CM, et al. Mortality risk in older men associated with changes in weight, lean mass and fat mass. *J Am Geriatr Soc.* 2011;59(2):233-240.

4. Pilgrim A, Robinson S, Sayer AA, Roberts H. An overview of appetite decline in older people. *Nurs Older People.* 2015;27(5):29-35.

5. Blanc-Bisson C, Fonck M, Rainfray M, et al. Undernutrition in elderly patients with cancer: target for diagnosis and intervention. *Crit Rev Oncol Hematol.* 2008;67:243-254.

6. Hays NP, Roberts SB. The anorexia of aging in humans. *Physiol Behav.* 2006;88:257-266.

7. White JV, Guenter P, Jensen G, et al. Consensus statement of the Academy of Nutrition and Dietetics/American Society for Parenteral and Enteral Nutrition: characteristics recommended for the identification and documentation of adult malnutrition (under-nutrition). *J Acad Nutr Diet.* 2012;112:730-738.

8. Guigoz Y, Lauque S, Vellas BJ. Identifying the elderly at risk for malnutrition: the mini-nutritional assessment. *Clin Geriatr Med.* 2002;18:737-757.

9. Vandewoude MFJ, Alish CJ, Sauer AC, Hegazi RA. Malnutrition-sarcopenia syndrome: is this the future of nutrition screening and assessment for older adults? *J Aging Res.* 2012;2012:651570.

10. Joint Commission on Accreditation of Healthcare Organizations. Standards frequently asked questions: nutritional, functional, and pain assessment and screens. Available at: https://www.jointcommission.org/standards_information/jcfaqdetails. aspx?StandardsFaqId=872&ProgramId=46. Accessed August 6, 2016.

11. Vellas B, Villars H, Abellan G, et al. Overview of the MNA®—its history and chal-lenges. *J Nutr Health Aging.* 2006;10:456-465.

12. Rubenstein LZ, Harker JO, Salva A, et al. Screening for undernutrition in geriatric practice: developing the Short-Form Mini Nutritional Assessment (MNA-SF). *J. Geront.* 2001;56A:M366-377.

13. Guigoz Y. The Mini-Nutritional Assessment (MNA®) review of the literature—what does it tell us? *J Nutr Health Aging.* 2006;10:466-487.

14. Kaiser MJ, Bauer JM, Ramsch C, et al. Validation of the Mini Nutritional Assessment Short-Form (MNA®-SF): a practical tool for identification of nutritional status. *J Nutr Health Aging.* 2009;13:782-788.

15. Banh L. Serum proteins as markers of nutrition: what are we treating? *Pract Gastroenterol.* 2006;43:46-64.

16. Cruz-Jentoft AJ, Baeyens JP, Bauer JM, et al. Sarcopenia: European consensus on definition and diagnosis. *Age Ageing.* 2010;39:412-423.

17. Liu CK, Leng X, Hsu FC, et al. The impact of sarcopenia on a physical activity intervention: the Lifestyle Interventions and Independence for Elders Pilot Study (LIFE-P). *J Nutr Health Aging.* 2014;18(1):59-64.

18. Boirie Y. Physiopathological mechanism of sarcopenia. *J Nutr Health Aging.* 2009;13(8):717-723.

19. Evans WJ. Skeletal muscle loss: cachexia, sarcopenia, and inactivity. *Am J Clin Nutr.* 2010;91(suppl):1123S-1127S.

20. Anker SD, Morley JE. Cachexia: a nutritional syndrome? *J Cachexia Sarcopenia Muscle.* 2015;6:269-271.

21. Fearon K, Strasser F, Anker SD, et al. Definition and classification of cancer cachexia: an international consensus. *Lancet Oncol.* 2011;12:489-495.

22. Locher JL, Ritchie CS, Roth DL, et al. Food choice among homebound older adults: motivations and perceived barriers. *J Nutr Health Aging.* 2009;13(8):659-664.

23. Desport JC, Gory-Delabaere G, Blanc-Vincent MP, et al. Standards, options and recommendations for the use of appetite stimulants in oncology (2000). *Brit J Cancer.* 2003;89(suppl 1):S98-S100.

24. Mendelsohn RB, Schattner MA. Cancer. In: Mueller C, ed. *The A.S.P.E.N. Adult Nutrition Support Core Curriculum.* Silver Spring, MD: American Society for Parenteral and Enteral Nutrition; 2012:568-571.

25. Bruera E, Macmillan K, Kuehn N, et al. A controlled trial of megestrol acetate on appetite, caloric intake, nutritional status, and other symptoms in patients with advanced cancer. *Cancer.* 1990;66:1279-1282.

26. Loprinzi CL, Kugler JW, Sloan JA, et al. Randomized comparison of megestrol acetate versus dexamethasone versus fluoxymesterone for the treatment of cancer anorexia/cachexia. *J Clin Oncol.* 1999;17:3299-3306.

27. Jatoi A, Windschitl HE, Loprinzi CL, et al. Dronabinol versus megestrol acetate versus combination therapy for cancer-associated anorexia: a North Central Cancer Treatment Group study. *J Clin Oncol.* 2002;20:567-573.

28. Volkert D, Berner YN, Berry E, et al. ESPEN guidelines on enteral nutrition: geriatrics. *Clin Nutr.* 2006;25:330-360.

29. Bozzetti F, Arends J, Lundholm K, et al. ESPEN guidelines on parenteral nutrition: non-surgical oncology. *Clin Nutr.* 2009;28:445-454.

Polypharmacy

Ginah Nightingale and Manpreet K. Boparai

BACKGROUND

Men and women aged 65 years or older are the biggest consumers of medications (1). Nearly one-third of community-dwelling adults aged 65 and older take more than five prescription medications, and almost 20% take 10 or more (1,2). Polypharmacy is a significant public health problem that disproportionately affects older adults, particularly those with multiple comorbid conditions. *Polypharmacy* is commonly defined as concurrent use of five or more medications, including prescription, nonprescription, and complementary and herbal supplements (3–5). Polypharmacy can also be defined by the use of potentially inappropriate medications (PIMs) which are associated with an increased risk for adverse drug effects in older adults. A publication by Bushardt and colleagues suggested that there are 24 distinct definitions of polypharmacy, encompassing concepts ranging from unnecessary or inappropriate medication use to the use of excessive numbers of medications (6).

Although the use of many medications may be good practice for the treatment of some chronic medical conditions, the addition of cancer-related therapy (to existing polypharmacy) adds to the prevalence of the use of multiple medications and/or the consumption of inappropriate medications. The multiple layers of specialists, primary care, and allied health professionals in the continuum of care make this population particularly prone to medication errors attributable to medication changes, complex regimens, and incomplete information hand-off between providers. As a consequence, there may be an increased risk for adverse drug events, drug–drug interactions, nonadherence, and in some cases an increased risk of hospitalization and increased health care utilization (7–13).

IMPORTANT CONSIDERATIONS WHEN PRESCRIBING FOR OLDER ADULTS

Prescribing for older adults presents unique challenges. Many medications must be used with caution due to age-related physiologic changes, and care must be taken when determining the appropriate dosages. Increased volume of distribution may result from the increase in body fat relative to skeletal muscle with aging. Lipophilic drugs (e.g., benzodiazepines) have an increased volume of distribution, taking longer to reach a steady state and longer to be eliminated.

Therefore, the starting doses should be decreased. A natural decline in renal function with age may result in decreased drug clearance. Decreased drug clearance and larger drug reservoirs prolong half-lives and lead to increased drug concentrations. Hepatic function also declines with age, further affecting drug metabolism and leading to adverse drug reactions (ADRs) (14).

POLYPHARMACY AND PIM USE

The National Comprehensive Cancer Network (NCCN) Older Adult Oncology Guidelines recommend a thorough evaluation of the medication list and PIMs, with subsequent discontinuation of nonessential or high-risk medications (15). Patients should also be asked about herbal medications, as patients may not volunteer this information nor recognize the importance of discussing this with the medical team. The prevalence of polypharmacy in the ambulatory older adult oncology population ranges from 48% to 80% and the prevalence of PIM use ranges from 8% to 51% (7–20). This variability may be attributed to the methodology used for the evaluation (e.g., self-reports, medical records extraction, pharmacist assessment), screening tools, and definitions of polypharmacy and inappropriate medications.

Similar to the heterogeneity that exists with defining polypharmacy, heterogeneity exists with identifying and categorizing PIMs. PIMs are largely referred to as medications lacking evidence-based indications, medications with treatment risks that outweigh benefits, medications that are significantly associated with ADRs, or those that may potentially interact with other medications or other diseases (21). The most current, evidence-based, validated criteria and screening tools to capture PIMs include the 2015 Beers Criteria (Table 8.1), the Screening Tool of Older Person's Prescriptions (STOPP), and the Medication Appropriateness Index (7–26) (Tables 8.2 and 8.3).

TABLE 8.1 Examples of PIMs—2015 Beers Criteria

High-Risk Medications	Rationale	Recommendations	Possible Alternatives
First-generation antihistamines Chlorpheniramine Diphenhydramine	Highly anticholinergic. Clearance reduced with advanced age. Greater risk of confusion, hallucinations, sleepiness, blurred vision, difficulty urinating, dry mouth, and constipation	**Avoid** Use of diphenhydramine for treating severe allergic reactions may be appropriate	For rhinitis: Steroid nasal sprays; e.g., fluticasone For allergies: Cetirizine, fexofenadine, loratadine For nausea: Ondansetron, prochlorperazine

(*continued*)

TABLE 8.1 Examples of PIMs—2015 Beers Criteria (*continued*)

High-Risk Medications	Rationale	Recommendations	Possible Alternatives
Antidepressants Amitriptyline Nortriptyline Paroxetine	Highly anticholinergic Sedating Cause orthostatic hypotension	**Avoid**	Consider antidepressant with less sedation and fewer anticholinergic effects (e.g., citalopram, escitalopram, sertraline, mirtazapine, bupropion, venlafaxine)
Benzodiazepines —Short-/intermediate-acting: Alprazolam, lorazepam, temazepam —Long-acting: Diazepam	Older adults have increased sensitivity to all benzodiazepines and decreased metabolism of long-acting agents All benzodiazepines increase risk of cognitive impairment, delirium, falls, fractures, and motor vehicle crashes	**Avoid** May be appropriate for seizure disorders, rapid eye movement sleep disorders, benzodiazepine withdrawal, ethanol withdrawal, severe generalized anxiety disorder, and periprocedural anesthesia	For anxiety: Buspirone SSRIs: Citalopram Sertraline For sleep: Nonmedication sleep hygiene techniques Trazodone (25–50 mg); may be used intermittently. Evidence suggests that trazodone does not affect REM sleep cycles
Pain Medication Non-COX selective NSAIDs: e.g., indomethacin and ketorolac	Increased risk of gastrointestinal bleeding and peptic ulcer disease in: High-risk groups (>75 years old) Taking oral or IV corticosteroids, anticoagulants, or antiplatelet agents Of all NSAIDs, indomethacin has most adverse effects	**Avoid** in CKD, chronic renal failure	**Moderate pain:** Acetaminophen Topical capsaicin products Lidocaine patches SNRIs: Duloxetine Venlafaxine
Pain Medication Meperidine	Not an effective oral analgesic in dosages commonly used Increased risk of neurotoxicity and delirium	**Avoid**	For moderate to severe pain: Tramadol Oxycodone immediate release with acetaminophen Morphine

(*continued*)

TABLE 8.1 Examples of PIMs—2015 Beers Criteria (*continued*)

High-Risk Medications	Rationale	Recommendations	Possible Alternatives
Megestrol	Minimal effect on weight; increases risk of thrombotic events and possible death in older adults	Avoid	Assist with eating (e.g., hand feeding or hand-over-hand technique) Social eating programs

COX, cyclo-oxygenase; NSAID, nonsteroidal anti-inflammatory drug; PIMs, potentially inappropriate medications; SNRIs, serotonin-norepinephrine reuptake inhibitors; SSRIs, selective serotonin reuptake inhibitors.

Source: Ref. (22). American Geriatrics Society 2015 Beers Criteria. American Geriatrics Society 2015 updated Beers criteria for potentially inappropriate medication use in older adults. *J Am Geriatr Soc.* 2015;63(11):2227-2246.

TABLE 8.2 Examples of PIMs—STOPP Criteria

Cardiovascular System	Avoid Use
Digoxin	Long-term use >125 µg/d with renal dysfunction
Loop diuretics	For dependent ankle edema only (no signs of HF); compression hosiery usually more appropriate
Thiazide diuretics	With history of gout (*may exacerbate gout*)
Noncardioselective beta-blockers	With COPD (*risk of increased bronchospasm*)
Diltiazem or verapamil	With NYHA class III or IV HF (*may worsen heart failure*)
Calcium channel blockers	With chronic constipation (may exacerbate constipation)

Central Nervous System/ Psychotropic Drugs	Avoid Use
Tricyclic antidepressants	With dementia (risk of worsening cognitive impairment)
Selective serotonin reuptake inhibitors	With hyponatremia

Gastrointestinal System	Avoid Use
Proton pump inhibitors	For PUD at full therapeutic doses for >8 weeks
Nonsteroid anti-inflammatory drugs	With moderate to severe hypertension or HF

COPD, chronic obstructive pulmonary disease; HF, heart failure; PIMs, potentially inappropriate medications; PUD, peptic ulcer disease; STOPP, Screening Tool of Older Person's Prescriptions.

Source: Adapted from Refs. (23–25).

TABLE 8.3 Medication Appropriateness Index Criteria

1. Is there an indication for the drug?

2. Is the medication effective for the condition?

3. Is the dosage correct?

4. Are the directions correct?

5. Are the directions practical?

6. Are there clinically significant drug–drug interactions?

7. Are there clinically significant drug–disease/condition interactions?

8. Is there unnecessary duplication with other drugs?

9. Is the duration of therapy acceptable?

10. Is this drug the least expensive alternative compared with others of equal usefulness?

Source: Ref. (26). Samsa GP, Hanlon JT, Schmader KE, et al. A summated score for the medication appropriateness index: development and assessment of clinimetric properties including content validity. *J Clin Epidemiol.* 1994;47(8):891-896.

a. The Beers Criteria is the most frequently used tool in the United States, supported and endorsed by the American Geriatrics Society (AGS). A consensus guideline, the Beers Criteria was first published in 1991 and last updated in 2015. It identifies 40 potentially problematic medications or classes of medications organized across five lists.

b. STOPP is a European-based tool developed on the basis of expert consensus and evidence-based criteria. It includes drug–drug and drug–disease interactions, drugs that adversely affect seniors at risk of falls, and medication duplications.

c. The Medication Appropriateness Index measures the appropriateness of prescribing using 10 criteria for *each* medication to determine whether it is appropriate, marginally appropriate, or inappropriate.

There are no head-to-head trials that recommend the use of one screening tool over another, so each of these tools is considered an option for use in practice. The AGS stated that the STOPP criteria should be used in a complementary manner with the Beers Criteria largely because there are some notable differences between the tools. It is important to highlight high-risk medications that have been associated with hospital admissions in older persons: insulin, warfarin, oral antiplatelet agents, and oral hypoglycemic agents. Especially careful attention is warranted with these agents (27).

MEDICATION ADHERENCE

Medication adherence has also become increasingly important in the setting of polypharmacy, especially given the acceleration expansion and development of oral chemotherapy. A systematic review of determinants and influences on adherence to oral chemotherapy drugs showed that older age was a factor (28). Barriers to adherence

TABLE 8.4 Interventions to Improve Medication Adherence

Patient education with behavioral support
Blister packaging
Incorporation of pill-taking into routine
Electronic monitoring (e.g., electronic caps for Rx vials)
Single dose vs. multiple doses prescribed
Reduction of treatment side effects
Telecommunications systems for monitoring and counseling
Selection of equivalent low-cost drugs to reduce out-of-pocket expenses

Source: Adapted from Ref. (14). Korc-Grodzicki B, Boparai MK, Lichtman SM. Prescribing for older patients with cancer. *Clin Adv Hematol Oncol.* 2014;12:309-318.

can occur on the individual or system level and interventions to improve adherence should be multifactorial (Table 8.4). The Morisky Medication Adherence Scale is a validated adherence assessment tool, which has been used for several chronic health conditions but has not been validated for use in oncology (29). Thus, a research gap exists regarding validated tools to measure medication adherence in the setting of polypharmacy and cancer.

PRESCRIBING AND DEPRESCRIBING

The medication use process comprises a series of stages including prescribing, communicating medication orders, dispensing, administering, and monitoring. Because of this multistage process, adequate patient-provider consultation time is needed to conduct comprehensive medication assessments, particularly at the initiation or modification of the patient's oncologic management, changes in clinical condition, and/or during transitions of care. The **brown bag** medication review method is highly recommended. It involves the patient/caregiver bringing in all medicines and supplements from home to the visit. During the visit, the provider should confirm medication indication (e.g., medication-condition matching), dosage (e.g., dosages appropriate for renal and/or liver function), and duration, and assess for drug duplication, drug–drug, drug–disease interactions, and adverse effects; in addition, the patient's ability to read medication label directions and to manage medications in an organized manner should be assessed. The provider should not only consider the pharmacologic properties of the medications, but should also consider the patient's comorbidities, cancer prognosis, and cognitive and functional status, as well as social, cultural, and economic factors. In this way, the prescribing process encompasses the patient's goals of care coupled with maintaining quality of life.

If polypharmacy or inappropriate medications are identified, **deprescribing** should be considered. *Deprescribing* is defined as the systematic process of identifying and discontinuing drugs in which existing or potential harms outweigh existing or potential benefits within the context of the patient's care goals, functional status, life expectancy, values, and preferences (30,31). Studies evaluating the positive effects of deprescribing have shown a reduction in overall medication number, reduction in the

TABLE 8.5 Considerations for Medication Discontinuation

1. Remaining life expectancy—may be considered

2. Time until benefit—medications like analgesics have a short time to benefit, and can be given to patients until and especially at the very end of life. Drugs used for primary and secondary prevention may not be helpful.

3. Goals of care—shared decision making among prescribers, patients, and families; differentiate between curative and palliative managements.

4. Treatment target that a medication may achieve: palliation, life prolongation, prevention of mortality and morbidity, maintenance of current state or function, treatment of acute illness.

Source: Adapted from Ref. (31). Bain KT, Holmes HM, Beers MH, et al. Discontinuing medications: a novel approach for revising the prescribing stage of the medication-use process. *J Am Geriatr Soc.* 2008;56(10):1946-1952.

number of inappropriate medications, reduction in hospital length of stay, association with global improvements in health, and improvements or slower declines in quality of life (7–33). Deprescribing may include substitution of a safer medication alternative. Hanlon and colleagues developed a list of evidence-based medication alternatives that may be used to replace high-risk medications (34). There are many challenges to successfully discontinuing medications, which include the complexity of the patient, limited consultation time, fragmented care, uncertainty about the benefits and harms, and the patient's psychological attachment to a medication. Table 8.5 lists considerations for medication discontinuation (31).

One approach to optimizing the prescribing and deprescribing process is through utilization of pharmacists as part of the health care delivery model for interprofessional, team-based care (35). The Institute of Medicine recognizes the significant role played by pharmacists in the areas of medication therapy management and medication safety, as well as the value of pharmacist-physician collaboration in patient care (7–38). Pharmacists have the professional education, training, skills, and medication use expertise crucial for this complex population that takes multiple medications.

CONCLUSION

Despite the fact that multiple medicine use is increasingly common among older adults, the term *polypharmacy* continues to lack a universally accepted definition. There is a need for validated approaches and interventions to reduce the prevalence of excessive and inappropriate medication use. Well-designed interventions aimed at improving medication use should extend far beyond reducing the number of medications. A multifaceted, patient-centered approach that incorporates an interprofessional health care team, promotes patient and provider education, and integrates information technology is vital to resolving and managing medication-related problems in this high-risk older adult population.

TAKE HOME POINTS

1. Start low and go slow when prescribing for older adults.
2. Use the "brown bag" approach when conducting medication reviews. Ask the patient to bring to the visit all prescribed, nonprescribed, and complementary/herbal supplements.
3. Use an evidence-based screening tool to assess medication appropriateness (e.g., Beers Criteria).
4. Consider deprescribing high-risk medications and initiating safer alternatives. Consider comorbidities, prognosis, functional status, and goals of care when modifying medications.
5. Maintain open and transparent communication between the patient and other health care providers. Include documentation indicating that a comprehensive medication evaluation was conducted and medication-related problems were identified and resolved.
6. Consider incorporating pharmacists as part of the interprofessional health care team to assist with optimizing medication management.

REFERENCES

1. Slone Epidemiology Center at Boston University. Patterns of Medication Use in the United States. Available at: http://www.bu.edu/slone/files/2012/11/SloneSurveyReport 2006.pdf.
2. Boyd CM, Darer J, Boult C, et al. Clinical practice guidelines and quality of care for older patients with multiple comorbid diseases: implications for pay for performance. *JAMA.* 2005;294(6):716-724.
3. Stewart RB. Polypharmacy in the elderly: a fait accompli? *DICP.* 1990;24:321-323.
4. Montamat SC, Cusack B. Overcoming problems with polypharmacy and drug misuse in the elderly. *Clin Geriatr Med.* 1992; 8:143-158.
5. Hajjar ER, Cafiero AC, Hanlon JT. Polypharmacy in elderly patients. *Am J Geriatr Pharmacother.* 2007;5:345-351.
6. Bushardt RL, Massey EB, Simpson TW, et al. Polypharmacy: misleading, but manageable. *Clin Interv Aging.* 2008;3(2):383-389.
7. Riechelmann RP, Tannock IF, Wang L, et al. Potential drug interactions and duplicate prescriptions among cancer patients. *J Natl Cancer Inst.* 2007;99:592-600.
8. Riechelmann RP, Zimmermann C, Chin SN, et al. Potential drug interactions in cancer patients receiving supportive care exclusively. *J Pain Symptom Manage.* 2008;35:535-543.
9. Riechelmann RP, Moreira F, Smaletz O, Saad ED. Potential for drug interactions in hospitalized cancer patients. *Cancer Chemother Pharmacol.* 2005;56:286-290.
10. Puts MT, Costa-Lima B, Monette J, et al. Medication problems in older, newly diagnosed cancer patients in Canada: how common are they? A prospective pilot study. *Drugs Aging.* 2009;26:519-536.
11. Scripture CD. Drug interactions in cancer therapy. *Nat Rev Cancer.* 2006;6:546-558.

12. Hilmer SN, Gnjidic D. The effects of polypharmacy in older adults. *Clin Pharmacol Ther.* 2009;85(1):86-88.

13. Fried TR, O'Leary J, Towle V, et al. Health outcomes associated with polypharmacy in community-dwelling older adults: a systematic review. *J Am Geriatr Soc.* 2014; 62(12):2261-2272.

14. Korc-Grodzicki B, Boparai MK, Lichtman SM. Prescribing for older patients with cancer. *Clin Adv Hematol Oncol.* 2014;12:309-318.

15. Network National Comprehensive Cancer. NCCN Clinical Practice Guidelines in Oncology: older adult oncology 2016. Available at: http://www.nccn.org/professionals/ physician_gls/pdf/senior.pdf. Accessed April 7, 2016.

16. Lichtman SM, Boparai MK. Geriatric medication management: evaluation of pharmacist interventions and potentially inappropriate medication (PIM) use in older cancer patients. *J Clin Oncol.* 2009;27:484 (suppl). Abstr 9507.

17. Maggiore RJ, Gross CP, Hardt M, et al. Polypharmacy, potentially inappropriate medications, and chemotherapy-related adverse events among older adults with cancer. *J Clin Oncol.* 2011 (suppl). Abstr e19501.

18. Prithviraj GK, Koroukian S, Margevicius S, et al. Patient characteristics associated with polypharmacy and inappropriate prescribing of medications among older adults with cancer. *J Geriatr Oncol.* 2012;3:228-237.

19. Nightingale G, Hajjar E, Swartz K, et al. Evaluation of a pharmacist-led medication assessment used to identify prevalence of and associations with polypharmacy and potentially inappropriate medication use among ambulatory senior adults with cancer. *J Clin Oncol.* 2015;33(13):1453-1459.

20. Maggiore RJ, Dale W, Gross CP, et al. Polypharmacy and potentially inappropriate medication use in older adults with cancer undergoing chemotherapy: effect on chemotherapy-related toxicity and hospitalization during treatment. *J Am Geriatr Soc.* 2014;62(8):1505-1512.

21. Dimitrow MS, Airaksinen MS, Kivelä SL, et al. Comparison of prescribing criteria to evaluate the appropriateness of drug treatment in individuals aged 65 and older: a systematic review. *J Am Geriatr Soc.* 2011;59(8):1521-1530.

22. American Geriatrics Society. American Geriatrics Society 2015 updated Beers criteria for potentially inappropriate medication use in older adults. *J Am Geriatr Soc.* 2015;63(11):2227-2246.

23. Gallagher P, O'Mahony D. STOPP (Screening Tool of Older Persons' potentially inappropriate Prescriptions): application to acutely ill elderly patients and comparison with Beers criteria. *Age Ageing.* 2008;37(6):673-679.

24. O'Mahony D, Gallagher P, Ryan C, et al. STOPP & START criteria: a new approach to detecting potentially inappropriate prescribing in old age. *Eur Geriatr Med.* 2010;1(1):45-51.

25. O'Mahony D, O'Sullivan D, Byrne S, et al. STOPP/START criteria for potentially inappropriate prescribing in older people: version 2. *Age Ageing.* 2015;44(2):213-218.

26. Samsa GP, Hanlon JT, Schmader KE, et al. A summated score for the medication appropriateness index: development and assessment of clinimetric properties including content validity. *J Clin Epidemiol.* 1994;47(8):891-896.

27. Budnitz DS, Lovegrove MC, Shehab N, Richards CL. Emergency hospitalizations for adverse drug events in older Americans. *N Engl J Med.* 2011;365(21):2002-2012.

28. Verbrugghe M, Verhaeghe S, Lauwaert K, et al. Determinants and associated factors influencing medication adherence and persistence to oral anticancer drugs: a systematic review. *Cancer Treat Rev.* 2013;39(6):610-621.

29. Morisky DE, Green LW, Levine DM. Concurrent and predictive validity of a self-reported measure of medication adherence. *Med Care.* 1986;24:67-74.

30. Scott IA, Hilmer SN, Reeve E, et al. Reducing inappropriate polypharmacy: the process of deprescribing. *JAMA Intern Med.* 2015;175(5):827-234.

31. Bain KT, Holmes HM, Beers MH, et al. Discontinuing medications: a novel approach for revising the prescribing stage of the medication-use process. *J Am Geriatr Soc.* 2008;56(10):1946-1952.

32. Garfinkel D, Mangin D. Feasibility study of a systematic approach for discontinuation of multiple medications in older adults: addressing polypharmacy. *Arch Intern Med.* 2010;170(18):1648-1654.

33. Tannenbaum C, Martin P, Tamblyn R, et al. Reduction of inappropriate benzodiazepine prescriptions among older adults through direct patient education: the EMPOWER cluster randomized trial. *JAMA Intern Med.* 2014;174(6):890-898.

34. Hanlon JT, Semla TP, Schmader KE. Alternative medications for use of high-risk medications in the elderly and potentially harmful drug–disease interactions in the elderly quality measures. *J Am Geriatr Soc.* 2015;63(12):e8-e18.

35. Holle LM, Michaud LB. Oncology pharmacists in health care delivery: vital members of the cancer care team. *J Oncol Pract.* 2014;10(3):e142-e145.

36. Kohn LT, Institute of Medicine. *Academic Health Centers: Leading Change in the 21st Century.* Washington, DC: National Academy Press; 2003.

37. Kohn LT, Corrigan JM, Donaldson MS. *To Err Is Human.* Washington, DC: National Academy Press; 2000.

38. Adams K, Corrigan JM, eds. *Priority Areas for National Action: Transforming Health Care Quality.* Washington, DC: National Academies Press; 2003.

9   Comorbidity in Cancer

Grant R. Williams and Holly M. Holmes

INTRODUCTION

Older adults with cancer respond differently to treatments than do younger patients. Older patients more often present with multiple medical conditions, in addition to their cancer diagnosis, that can complicate their oncologic treatment and tolerance. The majority of Medicare beneficiaries have two or more medical conditions and nearly 25% have four or more conditions (1). Over the last decade, the importance of comorbid medical conditions in cancer care has become more elucidated, yet due to stringent eligibility criteria and the lack of systematic measurement in clinical trials there is a limited evidence base for making informed decisions (2). Most clinical practice guidelines, including in oncology, are single-disease focused, with limited interpretability in patients with multiple comorbidities (3).

Historically, cancer has been considered an index condition and other diseases have been approached as comorbidities, defined as medical conditions that exist along with an index condition. A newer concept of "multimorbidity" has been used to reflect a model which shows that many diseases and treatments for disease impact other conditions and interact with each other to positively or negatively affect an individual's health, leading to overlapping medical conditions within the same patient (see Figure 9.1) (4,5).

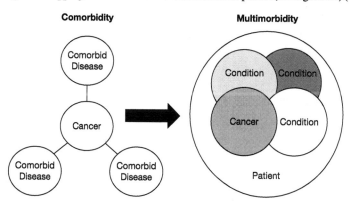

FIGURE 9.1 Conceptual differences between comorbidity and multimorbidity.

Source: Adapted from Ref. (4). Boyd C, Fortin, M. Future of multimorbidity research: how should understanding of multimorbidity inform health system design? *Public Health Rev.* 2010;32(2):451–474.

The approach to an individual with multimorbidity requires a new paradigm to provide individualized care that takes into account guiding principles that will be discussed later in this chapter. *Multimorbidity* is defined as the coexistence of two or more chronic conditions in which one is not necessarily more central than the others (6). As this chapter specifically focuses on comorbid illnesses within the context of cancer, we will frequently use the term *comorbidity* regardless of the number and severity of comorbid conditions.

RELEVANCE IN CANCER

Comorbid illnesses can impact cancer in a variety of ways, as the comorbid conditions themselves comprise a wide-range of heterogeneous conditions of varying severity and number. The majority of observational studies have found that cancer patients with increased comorbidities have poorer survival compared to those without comorbidity, with 5-year mortality hazard ratios ranging from 1.1 to 5.8 (7). The impact of comorbid conditions on survival in cancer partly depends on the aggressiveness and lethality of the cancer itself. The presence of moderate to severe comorbidities is of greatest prognostic importance in early stage and potentially curable patients, while in more aggressive cancers, where the mortality is dominated by the primary malignancy, there is often less impact (8).

Comorbidities can also impact the tolerability of cancer treatments. Patients with more comorbid conditions are at an increased risk of severe toxicity and hospitalization during chemotherapy treatment (9–11). In a study examining older adults undergoing adjuvant chemotherapy for breast cancer, patients with a Charlson Comorbidity Index (CCI) score of ≥1 were three times more likely to experience grade 3 or higher chemotherapy toxicities (11). Severe comorbid conditions (CCI ≥ 3) have been shown to be one of the strongest predictors of hospitalizations related to chemotherapy, with 10-fold higher hospitalization rates compared to patients with no comorbidities (10). Furthermore, comorbid patients are less likely to complete chemotherapy (12). As comorbid conditions can alter both the risk and benefit of cancer treatments, they can dramatically impact the risk/benefit balance of many treatments (2). The presence of comorbidities is one of the most frequent reasons cited in the medical chart for nonreceipt of cancer treatment (13,14).

ASSESSING COMORBIDITIES

There are many methods for assessing comorbidity in cancer, ranging from simple counts of conditions to weighted indices to system-based methods. Although comorbidity indices are frequently used in research settings, in the clinical setting a comprehensive history and physical with a list of comorbidities and their current treatments is frequently the only method used to assess comorbid illness. While this approach has some advantages and is already incorporated into our current clinical practice processes, there are additional advantages to using validated tools when assessing patients in the clinic. For one, describing comorbidity in terms of an index or tool makes communication about prognosis and impact on chemotherapy toxicity more standardized with patients and between colleagues caring for a patient. Validated tools also provide a more systematic description of the severity or burden of comorbidity than is used in a simple history and physical. For example, a heart attack might get more weight than a known history of coronary artery disease. Finally, using a comorbidity tool might help to frame a patient's likely outcome when extrapolating evidence from clinical trials, in which participants are only described in terms of an index.

There is no single gold standard to assess comorbidity, and a 2012 review identified 21 distinct approaches to assess comorbidity that have been used in cancer populations (15). The choice of comorbidity tool depends on the clinical setting and intended use of the instrument (2). For example, in a clinical setting primarily consisting of older patients with multimorbidity, a tool that allows capture of number and severity of comorbidities as well as the effect on daily function or quality of life might be most clinically useful. Some tools are simply not designed for clinic and are better suited for use with retrospective reviews of medical records or with claims data. See Table 9.1 for a list of selected comorbidity tools that are commonly used in oncology. There are many online calculator versions of several comorbidity tools, which may make them more usable in a clinic setting. Several detailed reviews of comorbidity methods are available for a more in-depth examination (15,26).

TABLE 9.1 Common Comorbidity Measurement Tools

Type	Index	Items and Rating
Summative		
	Elixhauser (16)	30 dichotomous conditions
Weighted		
	CCI (17)	19 conditions weighted 16
	NCI Comorbidity Index (18,19)	16 conditions weighted by empirically derived weights
Systems-based		
	CIRS (20)	13 or 14 organ system categories, each rated 0–4
	ICED (21)	Disease severity subindex: 14 diseases (rated 0–4). Functional severity subindex: 12 conditions (rated 0–2). Total: 0–3
	KFI (22)	12 conditions, each rated 0–3
	ACE-27 (23)	27 conditions, each rated 0–3
Cancer specific		
	WUHNCI (24)	7 conditions, each rated 0–4
	HCT-CI (25)	17 conditions, each rated 0–3

ACE-27, Adult Comorbidity Evaluation-27; CCI, Charlson Comorbidity Index; CIRS, Cumulative Illness Rating Scale; HCT-CI, hematopoietic cell transplantation-comorbidity index; ICED, Index of Coexistent Disease; KFI, Kaplan–Feinstein Index; WUHNCI, Washington University Head and Neck Comorbidity Index.

One of the most widely used and simplest comorbidity scales is the CCI. The index includes 19 conditions with individual weights (ranging from 1 to 6) based on the relative risk of death. In the CCI, myocardial infarction is weighted with 1 point, and metastatic cancer is weighted with 6 points. Patient-reported versions of the CCI have been validated that can be easily administered in the clinic, and an age-adjusted version has also been created (age-adjusted CCI) (27–29). Four of the items within the CCI are related to cancer and should be excluded if they apply to the cancer population in which they are used. For example, if the CCI is to be used in a clinic of solid tumor patients, the solid tumor would not be included; however, patients with lymphoma in addition to a solid tumor would still have points added for lymphoma. Although the range of scores is often small, with a highly skewed distribution toward lower scores (26), the CCI is a quick tool for systematic comorbidity measurement.

For a more detailed evaluation of comorbidity, many utilize the Cumulative Illness Rating Scale (CIRS). The CIRS categorizes comorbidities by organ system affected and rates them according to their severity from 0 to 4, similar to the Common Toxicity Criteria grading (none, mild, moderate, severe, and extremely severe/life-threatening) (20). More severe ratings also equate to greater functional burden as a result of the condition. Although the CIRS requires more training than the CCI in order to assess the severity of diseases, it can be performed in a few minutes by clinicians with a working familiarity of the manual (26).

The Older Americans Resources and Services Questionnaire (OARS) Physical Health subscale is frequently used as part of the patient-reported portion of the brief geriatric assessment developed by Hurria et al. (30,31). The OARS comorbidity scale is patient-reported and assesses 14 specific comorbid conditions and the degree to which each interferes with the participant's activities. The OARS questionnaire is unfortunately not easily available to clinicians for daily use, but is increasingly being incorporated in research studies and can be easily performed by patients without assistance. Finally, disease-specific comorbidity tools have been developed for use in certain cancers and can be particularly helpful when available (24,25,32). As choosing the right comorbidity measure depends on the clinical context, there is no single preferred method, but some form of systematic incorporation of comorbid conditions, such as the CCI, CIRS, or OARS, is highly recommended in older adults with cancer.

TREATING THE PATIENT WITH CANCER AND MULTIPLE COMORBIDITIES

A thorough assessment of comorbidities is necessary given their likely impact on cancer and cancer therapy. Once information on comorbid conditions has been obtained, there are several ways in which such information could be used clinically:

1. To adjust cancer regimens in light of comorbid illness. For example, dose adjustment of renally dosed chemotherapy in the setting of chronic kidney disease, or adjustments in anesthesia or surgical plan for patients with substantial cardiac or lung disease.
2. To anticipate higher risks for toxicity. For example, patients with comorbid peripheral neuropathy due to diabetes may have more difficulties with neurotoxic chemotherapy regimens.

3. To better optimize existing comorbid conditions during cancer therapy. Many patients who present with cancer may not have received regular primary care, and may need to have comorbid conditions more fully addressed and treated.
4. To better estimate prognosis independent of cancer. Patients with multiple severe comorbid illness have a lower likely remaining life expectancy than their age-matched peers with few illnesses. This information is a necessary first step to putting cancer-specific prognosis in perspective, particularly in the adjuvant treatment setting (33).

GUIDING CARE PRINCIPLES

In the absence of a substantial evidence base to guide clinical management and decision making in patients with multiple comorbidities, clinicians need practical guidance for a rational approach to manage these complicated patients (34). The American Geriatrics Society (AGS) convened an expert panel on the care of older adults with multimorbidity with the goal of developing an approach by which clinicians could provide optimal care for this challenging population (35). Based on a review of the literature and expert opinion, the panel developed a set of Guiding Principles for the Care of Older Adults with Multimorbidity. They include: (a) assessing patient preferences, (b) interpreting and applying available information, (c) estimating prognosis, (d) considering treatment feasibility, and (e) optimizing therapies and care plan. These are meant to provide a framework to help structure decision making and not as a formalized treatment "guideline." See Table 9.2 for an outline of how these principles can be applied to multimorbid patients with cancer (adapted and modified from Thompson et al. (34)). For a detailed review of adapting the principles into oncologic management, a recent "Geriatrics for Oncologists" article is available in the *Journal of Geriatric Oncology* (34) on how to best manage the care of older patients with cancer and multimorbidity.

TABLE 9.2 Guiding Principles for the Care of Older Adults With Cancer and Multimorbidity

1. **Assessing patient preferences**	Elicit and incorporate patient preferences into medical decision making. - *What outcomes are most important?* - *Which cancer treatments (if any) best align with that patient's goals?*
2. **Interpreting and applying available information**	Recognizing the limitations of the evidence base, interpret and apply the medical literature specifically to older adults with multimorbidity. - *Were multimorbid patients included in the study population of the proposed cancer therapy?* - *Is it known how the intervention will affect the patient's other chronic conditions?*

(continued)

TABLE 9.2 Guiding Principles for the Care of Older Adults With Cancer and Multimorbidity (*continued*)

3. **Estimating prognosis**	Frame clinical management decisions within the context of risks, burdens, benefits, and prognosis. - *How will the patient's other medical conditions impact outcomes?*
4. **Considering treatment feasibility**	Consider treatment complexity and feasibility when making clinical management decisions. - *Will cancer treatments limit adherence or contribute to polypharmacy?* - *Will cancer treatment lead to unwanted interactions with other medical conditions?*
5. **Optimizing therapies and care plan**	Use strategies for choosing therapies that optimize benefit, minimize harm, and enhance quality of life. - *How can other interprofessional and multidisciplinary team members or caregivers help to optimize the treatment plan?* - *Would the patient benefit from care coordination or geriatric assessment?*

Source: Adapted from Refs. (34), (35).

TAKE HOME POINTS

1. Given changing demographics, managing older adults with cancer and multiple comorbidities will become an increasingly routine issue for oncologists.
2. Multimorbidity is a newer concept used to reflect a model in which many diseases and treatments for diseases interact and often overlap within an individual patient.
3. Comorbidities can impact numerous cancer outcomes, including cancer treatment tolerability and overall survival.
4. Several tools are available to help quantify comorbidity measurement.
5. Adapting the AGS's Guiding Principles can provide a useful framework to help structure decision making regarding these complex patients.

REFERENCES

1. Wolff JL, Starfield B, Anderson G. Prevalence, expenditures, and complications of multiple chronic conditions in the elderly. *Arch Intern Med.* 2002;162(20):2269-2276.
2. Williams GR, Mackenzie A, Magnuson A, et al. Comorbidity in older adults with cancer. *J Geriatr Oncol.* 2015;7(4):249-257.
3. Boyd CM, Darer J, Boult C, et al. Clinical practice guidelines and quality of care for older patients with multiple comorbid diseases: implications for pay for performance. *JAMA.* 2005;294(6):716-724.
4. Boyd C, Fortin, M. Future of multimorbidity research: how should understanding of multimorbidity inform health system design? *Public Health Rev.* 2010;32(2):451-474.

5. Ritchie CS, Kvale E, Fisch MJ. Multimorbidity: an issue of growing importance for oncologists. *J Oncol Pract.* 2011;7(6):371-374.

6. Akker M, Buntinx F, Knottnerus JA. Comorbidity or multimorbidity: what's in a name? *Eur J Gen Pract.* 1996;2:65-70.

7. Sogaard M, Thomsen RW, Bossen KS, et al. The impact of comorbidity on cancer survival: a review. *Clin Epidemiol.* 2013;5(suppl 1):3-29.

8. Read WL, Tierney RM, Page NC, et al. Differential prognostic impact of comorbidity. *J Clin Oncol.* 2004;22(15):3099-3103.

9. Gronberg BH, Sundstrom S, Kaasa S, et al. Influence of comorbidity on survival, toxicity and health-related quality of life in patients with advanced non-small-cell lung cancer receiving platinum-doublet chemotherapy. *Eur J Cancer.* 2010;46(12):2225-2234.

10. Hassett MJ, Rao SR, Brozovic S, et al. Chemotherapy-related hospitalization among community cancer center patients. *Oncologist.* 2011;16(3):378-387.

11. Zauderer M, Patil S, Hurria A. Feasibility and toxicity of dose-dense adjuvant chemotherapy in older women with breast cancer. *Breast Cancer Res Treat.* 2009;117(1):205-210.

12. Neugut AI, Matasar M, Wang X, et al. Duration of adjuvant chemotherapy for colon cancer and survival among the elderly. *J Clin Oncol.* 2006;24(15):2368-2375.

13. O'Grady MA, Slater E, Sigurdson ER, et al. Assessing compliance with national comprehensive cancer network guidelines for elderly patients with stage III colon cancer: the Fox Chase Cancer Center Partners' initiative. *Clin Colorectal Cancer.* 2011;10(2):113-116.

14. Vinod SK, Sidhom MA, Gabriel GS, et al. Why do some lung cancer patients receive no anticancer treatment? *J Thorac Oncol.* 2010;5(7):1025-1032.

15. Sarfati D. Review of methods used to measure comorbidity in cancer populations: no gold standard exists. *J Clin Epidemiol.* 2012;65(9):924-933.

16. Elixhauser A, Steiner C, Harris DR, Coffey RM. Comorbidity measures for use with administrative data. *Med Care.* 1998;36(1):8–27 [Epub 1998/02/07].

17. Charlson ME, Pompei P, Ales KL, MacKenzie CR. A new method of classifying prognostic comorbidity in longitudinal studies: development and validation. *J Chronic Dis.* 1987;40(5):373-383.

18. Klabunde CN, Potosky AL, Legler JM, Warren JL. Development of a comorbidity index using physician claims data. *J Clin Epidemiol.* 2000;53(12):1258-1267.

19. Klabunde CN, Legler JM, Warren JL, et al. A refined comorbidity measurement algorithm for claims-based studies of breast, prostate, colorectal, and lung cancer patients. *Ann Epidemiol.* 2007;17(8):584-590.

20. Linn BS, Linn MW, Gurel L. Cumulative illness rating scale. *J Am Geriatr Soc.* 1968;16(5):622-626.

21. Greenfield S, Blanco DM, Elashoff RM, Ganz PA. Patterns of care related to age of breast cancer patients. *JAMA.* 1987;257(20):2766-2770.

22. Kaplan MH, Feinstein AR. The importance of classifying initial co-morbidity in evaluating the outcome of diabetes mellitus. *J Chronic Dis.* 1974;27(7-8):387-404.

23. Piccirillo JF, Tierney RM, Costas I, et al. Prognostic importance of comorbidity in a hospital-based cancer registry. *JAMA.* 2004;291(20):2441-2447.

24. Piccirillo JF, Lacy PD, Basu A, Spitznagel EL. Development of a new head and neck cancer-specific comorbidity index. *Arch Otolaryngol Head Neck Surg.* 2002;128(10):1172-1179.

25. Sorror ML, Maris MB, Storb R, et al. Hematopoietic cell transplantation (HCT)-specific comorbidity index: a new tool for risk assessment before allogeneic HCT. *Blood.* 2005;106(8):2912-2919.

26. Extermann M. Measuring comorbidity in older cancer patients. *Eur J Cancer.* 2000;36(4):453-471.

27. Katz JN, Chang LC, Sangha O, et al. Can comorbidity be measured by questionnaire rather than medical record review? *Med Care.* 1996;34(1):73-84.

28. Habbous S, Chu KP, Harland LT, et al. Validation of a one-page patient-reported Charlson comorbidity index questionnaire for upper aerodigestive tract cancer patients. *Oral Oncol.* 2013;49(5):407-412.

29. Charlson M, Szatrowski TP, Peterson J, Gold J. Validation of a combined comorbidity index. *J Clin Epidemiol.* 1994;47(11):1245-1251.

30. Fillenbaum GG, Smyer MA. The development, validity, and reliability of the OARS multidimensional functional assessment questionnaire. *J Gerontol.* 1981;36(4):428-434.

31. Hurria A, Gupta S, Zauderer M, et al. Developing a cancer-specific geriatric assessment: a feasibility study. *Cancer.* 2005;104(9):1998-2005.

32. Colinet B, Jacot W, Bertrand D, et al. A new simplified comorbidity score as a prognostic factor in non-small-cell lung cancer patients: description and comparison with the Charlson's index. *Br J Cancer.* 2005;93(10):1098-1105

33. Hurria A, Browner IS, Cohen HJ, et al. Senior adult oncology. *J Natl Compr Canc Netw.* 2012;10(2):162-209.

34. Thompson K, Dale W. How do I best manage the care of older patients with cancer with multimorbidity? *J Geriatr Oncol.* 2015;6(4):249-253.

35. Guiding principles for the care of older adults with multimorbidity: an approach for clinicians: American Geriatrics Society Expert Panel on the care of older adults with multimorbidity. *J Am Geriatr Soc.* 2012;60(10):E1-E25.

Cognitive Syndromes and Delirium

Reena Jaiswal and Yesne Alici

INTRODUCTION

Cognitive syndromes are commonly encountered among cancer patients, with the elderly being at higher risk (1). Factors such as primary or metastatic brain tumors, delirium, comorbid depression, or adverse effects of treatments such as chemotherapy and radiation can predispose patients to developing cognitive deficits (2). Cognitive deficits in older adults heavily impact outcomes in cancer care due to potential impairments in decision making and activities of daily living (e.g., ability to take medications). It is therefore important to systematically screen for cognitive impairment among elderly patients in oncology settings. In the absence of a structured screening tool for cognitive impairment, patients with cognitive syndromes are frequently underrecognized. Once a cognitive syndrome is identified, assessment of the underlying etiologies helps identify reversible and irreversible factors, as well as revising goals of care if needed. This chapter focuses on the cognitive assessment of older cancer patients and reviews the most commonly seen neurocognitive disorders (including delirium) in oncology settings.

DELIRIUM

Delirium is one of the most common and most serious neuropsychiatric complications seen in older adults with cancer. It is defined as an acute change in attention, level of alertness, cognition, and behavior secondary to a general medical condition or medications and is associated with significant distress, morbidity, and mortality (3). In elderly patients, delirium is associated with increased rates of cognitive decline, admission to institutions, increased health care costs, and mortality. The growing data on short-term and long-term outcomes of delirium highlight the importance of screening for it among all hospitalized cancer patients.

Older age and preexisting cognitive impairment are well-documented risk factors for delirium (4). Delirium is characterized by three subtypes based on the patient's level of psychomotor activity: hyperactive, hypoactive, or mixed (features of both hyperactive and hypoactive). Hyperactive delirium is associated with agitation and hallucinations, whereas patients with the hypoactive subtype appear lethargic with slowed movements. In older adults, the hypoactive form may be more common, but is under-recognized (5). Both subtypes of delirium are associated with increased morbidity and mortality in the medically ill and are significantly distressing to patients and caregivers (6). Therefore, timely diagnosis and management of delirium are essential regardless of the subtype.

Assessment for Delirium

The "gold standard" diagnosis of delirium is the clinician's assessment based on the *Diagnostic and Statistical Manual of Mental Disorders (DSM-5)* (7) delirium diagnostic criteria. Table 10.1 presents the highlights of delirium assessment in older patients with cancer. Several assessment and rating scales have been developed specifically for delirium, each with its own strengths and weaknesses (8,9). Commonly used delirium screening and assessment tools are reviewed in Table 10.2.

TABLE 10.1 Assessment of Delirium

- Delirium is an acute change in mental status with fluctuating course, attentional impairment, and disturbed level of alertness, accompanied by cognitive disturbances and/or delusions/perceptual disturbances due to medications or underlying medical etiologies.
- Clinical features may include psychomotor disturbances, sleep-wake cycle changes, agitation in the form of refusal of care, and affective ability.
- A timeline of when the symptoms began and how fast they are progressing is helpful in making the diagnosis. Rapid onset of cognitive impairment = delirium; gradual onset and progressive decline = dementia.
- Look for fluctuations in level of alertness; evaluate patients at different time points over 24 hr.
- Delirium may present with suicidal ideation, impulsivity, poor judgment, paranoia, and perceptual disturbances, which can increase risk of self-harm.
- Review the medication list for recent exposure to deliriogenic medications, especially anticholinergic agents, benzodiazepines, and opiates.
- Conduct a thorough physical exam. Look for signs of infection/sepsis or neurologic deficits.
- Laboratory and imaging testing should be ordered to identify infectious, metabolic, or endocrine disturbances.
- Consider neuroimaging in patients with new focal neurologic deficits, concerns for CNS infections, history of primary CNS cancer, or suspected CNS metastasis.
- Electroencephalography may help to diagnose nonconvulsive seizures as a cause of acute cognitive changes. Generalized slowing on an EEG can be seen in delirium or dementia, not in depression.

CNS, central nervous system; EEG, electroencephalogram.

TABLE 10.2 Commonly Used Delirium Screening and Assessment Tools

Confusion Assessment Method (10)	▪ Most commonly used delirium screening instrument in general medical settings, specifically among older adults. ▪ Four-item algorithm can be used to quickly screen for delirium. ▪ Requires well-trained raters. ▪ Excellent psychometric properties when used by well-trained raters. ▪ Cognitive testing is required to assess the cognitive items of the scale. ▪ Validated for use in a number of languages.
Delirium Rating Scale-R-98 (11)	▪ Includes 16 clinician-rated items, 13 for severity and 3 for diagnosis. The rating is applicable to the preceding 24 hr. ▪ Successfully differentiates delirium from dementia, depression, and schizophrenia. ▪ Administered by trained clinicians. ▪ Has excellent psychometric properties. ▪ Mostly used for research purposes. ▪ Has been validated in different languages.
Memorial Delirium Assessment Scale (12)	▪ Mainly used for assessment of the severity and subtype of delirium. ▪ MDAS has 10 items, rated from 0 (none) to 3 (severe), with a maximum possible score of 30. ▪ A score of 13 has been recommended as a cut-off for establishing the diagnosis of delirium in oncology settings. ▪ A cut-off score of 7 has yielded the highest sensitivity and specificity rates for delirium diagnosis in palliative care settings (1). ▪ Has excellent psychometric properties. ▪ Distinguishes between patients with delirium, dementia, or no cognitive impairment. ▪ Has been validated in a number of different languages. ▪ The most widely used delirium assessment scale in oncology and palliative care settings. ▪ Physician-rated. ▪ Takes about 10–15 min to administer.
Nursing Delirium Screening Scale (Nu-DESC) (13)	▪ Adapted from Confusion Rating Scale, a former delirium assessment tool. ▪ Comprised of five items including: orientation, behavior, communication, perceptual disturbances, and psychomotor retardation. ▪ Allows for continuous symptom assessment. ▪ Has been validated for use in oncology settings. ▪ Administered by nursing staff. ▪ Takes about 1–2 min. ▪ Has good psychometric properties. ▪ Has been validated in different languages.

Source: Adapted from Ref. (14). Breitbart W, Alici Y. Evidence-based treatment of delirium in patients with cancer. *J Clin Oncol.* 2012;30(11):1206-1214.

Prevention of Delirium

There is evidence to suggest that nonpharmacologic interventions reduce the incidence of delirium among hospitalized older patients (5). The American Geriatrics Society strongly recommends the implementation of multicomponent, nonpharmacologic interventions to prevent postoperative delirium in older adults (15). The essential components of preventive interventions include reorientation, minimizing polypharmacy, early mobilization, promotion of sleep, and maintenance of adequate hydration and nutrition (5). Antipsychotics, cholinesterase inhibitors, dexmedetomidine, and melatonin are the main pharmacologic interventions studied in the prevention of delirium in a variety of settings and in mixed age groups (16). There is currently not enough evidence to support the use of any of the pharmacologic interventions in the prevention of delirium in older adults with cancer (16).

Management and Treatment of Delirium

The treatment of delirium should first and foremost be to identify and correct the underlying etiologies. Nonpharmacologic interventions, such as those described in the preceeding section on Prevention of Delirium, should be included as first-line treatment strategies to reduce duration and severity of delirium (5). The current evidence supports short-term, low-dose use of antipsychotics to control symptoms of delirium (e.g., symptoms that put patients at risk of harm to themselves or others) with close monitoring of possible side effects in older adults with cancer (14). By using lower doses for short durations and monitoring closely for the development of side effects, adverse outcomes sometimes associated with antipsychotic use can be avoided. Table 10.3 includes a list of antipsychotics commonly used in the treatment of delirium.

DEMENTIA

Dementia is a progressive cognitive decline characterized by impairment in cognitive functioning (e.g., memory, language, executive functioning, visuospatial skills) that interferes with one's ability to perform activities of daily living independently. Although the exact prevalence is unknown, it is estimated that dementia affects between 2.4 and 5.5 million people in the United States (17). Cancer patients with cognitive impairment are at increased risk of functional dependence and medication nonadherence, and are at greater risk of death (18). Cognitive and functional assessments are recommended for all older adults with cancer to identify cognitive impairment (18). The National Comprehensive Cancer Network (NCCN) Senior Adult Oncology Guidelines provide recommendations on those assessment tools (19). The NCCN Senior Adult Oncology Guidelines (19) recommend that all cognitively impaired patients to be cared for by a multidisciplinary geriatric oncology team throughout their treatment. For patients with suspected cognitive impairment or for patients with

TABLE 10.3 Antipsychotic Medications Used Clinically in the Treatment of Delirium

Medication	Haloperidol	Chlorpromazine	Olanzapine	Risperidone	Quetiapine	Aripiprazole	Ziprasidone	Asenapine
Dose ranges for geriatric patients	0.25–2 mg every 2–12 hr	12.5–50 mg every 4–6 hr	2.5–5 mg every 12–24 hr	0.25–1 mg every 12–24 hr	12.5–100 mg every 12–24 hr	2–15 mg every 24 hr	10–40 mg every 12–24 hr	2.5–10 mg every 24 hr
Route of administration	PO, IV, IM SC	PO, IV, IM, SC, PR	PO,† IM	PO†	PO	PO,† IM	PO, IM	PO†
Adverse effects	-Extrapyramidal adverse effects can occur at higher doses -Monitor QT interval on ECG for potential prolongation	-More sedating and anti-cholinergic adverse effects compared with haloperidol -Monitor blood pressure for hypotension -More suitable for use in ICU settings where blood pressure can be closely monitored	Sedation is the main dose limiting adverse effect in short term use	Extrapyramidal adverse effects can occur with doses >6 mg/d	Sedation, orthostatic hypotension	Monitor for akathisia	Monitor QT interval on ECG	-Orthostasis -Dose-related akathisia -Sedation is a dose limiting factor -Not recommended for patients with severe hepatic impairment
Special considerations	-Remains the gold standard therapy for delirium -Can add lorazepam (0.25–1 mg every 2–4 hr) for agitated patients	-May be preferred in agitated patients due to its sedating effect	-Older age, pre-existing dementia, and hypoactive subtype of delirium have been associated with poor response -Doses over 10–15 mg per day may worsen delirium due to anti-cholinergic effect -IM preparation should never be combined with IM lorazepam due to risk of cardiovascular collapse	-May be associated with orthostatic hypotension	-Sedating effects may be helpful in patients with sleep-wake cycle disturbance -May be associated with orthostatic hypotension	-Evidence is limited -Might be more efficacious in patients with hypoactive subtype than the hyperactive subtype	-The literature on QT prolongation with ziprasidone makes it the least preferred agent in the medically ill	There is no evidence for use in delirium

ICU, intensive care unit; IM, intramuscular; IV, intravenous; PO, oral; PR, per rectum; SC, subcutaneous.

†Risperidone, olanzapine, and aripiprazole are available in orally disintegrating tablets.

All patients receiving antipsychotics should be monitored for QT prolongation.

Source: Adapted from Ref. (14). Breitbart W, Alici Y. Evidence-based treatment of delirium in patients with cancer. *J Clin Oncol.* 2012;30(11):1206-1214.

self-reported or family-reported concerns of cognitive impairment, a consultation with a cognitive disorders specialist is recommended. The NCCN guidelines also recommend periodic reassessment of cognitive functioning for those with cognitive impairment and for all older adults when considering changes to treatment plan.

Dementia: Screening and Assessment

The initial assessment of an individual suspected of having any cognitive impairment should start with a detailed history, with input from a collateral source that could provide information on the patient's previous level of functioning, as well as the temporal course and rate of cognitive decline (9). The time course and associated symptoms represent the key information to identify the type of dementia and to rule out underlying delirium or depression. For neurocognitive disorders such as dementia, the onset of symptoms is gradual and progressive as opposed to the abrupt and rapid onset usually seen in delirium. As part of the initial assessment, reviewing a patient's baseline and current ability to carry out his or her independent activities of daily living (IADLs) provides reliable information on cognitive functioning. It is important to determine what degree of the IADL impairment is secondary to physical impairment as opposed to cognitive deficits. Asking a caregiver if he or she has concerns for the patient's safety can also provide key information regarding the level of impairment.

The history should additionally include history of alcohol or illicit substance use, as well as exposure to toxins. A thorough review of medications, including use of supplements and over-the-counter drugs, must be completed. Cancer-related treatments, including chemotherapeutic agents, radiation, and hormone therapies, which have all been associated with cognitive changes, should be reviewed in detail. Clinicians should inquire about prior history of chronic medical conditions such as hypertension, vascular disease, hyperlipidemia, diabetes, obesity, and prior history of psychiatric illnesses. Patients with major depressive disorder can often present with mild forgetfulness, previously termed "pseudo-dementia." Feelings of sadness, hopelessness, anhedonia, amotivation, and suicidality are supportive of a diagnosis of depression. In depressed patients, cognitive impairments tend to be mild and would have not been present prior to development of the depressed mood. When answering cognitive assessment questions, the depressed patient often responds, "I don't know." Patients with dementia tend to express more distress over the impairment when asked questions. Patients with depression are expected to return to normal level of cognitive functioning once the depression is resolved. Fatigue secondary to cancer and cancer-related treatments is commonly encountered among elderly cancer patients and may contribute to cognitive dysfunction. Patients suffering from excessive fatigue could appear inattentive or sedated, and present with short-term memory impairments. Once the individual's fatigue is treated and rest is restored, these deficits should improve.

An important component of the evaluation is the objective assessment of an individual's cognitive abilities. Refer Table 10.4 for a brief summary of the cognitive assessment tools for patients with dementia. Repeated administration of the same assessment tool is important in tracking further declines in cognition. A structure-based performance evaluation administered by an occupational therapist and neuropsychological testing may be required to identify subtle deficits or those that present in an atypical pattern (9,20).

A comprehensive physical examination with focus on neurological signs should be performed. Information obtained during history and physical examination should guide clinicians as to the extent of laboratory testing and neuroimaging. Laboratory testing that includes a urinalysis, basic metabolic panel, lipid profile, liver function tests, thyroid function tests, HIV test, paraneoplastic panel, vitamin levels (including vitamin B_{12} and thiamine), neuroimaging, and examination of cerebrospinal fluid could be helpful in identifying causes of the cognitive impairment.

TABLE 10.4 Commonly Used Cognitive Assessment Tools

Features	MMSE	MoCA	Mini-Cog
Domains tested	Orientation, attention, comprehension, calculations, memory, language, visuospatial ability	Orientation, memory, clock, visuospatial ability, fluency, language, abstraction, calculations, executive function, attention	Memory, language comprehension, visual-motor skills, executive function
Advantages	Most widely used	Less likely to miss deficits in the well-educated; offers better estimate of executive functioning, more sensitive to mild impairment, available in many different languages	Not strongly influenced by education; quick to administer
Disadvantages	Can miss deficits in the well-educated; limited executive function testing	Does not distinguish between mild cognitive impairment and dementia	Scoring of clock drawing test is vulnerable to different interpretations
Time needed to administer	7–10 min	10–13 min	3 min

MMSE, Mini-Mental State Examination; MoCA, Montreal Cognitive Assessment.

Source: Adapted from Ref. (9). Scharre DW, Trzepacz PT. Evaluation of cognitive impairment in older adults. *Focus.* 2013;11(4):482–500.

Cancer or Cancer Therapy-Associated Cognitive Changes

Cancer or *cancer therapy-associated cognitive changes* refers to cognitive impairment during or following cancer diagnosis and treatments (21). Older patients, patients with low cognitive reserve, and individuals carrying certain genetic alleles (e.g., apolipoprotein E [*APOE4*]) have been shown to be at significantly increased risk for posttreatment cognitive changes (22). Routine screening for cognitive impairment is recommended for all older cancer patients. However, simple screening tools such as the Montreal Cognitive Assessment (MoCA) and the Mini-Mental State Examination (MMSE) may not capture the subtle cognitive changes reported by patients and families. Comprehensive neuropsychological testing can be utilized to help patients and providers make decisions regarding future treatment and need for cognitive rehabilitation or medications that target attention deficits, such as psychostimulants.

TAKE HOME POINTS

1. Cancer patients with cognitive impairment are at increased risk of treatment nonadherence, decline in independent functioning, and bad outcomes.
2. All older adults in oncology settings should be systematically screened for cognitive impairment because of the potential impact it can have on cancer care.
3. Delirium is one of the most commonly seen, serious neuropsychiatric complications in older adults with cancer. It is caused by an underlying medical condition or medications and is associated with significant morbidity and mortality.
4. Cognitive assessment tools such as the MoCA or Mini-Cog should be used to screen older adults for cognitive deficits; serial assessments with the same tool can help to track changes.
5. Older cancer patients with dementia would benefit from care by a multidisciplinary geriatric oncology team throughout their treatment.
6. Although cancer or cancer therapy-related cognitive changes are best diagnosed using comprehensive neuropsychological testing, serial assessments with brief, commonly used cognitive assessment tools are helpful in detecting any changes in cognitive functioning through the course of treatment, and after.

REFERENCES

1. Lawlor PG, Gagnon B, Mancini IL, et al. Occurrence, causes, and outcome of delirium in patients with advanced cancer: a prospective study. *Arch Intern Med.* 2000;160(6):786-794.
2. Andreotti C, Root JC, Alici Y, Ahles TA. Cognitive disorders and delirium. In: Holland JC, Wiesel TW, Nelson CJ, et al., eds. *Geriatric Psycho-Oncology.* Oxford, UK: Oxford University Press; 2015.

3. Witlox J, Eurelings LS, de Jonghe JF, et al. Delirium in elderly patients and the risk of postdischarge mortality, institutionalization, and dementia: a meta-analysis. *JAMA.* 2010;304(4):443-451.

4. Grover S, Kate N. Assessment scales for delirium: a review. *World J Psychiatr.* 2012; 2(4):58-70.

5. Inouye SK, Westendorp RG, Saczynski JS. Delirium in elderly people. *Lancet.* 2014;383(9920):911-922.

6. Breitbart W, Gibson C, Tremblay A. The delirium experience: delirium recall and delirium-related distress in hospitalized patients with cancer, their spouses/caregivers, and their nurses. *Psychosomatics.* 2002;43(3):183-194.

7. American Psychiatric Association. *Diagnostic and Statistical Manual of Mental Disorders: DSM-5.* Washington, DC: American Psychiatric Association; 2013.

8. Smith MJ, Breitbart WS, Platt MM. A critique of instruments and methods to detect, diagnose, and rate delirium. *J Pain Symptom Manage.* 1995;10(1):35-77.

9. Scharre DW, Trzepacz PT. Evaluation of cognitive impairment in older adults. *Focus.* 2013;11(4):482-500.

10. Inouye SK, van Dyck CH, Alessi CA, et al. Clarifying confusion: the Confusion Assessment Method. A new method for detection of delirium. *Ann Intern Med.* 1990;113(12):941-948.

11. Trzepacz PT, Mulsant BH, Dew MA, et al. Is delirium different when it occurs in dementia? A study using the Delirium Rating Scale. *J Neuropsychiatry Clin Neurosci.* 1998;10(2):199-204.

12. Breitbart W, Rosenfeld B, Roth A, et al. The Memorial Delirium Assessment Scale. *J Pain Symptom Manage.* 1997;13(3):128-137.

13. Gaudreau, JD, Gagnon P, Harel F, et al. Fast, systematic, and continuous delirium assessment in hospitalized patients: the Nursing Delirium Screening Scale. *J Pain Symptom Manage.* 2005;29(4):368-375.

14. Breitbart W, Alici Y. Evidence-based treatment of delirium in patients with cancer. *J Clin Oncol.* 2012;30(11):1206-1214.

15. American Geriatrics Society. American Geriatrics Society abstracted clinical practice guideline for postoperative delirium in older adults. *J Am Geriatr Soc.* 2015;63(1):142-150.

16. Korc-Grodzicki B, Root JC, Alici Y. Prevention of post-operative delirium in older patients with cancer undergoing surgery. *J Geriatr Oncol.* 2015;6(1):60-69.

17. Lin JS, O'Connor E, Rossom RC, et al. Screening for cognitive impairment in older adults: a systematic review for the US Preventive Services Task Force. *Ann Intern Med.* 2013;159(9):601-612.

18. Hurria, A, Wildes T, Blair SL, et al. Senior adult oncology, version 2.2014. *J Natl Compr Cancer Netw.* 2014;12(1):82-126.

19. Network NCC. NCCN Clinical Practice Guidelines in Oncology. *Senior Adult Oncology.* 2016. Available at: NCCN.org.

20. McCarten JR. The case for screening for cognitive impairment in older adults. *J Am Geriatr Soc.* 2013;61(7):1203-1205.

21. Ahles TA. Cognitive disorders and delirium. In: Holland JC, Weiss Wiesel T, Nelson CJ, et al., eds. *Geriatric Psycho-Oncology: A Quick Reference on the Psychosocial Dimensions of Cancer Symptom Management.* New York, NY: Oxford University Press; 2015.

22. Ahles TA. Brain vulnerability to chemotherapy toxicities. *Psychooncology.* 2012;21(11):1141-1148.

Anxiety and Depression in Older Cancer Patients

Rebecca Saracino, Christian J. Nelson, and Andrew J. Roth

INTRODUCTION

Older adults with cancer often develop symptoms of anxiety and depression, which are associated with decreased quality of life, significant deterioration in physical activities, relationship difficulties, and greater pain (1,2). Additionally, comorbid depression and anxiety are of great concern given their negative impact on treatment compliance and adherence (3,4). It is understandable that patients may experience symptoms of general distress, worry, and anxiety given the severity of a cancer diagnosis. However, distress is often experienced on a continuum from minor situational anxiety and transient depressive symptoms to more severe disorders that may interfere with daily functioning and require intervention and treatment.

Several barriers impede the identification of psychopathology in older patients with cancer. For example, the acceptance of significant mood symptoms in people with cancer as "normal" and "expected" by both patients and clinicians is common and therefore may go without mention, discussion, or treatment (5–7). Similarly, there is often pressure on those involved in the patient's care to "think positively." Depression may also be normalized in older adults, as somatic symptoms and depressive cognitions are viewed as a routine part of the aging process (8). However, depression, anxiety, and other forms of psychopathology are not an inevitable part of aging or a cancer experience. In fact, most adults report overall increases in well-being as they age (9,10). Therefore, careful consideration and evaluation of these symptoms are warranted in older adults with cancer.

DEPRESSION

The rates of depression in older cancer patients range from 15% to 37% (11–14). Unfortunately, depression can be difficult to recognize in older adults, as they are less likely to report depressed mood, and more likely to present with an anhedonic depression. Anhedonic depression occurs when people lose the capacity to experience pleasure, which must be distinguished from physical limitations of pleasurable behavior (15). The presence of cancer also complicates the ability of clinicians to accurately identify depressive symptoms (16,17). The difficulty in diagnosing depression lies in the overlap between the common symptoms of depression and symptoms of cancer and/or side effects of cancer treatment, such as changes in appetite, sleep, energy, and concentration (18–20). Thus, the same symptoms may arise from depression, from the cancer itself, from treatment side effects, or from some combination of the three, thereby leading to incorrect diagnostic assumptions (21–24).

Diagnostic Criteria

A diagnosis of major depressive disorder (MDD) in physically healthy people requires the presence of at least one of the two "gateway" symptoms (i.e., depressed mood, anhedonia) for a minimum period of 2 weeks, most of the day, most days, together with either distress or impaired functioning (25). Additional symptoms of MDD are bio-physical (i.e., weight loss or appetite changes, insomnia or hypersomnia, psychomotor agitation, or retardation) and cognitive (i.e., worthlessness or guilt, diminished concentration or indecisiveness, and recurrent thoughts of death or suicidal ideation). These symptoms are graded by severity (i.e., mild, moderate, severe). The diagnosis of depressive disorder due to another medical condition is given when an individual reports prominent depressed mood and/or anhedonia, and there is evidence from the history, physical examination, or laboratory findings that the disturbance is the direct pathophysiological consequence of another medical condition (25). In cancer, this might be the most appropriate diagnosis when the depressive disorder is clearly associated with the underlying disease or its treatment, even if all diagnostic criteria are not met for MDD.

Diagnostic Considerations for Older Adults With Cancer

Additional key symptoms in older patients that may be helpful to clinicians working in oncology settings (18,26) include "general malaise," as opposed to being depressed or having loss of interest due to pain or fatigue, or "general" aches and pains or stomach aches, as opposed to specific tumor-site pain or specific side effects of cancer treatment. Many patients with cancer express some hope for a meaningful future regardless of prognosis; thus, reports of little or no hope may be a sign of depression. Sleep may be problematic for all patients with cancer. If the patient wakes up in the middle of the night (middle insomnia), it is important to ask if this is due to a physical issue (e.g., pain, urination, or gastric distress). If the patient has difficulty getting back to sleep, and this is due to worry, ruminative thoughts, or feeling anxious, then this may be an indication of a depressive symptom. An older depressed patient may also report mood variation during the day as opposed to the typical picture of depression—mood may be worse in the morning and may improve as the day continues or vice versa.

ANXIETY

Recent studies found that 25% to 44% of older patients with cancer reported anxiety at levels high enough to warrant referral and treatment (11,12–14). As with sadness or depression, anxiety and stress may be a normal and adaptive initial reaction to a cancer diagnosis. Anxiety can motivate an individual to mobilize his or her practical

TABLE 11.1 Acute Anxiety Symptoms in the Cancer Setting

- Uneasiness, unpleasant feeling of arousal, restlessness
- Irritability
- Inability to relax; tendency to startle
- Difficulty falling asleep (leads to fatigue and low tolerance to frustration)
- Recurring, intrusive thoughts and images of cancer
- Occasionally, sense of impending doom
- Distractibility
- Helplessness and a sense of loss of control over one's own feelings
- Symptoms of autonomic arousal: rapid or forceful heartbeat, sweating, unpleasant tightness in stomach, shortness of breath, dizziness
- Vegetative disturbances: loss of appetite, decreased sexual interest
- Parasympathetically mediated symptoms: abdominal distress, nausea, diarrhea

Source: From Ref. (4). Die Trill M. Anxiety and sleep disorders in cancer patients. *EJC Suppl.* 2013;11(2):216-224.

and emotional coping resources in order to respond effectively to a cancer diagnosis. The course of anxiety typically vacillates in parallel with the illness course and events over time, such as awaiting a scan; waiting for the results of a scan or tumor marker test; finding out about a failed treatment or recurrence; or beginning a more aggressive treatment (4,27). However, prolonged and distressing symptoms of anxiety that interfere with an individual's ability to function optimally warrant intervention.

Anxiety Disorders

Anxiety symptoms include excessive worry, fear, panic, apprehension, and dread (see Table 11.1). Patients are diagnosed with an adjustment disorder when their initial anxiety symptoms do not dissipate over time. Given that cancer and its treatment have an uncertain course and present a real threat, it can be difficult for clinicians to disentangle "normal" from excessive anxiety. Nicholas (28) suggested that those with severe anxiety symptoms are unable to concentrate and to "turn off negative thoughts," have sleep problems most nights, and have crying spells that interfere with daily activities. They may also experience constant worries and have few ways of reducing anxiety. It is not surprising that this type of problematic anxiety can interfere with an individual's daily living and cause a disruption in functioning (25). Other anxiety disorders, including generalized anxiety disorder, a specific phobia, and panic disorder, may predate the cancer. Phobias may be seen as needle or MRI phobia, whereas panic attacks are experienced as tremor, shortness of breath, or palpitations with or without warning. A careful history should be obtained, however, as a pre-existing anxiety may be exacerbated in the context of a new stressor such as cancer. For an extensive review of other anxiety disorders in the context of cancer, see Traeger et al. (29).

Anxiety may also be due to a medical condition itself or a side effect of treatment. For example, poorly controlled pain, abnormal metabolic states, hormone-secreting tumors, anxiety-producing drugs, and anxiety-producing conditions may all precipitate anxiety in someone with cancer (Table 11.2) (30). These physical etiologies should be thoroughly addressed.

TREATMENT OF DEPRESSION AND ANXIETY

Older patients with cancer can benefit from many existing treatment modalities, including psychotherapeutic and psychopharmacologic interventions, or a combination of both. Psychotherapy techniques are listed in Table 11.3, although modalities may have to be adapted for patients' mobility, ability to get to sessions, cancer treatment schedules, diminished stamina or increased pain or discomfort that can make it difficult to sit for long periods.

When initiating pharmacologic intervention for older patients with cancer, the treating clinician should remember to "start low (doses), go slow." For the treatment of depression, selective serotonin reuptake inhibitors (SSRIs) and serotonin-norepinephrine reuptake inhibitors (SNRIs) are commonly prescribed. The first-line

TABLE 11.2 Medical Etiologies of Anxiety in the Cancer Setting

Medical Problem	Examples
Poorly controlled pain	Insufficient or as-needed pain medications
Abnormal metabolic states	Hypoxia, pulmonary embolus, sepsis, delirium, hypoglycemia, bleeding, coronary occlusion, or heart failure
Hormone-secreting tumors	Pheochromocytoma, thyroid adenoma or carcinoma, parathyroid adenoma, corticotropin-producing tumors, and insulinoma
Anxiety-producing drugs	Corticosteroids, neuroleptics used as antiemetics, thyroxine, bronchodilators, beta-adrenergic stimulants, antihistamines, and benzodiazepines (paradoxical reactions are often seen in older persons)
Anxiety-producing conditions	Substance withdrawal (from alcohol, opioids, or sedative-hypnotics)

Source: From Ref. (30). Roth AJ, Massie MJ. Anxiety and its management in advanced cancer. *Curr Opin Support Palliat Care.* 2007;1(1):50-56.

TABLE 11.3 Psychotherapy Modalities for Treating Depression and Anxiety in Older Patients

- Educational and emotional support from treatment team or from a therapist
- Cognitive-behavioral oriented therapy
- Insight-oriented therapy
- ACT
- PST
- Meaning-centered psychotherapy
- Dignity therapy

ACT, acceptance and commitment therapy; PST, problem-solving therapy.

anxiolytic drugs are benzodiazepines. However, they should be used with caution and require close monitoring, as older patients are at increased risk for confusion, drowsiness, falls, and depressed central nervous system effects.

CONCLUSION

Depression and anxiety are highly prevalent in older patients with cancer. In fact, in older patients with cancer, symptoms of anxiety often coexist with depression and mixed states, and are perhaps more common than anxiety or depression alone. Diagnosing depression and anxiety in older patients with cancer is challenging, even for mental health professionals. Therefore, clinicians need to be familiar with the unusual presentation of these symptoms in this population, as well as their potential underlying medical causes, in order to ensure optimal treatment and quality of life for the patient.

TAKE HOME POINTS

1. Older adults with cancer develop symptoms of anxiety and depression, which are associated with decreased quality of life, significant deterioration in physical activities, relationship difficulties, and greater pain.
2. Symptoms of significant anxiety and depression are often mistaken as a normal part of coping with cancer and therefore are not addressed.
3. In addition to depressed mood and the inability to experience pleasure unrelated to psychical symptoms, older adults with cancer may have somatic symptoms, general malaise, hopelessness, or sleep disturbance as key symptoms of depression.
4. Anxiety in older cancer patients can be experienced as worry, distress, restlessness, or panic symptoms.
5. Older cancer patients may benefit from psychotherapy or psychotropic medications for anxiety and depression, although both may have to be accommodated to particular needs of energy, travel, and cost.

REFERENCES

1. Deckx L, van Abbema DL, van den Akker M, et al. A cohort study on the evolution of psychosocial problems in older patients with breast or colorectal cancer: comparison with younger cancer patients and older primary care patients without cancer. *BMC Geriatr.* 2015;15:79.
2. Hopko DR, Bell JL, Armento ME, et al. The phenomenology and screening of clinical depression in cancer patients. *J Psychosoc Oncol.* 2008;26(1):31-51.
3. DiMatteo MR, Lepper HS, Croghan TW. Depression is a risk factor for noncompliance with medical treatment: meta-analysis of the effects of anxiety and depression on patient adherence. *Arch Intern Med.* 2000;160(14):2101-2107.
4. Die Trill M. Anxiety and sleep disorders in cancer patients. *EJC Suppl.* 2013;11(2):216-224.
5. Endicott J. Measurement of depression in patients with cancer. *Cancer.* 1984; 53(10 suppl):2243-2249.

6. Rhondali W, Perceau E, Berthiller J, et al. Frequency of depression among oncology outpatients and association with other symptoms. *Support Care Cancer.* 2012;20(11):2795-2802.

7. Weinberger MI, Bruce ML, Roth AJ, et al. Depression and barriers to mental health care in older cancer patients. *Int J Geriatr Psychiatry* 2011;26(1):21-26.

8. Fiske A, Wetherell JL, Gatz M. Depression in older adults. *Ann Rev Clin Psychol.* 2009;5:363-389.

9. Jeste DV, Savla GN, Thompson WK, et al. Association between older age and more successful aging: critical role of resilience and depression. *Am J Psychiatry.* 2013;170(2):188-196.

10. Jeste DV, Depp CA, Vahia IV. Successful cognitive and emotional aging. *World Psychiatry.* 2010;9(2):78-84.

11. Wiesel TRW, Nelson CJ, Tew WP, et al. The relationship between age, anxiety, and depression in older adults with cancer. *Psychooncology.* 2015;24(6):712-717.

12. Canoui-Poitrine F, Reinald N, Laurent M, et al. Geriatric assessment findings independently associated with clinical depression in 1092 older patients with cancer: the ELCAPA Cohort Study. *Psychooncology.* 2016;25(1):104-111.

13. Delgado-Guay M, Parsons HA, Li Z, et al. Symptom distress in advanced cancer patients with anxiety and depression in the palliative care setting. *Support Care Cancer.* 2009;17(5):573-579.

14. Nelson CJ, Balk EM, Roth AJ. Distress, anxiety, depression, and emotional well-being in African-American men with prostate cancer. *Psychooncology.* 2010;19(10):1052-1060.

15. Gallo JJ, Rabins PV, Lyketsos CG, et al. Depression without sadness: functional outcomes of nondysphoric depression in later life. *J Am Geriatr Soc.* 1997;45(5):570-578.

16. Simon GE, VonKorff M, Barlow W. Health care costs of primary care patients with recognized depression. *Arch Gen Psychiatry.* 1995;52(10):850-856.

17. Weinberger MI, Roth AJ, Nelson CJ. Untangling the complexities of depression diagnosis in older cancer patients. *Oncologist.* 2009;14(1):60-66.

18. Guo Y, Musselman DL, Manatunga AK, et al. The diagnosis of major depression in patients with cancer: a comparative approach. *Psychosomatics.* 2006;47(5):376-384.

19. Kathol RG, Mutgi A, Williams J, et al. Diagnosis of major depression in cancer patients according to four sets of criteria. *Am J Psychiatry.* 1990;147(8):1021-1024.

20. Passik SD, Lowery A. Psychological variables potentially implicated in opioid-related mortality as observed in clinical practice. *Pain Med.* 2011;12(suppl 2):S36-S42.

21. Koenig HG, George LK, Peterson BL, Pieper CF. Depression in medically ill hospitalized older adults: prevalence, characteristics, and course of symptoms according to six diagnostic schemes. *Am J Psychiatry.* 1997;154(10):1376-1383.

22. McDaniel JS, Musselman DL, Porter MR, et al. Depression in patients with cancer. Diagnosis, biology, and treatment. *Arch Gen Psychiatry.* 1995;52(2):89-99.

23. Akechi T, Ietsugu T, Sukigara M, et al. Symptom indicator of severity of depression in cancer patients: a comparison of the DSM-IV criteria with alternative diagnostic criteria. *Gen Hosp Psychiatry.* 2009;31(3):225-232.

24. Akechi T, Nakano T, Akizuki N, et al. Somatic symptoms for diagnosing major depression in cancer patients. *Psychosomatics.* 2003;44(3):244-248.

25. American Psychiatric Association. *Diagnostic and Statistical Manual of Mental Disorders.* Arlington, VA: American Psychiatric Publishing; 2013.

26. Saracino RM, Rosenfeld B, Nelson CJ. Towards a new conceptualization of depression in older adult cancer patients: a review of the literature. *Aging Ment Health.* 2015:1-13.

27. Cohen M. Depression, anxiety, and somatic symptoms in older cancer patients: a comparison across age groups. *Psychooncology.* 2014;23(2):151-157.

28. Nicholas DR. *Emotional side-effects of cancer: Distinguishing normal distress from mental disorders* [brochure]. Muncie, IN: Ball Memorial Hospital and Ball State University, 2008.

29. Traeger L, Greer JA, Fernandez-Robles C, et al. Evidence-based treatment of anxiety in patients with cancer. *J Clin Oncol.* 2012;30(11):1197-1205.

30. Roth AJ, Massie MJ. Anxiety and its management in advanced cancer. *Curr Opin Support Palliat Care.* 2007;1(1):50-56.

12

Social Isolation and Caregiver Burden

Linda Mathew and Carolyn Fulton

INTRODUCTION

More than 16 million Americans are currently living with a diagnosis of cancer; accordingly, the need for cancer caregiving have increased. Shorter hospital stays and the transition of cancer treatment to the ambulatory setting have only added to the complexity of this burden. Despite this fact, caregiver burden is greatly underidentified by medical professionals. Generally speaking, more women than men become caregivers and most caregivers are aged 55 years or older (1,2). Caregiving seems to affect genders differently. Women are at greater risk for isolation, loneliness, and decreased satisfaction and men are at greater risk of psychological distress (3).

CAREGIVER ROLE

The *caregiver* is defined as the primary person upon whom the patient relies for assistance with physical care, symptom management, and psychosocial needs and who does not receive financial remuneration for caregiving (4). The caregiver is not always a blood relative or a household member. Caregiving can be related to bonds of attachment and can be affected by cultural norms or feelings of guilt and obligation. Because many cancer patients are living longer due to improved treatments, the emotional implications of long-term caregiving are significant.

THE BURDEN OF CAREGIVING

Caregiver burden is the result of caring for someone with a chronic illness. Caregivers have their own emotional responses to patients' diagnoses and prognoses, and they may require problem-solving and emotional support separate from that offered to patients. Caregivers are often balancing work and family demands, along with emotional, physical, financial, and spiritual distress, as they help patients cope with cancer. Caregiver roles and caregiver burden are profoundly affected by a patient's prognosis, stage of illness, and goals of care. The physical and emotional demands of caregiving reach their peak as the disease progresses to the end-of-life phase. In the context of recurrent and advanced illness, the caregiver must meet a new set of challenges in dealing with increasing functional limitations and increasing dependence of the patient, as well as greater need for symptom management (4). In addition, uncertainty is a constant companion throughout all stages of disease. The trajectory of cancer is fraught with uncertainty and inflicts turmoil on everyday life. This uncertainty can increase caregivers' anxiety and stress levels, which in turn can impact the burden they feel placed on them. The high stress associated with this uncertainty, the demands of multiple medical appointments, and the physical needs of the patient add to this increased physiological and psychological burden as well. Acknowledgment of caregiver burden is often overlooked by clinicians who are treating the patients.

For cancer patients' caregivers, psychological and physical outcomes are mediated by the juxtaposition of the caregiver burden with the positive aspects of the role. Caregiver burden is associated with inadequate information and education, the disruptions it can cause to daily life, and the restrictions it imposes on outside activities that lead to social isolation (5). The physical effects in caregivers include behaviors such as not getting enough rest or exercise and neglecting their own health, which can sometimes mimic depression (6). The financial consequences of caregiving can include lost salaries, insurance deductibles, copayments, and uncovered services such as transportation and home care. Patients and caregivers have parallel spiritual tasks when dealing with cancer, such as finding meaning and hope in the disease process while also examining existential questions about life. As mentioned earlier, there are positive aspects to the role of caregiving, which can function as an opportunity for growth and satisfaction. It allows caregivers to become closer to the ones they are caring for, to repay care that they may have received earlier, can increase intimacy, and often provides an increased sense of purpose or meaning.

CAREGIVER-PATIENT DYAD EFFECTS ON CARE

An aspect that must be addressed is the parallel relationship that exists between caregivers' and patients' physical and emotional reactions to cancer. There is limited research focusing on this specific relationship, although a few studies have found that caregiver-patient responses to cancer were interdependent: each person affected the other's level of emotional and physical well-being (5). The research proposed that specific interventions can significantly improve patients' and caregivers' physical health, mental health, and communication and at the same time improve the caregivers' knowledge, preparedness, self-efficacy, and coping (7). Some interventions that were identified to help improve physical and emotional responses included: (a) psychoeducation that provides information about management of patient's symptoms, physical aspects, and emotional aspects of care; (b) skills training that addresses the development of caregivers' coping, communication, and problem-solving skills; and (c) therapeutic counseling that focuses on strengthening the patient-caregiver relationship.

SOCIAL ISOLATION

In a review of both geriatric and oncology literature, social isolation has been linked to an increased risk of mortality (8,9). Caregivers must cope with the combined challenge of aging and illness when they experience personal losses, such as a family member or friend. Caregivers can experience isolation from their social networks. Studies have shown that more than half of caregivers reported reduced socializing with others because of the demands of caregiving, and a lack of satisfaction with perceived levels of social support (10). This lack of social support is attributed to the older caregivers becoming enmeshed in the care situation; by doing so, they isolate themselves from social and family roles and are consumed with providing care. Caregivers also have limited time to engage in activities outside of the caregiving role, particularly when they are the only person available for the patient. This decrease in social activities also produces a sense of interpersonal loss for the caregiver and can lead to a lack of intimacy and affection; increased symptoms of depression and increased feelings of resentment can also occur (11). Caregivers speak about feeling very alone in the caregiving role even when they are engaging with family, friends, and members of their community (12).

A further element of social isolation in the context of caring for an older loved one is the inability to provide care in other areas of the caregiver's life. Many caregivers have partners and children, but because of the multiple demands primary caregivers have to manage, primary caregiving does not allow them to fully be present for any of their various roles. The inability to fully commit can increase feelings of stress, anxiety, anger, resentment, and extreme sadness (13). Unfortunately, these constraints, along with multiple levels of social isolation, make it difficult for caregivers to work on familial relationships. These tensions can manifest in the therapeutic setting, where it can be helpful to identify and normalize these challenging circumstances associated with caregiving.

One last component of social isolation relates to siblings or other family members. Caregivers may have to negotiate with siblings and family members in order to make medical decisions. This pressure often adds to the primary caregiver's distress and increases isolation, as the negotiation process can create challenges to relationships and communication within the family system (14).

The social impact of cancer and pain can be ameliorated by social support, financial security, and stability at work. It is clear that caregivers need guidance on how to respond to each of these elements of social support.

IMPLICATIONS FOR HEALTH CARE PROVIDERS

As the population continues to age, it will be crucial that we identify older adults who are caring for a patient with cancer. Integrating a geriatric caregiver assessment (see Box 12.1) at the initial patient visit might provide a way to identify those who have the greatest need (15). The complexities associated with loneliness, social isolation, and caregiver burden are all interconnected and must be supported and understood by medical professionals. The nature and quality of the preexisting patient-caregiver relationship are important considerations in the assessment and treatment of caregiver burden. If the impact of cancer caregiving is identified and assessed early on in the treatment trajectory, effective interventions to meet the needs of caregivers can be implemented.

BOX 12.1: Fundamental Principles for Caregiver Assessment

Caregiver Health:

Can you tell me a bit about how you are feeling/doing?
Is the patient aware of your caregiving situation?
Have you noticed that you are suffering from any emotional and/or physical health problems as a result of caregiving?

Quality of life:

How are you coping with these responsibilities?
Do you have any other caregiving responsibilities?
How often do you get out?
How do you rate your life satisfaction and/or quality of life?

Support:

Are there times when you really need help but don't ask, for fear of being a burden?
Do you have a social support network, or are you isolated?
Who else is involved in the support of (name of patient)?
Would you like more information about services and supports for caregivers?
What resources have you tried?

In Case of Emergency:

If anything should happen to you, have you made arrangements for someone to take care of (name of patient)?
Is anyone available to provide respite when you are unable to provide care?
Can you rely on their assistance?

TAKE HOME POINTS

1. The medical team may need to play a greater role in assessment of caregivers, in collaboration with oncology social work colleagues.
2. The medical team should explore caregivers' sense of well-being, assess their confidence in their ability to provide care, and identify their distress and need for additional support.
3. Refer caregivers to their oncology social worker, who can provide psychosocial support and connect them with a caregiver support group.
4. Attention to caregiving concerns is important in understanding how this major, unpaid segment of our health care and long-term care system works and determining what we can do to minimize the burdens of caregiving.

(continued)

(continued)

5. More attention should be focused on the potential conflicts caregivers face with other family members in relation to medical decision making and care planning.
6. Knowing when to link caregivers to family and/or couple therapy is an important intervention.

REFERENCES

1. Family Caregiver Alliance. Fact sheet: selected caregiver statistics. Available at: https://www .caregiver.org/caregiving.
2. National Cancer Institute. Stat Fact Sheet: all cancer sites. Available at: www.seer .cancer.gov/statfacts.
3. Njboer C, Tempelaar R, Sanderman R, et al. Cancer and caregiving: the impact on the caregiver's health. *Psycho oncology.* 1998;7:3-13.
4. Williams A. Psychosocial burden of family caregivers to adults with cancer. *Psycho oncology.* 2014;197:73-85.
5. Northhouse L, Williams A, Given B, McCorkle R. Psychosocial care for family caregivers of patients with cancer. *J Clin Oncol.* 2012;30(11):1227-1234.
6. Adelman RD, Tmanova LL, Delgado D, et al. Caregiver burden: a clinical review. *JAMA.* 2014;311(10):1052-1056.
7. Kent EE, Rowalnd JH, Northouse L, et al. Caring for caregivers and patients: research and clinical priorities for informal cancer caregiving. *Cancer.* 2016;122(13):1987-1995.
8. Haley WE. The costs of family caregiving: implications for geriatric oncology. *Crit Rev Oncol Hematol.* 2003;48:151-158.
9. Dickens AP, Richards SH, Greaves CJ, Campbell JL. Interventions targeting social isolation in older people: a systemic review. *BMC Public Health.* 2011;11:2-22.
10. Biordi DL, Nicholson NR. Social isolation. In: Larsen PD, Lubkin IM, eds. *Chronic Illness: Impact and Intervention.* 7th ed. Sudbury, MA: Jones & Bartlett; 2009:chap 5.
11. Given BA, Given CW, Sherwood P. The challenge of quality cancer care for family caregivers. *Semin Oncol Nurs.* 2012;28(4):205-212.
12. Weitzner MA, Haley WE, Chen H. The family caregiver of the older cancer patient. *Hematol Oncol Clin North Am.* 2000;14(1):269-281.
13. Rolland J. Cancer and the family: an integrative model. *Cancer.* 2005; 104(S11):2584-2595.
14. Bevans M, Sternberg EM. Caregiving burden, stress, and health effects among family caregivers of adult cancer patients. *JAMA.* 2012;307(4):394-403.
15. Schwartz S, Darlak L. *Selected Caregiver Assessment Measures: A Resource Inventory for Practitioners.* 2nd ed. San Francisco, CA: Family Caregiver Alliance; 2012.

13   Geriatric Assessment

Sincere McMillan and Beatriz Korc-Grodzicki

INTRODUCTION

A primary determination when considering appropriate therapy for an older patient with cancer is the patient's functional age. The aging process itself brings physiologic changes leading to a decline in organ function. The remodeling of physiologic reserve is influenced not only by genetic factors, but also by environmental factors, dietary habits, and the interaction of comorbidities and social conditions. Therefore, chronological age differs from functional age, and this difference must be captured and integrated in the decision-making process of cancer treatment. It is essential to identify those patients who are fit and potentially more resilient, because they are more likely to benefit from standard treatment, as opposed to patients who are more frail and vulnerable to adverse outcomes. This chapter describes how to assess geriatric syndromes through a comprehensive geriatric assessment (GA) and the association of GA results with cancer-related outcomes.

GERIATRIC ASSESSMENT

GA is a multidimensional, interdisciplinary evaluation. In older cancer patients, it is used to determine physiologic age, guide future diagnostic and therapeutic interventions, determine any reversible deficits, and devise treatment strategies to eliminate or mitigate such deficits and to risk-stratify patients prior to potentially high-risk therapy (1). Although there is no standard definition of a GA, a position paper by the International Society of Geriatric Oncology (SIOG) provided clarification regarding necessary elements of GA and guidance to tools that could be used for each element (1). The domains of a GA are shown in Table 13.1 along with examples of validated tools to measure those domains.

Assessment of Comorbidities

The incidence of pathology increases as we age. The presence of multiple chronic diseases or comorbidities represents a major difference between the younger and the older cancer patient. Frequent comorbidities in the elderly, such as cardiovascular disease, hypertension, diabetes, or dementia, influence the management of cancer. Comorbidities may increase the risk of complications, modify cancer behavior,

TABLE 13.1 Domains in GA and Examples of Tools Used for Each Domain

Domain	Tool
Social status and quality of life	Medical outcomes survey (2)
Comorbidity	CCI (3) CIRS-G (4)
Functional status	ADL (5) IADL (6)
Physical function	TUG (7) Short physical performance battery (8) Gait speed (9) Grip strength (10) 6-min walk (11)
Falls and falls risk	Tinetti Gait and Balance Scale (12)
Cognition	MMSE (13) MoCA (14) The BOMC Test (15) Mini-Cog (16)
Nutrition	BMI Unintentional weight loss MNA (17)
Medication management and polypharmacy	Use of inappropriate medications (such as the Beers list or screening tool for older persons' prescriptions) (18) Number of medications
Psychological status	GDS (19) Hospitalized Anxiety and Depression Scale (20) PHQ-9 (21) DT (22)

ADL, activities of daily living; BMI, body mass index; BOMC, blessed orientation-memory-concentration; CCI, Charlson Comorbidity Index; CIRS-G, Cumulative Illness Rating Scale–Geriatrics; DT, distress thermometer; GA, geriatric assessment; GDS, Geriatric Depression Scale; IADL, instrumental activities of daily living; MNA, Mini Nutritional Assessment; MMSE, Mini-Mental State Examination; MoCA, Montreal Cognitive Assessment; PHQ-9, patient health questionnaire-9; TUG, Timed Up and Go.

or mask symptoms with subsequent delays in cancer diagnosis. Conversely, cancer treatment may worsen comorbidities or increase the frequency of drug interactions.

Comorbidity burden is often measured using standardized indices such as the Charlson Comorbidity Index (CCI) (3) and the Cumulative Illness Rating Scale–Geriatrics (CIRS-G) (4). The CCI is based on the 1-year mortality of patients admitted to a medical hospital service. It is a simple instrument with well-defined rating criteria that has been validated in older cancer patients. The CCI can be used for large cohort studies; however, it may underdetect nonlethal endpoints. The geriatric version of the CIRS-G was designed for use in elderly populations. Although it details several geriatric concerns, the scale may overdetect minor problems, and it is quite complicated to rate.

Cognitive Assessment

Cancer patients with cognitive dysfunction represent a new challenge for oncologists. After age 65, the risk of developing Alzheimer disease doubles approximately every 5 years. By age 85, 37% of all people will have some signs of the disease (23). The increased rate of dementia in the elderly converges with the higher likelihood of developing cancer. For patients with cancer/dementia, overlap screening tends to be less standardized, which could lead to delayed diagnosis. Impaired cognition can result in significant difficulties in understanding and remembering treatment instructions, delayed diagnosis of complications, and decreased adherence to oral therapies and supportive treatments. An initial assessment of cognitive status is clinically important and could influence the choice of treatment and the modality of administration (Table 13.2).

The ability of patients to decide on a course of therapy in concert with the oncologist is critically important. Many oncologists are conflicted as to whether true informed consent for treatment can be obtained from older cancer patients when their cognitive abilities are impaired or unclear. It is imperative that health care providers who care for older adults with cancer be able to assess cognitive function, understand the implications of cognitive impairment when patients need to make decisions, address the potential for treatment-related cognitive decline, and be able to facilitate patient-centered cancer decision making.

TABLE 13.2 Common Instruments Validated for Cognitive Screening

MMSE (13)	Widely used screening tool covering multiple domains such as orientation, memory, attention, calculation, language, and constructional ability.
MoCA (14)	More sensitive test designed as a rapid screening instrument for mild cognitive dysfunction. It was found to provide additional information over the MMSE in brain tumor patients (24).
BOMC (15)	Brief, six-item scale frequently used in the geriatric oncology literature.
Mini-Cog assessment instrument (16)	Brief test that screens for cognitive impairment in a community sample of culturally, linguistically, and educationally heterogeneous older adults. It requires minimal training to administer, so it can be readily incorporated into general practice.

BOMC, blessed orientation-memory-concentration; MoCA, Montreal Cognitive Assessment; MMSE, Mini-Mental State Examination.

Medication Management and Polypharmacy

Pharmacotherapy in the elderly is often very complex due to age-related physiologic changes, multiple comorbidities, and multiple medications. In addition, cognitive impairment, functional limitations, and caregiver issues play a large role in adherence to medication regimens. Age-related physiologic changes and disease-related changes in organ function affect drug handling (pharmacokinetics) and response (pharmacodynamics), both of which significantly impact prescribing. Older cancer patients usually take multiple medications, not only for treatment of the cancer, but also for supportive care and the management of symptoms related to therapy-induced toxicity (25). Further discussion on medication management appears in Chapter 8.

Social Issues and Quality of Life

Social support has a substantial impact on cancer and cancer treatment outcomes. Evidence in breast cancer patients suggests that low social support is associated with development and progression of cancer (26). Once diagnosed, cancer has a substantial impact on quality of life and on social function at any age. Older patients with cancer may have additional requirements, such as the need for caregivers, transportation, and home care support, to be able to safely undergo cancer therapy. Social isolation and low levels of social support have been associated with an increased incidence of cancer as well as higher mortality risk in patients with cancer (27,28). Increased social isolation is also a risk factor for poor tolerance of the adverse effects of cancer treatment (29).

Assessment of Physical Function

Oncologists usually measure physical function using subjective scales such as the Eastern Cooperative Oncology Group (ECOG) or Karnofsky performance status scales. Physical function can also be assessed by objective measures of performance, including gait speed, grip strength, balance, and lower extremity strength, which are more sensitive. Decreases in these measures are associated with worse clinical outcomes (30). A commonly used test for gait speed is Timed Up and Go (TUG), which is brief and simple to implement in clinical settings (7). Gait speed is an important indicator in older persons, as it has been shown to be an independent predictor of mortality across numerous population-based studies (9). Grip strength is also important in cancer patients and is relatively quick and easy to assess; however, the availability of a handheld dynamometer may be a barrier. Grip strength is a measure that correlates with sarcopenia and has been shown to be associated with adverse outcomes in patients with cancer (31,32).

Falls

Falls are major events and major health concerns in the older population because they are related to the person's ability to live independently. More than one-third of persons

65 years of age or older fall each year, and in half of such cases the falls are recurrent (33). They are typically multifactorial and due to intrinsic factors (e.g., visual impairment, muscle weakness, poor balance, orthostasis), extrinsic factors (e.g., polypharmacy, medication side effects), or environmental factors (e.g., loose carpets, poor lighting). Falls should be thoroughly evaluated using a multidisciplinary approach (physical therapy, occupational therapy, home safety, medication evaluation, evaluation for cataracts, etc.) with the goal of minimizing the risks without compromising functional independence. The Tinetti Gait and Balance Scale is a rapid, reproducible assessment tool for the evaluation of fall risks, gait, and balance (12). The test is scored on the patient's ability to perform specific tasks. Time to complete is 10 to 15 minutes and interrater reliability was found to be greater than 85%.

Functional Status

An assessment of functional status includes daily living dependence scales and determination of whether a patient needs any assistance on instrumental activities of daily living (IADLs) or activities of daily living (ADLs). IADLs generally refer to tasks that are needed to live independently in the community and include shopping, transportation, using the telephone, managing finances, medication management, cooking, cleaning, and doing laundry (6). ADLs are basic self-care skills needed in order to live independently in the home (as opposed to an institutionalized setting), and include bathing, dressing, grooming, toileting, transferring, feeding, and continence (5). Assessing ADLs and IADLs captures additional information not obtained by assessing performance status alone.

Nutritional Status

The incidence of malnutrition in the elderly population is very significant. Nutritional status should be assessed as part of any GA, as malnutrition and weight are significant adverse factors in older patients and in patients with cancer. Although there is not one clear screening tool that is preferred, screening tools that have been used include body mass index (BMI), unintentional weight loss, or longer validated tools such as the Mini Nutrition Assessment (MNA) (17). The MNA is well validated and correlates highly with clinical assessment and objective indicators of nutritional status; because of its validity in screening and assessing the risk of malnutrition, the MNA should be integrated into the GA (34). Malnutrition is associated with treatment complications in patients receiving chemotherapy, radiation therapy, or surgery, and is also associated with increased mortality (35–40).

Psychological Status

Depression and psychological distress are common problems that impact patients with cancer and lead to poor quality of life, high caregiver burden, and functional decline. Although studies have suggested that anxiety may decrease with aging, there is a consistent relationship between depression and increased age (41). Depression is highly prevalent in older persons with cancer, with a range of 10% to 65% across different GA studies (42). Patients with cancer and depression are less likely to receive definitive treatment, and hence experience worse survival compared to those without depression (43). Brief screening tools may help clinicians in busy settings detect patients who are experiencing severe psychological distress. The distress thermometer (DT) is a single item that asks patients to rate their distress in the past week on a 0 ("no distress") to 10 ("extreme distress") scale (22). It offers an efficient means of identifying patients with advanced cancer who have severe distress. It has been used in psycho-oncology and validated for patients and cancer patients' families (44).

GA IN THE SURGICAL CANCER PATIENT

Geriatric surgical patients have unique vulnerabilities that require assessment beyond the traditional preoperative evaluation (45). Because the physiologic reserve of an elderly patient is not always apparent, established assessment tools such as the American Society of Anesthesiology Physical Status Classification System (ASA classification) are not sufficiently sensitive to predict differences in operative risks (46). GA has the potential for identifying patients at risk for postoperative adverse events such as mortality, disability, institutionalization, and cognitive decline, and it provides an opportunity to implement perioperative interventions.

The importance of GA in predicting surgical outcomes has been reported. Preoperative impaired cognition, low albumin level, previous falls, low hematocrit level, any functional dependence, and a high burden of comorbidities were most closely related to 6-month mortality and postdischarge institutionalization in patients undergoing major thoracic and abdominal operations (45). Baseline cognitive impairment is related to increased number of postoperative complications, length of stay, and long-term mortality (47). In the Preoperative Assessment of Cancer in the Elderly (PACE) study, functional dependency, fatigue, and abnormal performance status were associated with a 50% increase in the relative risk of postoperative complications (48). In patients greater than 65 years of age, lower Mini Mental Status Examination (MMSE) score and older age were significantly associated with the development of postcystectomy delirium, and those who developed delirium were more likely to face readmission and reoperation (49). In patients undergoing pancreaticoduodenectomy, older age and worse scores in GA predicted major complications, longer hospital stays, and surgical intensive care unit (ICU) admissions (50).

ASSOCIATION OF GA WITH CANCER TREATMENT OUTCOMES

Over the last decade, GA has been integrated into oncology care and has contributed to uncovering a substantial proportion of deficits in older cancer patients that would otherwise have gone unrecognized (42). Although results are difficult to compare, as different studies have used different components of GA, the most frequently assessed domains were functional status, comorbidity, depression, and cognition (51). GA has been found to influence treatment decisions, which included reducing the intensity of chemotherapy, lowering the amount of prescribed medications, or providing additional supportive care (1). GA not only helps to better inform treatment decision making, but also helps to better tailor individualized treatment to an older patient who might otherwise be at greater toxicity risk. A prospective multicentric study on the large-scale feasibility and usefulness of GA in clinical oncology showed that GA detected unknown geriatric problems in 51% of patients more than 70 years old, and when physicians became aware of the results, geriatric interventions and adapted treatment occurred in 25.7% and 25.3% of the patients, respectively (52).

GA is time consuming and requires close cooperation between oncologists and geriatricians. An important practical aspect of GA is the feasibility of incorporating it into a busy clinical oncology practice. Key considerations in performing the GA include the resources available (staff, space, and time), patient population (who will be assessed), what GA tools to use, and clinical follow-up (who will be responsible for using the GA results for the development of care plans and who will provide follow-up care). Important challenges in implementing GA in clinical practice include not having easy and timely access to geriatric expertise, patient burden of the additional hospital visits, and the need to establish collaboration between the GA team and oncologists regarding expectations of the population referred for GA and expected outcomes of the GA (53). A two-step approach has been suggested: the development of screening tools that would sort out who is an "older adult" with intact physiology and psychosocial conditions, and who is a vulnerable elder cancer patient in need of further multidisciplinary evaluation (see Chapter 14).

For risk stratification prior to chemotherapy, briefer tools based on GA such as the Cancer and Aging Research Group (CARG) (54) score and the Chemotherapy Risk Assessment Scale for High-Age Patients (CRASH) (55) score may be more efficient in determining a patient's predicted chemotoxicity risk.

1. The CARG score was developed in a prospective multicenter cohort study of 500 patients age 65 or older with cancer who were receiving chemotherapy. All patients underwent a GA that included measures of functional status, comorbidity, psychological state, social activity, social support, and nutrition. A predictive model was developed and validated (56), including GA variables along with patient demographic and clinical variables to predict grade 3 to 5 toxicity with chemotherapy administration. Higher risk scores were associated with increased chemotoxicity.
   www.mycarg.org/Chemo_Toxicity_Calculator

2. The CRASH score was developed in a prospective, multicenter study among patients 70 and older receiving chemotherapy. GA variables were included along with patient clinical variables and chemotoxicity risk, and predictive models were developed for grade 4 hematologic and for grade 3 to 4 nonhematologic toxicity (55).
   www.moffitt.org/eforms/crashscoreform/

TAKE HOME POINTS

1. The National Comprehensive Cancer Network (NCCN) and SIOG have recommended that some form of GA be conducted to help cancer specialists determine the best treatment for their older patients.
2. The results of GA can be used to risk-stratify patients, treat reversible conditions before cancer therapy, and guide cancer treatment decision making.
3. A two-step approach, with a brief screening tool followed by complete GA if needed, may be more efficient for a busy oncology practice.
4. Tools for risk stratification prior to chemotherapy have been developed and validated and are readily available online.
5. Surgeons treating elderly cancer patients should take into account that other factors, such as frailty, comorbidities, performance, and cognitive status, are important considerations when predicting outcomes.

REFERENCES

1. Wildiers H, Heeren P, Puts M, et al. International Society of Geriatric Oncology consensus on geriatric assessment in older patients with cancer. *J Clin Oncol.* 2014;32(24):2595-2603. doi:10.1200/jco.2013.54.8347.
2. Sherbourne CD, Stewart AL. The MOS social support survey. *Soc Sci Med.* 1991;32(6):705-714.
3. Charlson ME, Pompei P, Ales KL, MacKenzie CR. A new method of classifying prognostic comorbidity in longitudinal studies: development and validation. *J Chronic Dis.* 1987;40(5):373-383.
4. Salvi F, Miller MD, Grilli A, et al. A manual of guidelines to score the Modified Cumulative Illness Rating Scale and its validation in acute hospitalized elderly patients. *J Am Geriatr Soc.* 2008;56(10):1926-1931. doi:10.1111/j.1532-5415.2008.01935.x.
5. Katz S. Assessing self-maintenance: activities of daily living, mobility, and instrumental activities of daily living. *J Am Geriatr Soc.* 1983;31(12):721-727.
6. Lawton MP, Brody EM. Assessment of older people: self-maintaining and instrumental activities of daily living. *Gerontologist.* 1969;9(3):179-186.
7. Podsiadlo D, Richardson S. The timed "Up & Go": a test of basic functional mobility for frail elderly persons. *J Am Geriatr Soc.* 1991;39(2):142-148.
8. Guralnik JM, Simonsick EM, Ferrucci L, et al. A short physical performance battery assessing lower extremity function: association with self-reported disability and prediction of mortality and nursing home admission. *J Gerontol.* 1994;49(2):M85-94.
9. Studenski S, Perera S, Patel K, et al. Gait speed and survival in older adults. *JAMA.* 2011;305(1):50-58. doi:10.1001/jama.2010.1923.
10. Mathiowetz V, Kashman N, Volland G, et al. Grip and pinch strength: normative data for adults. *Arch Phys Med Rehabil.* 1985;66(2):69-74.
11. ATS Committee on Proficiency Standards for Clinical Pulmonary Function Laboratories. ATS statement: guidelines for the six-minute walk test. *Am J Respir Crit Care Med.* 2002;166(1):111-117. doi:10.1164/ajrccm.166.1.at1102.
12. Tinetti ME. Performance-oriented assessment of mobility problems in elderly patients. *J Am Geriatr Soc.* 1986;34(2):119-126.

13. Folstein MF, Folstein SE, McHugh PR. "Mini-mental state": a practical method for grading the cognitive state of patients for the clinician. *J Psychiatr Res.* 1975;12(3):189-198.

14. Nasreddine ZS, Phillips NA, Bedirian V, et al. The Montreal Cognitive Assessment, MoCA: a brief screening tool for mild cognitive impairment. *J Am Geriatr Soc.* 2005;53(4):695-699.doi:10.1111/j.1532-5415.2005.53221.x.

15. Katzman R, Brown T, Fuld P, et al. Validation of a short orientation-memory-concentration test of cognitive impairment. *Am J Psychiatry.* 1983;140(6):734-739.

16. Shephard JM, Kosslyn SM. The MiniCog rapid assessment battery: developing a "blood pressure cuff for the mind." *Aviat Space Environ Med.* 2005;76(6 suppl): B192-B197.

17. Oster P, Rost BM, Velte U, Schlierf G. Comparative nutrition evaluation with the Mini Nutritional Assessment and the Nutritional Risk Assessment Scale. *Nestle Nutr Workshop Ser Clin Perform Programme.* 1999;1:35-39; discussion 39-40.

18. American Geriatrics Society 2012 Beers Criteria Update Expert Panel. American Geriatrics Society updated Beers Criteria for potentially inappropriate medication use in older adults. *J Am Geriatr Soc.* 2012;60(4):616-631. doi:10.1111/j.1532-5415.2012.03923.x.

19. Yesavage JA, Brink TL, Rose TL, et al. Development and validation of a geriatric depression screening scale: a preliminary report. *J Psychiatr Res.* 1982;17(1):37-49.

20. Snaith RP. The Hospital Anxiety and Depression Scale. *Health Qual Life Outcomes.* 2003;1:29. doi:10.1186/1477-7525-1-29.

21. Kroenke K, Spitzer RL, Williams JB. The PHQ-9: validity of a brief depression severity measure. *J Gen Intern Med.* 2001;16(9):606-613.

22. Roth AJ, Kornblith AB, Batel-Copel L, et al. Rapid screening for psychologic distress in men with prostate carcinoma: a pilot study. *Cancer.* 1998;82(10):1904-1908.

23. Alzheimer's Association. 2014 Alzheimer's disease facts and figures. *Alzheimers Dement.* 2014;10(2). Available at: https://www.alz.org/downloads/facts_figures_ 2014.pdf.

24. Olson RA, Chhanabhai T, McKenzie M. Feasibility study of the Montreal Cognitive Assessment (MoCA) in patients with brain metastases. *Support Care Cancer.* 2008;16(11):1273-1278. doi:10.1007/s00520-008-0431-3.

25. Lichtman SM, Boparai MK. Anticancer drug therapy in the older cancer patient: pharmacology and polypharmacy. *Curr Treat Options Oncol.* 2008;9(2-3):191-203. doi:10.1007/s11864-008-0060-6.

26. Falagas ME, Zarkadoulia EA, Ioannidou EN, et al. The effect of psychosocial factors on breast cancer outcome: a systematic review. *Breast Cancer Res.* 2007;9(4):R44. doi:10.1186/bcr1744.

27. Ikeda A, Kawachi I, Iso H, et al. Social support and cancer incidence and mortality: the JPHC study cohort II. *Cancer Causes Control.* 2013;24(5):847-860. doi:10.1007/ s10552-013-0147-7.

28. Kroenke CH, Kubzansky LD, Schernhammer ES, et al. Social networks, social support, and survival after breast cancer diagnosis. *J Clin Oncol.* 2006;24(7):1105-1111. doi:10.1200/jco.2005.04.2846.

29. Penedo FJ, Traeger L, Benedict C, et al. Perceived social support as a predictor of disease-specific quality of life in head-and-neck cancer patients. *J Support Oncol.* 2012;10(3):119-123. doi:10.1016/j.suponc.2011.09.002.

30. Cesari M, Kritchevsky SB, Newman AB, et al. Added value of physical performance measures in predicting adverse health-related events: results from the Health, Aging and Body Composition Study. *J Am Geriatr Soc.* 2009;57(2):251-259. doi:10.1111/j.1532-5415.2008.02126.x.

31. Kilgour RD, Vigano A, Trutschnigg B, et al. Handgrip strength predicts survival and is associated with markers of clinical and functional outcomes in advanced cancer patients. *Support Care Cancer.* 2013;21(12):3261-3270. doi:10.1007/s00520-013-1894-4.

32. Chen CH, Ho C, Huang YZ, Hung TT. Hand-grip strength is a simple and effective outcome predictor in esophageal cancer following esophagectomy with reconstruction: a prospective study. *J Cardiothorac Surg.* 2011;6:98. doi:10.1186/1749-8090-6-98.

33. Tinetti ME. Clinical practice. Preventing falls in elderly persons. *N Engl J Med.* 2003;348(1):42-49. doi:10.1056/NEJMcp020719.

34. Guigoz Y, Lauque S, Vellas BJ. Identifying the elderly at risk for malnutrition: the Mini Nutritional Assessment. *Clin Geriatr Med.* 2002;18(4):737-757.

35. van der Schaaf MK, Tilanus HW, van Lanschot JJ, et al. The influence of preoperative weight loss on the postoperative course after esophageal cancer resection. *J Thorac Cardiovasc Surg.* 2014;147(1):490-495. doi:10.1016/j.jtcvs.2013.07.072.

36. Gourin CG, Couch ME, Johnson JT. Effect of weight loss on short-term outcomes and costs of care after head and neck cancer surgery. *Ann Otol Rhinol Laryngol.* 2014;123(2):101-110. doi:10.1177/0003489414523564.

37. Fiorelli A, Vicidomini G, Mazzella A, et al. The influence of body mass index and weight loss on outcome of elderly patients undergoing lung cancer resection. *Thorac Cardiovasc Surg.* 2014;62(7):578-587. doi:10.1055/s-0034-1373733.

38. Langius JA, Bakker S, Rietveld DH, et al. Critical weight loss is a major prognostic indicator for disease-specific survival in patients with head and neck cancer receiving radiotherapy. *Br J Cancer.* 2013;109(5):1093-1099. doi:10.1038/bjc.2013.458.

39. Ehrsson YT, Langius-Eklof A, Laurell G. Nutritional surveillance and weight loss in head and neck cancer patients. *Support Care Cancer.* 2012;20(4):757-765. doi:10.1007/s00520-011-1146-4.

40. Buskermolen S, Langius JA, Kruizenga HM, et al. Weight loss of 5% or more predicts loss of fat-free mass during palliative chemotherapy in patients with advanced cancer: a pilot study. *Nutr Cancer.* 2012;64(6):826-832. doi: 10.1080/01635581.2012.690062.

41. Weiss Wiesel TR, Nelson CJ, Tew WP, et al. The relationship between age, anxiety, and depression in older adults with cancer. *Psychooncology.* 2015;24(6):712-717. doi:10.1002/pon.3638.

42. Caillet P, Laurent M, Bastuji-Garin S, et al. Optimal management of elderly cancer patients: usefulness of the Comprehensive Geriatric Assessment. *Clin Interv Aging.* 2014;9:1645-1660. doi:10.2147/cia.s57849.

43. Goodwin JS, Zhang DD, Ostir GV. Effect of depression on diagnosis, treatment, and survival of older women with breast cancer. *J Am Geriatr Soc.* 2004;52(1):106-111.

44. Nelson CJ, Cho C, Berk AR, et al. Are gold standard depression measures appropriate for use in geriatric cancer patients? A systematic evaluation of self-report depression instruments used with geriatric, cancer, and geriatric cancer samples. *J Clin Oncol.* 2010;28(2):348-356. doi:10.1200/jco.2009.23.0201.

45. Robinson TN, Eiseman B, Wallace JI, et al. Redefining geriatric preoperative assessment using frailty, disability and co-morbidity. *Ann Surg.* 2009;250(3):449-455. doi:10.1097/SLA.0b013e3181b45598.

46. Kristjansson SR, Nesbakken A, Jordhoy MS, et al. Comprehensive geriatric assessment can predict complications in elderly patients after elective surgery for colorectal cancer: a prospective observational cohort study. *Crit Rev Oncol Hematol.* 2010;76(3):208-217. doi:10.1016/j.critrevonc.2009.11.002.

47. Robinson TN, Wu DS, Pointer LF, et al. Preoperative cognitive dysfunction is related to adverse postoperative outcomes in the elderly. *J Am Coll Surg.* 2012;215(1):12-17; discussion 7-8. doi:10.1016/j.jamcollsurg.2012.02.007.

48. Audisio RA, Pope D, Ramesh HS, et al. Shall we operate? Preoperative assessment in elderly cancer patients (PACE) can help. A SIOG surgical task force prospective study. *Crit Rev Oncol Hematol.* 2008;65(2):156-163. doi:10.1016/j.critrevonc.2007.11.001.

49. Large MC, Reichard C, Williams JT, et al. Incidence, risk factors, and complications of postoperative delirium in elderly patients undergoing radical cystectomy. *Urology.* 2013;81(1):123-128. doi:10.1016/j.urology.2012.07.086.

50. Dale W, Hemmerich J, Kamm A, et al. Geriatric assessment improves prediction of surgical outcomes in older adults undergoing pancreaticoduodenectomy: a prospective cohort study. *Ann Surg.* 2013;259(5):960-965. doi:10.1097/sla.0000000000000226.

51. Puts MT, Santos B, Hardt J, et al. An update on a systematic review of the use of geriatric assessment for older adults in oncology. *Ann Oncol.* 2014;25(2):307-315. doi:10.1093/annonc/mdt386.

52. Kenis C, Bron D, Libert Y, et al. Relevance of a systematic geriatric screening and assessment in older patients with cancer: results of a prospective multicentric study. *Ann Oncol.* 2013;24(5):1306-1312. doi:10.1093/annonc/mds619.

53. Sattar S, Alibhai SM, Wildiers H, Puts MT. How to implement a geriatric assessment in your clinical practice. *Oncologist.* 2014;19(10):1056-1068. doi:10.1634/theoncologist.2014-0180.

54. Hurria A, Togawa K, Mohile SG, et al. Predicting chemotherapy toxicity in older adults with cancer: a prospective multicenter study. *J Clin Oncol.* 2011;29(25):3457-3465. doi:10.1200/jco.2011.34.7625.

55. Extermann M, Boler I, Reich RR, et al. Predicting the risk of chemotherapy toxicity in older patients: the Chemotherapy Risk Assessment Scale for High-Age Patients (CRASH) score. *Cancer.* 2012;118(13):3377-3386. doi:10.1002/cncr.26646.

56. Hurria A, Mohile S, Gajra A, et al. Validation of a prediction tool for chemotherapy toxicity in older adults with cancer. *J Clin Oncol.* 2016;34(20):2366-2371. doi:10.1200/jco.2015.65.4327.

14   Screening Tools in Geriatric Oncology

Daniel W. Yokom, Cindy Kenis, Shabbir M. H. Alibhai, and Martine T. E. Puts

INTRODUCTION

The current gold standard for assessment of older adults with cancer is a comprehensive geriatric assessment (CGA). A CGA is a multidimensional, interdisciplinary process to determine the medical, psychosocial, and functional capabilities of an older person, with the aim of optimizing health and well-being (1,2). When applied to patients with cancer, CGA has been shown to identify previously unknown health problems, predict treatment-related toxicity, and predict oncologic outcomes, including overall survival and influence of cancer treatment decisions (2–4).

Implementing CGA in an oncology setting is resource intensive, which ultimately limits its widespread use. CGA requires an interdisciplinary team of specialized professionals to perform an assessment that can take up to 1 to 2 hours (5). Given that the majority of oncology patients are over age 65, in most clinical oncology settings it is not practical to perform a CGA for all older patients. Therefore, it has been suggested to restrict the use of CGA specifically to complex older adults (6–8). To select patients who would benefit from a CGA, a number of clinical screening tools have been developed.

The primary purpose of a screening tool in geriatric oncology is to provide a busy clinician with a means to quickly identify patients in need of a CGA. Screening tools are commonly short questionnaires administered by any health care provider, not necessarily a geriatric specialist, and some tools can be administered by the patients themselves (9). CGA assesses multiple domains, commonly: functional status, falls, cognition, mood, comorbidities and polypharmacy, social and financial support, preferences, and goals of care. Conversely, screening tools typically assess only a few domains from the CGA or assess each of the domains superficially. Certain screening tools, including the G8 and Vulnerable Elders Survey (VES-13), have also been assessed for their ability to predict chemotherapy toxicity; however, this is not their primary purpose. More specific chemotherapy toxicity prediction tools have been developed, including the Cancer and Aging Research Group (CARG) tool (10,11) and the Chemotherapy Risk Assessment Scale for High-Age patients (CRASH) score (12). Both the CARG and CRASH tools are more accurate at predicting risk of chemotherapy and have been validated in larger prospective cohort studies. CARG and CRASH are discussed further in Chapter 13.

The International Society for Geriatric Oncology (SIOG) provided a consensus statement to recommend the use of screening tools to identify patients who should be further assessed with a CGA. At least 17 different screening tools for older oncology patients have been developed; however, the G8 and VES-13 are the mostly widely studied (9,13). There are a variety of benefits and challenges with each screening tool that must be weighed against one another. No particular screening tool was recommended by SIOG; rather, it is left to the discretion of the health care providers to choose the tool that fits best with their practice model and patient population. The caveat to the SIOG statement is that screening tools cannot replace the CGA: an abnormal screening result should always be followed up with a CGA (9). In this chapter, we:

- Outline the G8, VES-13, and other screening tools used for older adults with cancer
- Discuss the evidence for the benefits and limitations of these screening tools
- Provide recommendations for how to implement geriatric screening tools into routine oncology practice

SCREENING TOOLS

G8

The G8 (Table 14.1) is a screening tool that was specifically developed for use in adults with cancer over age 70 on first-line chemotherapy (14,15). It can be administered by any health care professional and takes about 5 minutes to complete (16). The G8 covers a number of domains from the CGA, including functional capacity, health, nutritional status, and cognitive impairment, as well as self-rated health. The maximum total score for the G8 is 17 and a score of 14 or lower is considered abnormal (14).

Compared to other screening tools, the G8 is one of the most sensitive screening tools; however, it has only modest specificity (9). A systematic review of different screening tests showed that among seven studies on the accuracy of the G8, the average sensitivity was 82.8% (65%–95%) and specificity was 61.1% (3%–75%) (9). Variations of the G8 have been developed to improve the specificity, but these versions have not been widely studied, validated, or accepted in clinical practice (17,18).

When using the G8, it is important to acknowledge a few of its limitations. To begin, the G8 includes a score for "neuropsychological problems." Although this item is very important, the definition of a neuropsychological problem is open to interpretation and may require further cognitive or psychological assessment or access to prior assessments. Furthermore, the G8 may not yield similar results across tumor types and stages. For example, one study showed that the sensitivity of the G8 was 95% for upper gastrointestinal (GI) cancers whereas it was only 65% sensitive for prostate cancer (19).

TABLE 14.1 The G8 Screening Tool

Items		Points
1	Has food intake declined over the past 3 months due to loss of appetite, digestive problems, chewing or swallowing difficulties?	0: severe decrease in food intake 1: moderate decrease in food intake 2: no decrease in food intake
2	Weight loss during the last 3 months	0: weight loss >3 kg 1: does not know 2: weight loss between 1 kg and 3 kg 3: no weight loss
3	Mobility	0: bed- or chair-bound 1: able to get out of bed/chair but does not go out 2: goes out
4	Neuropsychological problems	0: severe dementia or depression 1: mild dementia or depression 2: no psychological problems
5	BMI (weight [kg]/height [m²])	0: BMI < 19 1: BMI = 19 to BMI < 21 2: BMI = 21 to BMI < 23 3: BMI = ≥ 23
6	Takes more than three medications per day	0: yes 1: no
7	In comparison with other people of the same age, how does the patient consider his or her health status?	0: not as good 0.5: does not know 1: as good 2: better
8	Age	0: >85 1: 80–85 2: <80
	TOTAL SCORE	0–17
	Abnormal score	≤14

BMI, body mass index.

Source: Ref. (15). G8 screening tool. Available at: http://siog.org/content/comprehensive-geriatric-assessment-cga-older-patient-cancer.

In addition to being used as a screening tool, the G8 has also been studied to predict the following:

1. Treatment toxicity: Several studies assessing its usefulness in predicting chemotherapy-related toxicity have shown mixed results (20,21).
2. Functional decline and falls: Two prospective studies have shown that an abnormal G8 is predictive of falls or functional decline within 3 months of a cancer treatment decision (22,23).
3. Overall survival: Multiple studies have determined that an abnormal G8 is associated with worse overall survival compared to patients with a normal G8 (16,19,22).

Although the G8 requires some experience to administer correctly, it is an effective, highly sensitive tool to predict for an abnormal CGA.

Vulnerable Elders Survey-13

The VES-13 (Table 14.2) was originally designed to assess adults over age 65 living in the community who were at increased risk of functional decline (24,25). Domains of the CGA included in the VES-13 are limited to functional capacity, although this is covered in more detail than the G8. Self-reported health and age are also included. The maximum score is 10, with a score of 3 or higher considered abnormal. Notably, an age of 85 or older scores 3 points, which automatically puts those patients into an abnormal range.

Unlike most screening tools, the VES-13 is a self-administered test, which means a health care professional is not required to administer the tool. The VES-13 can be mailed to patients prior to an appointment and takes 4 to 5 minutes to complete (16,26). A small percentage of patients may not be able to complete the survey independently due to a language barrier, cognitive impairment, or low level of education (27,28).

The SIOG systematic review of 10 studies that compared VES-13 to CGA found these studies to have an average sensitivity of 68.3% (39%–87%) and specificity of 71.6% (61%–100%) (16,26,29–35). This review determined that the VES-13 is less sensitive but more specific for an abnormal CGA compared to other screening tools (9).

Investigators have also assessed the predictive ability of the VES-13 in older patients with cancer:

■ Treatment-related toxicity: A pooled analysis of four observational and prospective studies involving 648 patients over age 65 showed that patients with an abnormal VES-13 were at double the risk of chemotherapy toxicity (36).
■ Overall survival: Two studies have shown mixed results regarding the prognostic value of the VES-13 (16,37).

The VES-13 tool is specific for an abnormal CGA, with the added advantage of being self-administered, which allows this tool to be easily incorporated into any clinical practice. These benefits must be balanced by a lower sensitivity, meaning that a number of patients with a normal screening VES-13 would have an abnormal CGA.

TABLE 14.2 VES-13 Screening Tool

Items		Points
1	Age	0: 65–74 1: 75–84 3: ≥85
2	In general, compared to other people of your age, would you say your health is: ☐ Poor ☐ Fair ☐ Good ☐ Very Good ☐ Excellent	0: Answer of Good, Very Good or Excellent 1: Answer of Poor or Fair
3	How much difficulty, on average, do you have with the following activities (each scored as none, a little, some, a lot, or unable)? a. Stooping, crouching, or kneeling b. Lifting, or carrying, objects as heavy as 10 pounds c. Reaching or extending arms above shoulder level d. Writing, or handling, and grasping small objects e. Walking a quarter mile f. Heavy housework such as scrubbing floors or washing windows	1: For each answer of "a lot" or "unable" Maximum of 2 points

4	Because of your health or physical condition, do you have any difficulty:
	a. Shopping for personal items (like toilet items or medicines)?
	  YES → Do you get help with shopping? ☐ Yes ☐ No
	  NO
	  DON'T DO → Is that because of your health? ☐ Yes ☐ No
	b. Managing money (like keeping track of expenses or paying bills)?
	  YES → Do you get help with managing money? ☐ Yes ☐ No
	  NO
	  DON'T DO → Is that because of your health? ☐ Yes ☐ No
	c. Walking across the room? Use of a cane or walker is okay.
	  YES → Do you get help with walking? ☐ Yes ☐ No
	  NO
	  DON'T DO → Is that because of your health? ☐ Yes ☐ No
	d. Doing light housework (like washing dishes, straightening up, or light cleaning)?
	  YES → Do you get help with light housework? ☐ Yes ☐ No
	  NO
	  DON'T DO → Is that because of your health? ☐ Yes ☐ No
	e. Bathing or showering?
	  YES → Do you get help with bathing or showering? ☐ Yes ☐ No
	  NO
	  DON'T DO → Is that because of your health? ☐ Yes ☐ No
		4: For each checkbox answer of "Yes"
		Maximum of 4 points

(continued)

TABLE 14.2 VES-13 Screening Tool (*continued*)

Items	Points
TOTAL SCORE	0–10
Abnormal score	≥3

VES-13, Vulnerable Elders Survey.

Source: Ref. (25). Vulnerable Elders Survey (VES-13). Available at: www.rand.org/health/projects/acove/survey.html.

TABLE 14.3 Comparing G8 and VES-13

	G8	VES-13
Original target population	Oncology patients over age 70 scheduled for first-line chemotherapy	Community general geriatric patients 65 and over
Who administers the test	Health care professional	Self-administered ± health care professional
Location of administration	Clinic	Home Waiting room Clinic
Cost of the test	Free	Free
Domains covered	Functional status Self-rated health Comorbidities Nutrition Cognitive function	Functional status Self-rated health
Time to perform	~5 min	4–5 min
Number of studies comparing to CGA	8	11
Average sensitivity for an abnormal CGA (range)	82.8 (65–92)	61.1 (39–87)
Average specificity for an abnormal CGA (range)	68.3 (3–75)	71.6 (62–100)
Abnormal score predictive for:		
Chemotherapy-related toxicity	Mixed results	Yes
Functional decline	Yes	Not studied
Falls	Yes	Not studied
Abnormal score prognostic for overall survival	Yes	Mixed results
Limitations	May require special assessment regarding "neuropsychosocial problems"	Some patients may be unable to self-administer test

CGA, comprehensive geriatric assessment; VES, Vulnerable Elders Survey.

Other Geriatric Oncology Screening Tools

A number of other screening tools for CGA have been studied. The Flemish version of the Triage Risk Screening Tool (fTRST) is a short survey administered by a health care professional using only five questions. In a prospective trial of older adults with cancer, the fTRST and G8 had similar sensitivity and specificity for an abnormal CGA (22). The advantage of the fTRST is that it requires significantly less time to administer—about 2 minutes compared to 5 minutes for the G8 (9,38). The Groningen Frailty Indicator (GFI) screening tool is a longer questionnaire comprised of 15 questions (39). The GFI has been compared to CGA in three studies of older adults with cancer and found to have a lower sensitivity than other tests, 39% to 66%, but a high specificity of 86% to 87% (25,40,41). In addition to screening tools that assess health metrics, other tools such as the Fried Frailty Criteria incorporate frailty markers such as gait speed and grip strength (42). At this time, frailty markers as well as the fTRST and GFI are still in the early stages of investigation and have not been accepted in everyday clinical oncology practice.

LIMITATIONS OF SCREENING TOOLS

Screening tools in geriatric oncology have a number of important limitations:

■ The minimum age (65 or 70) at which to start applying these tools is unclear, with both age cutoffs used in clinical studies and conflicting guideline recommendations (9,43,44).

■ Unlike a CGA, screening tools do not identify modifiable risks that can be acted on and followed up.

■ For centers that do not have access to geriatric expertise, an abnormal result on the screening tool should be followed by a referral to a geriatric team outside the center; this may cause delays in treatment decision making and planning. A normal result on the screening tool has value in reassuring the treating team that the patient would likely not have an abnormal CGA and therefore could tolerate standard treatment.

HOW TO IMPLEMENT SCREENING TOOLS IN GERIATRIC ONCOLOGY INTO ROUTINE ONCOLOGY PRACTICE

When deciding to incorporate a screening tool into your practice, there are a number of important considerations:

1. Ease of use: Who administers the test, time to assess, whether other information is needed
2. Cost: Price of using the screening tool, resource utilization, time
3. How well the test performs for the purpose
4. If the result on the screening tool is abnormal, who the patient will be referred to for further assessment (this will depend on local expertise and resources)

Currently, all of the screening tools discussed in this chapter are freely available online (15,25).

Figure 14.1 shows a suggested flow diagram for how screening tools could be used in a routine oncology practice. The VES-13 could even be used to screen patients prior to an appointment, to help facilitate early referral for CGA or customize the initial assessment. To give the reader an idea of what to expect when using either the G8 or VES-13 in practice, Table 14.4 outlines the possible results and illustrates the trade-offs between these two screening tools. On average, using the G8 results in 73% of patients having an abnormal screening test, compared to 54% having abnormal screening tests when using the VES-13. Due to lower sensitivity, screening with the VES-13 results in more "false negative" results, or normal screening score in patients who would have an abnormal CGA. In contrast, using the G8 would result in more "false positive" results, or abnormal screening score in patients who would have a normal CGA. Both tools are comparable in terms of correctly identifying patients who do not require a CGA.

The decision of which tool to use ultimately comes down to personal preference, availability of resources, and tolerance for false negative or false positive results.

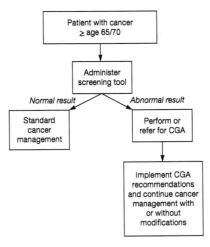

FIGURE 14.1 Flow diagram of how screening tools can fit into the care for older adults with cancer.

CGA, comprehensive geriatric assessment.

TABLE 14.4 Expected Results* of Implementing G8 or VES-13 for 100 Older Patients With Cancer

100 Patients Assessed	Abnormal CGA (73%)	Normal CGA (27%)
Number of patients with an abnormal screening score G8 = 73 VES-13 = 54	**True Positive (True Abnormal)** Number of patients who will be referred for CGA based on an abnormal screening score and found to require	**False Positive (False Abnormal)** Number of patients who would be referred for CGA unnecessarily based on an

(continued)

TABLE 14.4 Expected Results* of Implementing G8 or VES-13 for 100 Older Patients With Cancer (*continued*)

100 Patients Assessed	Abnormal CGA (73%)	Normal CGA (27%)
	some interventions prior to treatment.	abnormal screening score but would subsequently be found to be fit by CGA and can proceed with standard treatment without intervention.
	G8: 60 **VES-13: 50**	
		G8: 13 **VES-13: 4**
Number of patients with a normal screening score G8 = 27 VES-13 = 46	**False Negative (False Normal)** Number of patients who would not be referred for CGA based on a normal screening result but would have been found to have an abnormal CGA. These patients should have had some intervention prior to treatment.	**True Negative (True Normal)** Number of patients who have a normal screening score and would not be shown to have an abnormal CGA and therefore are likely able to tolerate standard treatment without any intervention.
	G8: 11 **VES-13: 27**	**G8: 16** **VES-13: 19**

CGA, comprehensive geriatric assessment; SIOG, International Society for Geriatric Oncology; VES, Vulnerable Elders Survey.

*Assuming a population in which 73% of people would have an abnormal CGA, the G8 has 73% abnormal scores, sensitivity of 82.8%, specificity of 61.1% and the VES-13 has 54% abnormal scores, sensitivity of 68.3%, and specificity of 71.6%. Based on the SIOG systematic review of screening tools (9).

TAKE HOME POINTS

1. Screening tools are easy to use in a general oncology practice and allow for rapid assessment of older patients with cancer to determine if they are in need of a CGA.
2. The G8 and VES-13 are both acceptable screening tools with practical trade-offs. Preference for which test to use may vary based on the patient population and clinical setting.
3. Screening tools can provide important information about treatment-related toxicity, risk of functional decline, and overall survival, but are not a substitute for a CGA.

REFERENCES

1. Reuben DB, Borok GM, Wolde-Tsadik G, et al. A randomized trial of comprehensive geriatric assessment in the care of hospitalized patients. *N Engl J Med.* May 18, 1995;332(20):1345-1350.

2. Wildiers H, Heeren P, Puts M, et al. International Society of Geriatric Oncology consensus on geriatric assessment in older patients with cancer. *J Clin Oncol.* August 20, 2014;32(24):2595-2603.

3. Kenis C, Bron D, Libert Y, et al. Relevance of a systematic geriatric screening and assessment in older patients with cancer: results of a prospective multicentric study. *Ann Oncol.* May 2013;24(5):1306-1312.

4. Puts MTE, Santos B, Hardt J, et al. An update on a systematic review of the use of geriatric assessment for older adults in oncology. *Ann Oncol.* February 1, 2014;25(2):307-315.

5. Puts MTE, Hardt J, Monette J, et al. Use of geriatric assessment for older adults in the oncology setting: a systematic review. *J Natl Cancer Inst.* August 8, 2012;104(15):1133-1163.

6. Extermann M. Integrating a geriatric evaluation in the clinical setting. *Semin Radiat Oncol.* 2012;22(4):272-276.

7. Van Cleave JH, Kenis C, Sattar S, et al. A research agenda for gero-oncology nursing. *Semin Oncol Nurs.* February 2016;32(1):55-64.

8. Extermann M. Geriatric oncology: an overview of progresses and challenges. *Cancer Res Treat.* June 2010;42(2):61-68.

9. Decoster L, Van Puyvelde K, Mohile S, et al. Screening tools for multidimensional health problems warranting a geriatric assessment in older cancer patients: an update on SIOG recommendations. *Ann Oncol.* 2015;26(2):288-300.

10. Hurria A, Mohile S, Gajra A, et al. Validation of a prediction tool for chemotherapy toxicity in older adults with cancer. *J Clin Oncol.* July 10, 2016;34(20):2366-2371.

11. Hurria A, Togawa K, Mohile SG, et al. Predicting chemotherapy toxicity in older adults with cancer: a prospective multicenter study. *J Clin Oncol.* 2011; 29(25):3457-3465.

12. Extermann M, Boler I, Reich RR, et al. Predicting the risk of chemotherapy toxicity in older patients: the Chemotherapy Risk Assessment Scale for High-Age Patients (CRASH) score. *Cancer.* 2012;118(13):3377-3386.

13. Hamaker ME, Jonker JM, de Rooij SE, et al. Frailty screening methods for predicting outcome of a comprehensive geriatric assessment in elderly patients with cancer: a systematic review. *Lancet Oncol.* October 2012;13(10):e437-e444.

14. Bellera CA, Rainfray M, Mathoulin-Pélissier S, et al. Screening older cancer patients: first evaluation of the G-8 geriatric screening tool. *Ann Oncol.* August 2012;23(8):2166-2172.

15. G8 screening tool. Available at: http://siog.org/content/comprehensive-geriatric-assessment-cga-older-patient-cancer. Accessed March 16, 2017.

16. Soubeyran P, Bellera C, Goyard J, et al. Screening for vulnerability in older cancer patients: the ONCODAGE Prospective Multicenter Cohort Study. *PLoS One.* January 11, 2014;9(12):e115060.

17. Martinez-Tapia C, Canoui-Poitrine F, Bastuji-Garin S, et al. Optimizing the G8 screening tool for older patients with cancer: diagnostic performance and validation of a six-item version. *Oncologist.* January 13, 2016;21(2):188-195.

18. Petit-Monéger A, Rainfray M, Soubeyran P, et al. Detection of frailty in elderly cancer patients: improvement of the G8 screening test. *J Geriatr Oncol.* February 8, 2016;7(2):99-107.

19. Liuu E, Canouï-Poitrine F, Tournigand C, et al. Accuracy of the G-8 geriatric-oncology screening tool for identifying vulnerable elderly patients with cancer according to tumour site: the ELCAPA-02 study. *J Geriatr Oncol.* 2014;5(1):11-19.

20. Dubruille S, Bron D, Roos M, et al. The respective usefulness of the G8 and a comprehensive geriatric assessment (CGA) to predict intolerance to chemotherapy and survival of fit and vulnerable older patients with hematological malignancies. *J Geriatr Oncol.* October 1, 2013;4:S56.

21. Stokoe JM, Pearce J, Sinha R, Ring A. G8 and VES-13 scores predict chemotherapy toxicity in older patients with cancer. *J Geriatr Oncol.* October 1, 2012;3:S81.

22. Kenis C, Decoster L, Van Puyvelde K, et al. Performance of two geriatric screening tools in older patients with cancer. *J Clin Oncol.* January 1, 2014;32(1):19-26.

23. Vande Walle N, Kenis C, Heeren P, et al. Fall predictors in older cancer patients: a multicenter prospective study. *BMC Geriatr.* January 2014;14:135.

24. Saliba D, Elliott M, Rubenstein LZ, et al. The Vulnerable Elders Survey: a tool for identifying vulnerable older people in the community. *J Am Geriatr Soc.* December 2001;49(12):1691-1699.

25. Vulnerable Elders Survey (VES-13). Available at: http://www.rand.org/health/projects/acove/survey.html. Accessed March 16, 2017.

26. Mohile SG, Bylow K, Dale W, et al. A pilot study of the Vulnerable Elders Survey-13 compared with the comprehensive geriatric assessment for identifying disability in older patients with prostate cancer who receive androgen ablation. *Cancer.* 2007;109(4):802-810.

27. Bononi A, Stievano L, Modena Y, et al. P9 comparison of three different CGA screening tests in daily practice: preliminary results. *Crit Rev Oncol Hematol.* October 1, 2009;72(1):S22.

28. Monfardini S, Basso U, Fiduccia P, et al. Can the short screening test Vulnerable Elders Survey 13 (VES-13) substitute for the time-consuming comprehensive geriatric assessment (CGA) to identify vulnerable/frail elderly breast cancer patients? [meeting abstracts]. *J Clin Oncol.* 2010;28(15 suppl):9114.

29. Pottel L, Boterberg T, Pottel H, Goethals L. Determination of an adequate screening tool for identification of vulnerable elderly head and neck cancer patients treated with radio(chemo)therapy. *J Geriatr Oncol.* 2012;3(1):24-32.

30. Luciani A, Ascione G, Bertuzzi C, et al. Detecting disabilities in older patients with cancer: comparison between comprehensive geriatric assessment and Vulnerable Elders Survey-13. *J Clin Oncol.* 2010;28(12):2046-2050.

31. Biganzoli L, Boni L, Becheri D, et al. Evaluation of the cardiovascular health study (CHS) instrument and the Vulnerable Elders Survey-13 (VES-13) in elderly cancer patients: are we still missing the right screening tool? *Ann Oncol.* 2013;24(2):494-500.

32. Owusu C, Koroukian SM, Schluchter M, et al. Screening older cancer patients for a comprehensive geriatric assessment: a comparison of three instruments. *J Geriatr Oncol.* 2011;2(2):121-129.

33. Molina-Garrido MJ, Guillen-Ponce C. Comparison of two frailty screening tools in older women with early breast cancer. *Crit Rev Oncol Hematol.* 2011;79(1):51-64.

34. Kellen E, Bulens P, Deckx L, et al. Identifying an accurate pre-screening tool in geriatric oncology. *Crit Rev Oncol Hematol.* September 1, 2010;75(3):243-248.

35. Falci C, Basso U, Fiduccia P, et al. P4 is Vulnerable Elders Survey 13 (VES-13) a sensitive and specific screening tool for identifying vulnerable/frail elderly cancer patients compared to full comprehensive geriatric assessment (CGA)? *Crit Rev Oncol Hematol.* October 1, 2009;72(1):S19-S20.

36. Luciani A, Biganzoli L, Colloca G, et al. Estimating the risk of chemotherapy toxicity in older patients with cancer: the role of the Vulnerable Elders Survey-13 (VES-13). *J Geriatr Oncol.* 2015;6(4):272-279.

37. Kitamura H, Nagashima F, Miyajima K, et al. Continuous comprehensive geriatric assessment could predict the prognosis in elderly cancer patients. *J Geriatr Oncol.* October 1, 2013;4:S82-S83.

38. Meldon SW, Mion LC, Palmer RM, et al. A brief risk-stratification tool to predict repeat emergency department visits and hospitalizations in older patients discharged from the emergency department. *Acad Emerg Med.* March 2003;10(3):224-232.

39. Schuurmans H, Steverink N, Lindenberg S, et al. Old or frail: what tells us more? *J Gerontol A Biol Sci Med Sci.* September 1, 2004;59(9):M962-M965.

40. Baitar A, Van Fraeyenhove F, Vandebroek A, et al. Evaluation of the Groningen Frailty Indicator and the G8 questionnaire as screening tools for frailty in older patients with cancer. *J Geriatr Oncol.* January 2013;4(1):32-38.

41. Kenis C, Schuermans H, Van Cutsem E, et al. Screening for a geriatric risk profile in older cancer patients: a comparative study of the predictive validity of three screening tools. *Crit Rev Oncol Hematol.* October 1, 2009;72(1):S22.

42. Fried LP, Tangen CM, Walston J, et al. Frailty in older adults: evidence for a phenotype. *J Gerontol A Biol Sci Med Sci.* March 2001;56(3):M146-M156.

43. NCCN. Older adult oncology. 2015. Available at: www.nccn.org. Accessed September 17, 2015.

44. Pallis AG, Fortpied C, Wedding U, et al. EORTC elderly task force position paper: approach to the older cancer patient. *Eur J Cancer.* 2010;46(9):1502-1513.

IV Select Cancers in the Elderly

15 Breast Cancer

Shlomit Strulov Shachar, Trevor A. Jolly, Noam VanderWalde, and Hyman B. Muss

INTRODUCTION

Major advances in medical care and public health have resulted in dramatic increases in life expectancy. A woman born now has a life expectancy of 81 years, and the U.S. female population 65 years and older will grow from 26.4 million in 2015 to 46.2 million in 2050 (1). This surge in the aging female population corresponds to a striking rise in breast cancer (BC) cases, as the incidence of BC increases dramatically with age. BC is the most common cancer among women in the United States, accounting for nearly one in three female cancers. It is also the second leading cause of cancer death among women after lung cancer (2).The average age at diagnosis of BC is 62 years, and the majority of woman who die of BC are older than 65 years. The combination of an aging population with an increased incidence of BC and other comorbidities related to aging make management of this expanding group of older patients a major challenge. Treatment of BC in the elderly is especially challenging because older adults, even those with normal performance status, are more likely to have physiologic changes, functional deficits, comorbid medical conditions, and polypharmacy, which increase the risk of treatment toxicity (3). Geriatric assessment can identify such deficits, predict treatment toxicity, and may lead to interventions that improve quality of life (QoL) and preserve function (4).

SCREENING MAMMOGRAPHY

The American Cancer Society recommends that women should continue mammography screenings as long as their overall health is good and they have a life expectancy of 10 years or longer (qualified recommendation) (5). The U.S. Preventive Services Task Force has no recommendation for women older than 75, as there is insufficient evidence to support any firm recommendation (6). In a large study based on Surveillance, Epidemiology, and End Results (SEER) data, Black and White women aged 75 to 84 years who had annual mammography had lower 10-year BC mortality than corresponding women who had biennial or no/irregular mammographies (7). We recommend screening in women above 65 annually or biennially provided they have at least a 10-year average life expectancy, and after discussion of the risks and benefits. An excellent review of this topic is available (8) and a web-based model (cancerscreening.eprognosis.org/) can help in decision making (9).

BC PHENOTYPES

After age, life expectancy, and the goals of treatment are taken into account, BC treatment decisions can be made on the basis of stage, histologic subtype, tumor grade, and phenotype. For simplicity's sake, BC can be divided into three major phenotypes: (a) hormone receptor (HR) (estrogen and/or progesterone receptor) positive and human epidermal growth factor receptor-2 (HER-2) negative tumors, which are found in the majority of patients; (b) HR negative and HER-2 negative tumors (so called "triple negative" BC); (c) HER-2 positive tumors (with any HR status). HR positive and HER-2 negative tumors increase with age and account for about 75% of tumors in women aged 70 and above, and most relapses occur 5 years after diagnosis. Patients with HER-2 positive and triple negative BC who relapse generally do so within 5 years of diagnosis. More recently, genetic assays of tumor tissue have divided BC into several major subtypes (10). Although the frequency of more favorable subtypes (luminal A and B tumors) increases with age, many older women have high-risk subtypes—an important finding because prognosis and treatment outcomes are similar and independent of age once subtype is accounted for (11).

MANAGEMENT OF THE PRIMARY LESION

Primary Endocrine Therapy

The majority of older patients will have HR positive, HER-2 negative tumors and comorbidities associated with aging that sometimes lead to life expectancies of only several months or years. Primary endocrine therapy can be an excellent option for such patients. This strategy is also appropriate for those with HR positive, HER-2 negative unresectable primary lesions, for which preoperative endocrine therapy can decrease tumor size and allow for either mastectomy or breast preservation. We prefer aromatase inhibitors (AIs) in this setting, due to their more favorable treatment effect and toxicity profiles, and because unlike tamoxifen, there is no increased risk of uterine cancer or thromboembolism (12). Primary endocrine therapy controls tumor growth for about 18 to 24 months on average (13), making it an appropriate treatment for patients with a short life expectancy. Although time to onset of a response may take several months or longer (14), many patients will have continuous disease control throughout the rest of their lives. However, the cornerstone of early BC treatment at any age remains surgery, unless the patient has a short life expectancy, declines surgery, or is not a suitable surgical candidate (15).

Surgery

Elderly patients generally tolerate surgery well and with low complication rates (16). Most older women will be candidates for breast preservation. Sentinel node biopsy is a safe and accurate procedure (17) and should be offered to women with clinically negative axilla, provided the information will help in decision making. Axillary lymph node dissection should be considered in patients with clinically involved axillary nodes, provided such patients have a reasonable life expectancy.

Radiation Therapy

Adjuvant radiation therapy (RT) plays an important role in the treatment of most women undergoing breast conservation surgery for early stage BC. The Early Breast Cancer Trialists, Group (EBCTG) meta-analysis demonstrates that the addition of radiotherapy to breast conservation surgery decreased recurrence by 15.7% (35.0% vs. 19.3%) at 10 years and BC-related death by 3.8% (25.2% vs. 21.4%) at 15 years for all patients (18). However, for older patients with potentially lower risks of recurrence and a higher likelihood of death from comorbid conditions, many questioned the value of breast irradiation, leading to at least five large randomized studies of older women with early stage BC comparing adjuvant RT to no RT (19–23). Arguably, the most impactful of these studies thus far has been Cancer and Leukemia Group B (CALGB) 9343. At 10 years, locoregional recurrence rates were 10% in those not receiving RT, compared to 2% in those who received RT ($P < .001$). No difference in disease-specific or overall survival was found, and the vast majority of deaths were due to non-BC causes (21). Due to the relatively low risk of locoregional recurrence even without RT, this and other studies have been used to justify the omission of RT in older women with T1N0 hormone positive BC (24). Care should be taken not to extrapolate the results of these studies to patients who do not meet the strict eligibility criteria for study entry; higher risks of locoregional recurrence have been found among patients with larger, higher grade, and/or hormone-negative tumors (25).

Locoregional radiation should also be considered for women postmastectomy who have large tumors and/or nodal involvement; in this setting, radiation can substantially decrease locoregional recurrence and improve survival. Multidisciplinary consultations with breast surgeons, medical oncologists, and radiation oncologists for all older patients are recommended (see Table 15.1 for more details).

ADJUVANT SYSTEMIC THERAPY

The purpose of adjuvant systemic therapy in patients with early BC is to increase the chances for long-term disease-free survival. Goals of treatment, assessment of life expectancy, and geriatric assessment should be performed before making systemic treatment decisions. The estimation of the potential value of endocrine therapy, chemotherapy, and anti-HER-2 directed therapies can be made using online calculators (e.g., www.adjuvantonline.com, and www.predict.nhs.uk/predict.html—see Table 15.2), and detailed review is available (26). The PREDICT model also estimates the absolute benefit in overall survival of trastuzumab-based regimens in patients with HER-2 positive tumors and can accurately predict 5-year survival in the elderly (27). However, the added value of chemotherapy appears to be overestimated in Adjuvant! (28). General recommendations for use of systemic therapy are shown in Figure 15.1. International Society of Geriatric Oncology (SIOG) guidelines (30) and current reviews, including one on management of BC in women older than 80 years, are available (31,32).

TABLE 15.1 Adjuvant Radiation Studies

Study	Key Eligibility Criteria	Study Arms	Local Recurrence Results	Overall Survival Results
Princess Margaret Hospital (19)	Age 50 and above BCS Negative margins T1 or T2 (5 cm or less) Negative nodes No adjuvant chemotherapy allowed	Tamoxifen alone (n = 383) vs. RT + tamoxifen (n = 386)	5 y rate: 7.7% vs. 0.6% (P < .001)	5 y rate: 93.2% vs. 92.8% (P = .83)
ABCSG 8A (20)	Postmenopausal women BCS Negative margins T1 or T2 (<3 cm) Hormone positive Negative nodes Grade 1 or 2	Tamoxifen or anastrozole (n = 417) vs. RT + Tamoxifen or anastrozole (n = 414)	5 y rate: 5.1% vs. 0.4% (P < .001)	5 y rate: 94.5% vs. 97.9% (P = .18)
RT 55–75 Trial (23)	Postmenopausal women, age 55–75 Size < 2.5 cm No extensive intraductal component or LVSI Up to two axillary nodes allowed	Quandretectomy alone vs. postop RT	5 y rate: 2.5% vs. 0.7% (P = .07)	5 y rate 96% vs. 95%
CALGB 9343 (21)	Age 70 and above BCS Negative margins T1 (2 cm or less) Hormone positive or unknown Negative nodes	Tamoxifen alone (n = 319) vs. RT + tamoxifen (n = 317)	Locoregional recurrence: 5 y rate: 4% vs. 1% (P < .001) 10 y rate: 9% vs. 2% (P < .001)	5 y rate: 86% vs. 87% (P = .94) 10 y rate: 66% vs. 67% (P = .64)

TABLE 15.1 Adjuvant Radiation Studies (continued)

Study	Key Eligibility Criteria	Study Arms	Local Recurrence Results	Overall Survival Results
PRIME II (22)	Age 65 and above BCS Negative margins T1 or T2 (<3 cm) Negative nodes Hormone positive Grade 3 or LVSI but not both	Endocrine therapy + RT (n = 658) vs. Endocrine therapy, no RT (n = 668)	5 y rate: 4% vs. <1% (P < .001)	5 y rate: 94% vs. 95% (P = .34)

ABCSG, Austrian Breast & Colorectal Cancer Study Group; BCS, breast-conserving surgery; CALGB, Cancer and Leukemia Group B; LVSI, lymphovascular invasion; RT, radiation therapy.

TABLE 15.2 Web-Based Calculators for Treatment Benefit, Toxicity Risk, and Life Expectancy

Name	Details
BC predictive websites	
Adjuvant!* www.adjuvantonline.com	Calculator that estimates benefits of adjuvant therapy. Also consider comorbidities.
PREDICT www.predict.nhs.uk	Calculates benefits of adjuvant therapy for patients with BC. Does not consider comorbidities. Does consider anti-HER-2 treatment benefits.
Screening benefits, life expectancy, and toxicity prediction calculators	
ePrognosis eprognosis.ucsf.edu/default.php	Calculator for estimating life expectancy.
ePrognosis cancerscreening.eprognosis.org/	Calculator for estimating cancer screening benefit.
Moffitt Cancer Center Senior Adult Oncology Program Tools moffitt.org/cancer-types –treatment/cancers-we-treat/ senior-adult-oncology-program-tools	Calculator for estimating chemotherapy toxicity.
CARG (Cancer and Aging Research Group) www.mycarg.org/	Calculator for estimating chemotherapy toxicity.

BC, breast cancer; HER-2, human epidermal growth factor receptor-2

*Registration and password needed.

Endocrine Therapy

For HR positive tumors, endocrine therapy with an AI for 5 years or tamoxifen for 2 to 3 years followed by an AI should be considered. Both AIs and tamoxifen are usually well tolerated in older patients (33). Recent data suggest that longer durations of endocrine therapy are associated with superior outcomes: In older patients decisions on extending endocrine treatment should be made on a case-by-case basis. We favor AI therapy, as relapse rates are a few percent lower when compared to tamoxifen; also, there is a small survival advantage (34) and a more favorable toxicity profile. Numerous studies have shown that compliance with and adherence to endocrine therapy is a major problem (35). Patients should be queried to confirm that they are taking their medications as directed.

Chemotherapy

Chemotherapy should be considered for most patients with triple negative BCs unless the tumors are very small or the patient has a life expectancy less than 5 years. For patients with HR positive and HER-2 negative tumors, chemotherapy should be considered for those with large tumors and/or lymph node involvement. For older patients with this phenotype and with life expectancies at least 5 years or longer, who have node-negative tumors less than 5 cm, genetic-based assays should be considered to determine the added value of chemotherapy to endocrine therapy (36). All treatment decisions should take into account patient preferences and goals of treatment as well as the risks and benefits of treatment. In general, we favor nonanthracycline-based chemotherapy unless more beneficial but more toxic anthracycline and taxane regimens improve 5-year survival by more than 3% compared to nonanthracycline regimens in the PREDICT calculator. The benefits of newer chemotherapy regimens are similar among older and younger patients, but older patients have higher rates of hematological toxicity (37). For those with HER-2 positive tumors, an absolute survival improvement of a few percent or more should be the basis for offering chemotherapy and trastuzumab.

Several calculators are available (see Table 15.1) to estimate grade 3 and greater chemotherapy toxicity, and can help in the chemotherapy treatment decision for both patients with early stage and metastatic disease (4,38).

METASTATIC DISEASE

In the United States in 2016, 41,000 estimated deaths were from metastatic BC (39). Overall, the prognosis of patients with metastatic breast cancer (MBC) remains poor, with 5- and 10-year survival rates approximating 25% and 10%, respectively (40). As MBC is incurable with current treatments, the ultimate goal of therapy is to delay symptom onset, palliate symptoms, slow disease progression, maintain or improve QoL, and when possible prolong overall survival. No standard treatment exists for MBC and therapy should be tailored to the individual patient based on tumor phenotype, disease tempo, organ function, comorbidities, sites of metastases, tumor volume, functional status, and patient preference. In general, patients with HR positive disease without evidence of visceral crisis are treated with endocrine therapy until endocrine resistance develops, and then chemotherapy if appropriate and in keeping with treatment goals. The addition of newer biologic agents (everolimus and palbociclib) to standard endocrine treatments improves the duration of disease control, but the safety of these agents in older patients is uncertain. HER-2 overexpressing tumors are generally treated with anti-HER-2 directed therapy (trastuzumab, pertuzumab, ado-trastuzumab emtansine), either alone or in addition to chemotherapy. Chemotherapy is the main treatment option for metastatic triple negative BC.

Supportive and palliative care is an integral part of treating MBC in all patients. A detailed review on the management of MBC is available (41).

CONCLUSION

Figure 15.1 provides a schema for the treatment for a woman over 70 years newly diagnosed with BC. Screening older women without BC and optimizing treatment decisions for those who do have BC should be based on life expectancy, patient goals, the potential benefits and risks of treatment, and the effects of treatment on function

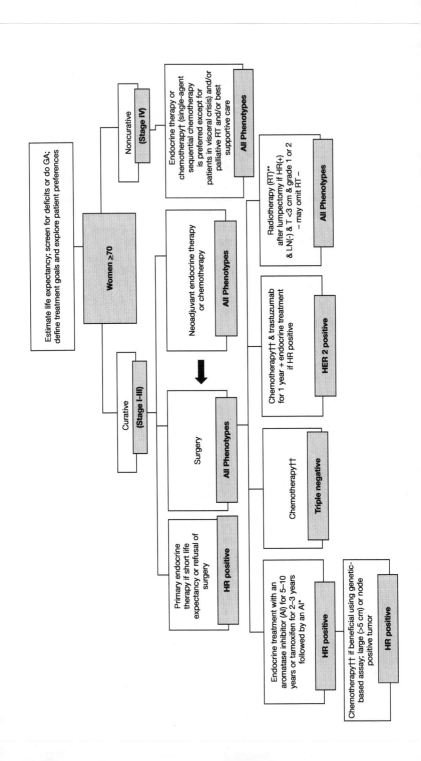

Estimate life expectancy; screen for deficits or do GA; define treatment goals and explore patient preferences

Women ≥70

Curative (Stage I-III)

Noncurative (Stage IV)

Endocrine therapy or chemotherapy† (single-agent sequential chemotherapy is preferred except for patients in visceral crisis) and/or palliative RT and/or best supportive care

All Phenotypes

Primary endocrine therapy if short life expectancy or refusal of surgery

HR positive

Neoadjuvant endocrine therapy or chemotherapy

All Phenotypes

Surgery

All Phenotypes

Radiotherapy (RT)** after lumpectomy if HR(+) & LN(−) & T <3 cm & grade 1 or 2 – may omit RT –

All Phenotypes

Chemotherapy† & trastuzumab for 1 year + endocrine treatment if HR positive

HER 2 positive

Chemotherapy†

Triple negative

Endocrine treatment with an aromatase inhibitor (AI) for 5-10 years or tamoxifen for 2-3 years followed by an AI*

HR positive

Chemotherapy† if beneficial using genetic-based assay; large (>5 cm) or node positive tumor

HR positive

FIGURE 15.1 Flow diagram for BC treatment in women 70 years and older.

BC, breast cancer; GA, geriatric assessment; HR, hormone receptor; LN, lymph nodes; RT, radiation therapy; T, tumor.

†Combination chemotherapy leads to higher response rates and progression-free survival and is preferred in patients in visceral crisis, but may not confer a survival advantage (29).

††For specific chemotherapy options, potential toxicities such as decreased ejection fraction and congestive heart failure (anthracyclines, trastuzumab), neuropathy (taxanes), and myelodysplasia and acute leukemia (anthracyclines) should be taken into consideration. Cardiac function should be assessed prior to anthracycline and/or trastuzumab administration and during trastuzumab therapy. The decision to incorporate white cell growth factors into treatment plans, hepatic, renal, and cardiac function, and attention to dose and scheduling, are all important considerations in selecting and delivering the safest treatment.

*Should be considered for most elderly women unless they have small (<1 cm) low-grade, node-negative tumors or extremely short life expectancy.

**Source: Adapted from Refs. (21,22)

and QoL. A major drawback to decision making is the paucity of data on older patients from clinical trials (42). Above all, older patients who are eligible for trials should be encouraged to participate.

TAKE HOME POINTS

1. Mammographic screening recommendations should be based on life expectancy and the pros and cons of the procedure.
2. Endocrine therapy is the mainstay adjuvant treatment for older women with early stage BC and HR positive tumors.
3. Older patients with BC have similar benefits from chemotherapy as younger patients, but are at greater risk from toxicity.
4. Adjuvant breast radiation might be omitted in older patients with small, node negative, HR positive tumors, provided they are compliant with endocrine therapy.
5. In MBC, endocrine therapy is the cornerstone of treatment for HR positive tumors and chemotherapy for triple negative tumors.

REFERENCES

1. United Nations. World population ageing 2015. 2015. Available at: http://www.un.org/en/development/desa/population/theme/ageing/WPA2015.shtml. Accessed February 1, 2016.
2. DeSantis C, Ma J, Bryan L, Jemal A. Breast cancer statistics, 2013. *CA Cancer J Clin.* 2014;64(1):52-62.
3. Jolly TA, Deal AM, Nyrop KA, et al. Geriatric assessment-identified deficits in older cancer patients with normal performance status. *Oncologist.* 2015;20:379-385.
4. Hurria A, Togawa K, Mohile SG, et al. Predicting chemotherapy toxicity in older adults with cancer: a prospective multicenter study. *J Clin Oncol.* 2011;29(25):3457-3465.
5. Oeffinger KC, Fontham ET, Etzioni R, et al. Breast cancer screening for women at average risk: 2015 guideline update from the American Cancer Society. *JAMA.* 2015;314(15):1599-1614.
6. Siu AL. Screening for breast cancer: U.S. Preventive Services Task Force recommendation statement. *Ann Intern Med.* 2016;164(4):279-296.
7. Sanderson M, Levine RS, Fadden M, et al. Mammography screening among the elderly: a research challenge. *Am J Med.* 2015;128(12):1362.e7-1362.e14.
8. Walter LC, Schonberg MA. Screening mammography in older women: a review. *JAMA.* 2014;311(13):1336-1347.
9. Cruz M, Covinsky K, Widera EW, et al. Predicting 10-year mortality for older adults. *JAMA.* 2013;309(9):874-876.
10. Perou CM, Parker JS, Prat A, et al., Clinical implementation of the intrinsic subtypes of breast cancer. *Lancet Oncol.* 2010;11(8):718-719.
11. Jenkins EO, Deal AM, Anders CK, et al. Age-specific changes in intrinsic breast cancer subtypes: a focus on older women. *Oncologist.* 2014;19(10):1076-1083.
12. Muss HB, Tu D, Ingle JN, et al. Efficacy, toxicity, and quality of life in older women with early-stage breast cancer treated with letrozole or placebo after 5 years of tamoxifen: NCIC CTG intergroup trial MA.17. *J Clin Oncol.* 2008;26(12):1956-1964.

13. Hind D, Wyld L, Beverley CB, Reed MW. Surgery versus primary endocrine therapy for operable primary breast cancer in elderly women (70 years plus). *Cochrane Database Syst Rev.* 2006;25(1):CD004272.

14. Dixon JM, Wyld L, Beverley CB, Reed MW. Increase in response rate by prolonged treatment with neoadjuvant letrozole. *Breast Cancer Res Treat.* 2009;113(1):145-151.

15. Hind D, Wyld L, Reed MW. Surgery, with or without tamoxifen, vs tamoxifen alone for older women with operable breast cancer: Cochrane Review. *Br J Cancer.* 2007;96(7):1025-1029.

16. Kemeny MM. Surgery in older patients. *Semin Oncol.* 2004;31(2):175-184.

17. Gennari R, Rotmensz N, Perego E, et al. Sentinel node biopsy in elderly breast cancer patients. *Surg Oncol.* 2004;13(4):193-196.

18. Early Breast Cancer Trialists' Collaborative Group. Effect of radiotherapy after breast-conserving surgery on 10-year recurrence and 15-year breast cancer death: meta-analysis of individual patient data for 10,801 women in 17 randomised trials. *Lancet.* 2011;378(9804):1707-1716.

19. Fyles AW, McCready DR, Manchul LA, et al. Tamoxifen with or without breast irradiation in women 50 years of age or older with early breast cancer. *N Engl J Med.* 2004;351(10):963-970.

20. Potter R, Gnant M, Kwasny W, et al. Lumpectomy plus tamoxifen or anastrozole with or without whole breast irradiation in women with favorable early breast cancer. *Int J Radiat Oncol Biol Phys.* 2007;68(2):334-340.

21. Hughes KS, Schnaper LA, Bellon JR, et al. Lumpectomy plus tamoxifen with or without irradiation in women age 70 years or older with early breast cancer: long-term follow-up of CALGB 9343. *J Clin Oncol.* 2013;31(19):2382-2387.

22. Kunkler IH, Williams LJ, Jack WJ, et al. Breast-conserving surgery with or without irradiation in women aged 65 years or older with early breast cancer (PRIME II): a randomised controlled trial. *Lancet Oncol.* 2015;16(3):266-273.

23. Tinterri C, Gatzemeier W, Zanini V, et al. Conservative surgery with and without radiotherapy in elderly patients with early-stage breast cancer: a prospective randomised multicentre trial. *Breast* 2009;18(6):373-377.

24. National Comprehensive Cancer Network. *Clinical Practice Guidelines in Oncology: Breast Cancer.* 2014. Available at: http://www.nccn.org. Accessed February 1, 2016.

25. Smith BD, Gross CP, Smith GL, et al. Effectiveness of radiation therapy for older women with early breast cancer. *J Natl Cancer Inst.* 2006;98(10):681-690.

26. Shachar SS, Muss HB. Internet tools to enhance breast cancer care. *NPJ Breast Cancer.* 2016;2:16011.

27. de Glas NA, Bastiaannet E, Engels CC, et al. Validity of the online PREDICT tool in older patients with breast cancer: a population-based study. *Br J Cancer.* 2016;114(4):395-400.

28. de Glas NA, van de Water W, Engelhardt EG, et al. Validity of Adjuvant! Online program in older patients with breast cancer: a population-based study. *Lancet Oncol.* 2014;15(7):722-729.

29. Miles DG, von Minckwitz G, Seidman AD. Combination versus sequential single-agent therapy in metastatic breast cancer. *Oncologist.* 2002;7(suppl 6):13-19.

30. Biganzoli L, Wildiers H, Oakman C, et al. Management of elderly patients with breast cancer: updated recommendations of the International Society of Geriatric Oncology (SIOG) and European Society of Breast Cancer Specialists (EUSOMA). *Lancet Oncol.* 2012;13(4):e148-e160.

31. Shachar SS, Hurria A, Muss HB. Breast cancer in women older than 80 years. *J Oncol Pract.* 2016;12(2):123-132.

32. Jolly TA, Williams GR, Bushan S, et al. Adjuvant treatment for older women with invasive breast cancer. *Womens Health (Lond)*. 2016;12(1):129-146.

33. Crivellari D, Sun Z, Coates AS, et al. Letrozole compared with tamoxifen for elderly patients with endocrine-responsive early breast cancer: the BIG 1-98 trial. *J Clin Oncol*. 2008;26(12):1972-1979.

34. Early Breast Cancer Trialists' Collaborative Group. Aromatase inhibitors versus tamoxifen in early breast cancer: patient-level meta-analysis of the randomised trials. *Lancet*. 2015;386(10001):1341-1352.

35. Hershman DL, Kushi LH, Shao T, et al. Early discontinuation and nonadherence to adjuvant hormonal therapy in a cohort of 8,769 early-stage breast cancer patients. *J Clin Oncol*. 2010;28(27):4120-4128.

36. Zelnak AB, O'Regan RM. Genomic subtypes in choosing adjuvant therapy for breast cancer. *Oncology (Williston Park)*. 2013;27(3):204-210.

37. Muss HB, Berry DA, Cirrincione C, et al. Toxicity of older and younger patients treated with adjuvant chemotherapy for node-positive breast cancer: the Cancer and Leukemia Group B Experience. *J Clin Oncol*. 2007;25(24):3699-3704.

38. Extermann M, Boler I, Reich RR, et al. Predicting the risk of chemotherapy toxicity in older patients: the Chemotherapy Risk Assessment Scale for High-Age Patients (CRASH) score. *Cancer*. 2012;118(13):3377-3386.

39. Siegel RL, Miller KD, Jemal A. Cancer statistics, 2016. *CA Cancer J Clin*. 2016;66(1):7-30.

40. SEER stat fact sheets. Available at: http://seer.cancer.gov/statfacts. Accessed February 1, 2016.

41. Jolly T, Williams GR, Jones E, Muss HB. Treatment of metastatic breast cancer in women aged 65 years and older. *Womens Health (Lond)*. 2012; 8(4):455-469;quiz 470-471.

42. Lewis JH, Kilgore ML, Goldman DP, et al. Participation of patients 65 years of age or older in cancer clinical trials. *J Clin Oncol*. 2003;21(7):1383-1389.

16

Prostate Cancer in Elderly Patients

Pedro Recabal, Chung-Han Lee, and Dana E. Rathkopf

INTRODUCTION

Prostate cancer (PCa) is the most common malignancy among men, and the second leading cause of cancer death in the United States (1); the American Cancer Society estimates more than 180,000 new cases and more than 26,000 deaths in 2016. The disease burden is expected to increase along with aging of the population. More than half of men diagnosed with PCa (2) meet the conventional definition of *elderly person* (≥65 years old) (3); for this chapter, *elder* will be defined as greater than 70 years old. The prevalence of incidental PCa increases with age (59% in autopsies of men ≥ 79) (4). Elders are more likely than younger patients to present with high-risk features, including higher Gleason grade (5,6), and metastatic disease; these patients account for more than half of all PCa deaths (7). A study (8) estimated that around one-third of avoidable cancer deaths would be diagnosed in elders. However, current evidence-based recommendations suggest that prostate-specific antigen (PSA) screening should end at age 70, unless a man is very healthy and has a higher than average PSA, and at 75 for all men (9).

LIFE EXPECTANCY AND HEALTH STATUS ASSESSMENT

For therapeutic decisions, the survival benefit of treatments must be weighed against the patient's life expectancy, for which a predictive model has been validated for patients with localized PCa, and is available online (10). Age by itself is a poor predictor of survival (11), and comorbidity is a stronger predictor of noncancer mortality than age (12). The current International Society of Geriatric Oncology (SIOG) guidelines recommend individualized management of PCa patients who are 70 or more years old, stratifying health status into three groups (healthy, vulnerable, and frail) based on comorbidities, dependence, nutritional status, and cognitive and physical functions (13) using the G-8 screening tool (see Chapter 14 and Figure 16.1).

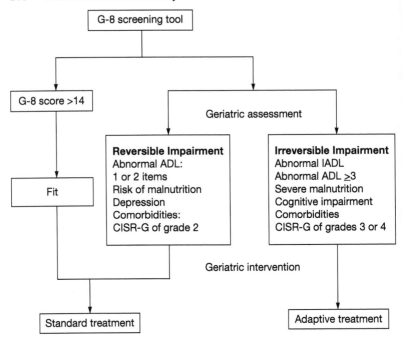

FIGURE 16.1 SIOG guidelines for treatment of PCa according to health status.

ADL, activities of daily living; IADL, instrumental activities of daily living; CISR-G, cumulative illness score rating-geriatrics; SIOG, International Society of Geriatric Oncology.

CLINICAL STATES OF THE DISEASE

The long natural history of PCa and evolving therapeutic alternatives have been the rationale for developing a model that partitions the disease continuum into dynamic clinical states characterized by the status of the primary tumor, presence of metastases, prior and current treatment, and testosterone levels (Figure 16.2). This model aids in assessing the prognosis at different clinical states—information not accounted for in nomograms or traditional staging systems (14).

DISEASE RISK STRATIFICATION

The TNM staging system, along with the Gleason score and the PSA, are used in combination to assess the risk of progression, recurrence, and cancer-related death. Different classification systems are available. These cluster patients according to cutoffs for each variable. The National Comprehensive Cancer Network (NCCN) risk groups (15) and criteria are presented in Table 16.1. Several nomograms have

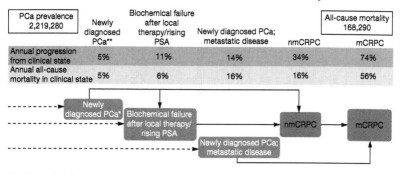

PCa prevalence 2,219,280	Newly diagnosed PCa**	Biochemical failure after local therapy/rising PSA	Newly diagnosed PCa; metastatic disease	nmCRPC	All-cause mortality 168,290 mCRPC
Annual progression from clinical state	5%	11%	14%	34%	74%
Annual all-cause mortality in clinical state	5%	6%	16%	16%	56%

FIGURE 16.2 Clinical states of disease.

mCRPC, metastatic castration-resistant prostate cancer; nmCRPC, non metastatic, castration-resistant prostate cancer; PCa, prostate cancer; PSA, prostate-specific antigen.

*Weighted averages of patients diagnosed with localized, locally advanced, and metastatic disease.

**Localized disease or locally advanced disease.

also been published which provide a better estimation of an individual's risk. However, the risk estimation provided by these tools may not be generalizable. For example, the accuracy of a nomogram predicting recurrence after surgery may vary from institution to institution.

TREATMENT: NEWLY DIAGNOSED LOCALIZED/LOCALLY ADVANCED PCa

Treatment decisions in older PCa patients should consider the risk of cancer and noncancer mortality, the side effect profile of treatments, and patient preference. Elders classified as healthy (G-8 score > 14) and vulnerable patients with reversible causes of impairment may benefit from treatment of the primary tumor according to cancer risk stratification; in contrast, frail patients should be spared from curative treatments, and expectant management is preferred, especially for low-risk tumors and men with a short life expectancy.

For elders selecting radical prostatectomy (RP), comorbidity is a better predictor of morbidity and mortality than age; healthy men have low operative mortality (0.66% in men between 70 and 79 years old [17]) and good long-term overall survival (18). Most men can recover urinary and sexual function after surgery; however, age has a negative impact on functional recovery. In a large retrospective study, 1-year continence rates for age groups less than 65, 65 to 70, 70 to 75, and greater than 75 were 93.2%, 90.8%, 86.0%, and 86.5%, and 1-year potency rates were 59.3%, 46.9%, 44.4%, and 31.3% (19). In men 70 years of age or older, minimally invasive RP is feasible, and has been associated with decreased rates of transfusions, postoperative complications, and anastomotic stricture compared to the open approach (20).

Radiotherapy (RT) is also a viable treatment for older healthy or vulnerable patients with localized intermediate or high-risk tumors (21). Randomized control

TABLE 16.1 NCCN Cancer Risk Stratification and Treatment Options for Newly Diagnosed PCa

Disease Presentation	Clinically Localized					Locally Advanced	Metastatic Hormone Naïve	
Risk Group	**Very Low**	**Low**	**Intermediate**		**High**	**Very High**	**Oligometastatic**	**High-volume Metastasis**
CT stage	T1c	T1-T2a	T2b-T2c		T3a	T3b-T4	Any T	Any T
Gleason score	6	6	3+4	4+3	8-10	Primary Gleason pattern 5	Any Gleason score	Any Gleason score
PSA	<10 ng/mL	<10 ng/mL	10–20 ng/mL		>20 ng/mL			
Other characteristics	<3 biopsy cores positive, 50% cancer in each core					>4 cores with Gleason score 8–10	N1 or M1	visceral metastases or ≥4 bone lesions with ≥1 beyond the vertebral bodies and pelvis*
	PSA density <0.15 ng/mL/g					Two or more high-risk criteria		
Treatment options	AS/WW	AS/WW						
		FT	FT					
			RT	RT	RT			
					RP + LND	RP + LND		
					RT + ADT	RT + ADT		
							ADT	ADT
								ADT + CT

ADT, androgen deprivation therapy; AS, active surveillance; FT, focal therapy; LND, lymph node dissection; NCCN, National Comprehensive Cancer Network; PCa, prostate cancer; PSA, prostate-specific antigen; RP, radical prostatectomy; RT, radiotherapy; WW, watchful waiting.

Source: Data from Ref. (16). Sweeney CJ, Chen YH, Carducci M, et al. Chemohormonal therapy in metastatic hormone-sensitive prostate cancer. *N Engl J Med.*

trials (RCTs) demonstrate a survival benefit of RT plus androgen-deprivation therapy (ADT) over ADT alone (22); however, elderly populations are underrepresented in those trials. In a cohort study, the combination of RT and ADT was associated with reduced cause-specific and all-cause mortality in older men compared to ADT alone (23). In contrast, for men older than 70, adjuvant radiation after RP may have a detrimental effect (24).

ADT has been used as primary therapy in unfit patients with nonmetastatic high-risk PCa. In this group (T0-4 N0-2 M0), immediate ADT provided a small but significant benefit in overall survival (but not in symptom-free or cancer-specific survival) compared to deferred ADT (25). This benefit should be weighed against the side effects of ADT, which can include decreased bone mineral density; metabolic changes such as weight gain, decreased muscle mass, and increased insulin resistance; decreased libido and sexual dysfunction; hot flashes; gynecomastia; reduced testicle size; anemia; and fatigue (26).

RISING PSA (BIOCHEMICAL FAILURE AFTER LOCAL THERAPY)

Treatment decisions should be preceded by a health status assessment in older men with a rising PSA (27). Early salvage RT can improve survival, although the benefit for older patients is unclear, and age is an independent predictor of long-term grade 3 urinary toxicity. Early ADT at biochemical recurrence has no proven benefit in survival. It should be reserved for those at highest risk of progression (PSA-DT < 6–12 months; Gleason score > 7, and long life expectancy) (28).

METASTATIC NONCASTRATE PCa

ADT has been the mainstay of treatment in this setting for decades, despite the lack of RCTs (21). Level 1b evidence supports the role of ADT to palliate symptoms and improve quality of life (QoL). Complete androgen blockade provides a small survival benefit but increases toxicity (28). Seven phase III trials testing continuous versus intermittent ADT have reached inconclusive results (29–31).

Recent studies have found that chemo-hormonal treatment with six cycles of docetaxel combined with continuous ADT is associated with overall and progression-free survival advantage in castration-sensitive metastatic patients (especially for men with "high-volume disease," defined as visceral metastases or ≥4 bone lesions with ≥1 beyond the vertebral bodies and pelvis) (16). This benefit may extend to healthy older patients who are fit for chemotherapy (30).

METASTATIC CASTRATION-RESISTANT PCa (mCRPC)

Several new agents that may affect survival have been approved for treatment of mCRPC in recent years. The survival benefit of taxane chemotherapy appears to be independent of patient age, with acceptable toxicity (32–34). In the elderly, the next-generation androgen-targeted agents abiraterone (35) and enzalutamide (36) have also been shown to improve survival. Additional agents have been approved based on a survival benefit for patients with mCRPC (although studies in elderly patients are ongoing), including immunotherapy (Sipuleucel-T) and radiopharmaceuticals (radium-223) (37). The optimal sequence for these newly approved agents and appropriate patient selection remains uncertain at present (38).

PALLIATIVE CARE

Palliative care should be offered to patients with advanced PCa concurrently with disease-directed treatment. Palliative care teams can collaborate with cancer clinicians to manage complex pain, fatigue, depression, anxiety, caregiver distress, and existential crisis (39).

TAKE HOME POINTS

1. Geriatric evaluation is essential for appropriate management of PCa in older patients.
2. Screening tools can identify healthy older patients who may benefit from standard treatments in accordance with risk and clinical state of the disease.
3. Vulnerable patients with reversible impairment may be eligible for standard treatment.
4. Frail patients should be spared from curative treatments and receive adjusted management.
5. Palliative care, including symptom management, should be offered to patients with advanced PCa concurrently with disease-directed treatment.

REFERENCES

1. Siegel R, Miller K, Jemal A. Cancer statistics, 2016. *CA Cancer J Clin.* 2016;66:7-30.
2. Barbosa PV, Thomas IC, Srinivas S, et al. Overall survival in patients with localized prostate cancer in the US Veterans Health Administration: is PIVOT generalizable? *Eur Urol.* February 29, 2016;pii:S0302-2838(16)00215-3.
3. Orimo H, Ito H, Suzuki T, et al. Reviewing the definition of "elderly." *Geriatr Gerontol Int.* 2006;6(3):149-158. doi:10.1111/j.1447-0594.2006.00341.x.
4. Bell KJL, Del Mar C, Wright G. Prevalence of incidental prostate cancer: a systematic review of autopsy studies. *Int J Cancer.* 2015;137:1749-1757.
5. Pepe P, Pennisi M. Gleason score stratification according to age at diagnosis in 1028 men. *Contemp Oncol (Pozn).* 2015;19(6):471-473.
6. Muralidhar V, Ziehr DR, Mahal BA, et al. Association between older age and increasing Gleason score. *Clin Genitourin Cancer.* December 2015;13(6):525-30.e1-3.
7. Scosyrev E, Messing EM, Mohile S, et al. Prostate cancer in the elderly: frequency of advanced disease at presentation and disease-specific mortality. *Cancer.* June 15, 2012;118(12):3062-3070.

8. Gulati R, Tsodikov A, Etzioni R, et al. Expected population impacts of discontinued prostate-specific antigen screening. *Cancer.* November 15, 2014;120(22):3519-3526.

9. Vickers AJ, Eastham JA, Scardino PT, et al. The Memorial Sloan Kettering Cancer Center recommendations for prostate cancer screening. *Urology.* February 2, 2016;pii:S0090-4295(16)00070-4.

10. Kent M, Penson DF, Albertsen PC, et al. Successful external validation of a model to predict other cause mortality in localized prostate cancer. *BMC Med.* February 9, 2016;14(1):25.

11. Walter LC, Covinsky KE. Cancer screening in elderly patients: a framework for individualized decision making. *JAMA.* June 6, 2001;285(21):2750-2756.

12. Daskivich TJ, Chamie K, Kwan L, et al. Comorbidity and competing risks for mortality in men with prostate cancer. *Cancer.* October 15, 2011;117(20): 4642-4650.

13. Droz JP, Aapro M, Balducci L, et al. Management of prostate cancer in older patients: updated recommendations of a working group of the International Society of Geriatric Oncology. *Lancet Oncol.* August 2014;15(9):e404-414.

14. Scher HI, Solo K, Valant J, et al. Prevalence of prostate cancer clinical states and mortality in the United States: estimates using a dynamic progression model. *PLOS ONE.* October 13, 2015;10(10):e0139440.

15. Mohler JL, Armstrong AJ, Bahnson RR, et al. Prostate cancer, version 1.2016. *J Natl Compr Canc Netw.* January 2016;14(1):19-30.

16. Sweeney CJ, Chen YH, Carducci M, et al. Chemohormonal therapy in metastatic hormone-sensitive prostate cancer. *N Engl J Med.* August 20, 2015;373(8):737-746. doi:10.1056/NEJMoa1503747.

17. Alibhai SM, Leach M, Tomlinson G, et al. 30-day mortality and major complications after radical prostatectomy: influence of age and comorbidity. *J Natl Cancer Inst.* October 19, 2005;97(20):1525-1532.

18. Mandel P, Kriegmair MC, Kamphake JK, et al. Tumor characteristics and oncological outcome after radical prostatectomy in men 75 years and older. *J Urol.* January 18, 2016; pii:S0022-5347(16)00038-0.

19. Mandel P, Graefen M, Michl U, et al. The effect of age on functional outcomes after radical prostatectomy. *Urol Oncol.* May 2015;33(5):203.e11-203.e18.

20. Adejoro O, Gupta P, Ziegelmann M, et al. Effect of minimally invasive radical prostatectomy in older men. *Urol Oncol.* January 12, 2016;pii:S1078-1439(15)00568-2.

21. Kunkler IH, Audisio R, Belkacemi Y, et al. Review of current best practice and priorities for research in radiation oncology for elderly patients with cancer: the International Society of Geriatric Oncology (SIOG) task force. *Ann Oncol.* November 2014;25(11):2134-2146.

22. Mason MD, Parulekar WR, Sydes MR, et al. Final report of the intergroup randomized study of combined androgen-deprivation therapy plus radiotherapy versus androgen-deprivation therapy alone in locally advanced prostate cancer. *J Clin Oncol.* July 1, 2015;33(19):2143-2150.

23. Bekelman JE, Mitra N, Handorf EA. Effectiveness of androgen-deprivation therapy and radiotherapy for older men with locally advanced prostate cancer. *J Clin Oncol.* March 1, 2015;33(7):716-722.

24. Bolla M, van Poppel H, Tombal B, et al. Postoperative radiotherapy after radical prostatectomy for high-risk prostate cancer: long-term results of a randomised controlled trial (EORTC trial 22911). *Lancet.* December 8, 2012;380(9858): 2018-2027.

25. Studer UE, Whelan P, Albrecht W, et al. Immediate or deferred androgen deprivation for patients with prostate cancer not suitable for local treatment with curative intent: European Organisation for Research and Treatment of Cancer (EORTC) trial 30891. *J Clin Oncol.* April 20, 2006;24(12):1868-1876.

26. Nguyen PL, Alibhai SM, Basaria S, et al. Adverse effects of androgen deprivation therapy and strategies to mitigate them. *Eur Urol.* May 2015;67(5):825-836.

27. Goineau A, d'Aillières B, de Decker L, et al. Integrating geriatric assessment into decision-making after prostatectomy: adjuvant radiotherapy, salvage radiotherapy, or none? *Front Oncol.* October 15, 2015;5:227.

28. van den Bergh RC, van Casteren NJ, van den Broeck T, et al. Role of hormonal treatment in prostate cancer patients with nonmetastatic disease recurrence after local curative treatment: a systematic review. *Eur Urol.* December 12, 2015;pii:S0302-2838(15)01178-1.

29. Bernard B, Sweeney CJ. Management of metastatic hormone-sensitive prostate cancer. *Curr Urol Rep.* March 2015;16(3):14.

30. Heidenreich A, Bastian PJ, Bellmunt J, et al. EAU guidelines on prostate cancer. Part II: treatment of advanced, relapsing, and castration-resistant prostate cancer. *Eur Urol.* February 2014;65(2):467-479.

31. Hussain M, Tangen C, Higano C, et al. Evaluating intermittent androgen-deprivation therapy phase III clinical trials: the devil is in the details. *J Clin Oncol.* January 20, 2016;34(3):280-285.

32. Miller RE, Sweeney CJ. Chemotherapy for metastatic castrate-sensitive prostate cancer. *Prostate Cancer Prostatic Dis.* June 2016;19(2):139-144.

33. Droz JP, Efstathiou E, Yildirim A, et al. First-line treatment in senior adults with metastatic castration-resistant prostate cancer: a prospective international registry. *Urol Oncol.* January 14, 2016;pii:S1078-1439(15)00583-9.

34. Veccia A, Caffo O, De Giorgi U, et al. Clinical outcomes in octogenarians treated with docetaxel as first-line chemotherapy for castration-resistant prostate cancer. *Future Oncol.* February 2016;12(4):493-502.

35. Smith MR, Rathkopf DE, Mulders PF, et al. Efficacy and safety of abiraterone acetate in elderly (75 years or older) chemotherapy naïve patients with metastatic castration resistant prostate cancer. *J Urol.* November 2015;194(5):1277-1284.

36. Sternberg CN, de Bono JS, Chi KN, et al. Improved outcomes in elderly patients with metastatic castration-resistant prostate cancer treated with the androgen receptor inhibitor enzalutamide: results from the phase III AFFIRM trial. *Ann Oncol.* February 2014;25(2):429.

37. Parker C, Nilsson S, Heinrich D, et al. Alpha emitter radium-223 and survival in metastatic prostate cancer. *N Engl J Med.* July 18, 2013;369(3):213-223.

38. Gillessen S, Omlin A, Attard G, et al. Management of patients with advanced prostate cancer: recommendations of the St Gallen Advanced Prostate Cancer Consensus Conference (APCCC) 2015. *Ann Oncol.* August 2015;26(8):1589-1604.

39. Rabow MW, Lee MX. Palliative care in castrate-resistant prostate cancer. *Urol Clin North Am.* November 2012;39(4):491-503.

17   Colorectal Cancer

Armin Shahrokni

INTRODUCTION

Every year about 140,000 patients are diagnosed with colorectal cancer (1). Older cancer patients are disproportionally affected by it. About 29% and 43% of deaths related to colorectal cancer occur in men and women older than age 80, respectively (2). Although individuals older than age 65 are minority compared to the whole population, 60% of colorectal cancer cases are diagnosed in this age group (2). Although the incidence and mortality from colorectal cancer have decreased in the aging population, due to colorectal cancer screening and surgical treatment of localized cancer, the number of older colorectal cancer patients requiring treatment still remains very high (2).

Treatment of older colorectal cancer patients presents different challenges than treatment of younger patients. In general, as patients become older, they develop more comorbid conditions, take more medications, lose their independence, and become more socially isolated. As a result, applying standard of care without addressing these issues may cause more harm rather than achieving benefit.

In this chapter, we briefly discuss the concept of frailty as it impacts chemotherapy decision making, and review some of the most common challenges that may be faced by medical oncologists taking care of older colorectal cancer patients.

INTERSECTION OF FRAILTY AND AGING-RELATED PHYSIOLOGICAL CHANGES (FIGURE 17.1)

- Geriatric assessment (GA) is a multidimensional assessment of older patients that captures their functional activity, psychosocial well-being, cognitive function, polypharmacy, and nutritional status.
- Patients with more deficits based on GA are considered to be frail.
- Less time-consuming screening versions of GA are available (3).
- Cancer treatment decision making will be based on GA and organ function of older colorectal cancer patients.

ADJUVANT TREATMENT FOR LOCALIZED COLORECTAL CANCER (FIGURE 17.2)

1. **Assessment of frailty/fitness:** Various definitions and screening tools for fitness/ frailty assessment exist. In a broad definition, a *fit patient* is a patient with no or just

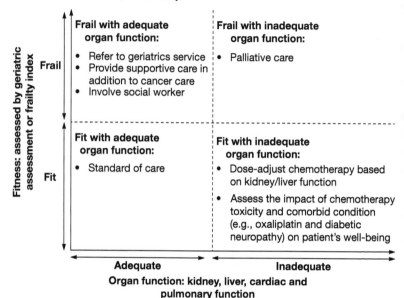

FIGURE 17.1 The impact of frailty and organ dysfunction on treatment decision making.

one comorbid condition who is independent in basic and instrumental activities of daily living (see Chapters 3 and 13).

2. **Assessment of patient's life expectancy:** Older patients are more likely to die from noncancer causes than younger patients (4). Consider administering adjuvant chemotherapy in patients with life expectancy of greater than 5 years or in those with high lymph node involvement. A comorbidity-adjusted life expectancy table (5) is useful in this assessment. Other useful methods for calculating life expectancy are the Schonberg mortality index (6), and e-prognosis (7).

3. **Chemotherapy toxicity calculators for older adults with cancer:** At least two chemotherapy toxicity prediction models have been validated among older cancer patients. In the Cancer and Aging Research Group (CARG) calculator (8), the toxicity is assessed by aging-related deficits, hemoglobin and kidney function, and the number of chemotherapy agents. In the Chemotherapy Risk Assessment Scale for High-Age Patients (CRASH) calculator (9), the risk is assessed by aging-related deficits, diastolic blood pressure, lactate dehydrogenase (LDH), and the toxicity risk associated with certain chemotherapy agents and regimens. The CRASH calculator estimates hematological and nonhematological toxicity risk, whereas the CARG calculator provides only one risk score.

4. **Capecitabine versus fluorouracil (5-FU): A**—5-FU and capecitabine have similar efficacy in improving patient outcomes (10). **B**—The decision for choosing 5-FU versus capecitabine should be based on their toxicity profiles and ease of use based on the patient's overall status. **C**—About 30% of patients only receive 1 to 4 months

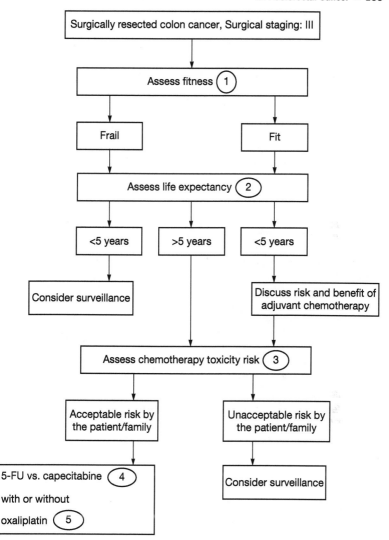

FIGURE 17.2 Treatment decision making for older cancer patients with localized colorectal cancer.

5-FU, fluorouracil.

of adjuvant chemotherapy (11). These patients are two times more likely to die compared to those who complete the adjuvant chemotherapy. This emphasizes the importance of the proper selection of older colon cancer patients for adjuvant chemotherapy, proper decision making on single versus doublet chemotherapy and 5-FU versus capecitabine, and providing support for older colon cancer patients.

5. **Use of oxaliplatin: A**—oxaliplatin has limited benefits in improving outcomes of older patients with colon cancer. The probability of 5-year survival was 75.8% for patients who received 5-FU and oxaliplatin compared to 76.1% for patients who only received 5-FU/Leucovorin (LV) (12). **B**—Despite lack of solid benefit, in the community, 50% of patients age 70 to 79, 33% of patients age 80 to 84, and 13% of patients older than age 85 have received oxaliplatin as a part of their adjuvant treatment (13). **C**—Strongly consider omitting oxaliplatin in patients with diabetes and/or diabetic neuropathy, with history of multiple falls, or with other sensory deficits (e.g., poor vision).

METASTATIC COLORECTAL CANCER; TREATMENT DECISION MAKING (FIGURE 17.3)

1. Refer to chemotherapy toxicity calculators for older adults with cancer in the previous section.
2. For selecting between single-agent 5-FU versus capecitabine or irinotecan, refer to Table 17.1.
3. For making decisions on administering oxaliplatin, refer to point 5 of the previous section.
4. One study showed that among patients unfit for standard-dose chemotherapy, starting with 80% dose-reduced chemotherapy is an acceptable option leading to less toxicity and no significant change in overall survival (14).

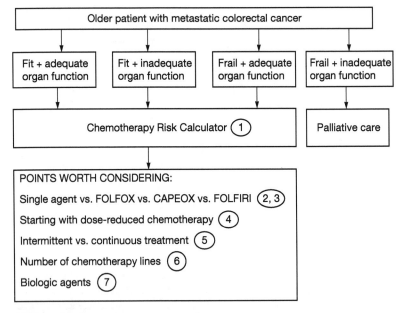

FIGURE 17.3 Treatment decision making for older patients with metastatic colorectal cancer.

TABLE 17.1 Barriers and Benefits of Capecitabine, 5-FU, and Irinotecan

	Capecitabine	**5-FU**	**Irinotecan**
Main side effect	Hand and foot syndrome	Neutropenia	Diarrhea, hair loss
Advantage	May require fewer office visits given the 3-wk schedule	Patients with poly-pharmacy are not required to take additional chemotherapy pills	No need for port placement
Not very helpful in	Patients with cognitive impairment, patients already suffering from polypharmacy	Inability to maintain port hygiene/ patients with lack of proper access for chemotherapy infusion every 2 wk	Patients concerned about hair loss
Dose adjustment	Kidney failure	Liver failure	Liver failure

5-FU, fluorouracil.

5. Two studies showed that stopping treatment after 12 weeks of treatment, and restarting the treatment after the disease progressed, does not impact patients' outcome and may lead to better quality of life (15,16).

6. A study on older patients with metastatic colon and rectal cancer who received treatment between the years 2000 and 2009 showed that the addition of three or more lines of treatment led only to an additional month of survival for patients older than age 75. For those 65 to 74 years of age, the increased survival was 6 months for colon cancer patients and 10 months for rectal cancer patients (17).

7. Adding bevacizumab to the first line of treatment leads to an increase in progression-free survival of approximately 3 months in older patients with metastatic colorectal cancer. Patients receiving bevacizumab are at higher risk for arterial thromboembolic events, gastrointestinal perforation, slower wound healing, and increase in blood pressure (18). As a result, it is important to evaluate comorbid conditions of older patients with metastatic colorectal cancer very carefully. Cetuximab and panitumumab are antibodies toward epidermal growth factor receptors. Patients with metastatic colorectal cancer with wild-type V-Ki-ras2 Kristen rat sarcoma (KRAS) status benefit from addition of cetuximab or panitumumab to combination chemotherapy (19,20). For those who progress on previous lines of chemotherapy, cetuximab or panitumumab can be used as single agent if patients have not received them before. In this setting, their benefit is about prolonging life by about 1.5 months (21) or not at all, partially explained by a crossover study (22). These agents can cause skin rash, diarrhea, and fatigue (23). In our experience, we use triplet treatment as the first line of treatment for metastatic colorectal cancer patients if they are fit and have low volume of metastatic disease; surgery is considered curative following chemotherapy.

TAKE HOME POINTS

1. Assess older colorectal cancer patients' fitness level and organ function in order to make treatment decisions.
2. Frail older patients with inadequate organ function should receive surveillance and best supportive care. If these patients have metastatic disease, they should also be offered palliative care.
3. Be cautious about the use of oxaliplatin in the adjuvant setting (limited benefit) and in metastatic disease, especially if the patient suffers from neuropathy.
4. Utilize chemotherapy toxicity calculators when deciding on number and dose of agents.
5. Administering more than two lines of chemotherapy to metastatic colorectal cancer patients older than age 75 has extremely limited benefit. Consider discussing goals of care in this setting.

REFERENCES

1. Siegel RL, Miller KD, Jemal A. Cancer statistics, 2015. *CA Cancer J Clin.* 2015;65(1):5-29.
2. Siegel R, DeSantis C, Jemal A. Colorectal cancer statistics, 2014. *CA Cancer J Clin.* 2014;64(2):104-117.
3. Wildiers H, Heeren P, Puts M, et al. International Society of Geriatric Oncology Consensus on geriatric assessment in older patients with cancer. *J Clin Oncol.* 2014; 32(24):2595-2603.
4. Sargent DJ, Goldberg RM, Jacobson SD, et al. A pooled analysis of adjuvant chemotherapy for resected colon cancer in elderly patients. *N Engl J Med.* 2001;345(15):1091-1097.
5. Cho H, Klabunde CN, Yabroff KR, et al. Comorbidity-adjusted life expectancy: a new tool to inform recommendations for optimal screening strategies. *Ann Intern Med.* 2013;159(10):667-676.
6. Schonberg MA, Davis RB, McCarthy EP, Marcantonio ER. External validation of an index to predict up to 9-year mortality of community-dwelling adults aged 65 and older. *J Am Geriatr Soc.* 2011;59(8):1444-1451.
7. Diab SG, Elledge RM, Clark GM. Tumor characteristics and clinical outcome of elderly women with breast cancer. *J Natl Cancer Inst.* 2000;92(7):550-556.
8. Rollig C, Thiede C, Gramatzki M, et al. A novel prognostic model in elderly patients with acute myeloid leukemia: results of 909 patients entered into the prospective AML96 trial. *Blood.* 2010;116(6):971-918.
9. Luciani A, Balducci L. Multiple primary malignancies. *Semin Oncol.* 2004;31(2):264-273.
10. Twelves C, Wong A, Nowacki MP, et al. Capecitabine as adjuvant treatment for stage III colon cancer. *N Engl J Med.* 2005;352(26):2696-2704.
11. Neugut AI, Matasar M, Wang X, et al. Duration of adjuvant chemotherapy for colon cancer and survival among the elderly. *J Clin Oncol.* 2006;24(15):2368-2375.

12. Tournigand C, André T, Bonnetain F, et al. Adjuvant therapy with fluorouracil and oxaliplatin in stage II and elderly patients (between ages 70 and 75 years) with colon cancer: subgroup analyses of the Multicenter International Study of Oxaliplatin, Fluorouracil, and Leucovorin in the Adjuvant Treatment of Colon Cancer trial. *J Clin Oncol.* 2012;30(27):3353-3360.

13. Lund JL, Stürmer T, Sanoff HK, et al. Determinants of adjuvant oxaliplatin receipt among older stage II and III colorectal cancer patients. *Cancer.* 2013;119(11): 2038-2047.

14. Seymour MT, Thompson LC, Wasan HS, et al. Chemotherapy options in elderly and frail patients with metastatic colorectal cancer (MRC FOCUS2): an open-label, randomised factorial trial. *Lancet.* 2011;377(9779):1749-1759.

15. Maughan TS, James RD, Kerr DJ, et al. Comparison of intermittent and continuous palliative chemotherapy for advanced colorectal cancer: a multicentre randomised trial. *Lancet.* 2003;361(9356):457-464.

16. Adams RA, Meade AM, Seymour MT, et al. Intermittent versus continuous oxaliplatin and fluoropyrimidine combination chemotherapy for first-line treatment of advanced colorectal cancer: results of the randomised phase 3 MRC COIN trial. *Lancet Oncol.* 2011;12(7):642-653.

17. Bradley CJ, Yabroff KR, Warren JL, et al. Trends in the treatment of metastatic colon and rectal cancer in elderly patients. *Med Care.* 2016;54(5):490-497.

18. Kabbinavar FF, Hurwitz HI, Yi J, et al. Addition of bevacizumab to fluorouracil-based first-line treatment of metastatic colorectal cancer: pooled analysis of cohorts of older patients from two randomized clinical trials. *J Clin Oncol.* 2009;27(2):199-205.

19. Van Cutsem E, Köhne CH, Láng I, et al. Cetuximab plus irinotecan, fluorouracil, and leucovorin as first-line treatment for metastatic colorectal cancer: updated analysis of overall survival according to tumor KRAS and BRAF mutation status. *J Clin Oncol.* 2011:29(15):2011-2019.

20. Douillard JY, Siena S, Cassidy J, et al. Randomized, phase III trial of panitumumab with infusional fluorouracil, leucovorin, and oxaliplatin (FOLFOX4) versus FOL-FOX4 alone as first-line treatment in patients with previously untreated metastatic colorectal cancer: the PRIME study. *J Clin Oncol.* 2010;28(31):4697-4705.

21. Jonker DJ, O'Callaghan CJ, Karapetis CS, et al. Cetuximab for the treatment of colorectal cancer. *N Engl J Med.* 2007;357(20):2040-2048.

22. Hecht JR, Patnaik A, Berlin J, et al. Panitumumab monotherapy in patients with previously treated metastatic colorectal cancer. *Cancer.* 2007;110(5):980-988.

23. Widakowich C, de Castro G, Jr, de Azambuja E, et al. Review: side effects of approved molecular targeted therapies in solid cancers. *Oncologist.* 2007;12(12):1443-1455.

Lung Cancer

Shreya Sinha, Mariam Alexander, and Ajeet Gajra

INTRODUCTION

Lung cancer is the leading cause of cancer death in the United States (1). It was estimated that 224,390 new cases of lung cancer would be diagnosed in 2016, with 158,080 deaths expected. Even though lung cancer accounts for 14% of all new cancer diagnoses, it is the leading cause of cancer-related mortality in both men and women. In addition, more than 50% of lung cancers are diagnosed in patients aged 65 and older; less than 2% of cases occur in individuals less than 45 years of age (1,2).

PATHOPHYSIOLOGY

Lung cancer can be broadly divided into non–small-cell lung cancer (NSCLC) and small cell lung cancer (SCLC) based on the cell type of origin. Malignant transformation of neuroendocrine cells leads to SCLC, whereas NSCLC originates from epithelial cells. Based on histopathological analysis, NSCLC is further classified into broad categories of adenocarcinoma, squamous cell carcinoma, and large cell carcinoma, with adenocarcinoma accounting for more than half of all cases of lung cancer (3). There are numerous molecular pathways involved in the pathogenesis of NSCLC. Of these, mutations in genes encoding epidermal growth factor receptor (EGFR) and anaplastic lymphoma kinase (ALK) are best characterized for targeted therapies (4). Other proteins that are currently targeted in NSCLC, albeit at lower frequencies, include ROS1, HER2, BRAF, MET, and RET (5,6). While EGFR mutations are commonly encountered in older patients, especially women with no smoking history, recent data analyzing NSCLC suggest that overall, older patients may be more likely to harbor MET mutations than EGFR or KRAS mutations (7). There are no currently available inhibitors against the MET pathway, though trials are ongoing.

CLINICAL FEATURES

Signs and symptoms that are initially encountered in the patient will depend on the subtype, location, and distant metastasis. Presenting symptoms in the elderly may include weight loss, chest pain, ongoing cough, dyspnea, chronic pneumonia, or hemoptysis (8). Mediastinal involvement can manifest as superior vena cava syndrome, pericardial effusion, pleural effusion, and dysphagia. Apical growth or Pancoast tumor can cause brachial plexus compression and Horner syndrome. Paraneoplastic syndromes can be seen in both SCLC (e.g., Cushing syndrome, syndrome of inappropriate antidiuretic hormone secretion [SIADH]) and NSCLC (hypercalcemia, hypertrophic osteoarthropathy, and digital clubbing) (9). Frequent sites of metastasis are brain, bone, liver, and adrenal glands.

INITIAL EVALUATION AND STAGING

All patients with lung cancer, especially those with early stage, potentially operable disease, should undergo a PET/CT scan to evaluate mediastinal and occult disease. A cytologic or histopathological evaluation of the tumor is necessary for diagnosis and molecular analysis of the cancer. Tissue can be obtained through flexible bronchoscopy, transthoracic needle biopsy, or pleural fluid analysis. Mediastinal nodal sampling can be accomplished by mediastinoscopy or endobronchial ultrasound (EBUS)-guided nodal sampling. Tumor factors (stage, histological subtype, specific molecular profile) and patient factors (performance status [PS]; comorbidity, nutritional, cognitive, and psychological status; as well as social support) dictate treatment options, likely outcomes, and overall prognosis, especially in the elderly. This is the reason geriatric assessment (GA) tools, as described later in the chapter, can assist clinicians and patients with treatment decisions. Lung cancer is staged based on the TNM system where T defines the extent of the tumor, N is regional lymph node involvement, and M is metastasis (10). Historically, SCLC was staged as limited and extensive stage. *Limited stage* is defined as tumor being confined to one hemithorax and ipsilateral lymph nodes, which can be included in a single radiation port; tumor extent beyond this definition is designated as *extensive stage*.

MANAGEMENT

Management strategies for NSCLC vary depending on the stage (Table 18.1).

Early Stage NSCLC: Stages I and II

The primary modality of treatment for stage I disease is surgical resection. In a Surveillance, Epidemiology, and End Results (SEER) database study, lobectomy was found to have better long-term survival rates compared to sublobar resection, conventional radiation, observation, and stereotactic body radiation therapy (SBRT) (10). However, the elderly population is offered surgery less often due to poor postsurgical outcomes secondary to age (11,12).

Stage II disease has limited regional spread of the tumor and is still amenable to surgery with the addition of adjuvant platinum-based chemotherapy. All patients with stage II or III and stage IB (≥4 cm) should be offered platinum-based adjuvant chemotherapy for four cycles. Of the trials done to establish the efficacy of adjuvant chemotherapy in patients with early stage NCSLC, none had adequate representation of the elderly (13–15). Age-based post hoc analysis of the patients from these trials did demonstrate an overall survival benefit in the elderly patients who received adjuvant platinum-based therapy (Table 18.2). A separate pooled analysis of elderly patients

TABLE 18.1 Treatment Options for NSCLC Based on Staging for the Elderly

Stages	Stage IA/IB	Stage IIA/IIB	Stage IIIA/IIIB	Stage IV
	Early	Early with limited spread	Locally/regionally advanced	Distant metastasis
First-line therapy	Surgery	Surgery followed by adjuvant chemotherapy (cisplatin-based)	For tumors not amenable to surgery, concurrent chemoradiation	Cytotoxic chemotherapy with or without biologic/targeted therapy
Alternate therapy	Radiation or SBRT	■ If not a surgical candidate, radiation ± chemotherapy ■ Cisplatin-based adjuvant chemotherapy after surgery; carboplatin-based if not candidate for cisplatin	■ Radiation then chemotherapy ■ Radiation therapy with curative or palliative intent	Palliative care

NSCLC, non–small-cell lung cancer; SBRT, stereotactic body radiation therapy.

TABLE 18.2 Major Trials of Adjuvant Chemotherapy in NSCLC

Trial (Ref.)	ANITA (14)	IALT (12)	JBR.10 (13)
Total (n)	840	1867	482
Age >65–69 (%)	170 (20)	328 (18)	84 (17)
Age >70 (%)	64 (8)	168 (9)	71 (15)
Stage Inclusion	IB-IIIA	I-III	IB-II
PS Inclusion	0–2	0–2	0,1
Cisplatin dose in mg/sqm	400	300–400	400
OS Increase at 5 y (%)	8.6	4.1	15

ANITA, Adjuvant Navelbine International Trialist Association; IALT, International Adjuvant Lung Cancer Trial; NSCLC, non–small-cell lung cancer; OS, overall survival; PS, performance status.

A subset analysis of all three studies mentioned earlier showed survival advantage for older adults when they received platinum-based doublet as adjuvant therapy.

receiving adjuvant cisplatin-based chemotherapy revealed no difference in toxicity rates in the elderly (>70) compared to young patients (<65) (16). There was significant benefit despite reduction in dose due to toxicity. Platinum-based chemotherapy is now the standard of care in elderly patients except in patients aged 80 or older, a group that has not been studied (17,18). It is reasonable to consider carboplatin-based chemotherapy in the elderly who have contraindications to cisplatin (19).

SBRT: SBRT is a treatment option for inoperable early stage NSCLC. SBRT uses small, focused radiation beams tracking the tumor, typically in three to five treatments. In a study of elderly patients with T1-T3N0M0 NSCLC, SBRT was shown to lower risk of death compared to those who did not receive any treatment; thus, SBRT should be offered to patients who are not candidates for surgical resection (20).

Locally Advanced Disease: Stage III

Almost a third of NSCLC patients have stage III or locally advanced disease (2). In the United States, a minority of such patients undergo resection depending on tumor volume, lung function, comorbidity, and PS, and these patients should be offered adjuvant chemotherapy. The gold standard for patients with good PS irrespective of age is concurrent chemoradiotherapy. In age-unspecified trials, older patients with good PS have shown improved survival with chemoradiation compared to radiation alone, although elderly-specific prospective trials are scarce (21–23). Concurrent chemoradiation can be complicated by radiation esophagitis; thus, special attention to nutritional status is essential. Other acute complications include myelosuppression and infections, and esophageal stricture, malnutrition, and radiation pneumonitis can occur later in the course. Frail elderly with high comorbid burden are not candidates for concurrent chemoradiation and should be treated with radiation therapy alone (24).

Metastatic/Palliative Disease: Stage IV NSCLC

Treatment options for stage IV disease are either single-agent chemotherapy or platinum-based doublet cytotoxic therapy based on the patient's PS. It has been shown that single-agent chemotherapy improves outcomes in elderly patient compared to best supportive care alone (25). Data are conflicting regarding benefit of chemotherapy doublets, although one trial limited to the elderly did demonstrate benefit for a paclitaxel and carboplatin combination compared to single-agent chemotherapy in fit elderly (26–29) (Table 18.3). There are no data specific to the elderly regarding the use of maintenance chemotherapy. The role of bevacizumab is limited because older patients do not appear to derive the same amount of benefit as younger patients and suffer more toxicity (30). All patients with advanced adenocarcinoma of the lung should be tested for mutations in the EGFR, ALK, and ROS1 genes. If such driver mutations are detected, then an appropriate oral targeted agent should be the first line of therapy: EGFR (erlotinib, gefitinib or afatanib), ALK (crizotinib, ceritinib, or alcetinib), and ROS1 (crizotinib).

Immunotherapy in Older Adults for NSCLC

The recent advent of immune checkpoint inhibition for NSCLC has offered additional treatment options. These inhibitors work to enhance the response of the immune system to tumor cells by targeting proteins that regulate the immune system, such as

TABLE 18.3 Important Trials Specific to Elderly in Advanced NSCLC

Study, Year of Publication (Ref.)	Total n	Regimen	Median OS (month)
ELVIS, 1999 (25)	161	Vinorelbine vs. BSC	6.5* 4.9
Frascl et al., 2000 (26)	120	Gem + Vin vs. Vin	6.7* 4.2
Gridelli et al., MILES trial (27)	698	Gem Vin vs. Gem+ Vin	5.1 4.0 4.3
WJCOG0803/WJOG4307L, 2011 (28)	276	Doc vs. Doc + Cis	17.3 13.3
IFCT-0501, 2011 (29)	451	Pac + Carbo vs. Vin or Gem	10.3* 6.2

Carbo, carboplatin; Cis, cisplatin; Doc, docetaxel; Gem, gemcitabine; MILES, Multicenter Italian Lung cancer in the Elderly Study; NSCLC, non–small-cell lung cancer; Pac, paclitaxel; Vin, vinorelbine.

*Statistically significant difference.

programmed cell death protein 1 (PD-1). In two recently reported trials, one limited to patients with squamous NSCLC and the other to nonsquamous NSCLC, patients with progression after chemotherapy were randomized to a PD-1 antibody (nivolumab) or docetaxel (31,32). In these trials, 42% to 44% of patients were aged more than 65 and 7% to 11% were older than 75 years of age. Nivolumab was associated with improved overall survival in both trials (9.2 vs. 6 months in squamous, $P < .001$ and 12.2 vs. 9.4 months in nonsquamous trial, $P = .002$). Pembrolizumab, another anti-PD-1 monoclonal antibody, was recently approved as first-line treatment of untreated advanced NSCLC with PD-L1 expression on at least 50% of tumor cells, based on higher progression-free survival and response rates when compared to platinum-based chemotherapy (33). In this trial, 54% patients were age 65 or older and experienced the same benefit with immunotherapy as younger patients. Although the toxicity profile of these agents differs from that of cytotoxic chemotherapy, these are fairly well tolerated in older adults with good PS.

Small Cell Lung Cancer

Although SCLC has a lower rate of incidence (12%–15% of all lung cancer), it is more aggressive and has higher rates of recurrence. There has been little improvement in the enrollment of older adults to trials in SCLC over the past two decades (34). SCLC is more chemosensitive compared to NSCLC. The cornerstone in the treatment of SCLC is chemotherapy with a platinum agent (cisplatin or carboplatin) combined with a topoisomerase inhibitor (etoposide or irinotecan). Thoracic radiation is added concurrently for limited-stage disease in patients with good PS. Given the high toxicity associated with cisplatin (emetogenecity, ototoxicity, neuropathy, and nephrotoxicity), carboplatin is commonly substituted for older adults. SCLC has a high propensity to metastasize to the brain and hence prophylactic cranial irradiation is recommended in patients with limited disease with good response to chemotherapy. The Food and Drug Administration (FDA)-approved second-line agent topotecan has limited efficacy and high toxicity. Other agents, like taxanes and gemcitabine, may be used with palliative intent in the relapse setting. The combination of immunotherapeutic agents nivolumab and ipilumumab has shown some early promise in relapsed disease (35).

GA TOOLS

GA and its abridged versions can assist in risk stratification and thus improve decision making and outcomes in elderly patients with lung cancer. Various GA domains have been associated with poor survival in lung cancer, including Eastern Cooperative Oncology Group (ECOG) PS, instrumental activity of daily living (IADL) I dependency, dementia, depression, weight loss, albumin level, and frailty (36). In a study specific to elderly with advanced NSCLC, higher scores for pretreatment quality of life and IADLs were associated with better prognosis, whereas another found association between comorbidity and survival (26,37). In early stage disease, preoperative GA can predict postoperative morbidity and mortality: In a prospective study, preoperative cognitive dysfunction increased the risk for postoperative complications, delirium, and dependency for activities of daily living (ADLs) (38). In one study, it changed therapeutic decisions in half of the vulnerable patients with lung cancer (39). Though not specific to lung cancer, other GA-based tools have demonstrated the ability to predict chemotherapy-associated toxicity in the elderly, allowing for improved decision making and limiting toxicity (40,41). A multicenter trial confirmed that there is decreased toxicity with no decrement in survival when GA-based treatment allocation strategy is used in elderly patients with advanced lung cancer (42). Because these assessment tools have shown good predictive ability for toxicity, it is recommended that some form of GA be included in the initial assessment of an older adult.

ROLE OF PALLIATIVE CARE

Currently, palliative care is typically consulted only in later stages and late in the course of disease. However, studies have shown that early utilization of palliative care is associated with improvement in mood, quality of life, and survival (43). These findings may have some variations based on age and gender (44).

SCREENING RECOMMENDATIONS

Smoking causes 85% to 90% of lung cancers (45). The National Lung Screening Trial found that low-dose CT screening significantly reduces mortality from lung cancer (46). The United States Preventive Services Task Force now recommends annual low-dose helical CT scan of the thorax for patients age 55 to 80 with a history of smoking at least 30 pack-years, or if they were previous smokers and have quit within the past 15 years (47). Plain chest radiograph has been shown to be an ineffective tool for screening and should not be used (48).

TAKE HOME POINTS

1. Older adults with good PS (ECOG 0, 1) should be treated like their younger counterparts.
2. GA-based tools should be utilized by clinicians for better risk stratification and to aid with treatment decision making.
3. Older patients should be treated with an appropriate targeted agent in the setting of a targetable mutation, as well as immunotherapy when indicated.
4. Early integration of palliative care is an important intervention in the appropriate management of patients with advanced lung cancer, especially older adults.
5. Lung cancer screening for risk-defined patients up to 80 years of age is recommended.

REFERENCES

1. Siegel RL, Miller KD, Jemal A. Cancer statistics, 2016. *CA Cancer J Clin.* 2016;66(1):7-30.
2. American Cancer Society. *Cancer Facts & Figures 2016.* Atlanta, GA: American Cancer Society; 2016.
3. Molina JR, Yang P, Cassivi SD, et al. Non–small cell lung cancer: epidemiology, risk factors, treatment, and survivorship. *Mayo Clin Proc.* May 2008;83(5):584-594.
4. Roviello G. The distinctive nature of adenocarcinoma of the lung. *Onco Targets Ther.* September 2, 2015;8:2399-2406.
5. Herbst RS, Heymach JV, Lippman SM. Lung cancer. *N Engl J Med.* September 25, 2008;359:1367-1380.
6. Larsen JE, Minna JD. Molecular biology of lung cancer: clinical implications. *Clin Chest Med.* December 2011;32:703-740.
7. Awad MM, Oxnard GR, Jackman DM, et al. MET Exon 14 mutations in non–small-cell lung cancer are associated with advanced age and stage-dependent MET genomic amplification and c-Met overexpression. *J Clin Oncol.* March 1, 2016;34(7):721-730. doi:10.1200/JCO.2015.63.4600. Epub 2016 January 4. PMID: 26729443.
8. Nadpara P, Madhavan SS, Tworek C. Guideline concordant timely lung cancer care and prognosis among elderly patients in the United States: a population-based study. *Cancer Epidemiol.* December 2015;39:1136-1144.
9. Pelosof LC, Gerber DE. Paraneoplastic syndromes: an approach to diagnosis and treatment. *Mayo Clin Proc.* September 2010;85:838-854.
10. Nicholson AG, Chansky K, Crowley J, et al. The International Association for the Study of Lung Cancer lung cancer staging project: proposals for the revision of the clinical and pathologic staging of small cell lung cancer in the forthcoming eighth edition of the TNM classification for lung cancer. *J Thorac Oncol.* March 2016;11(3):300-311.
11. Shrivani S, Jiang J, Chang JY, et al. Comparative effectiveness of 5 treatment strategies for early-stage non-small cell lung cancer in the elderly. *Int J Radiat Oncol Biol Phys.* 2012;84:1060-1070.

12. Mery CM, Pappas AN, Bueno R, et al. Similar long-term survival of elderly patients with non–small cell lung cancer treated with lobectomy or wedge resection within the surveillance, epidemiology, and end result database. *Chest.* 2005;128:237-245.

13. Arriagada R, Bergman B, Dunant A, et al. Cisplatin-based adjuvant chemotherapy in patients with completely resected non-small-cell lung cancer. *N Engl J Med.* 2004;350:351-360.

14. Winton T, Livingston R, Johnson D, et al. Vinorelbine plus cisplatin vs. observation in resected non-small-cell lung cancer. *N Engl J Med.* 2005;352:2589-2597.

15. Douillard JY, Rosell R, De Lena M, et al. Adjuvant vinorelbine plus cisplatin versus observation in patients with completely resected stage IB–IIIA non-small-cell lung cancer (Adjuvant Navelbine International Trialist Association [ANITA]): a randomized controlled trial. *Lancet Oncol.* 2006;7(9):719-727.

16. Fruh M, Rolland E, Pignon J-P, et al. Pooled analysis of the effect of age on adjuvant cisplatin based chemotherapy for completely resected non-small cell lung cancer. *J Clin Oncol.* 2008;26:3573-3581.

17. Poudel A, Sinha S, Gajra A. Navigating the challenges of adjuvant chemotherapy in older patients with early-stage non-small cell lung cancer. *Drugs Aging.* April 2016;33(4):223-232. doi:10.1007/s40266-016-0350-9.

18. Cuffe S, Booth CM, Peng Y, et al. Adjuvant chemotherapy for non-small cell lung cancer in the elderly: a population-based study in Ontario, Canada. *J Clin Oncol.* 2012;30(15):1813-1821.

19. Ganti AK, Williams CD, Gajra A, Kelley MJ. Effect of age on the efficacy of adjuvant chemotherapy for resected non-small cell lung cancer. *Cancer.* August 1, 2015;121(15):2578-2585.

20. Nanda RH, Liu Y, Gillespie TW, et al. Stereotactic body radiation therapy versus no treatment for early stage non-small cell lung cancer in medically inoperable elderly patients: a National Cancer Data Base analysis. *Cancer.* De 1, 2015;121(23):4222-4230.

21. Schild SE, Mandrekar SJ, Jatoi A, et al. The value of combined-modality therapy in elderly patients with stage III nonsmall cell lung cancer. *Cancer.* 2007;110(2):363-368.

22. Rocha-Lima CM, Herndon JE, Kosty M, et al. Therapy choices among older patients with lung carcinoma: an evaluation of two trials of the Cancer and Leukemia Group B. *Cancer* 2002;94(1):181-187.

23. Atagi S, Kawahara M, Yokoyama A, et al. Thoracic radiotherapy with or without daily low-dose carboplatin in elderly patients with non-small-cell lung cancer: a randomised, controlled, phase 3 trial by the Japan Clinical Oncology Group (JCOG0301). *Lancet Oncol.* 2012;13(7):671-678.

24. Lee JH, Wu HG, Kim HJ, et al. Influence of comorbidities on the efficacy of radiotherapy with or without chemotherapy in elderly stage III non-small cell lung cancer patients. *Cancer Res Treat.* 2012;44:242-250.

25. Gridelli C. Effects of vinorelbine on quality of life and survival of elderly patients with advanced non-small-cell lung cancer: The Elderly Lung Cancer Vinorelbine Italian Study Group. *J Natl Cancer Inst.* 1999;91:66-72.

26. Frasci G, Lorusso V, Panza N, et al. Gemcitabine plus vinorelbine versus vinorelbine alone in elderly patients with advanced non-small-cell lung cancer. *J Clin Oncol.* 2000;18(13): 2529-2536.

27. Gridelli C, Perrone F, Gallo C, et al. Chemotherapy for elderly patients with advanced nonsmall-cell lung cancer: the Multicenter Italian Lung Cancer in the Elderly Study (MILES) phase III randomized trial. *J Natl Cancer Inst.* 2003;95:362-372.

28. Abe T, Yokoyama A, Takeda K, Ohe Y. Randomized phase III trial comparing weekly docetaxel (D)-cisplatin (P) combination with triweekly D alone in elderly patients (pts) with advanced non-small cell lung cancer (NSCLC): an intergroup trial of JCOG0803/WJOG4307L. *J Clin Oncol.* 2011;29(suppl 15). Abstract 7509.

29. Quoix E, Zalcman G, Oster JP, et al. Carboplatin and weekly paclitaxel doublet chemotherapy compared with monotherapy in elderly patients with advanced non-small-cell lung cancer: IFCT-0501 randomised, phase 3 trial. *Lancet.* 2011;378:1079-1088.

30. Ramalingam SS, Dahlberg SE, Langer CJ, et al. Outcomes for elderly, advanced-stage non small-cell lung cancer patients treated with bevacizumab in combination with carboplatin and paclitaxel: analysis of Eastern Cooperative Oncology Group Trial 4599. *J Clin Oncol.* 2008;26:60-65.

31. Brahmer J, Reckamp KL, Baas P, et al. Nivolumab versus docetaxel in advanced squamous-cell non-small-cell lung cancer. *N Engl J Med.* July 9, 2015;373(2): 123-135.

32. Borghaei H, Paz-Ares L, Horn L. Nivolumab versus docetaxel in advanced nonsquamous non-small-cell lung cancer. *N Engl J Med.* October 22, 2015;373(17):1627-1639.

33. Reck M, Rodríguez-Abreu D, Robinson AG, et al. Pembrolizumab versus chemotherapy for PD-L1-positive non-small-cell lung cancer. *N Engl J Med.* October 8, 2016;375:1823-1833.

34. Pang HH, Wang X, Stinchcombe TE, et al. Enrollment trends and disparity among patients with lung cancer in National Clinical Trials, 1990 to 2012. *J Clin Oncol.* September 19, 2016;pii:JCO677088. [Epub ahead of print]

35. Antonia SJ, López-Martin JA, Bendell J, et al. Nivolumab alone and nivolumab plus ipilimumab in recurrent small-cell lung cancer (CheckMate 032): a multicentre, open-label, phase 1/2 trial. *Lancet Oncol.* July 2016;17(7):883-895. doi:10.1016/S1470-2045(16)30098-5.

36. Gironés R, Torregrosa D, Maestu I, et al. Comprehensive Geriatric Assessment (CGA) of elderly lung cancer patients: a single-center experience. *J Geriatr Oncol.* 2012;3(2):98-103.

37. Maione P. Pretreatment quality of life and functional status assessment significantly predict survival of elderly patients with advanced non-small-cell lung cancer receiving chemotherapy: a prognostic analysis of the multicenter Italian lung cancer in the elderly study. *J Clin Oncol.* 2005;23(28):6865-6872.

38. Fukuse, T, Naoki S, Kyoko H, Fujinaga T. Importance of a comprehensive geriatric assessment in prediction of complications following thoracic surgery in elderly patients. *Chest.* 2005;127(3):886-891.

39. Aliamus V, Adam C, Druet-Cabanac M, et al. Geriatric assessment contribution to treatment decision-making in thoracic oncology. *Rev Mal Respir* 2011;28(9):1124-1130.

40. Hurria A, Togawa K, Mohile SG, et al. Predicting chemotherapy toxicity in older adults with cancer: a prospective multicenter study. *J Clin Oncol.* September 1, 2011;29(25):3457-3465.

41. Extermann M, Boler I, Reich RR, et al. Predicting the risk of chemotherapy toxicity in older patients: the Chemotherapy Risk Assessment Scale for High-Age Patients (CRASH) score. *Cancer.* July 1, 2012;118(13):3377-3386.

42. Corre R, Greillier L, Le Caër H, et al. Use of a comprehensive geriatric assessment for the management of elderly patients with advanced non-small-cell lung cancer: the phase III randomized ESOGIA-GFPC-GECP 08-02 study. *J Clin Oncol.* 2016;34(13):1476-1483.

43. Temel J, Greer J, Muzikansky A, et al. Early palliative care for patients with metastatic non–small-cell lung cancer. *N Engl J Med.* 2010;363:733-742.

44. Nipp RD, Greer JA, El-Jawahri A, et al. Age and gender moderate the impact of early palliative care in metastatic non-small cell lung cancer. *Oncologist.* January 2016;21(1):119-126. doi:10.1634/theoncologist.2015-0232.

45. Alberg AJ, Samet JM. Epidemiology of lung cancer. *Chest.* 2003;123(suppl 1):21S.

46. National Lung Screening Trial Research Team. Reduced lung-cancer mortality with low-dose computed tomographic screening. *N Engl J Med.* 2011;365(5):395-409.

47. U.S. Preventive Services Task Force. Final Recommendation Statement: Lung Cancer: Screening. July 2015. Available at: http://www.uspreventiveservicestaskforce.org/Page/Document/UpdateSummaryFinal/lung-cancer-screening.

48. Manser R, Lethaby A, Irving LB, et al. Screening for lung cancer. *Cochrane Database Syst Rev.* 2013;6:CD001991.

Ovarian Cancer in the Older Woman

William P. Tew

BACKGROUND

Ovarian cancer is recognized as a disease of aging, with more than 30% of new cases being diagnosed in women older than 70 (1). The rate of older women with ovarian cancer is expected to increase as our population ages and life expectancy improves (2–4). Outcomes steadily worsen with aging: the relative survival rates at 1 year are 57% for women aged 65 to 69 years, 45% for those aged 70 to 74 years, and 33% for those aged 80 to 84 years (5). Various theories have been put forward to account for the decreased survival in older women, including: (a) more aggressive cancer biology with higher grade and more advanced stage; (b) inherent resistance to chemotherapy; (c) patient factors leading to greater toxicity with therapy such as multiple concurrent medical problems, polypharmacy, functional dependence, cognitive impairment, depression, frailty, and poor nutrition; and (d) physician and health care biases that lead to inadequate surgery, suboptimal chemotherapy, and poor enrollment in clinical trials (6). Guidelines have been developed to help inform oncologists about caring for the older adult (7).

GERIATRIC ASSESSMENT

Geriatric assessment (GA) provides clinicians with information about a patient's functional status, comorbid medical conditions, cognition, psychological status, social functioning and support, and nutritional status (refer to Chapter 13). Several studies have demonstrated the predictive value of GA for estimating the risk of severe toxicity from chemotherapy and surgery (8,9). GA instruments used specifically for women with gynecological cancer (see Table 19.1) include the Cancer and Aging Research Group (CARG) score (9,10), Geriatric Vulnerability Scale (11), instrumental activities of daily living (IADLs) in GOG 273 (12), and the Gynecologic Oncology Group (GOG) GA/Preoperative Scores. Functional assessment specifically with IADLs appears to be most predictive and is included in all the scores.

TABLE 19.1 GA Tools Used in Clinical Trials for Older Ovarian Cancer Patients

	NRG-CC002: GOG Preoperative Assessment Study	GOG 273 IADL Score	NRG-GOG GAS	GINECO: GVS
Setting	Preoperative	Prechemotherapy	Prechemotherapy	Prechemotherapy
Population	GOG study underway. Newly diagnosed ovarian cancer older than 70 y.	GOG 273 Arm 1 and 2 Newly diagnosed ovarian cancer older than 70 y.	GOG 273 Arm 3 Newly diagnosed ovarian cancer older than 70 y.	
Variables	Measures to be collected: 1. Function (ADL, IADL, PS, Fall Hx) 2. Comorbidity (physical health section of OARS) 3. Psychological (Mental Health Inventory-17) 4. Social activity/support (MOS surveys) 5. Brief Fatigue Inventory 6. Nutrition (BMI, weight loss) 7. Medication list A GYN-GA score will be calculated same as CARG model EXCEPT the following variables are removed: cancer type (GI or GU), standard dosing, and poly-chemotherapy.		Measures to be collected: 1. Function (ADL, IADL, PS) 2. Comorbidity (Charlson Score, hearing loss, falls) 3. FACT-O 4. FACT/ GOG-NTX-4 5. Nutrition (BMI, weight loss) GA score same as CARG model EXCEPT the following variables are removed: cancer type (GI or GU), standard dosing, and poly-chemotherapy	If yes to below—a graded value is added to a toxicity score (GVS): 1. low albumin (<35 g/L) 2. low ADL score (<6) 3. low IADL score (<25) 4. Lymphopenia (<1G/L) 5. HADS score (>14)
Study conclusion	Final report underway.		Final report underway.	Accrual underway.

ADL, activities of daily living; BMI, body mass index; CARG, Cancer and Aging Research Group; FACT-O, functional assessment of cancer therapy for ovarian cancer; FACT/GOG-NTX-4, functional assessment of cancer therapy for neurotoxicity; GA, Geriatric Assessment; GI, gastrointestinal; GOG, Gynecologic Oncology Group; GU, genitourinary; GVS, geriatric vulnerability score; HADS, Hospital Anxiety and Depression Scale; Hx, history; IADL, instrumental activities of daily living; MOS, medical outcomes study; OARS, older American resources and services; PS, performance status.

SURGERY

Surgery plus platinum-based chemotherapy are standard treatments for women with advanced ovarian cancer. Older patients, particularly those older than 80 years, are less likely to receive any surgery at all, and those who undergo surgery develop higher surgical morbidity, achieve lower rates of optimal cytoreduction, and likely did not see a specialized gynecologic oncologist (13,14). A Surveillance, Epidemiology, and End Results (SEER) analysis of older women who underwent primary cytoreductive surgery (CRS) ($n = 4,517$) showed a 30-day mortality of 5.6%. Those admitted emergently had a 30-day mortality of 20.1%. Those aged 75 and older with either stage IV disease or stage III disease and a comorbidity score of 1 or more had a 30-day mortality of 12.7% even when admitted electively (15). In addition, there is concern that toxicities of surgery may prevent older women from receiving chemotherapy. One retrospective report on 85 patients over the age of 80 undergoing CRS (mostly primary) showed that 13% died prior to discharge and 20% died within 60 days of surgery. Thirteen percent never received adjuvant therapy, and of those treated 43% completed less than three cycles of therapy (16).

These and other data on the increased toxicity of primary CRS in the elderly have led to the increased use of neoadjuvant chemotherapy (NACT) and interval CRS in older patients. The ability to assess who is fit enough to undergo aggressive CRS followed by chemotherapy and who should be offered an alternative pathway such as NACT and interval CRS or primary chemotherapy alone is an unmet need. Aletti identified a high-risk group of women who do not appear to benefit from primary surgery. Risk features included stage IV disease, high initial tumor distribution, poor performance status (PS) (ASA score ≥ 3), poor nutritional status (albumin < 3.0g/dL), and older age (≤75 years) (17). Although each patient plan must be individualized, at this time it is reasonable to use these criteria as guidelines for a NACT approach. The American Society of Oncology (ASCO) and Society of Gynecologic Oncology (SGO) jointly developed guidelines to help oncologists select patients for primary surgery versus NACT (18).

CHEMOTHERAPY

Background

First-line chemotherapy improves survival in older women with ovarian cancer. Platinum-based chemotherapy among women over 65 years was associated with a 38% improvement in survival outcomes compared with the use of no chemotherapy (18, 19). However, only half of this population received platinum-based chemotherapy. A SEER review, which included almost 8,000 women older than 65 years with stage III or IV epithelial ovarian cancer, suggested that while patients who underwent surgery only had similar survival compared with patients who received no treatment (2.2 vs. 1.7 months), patients receiving chemotherapy as the sole treatment for their disease had a better overall survival (OS) (14.4 months) (20). Those who received debulking surgery and optimal chemotherapy (six cycles within an appropriate time frame) had the best OS (39 months), an association that was maintained after multivariate analysis controlling for demographics, cancer type, and comorbidities.

Older patients are more vulnerable to certain chemotherapy toxicities. The most common toxicities of platinum-taxane regimens, the usual first-line therapy for ovarian cancer, are cytopenias and neuropathy. This was highlighted in a large retrospective analysis of outcomes and toxicities seen in the 620 patients aged 70 years and older enrolled in GOG 182, a phase III trial studying triplet-chemotherapy regimens for patients with newly diagnosed ovarian cancer (21). Older women enrolled in this trial were likely to be healthier than the average older woman with ovarian cancer, but older patients still had poorer PS, lower completion rates of all eight chemotherapy cycles, and increased toxicities, particularly grade 3+ neutropenia and grade 2+ neuropathy (36% vs. 20% for older vs. younger women on the standard carboplatin/paclitaxel arm). Although the difference in median time to disease progression was only 1 month, older women had significantly shorter median OS than younger women (37 vs. 45 months, $P < .001$).

A number of prospective ovarian cancer trials have enrolled exclusively older women, or have analyzed their older subjects separately. Modified regimens studied or being studied in vulnerable populations include increased use of growth factor, single-agent carboplatin chemotherapy, and weekly low-dose chemotherapy.

Chemotherapy—First Line

European Studies: The French National Group of Investigators for the study of Ovarian and Breast Cancer (GINECO) has performed a series of front-line chemotherapy trials for patients aged 70 years and older with advanced ovarian cancer, and used them to develop a decision aid (Geriatric Vulnerability Score [GVS]) for identifying which patients will not tolerate aggressive chemotherapy (11,22–24). The trials used carboplatin/cyclophosphamide, paclitaxel/cyclophosphamide, and single-agent carboplatin. Rates of completion of six cycles of chemotherapy were 75.6%, 68.1%, and 74% for the three trials respectively. OS for each of the trials was 21.6 months/25.9 months/17.4 months. The GVS score is being used in the ongoing Elderly Women in Ovarian Cancer (EWOC) trial that randomizes newly diagnosed ovarian cancer patients with a GVS of three or higher to treatment with single-agent carboplatin AUC 5-6, every 3 week carboplatin AUC 5-6 plus every 3 week paclitaxel 175 mg/m^2, and carboplatin AUC 2 plus paclitaxel 60 mg/m^2 both administered weekly for 3 weeks on an every 4 week schedule.

Weekly dosing of chemotherapy is particularly of interest. A carboplatin and paclitaxel combination was explored in the phase II Multicenter Italian Trial in Ovarian cancer (MITO-5) study, which included 26 vulnerable patients aged 70 years or older (25). The response rate was 38.5%, and median OS was 32.0 months. Toxicity was low, with 23 patients (89%) treated without experiencing serious adverse events. Though not specific to older adult women, these data were confirmed in a subsequent phase III MITO-7 study that compared carboplatin (AUC 6) with paclitaxel (175 mg/m^2) every 3 weeks to a weekly carboplatin (AUC 2) and weekly paclitaxel (60 mg/m^2) regimen given over 18 weeks in more than 800 women with newly diagnosed ovarian cancer at any age (median 59 and 60 years, respectively) and any stage (more than 80% with stage III to IV disease) (26). Compared with the women in the every-3-week arm, there was no difference in progression-free survival (PFS) with weekly dosing (median, 17.3 vs. 18.3 months, HR 0.96, P = .066). However, weekly dosing was associated with better quality of life scores and lower toxicities, including grade 2 or worse neuropathy, and serious (grade 3 to 4) hematologic toxicity. **These data suggest that weekly dosing of carboplatin and paclitaxel may be a more reasonable option for older patients, especially those deemed to be at higher risk for treatment-related toxicities** (25).

US Studies: The administration of reduced doses of carboplatin and paclitaxel was evaluated retrospectively in a group of patients older than 70 years (27). Compared with treatment using reduced doses, standard administration of chemotherapy resulted in a significantly higher incidence of grade 3 to 4 neutropenia (54% vs. 19%). In addition, those patients treated with standard doses were more likely to experience cumulative toxicity and require treatment delays. Importantly, there were no differences in PFS or OS between cohorts.

VonGruenigen led a trial of women 70 years and older with newly diagnosed ovarian cancer receiving first-line platinum-based chemotherapy (GOG 273) (12). Patients and their physicians selected from two different regimens: (Arm 1) every 3 week carboplatin AUC 5, paclitaxel 135 mg/m², and pegfilgrastim support; or (Arm 2) every 3 week single-agent carboplatin AUC 5. Patients could be enrolled either after CRS or prior to any surgical intervention. One hundred fifty-three women enrolled into Arm 1 and 59 into Arm 2. Women on Arm 2 were older (median age 83 vs. 77 years), had lower PS (PS2-3: 37% vs. 11%), were more likely to receive chemotherapy prior to surgery (58% vs. 49%) and less likely to complete all four cycles without dose reduction or a more than 7-day delay (54% vs. 82%). However, in general, overall completion of four cycles of chemotherapy was high (Arm 1: 92% and Arm 2: 75%). The ability to complete four cycles of chemotherapy without dose reduction or delay was significantly related to independence in ADLs, improved social activity and higher quality of life. IADL dependency was associated with reduced survival and higher toxicity from chemotherapy. With both regimens, patient-reported outcomes including quality of life, social activity, and function (ADLs) improved over time with cumulative chemotherapy cycles. **This suggests an important symptomatic benefit of chemotherapy even in the oldest age groups.**

After Arm 1 and 2 completed enrollment, Tew and colleagues explored the widely used dose-dense paclitaxel regimen. Patients were treated with carboplatin (AUC 5) every 3 weeks and dose-reduced weekly paclitaxel (60 mg/m²) on an every 3 week cycle; this arm was designed to test the hypothesis that the GOG GAS will predict ability to tolerate chemotherapy.

NACT is the delivery of chemotherapy prior to CRS. NACT use is gaining popularity in both the United States and Europe, particularly for older and vulnerable patients, because it is associated with less surgical toxicity. In an analysis of Medicare patients with stage II–IV ovarian cancer who survived at least 6 months from diagnosis, use of NACT had increased from 19.7% in 1991 to 31.8% in 2007, and is likely higher now (28). Randomized trial data suggest that outcomes with NACT and primary surgery are similar overall, though different subgroups may benefit from different approaches. A prospective randomized study of NACT (29) randomly assigned 632 patients with newly diagnosed stage IIIC or IV epithelial ovarian cancer to either primary CRS followed by six cycles of platinum-based chemotherapy or three cycles of platinum-based NACT followed by an interval CRS followed by an additional three cycles of platinum-based chemotherapy. The median age was 62 years (25–86) in the primary surgery group and 63 years (33–81) in the NACT group. Survival outcomes in the two arms were similar, with a median OS of 29 months in the primary surgery group and 30 months in those assigned to NACT. Surgical complications were higher in the primary surgery group, with postoperative death in 2.5% versus 0.7% and infection in 8.1% and 1.7% of participants respectively. Similar results were seen in a preliminary report from the MRC CHORUS trial, which involved an identical randomization and showed 12-month survival rates of 70% for primary surgery and 76% for NACT (30). Exploratory subgroup analyses of the EORTC trial did not show differences in benefit by age: 5-year survival rates of patients over the age of 69 (*n* = 166) were 20% with primary surgery and 18% with NACT (31). **Interestingly, patients with stage IV tumors and large tumor volume appeared to do better with NACT, whereas patients with low tumor burden appeared to do better with primary surgery.**

Intraperitoneal Chemotherapy (IP): IP chemotherapy has shown a survival benefit in multiple randomized trials of patients with optimally cytoreduced ovarian cancer (32–34). Only a small fraction of the women enrolled in these trials were over the age of 70 years. All of the randomized trials used cisplatin, which has more nephrotoxicity, neurotoxicity, and ototoxicity than carboplatin—side effects concerning for an older patient. Although some reports have suggested that healthy fit older patients can tolerate IP chemotherapy (35), one small report on women over age 75 treated with aggressive surgery followed by hyperthermic IP found a 78% morbidity rate (36).

Chemotherapy for Recurrent Disease

For patients with platinum-sensitive disease (>6 months in remission since last platinum treatment), randomized trials show a PFS advantage to a doublet combination with carboplatin and either paclitaxel, gemcitabine (37), or liposomal doxorubicin (38) versus treatment with carboplatin alone; platinum-based doublet therapy is therefore standard. In one retrospective study, however, older women had less secondary surgery, more frequent single-agent chemotherapy, and lower response rates to chemotherapy (67.2% vs. 46.5%) (39). Choice of regimen is often based on the toxicity profile, and in older patients, gemcitabine can produce higher rates of cytopenias and paclitaxel higher rates of neuropathy. A subset analysis of patients aged 70 years and older treated on the CALYPSO trial (carboplatin/paclitaxel [CP] vs. carboplatin/liposomal doxorubicin [CD]) showed that elderly patients completed the planned six cycles at the same rate as younger patients (79% for CP and 82% for CD), and had similar rates of hematologic toxicity. Grade 2 or greater peripheral neuropathy was greater among older patients treated with paclitaxel (36% vs. 24% for younger patients) and, interestingly, carboplatin hypersensitivity reactions were significantly less common in older women (40).

For platinum-resistant disease, chemotherapy is typically given as single agent and responses range from 10% to 25% with a median duration from 4 to 8 months. Common options include liposomal doxorubicin, topotecan, gemcitabine, weekly paclitaxel, and vinorelbine (41). Liposomal doxorubicin or gemcitabine are reasonable choices for older patients with platinum-resistant disease, given their relatively good toxicity profiles. However, because these chemotherapy options only offer a low chance of disease palliation, it may be reasonable to focus on better supportive measures, rather than more chemotherapy, in the setting of platinum-resistant disease. Disease progression on two consecutive lines of therapy has been recommended as a guide to stop therapy (42). In one study, there was a significant cost difference with no appreciable improvement in survival between ovarian cancer patients treated aggressively with chemotherapy versus those enrolled in hospice at the final months of their life. **The authors suggest that earlier hospice enrollment is beneficial, particularly in older frail patients** (43).

Targeted Agents

The targeted agents currently of most relevance to the treatment of ovarian cancer are the Poly (ADP-ribose) polymerase (PARP) inhibitors and antiangiogenic agents. There are no elderly-specific data on PARP inhibitors, but they appear generally to be well tolerated (low-grade fatigue, GI symptoms, anemia, and rash) (44). PARP inhibitors have increased activity in women with a BRCA mutation. Although BRCA-linked hereditary ovarian cancers, particularly BRCA1-associated cancers, tend to occur at a younger age than nonhereditary/sporadic ovarian cancer, the mean age at time of ovarian cancer diagnosis for mutation carriers ranges significantly (BRCA1: 54 years [31–79], BRCA2: 62 years [44–77], and sporadic: 63 years [25–87]) (45). Genetic counseling and consideration of PARP inhibitor therapy are appropriate regardless of age.

Antiangiogenic agents require more caution in the older population. Although the effect of bevacizumab on survival outcomes appears to be similar in older and younger patients with ovarian cancer (46), a variety of toxicities are increased in the older population. Of particular concern are vascular events. The package insert for bevacizumab as of September 2014 notes that in an exploratory pooled analysis of 1,745 patients treated in five randomized controlled studies, the rate of arterial thromboembolic events in bevacizumab-treated patients was 8.5% for those aged 65 years and older versus 2.9% for those younger than 65 years of age (47). Patients with a history of prior stroke or transient ischemic attack (TIA) should not receive bevacizumab, and close attention must be paid to blood pressure control. Mohile et al. conducted a prospective analysis of toxicity in older patients receiving bevacizumab in combination with chemotherapy for colon cancer or non–small-cell lung cancer (NSCLC). The addition of bevacizumab increased toxicity, particularly grade 3 hypertension, but no GA variables were found to be associated with increased toxicity (48). Anti-VEGF tyrosine kinase inhibitors are of increasing interest in ovarian cancer, but significant side effects have been observed in older adults (fatigue, diarrhea, and hypertension) (49–53).

TAKE HOME POINTS

1. Older patients with ovarian cancer have poorer survival, higher complications with surgery and chemotherapy, and reduced usage of standard treatment.
2. Modification in chemotherapy dosing, scheduling, and timing (neoadjuvant or postoperative) should be considered to reduce toxicity in the more vulnerable patients.
3. GA, especially functional dependency with IADLs, can help predict patients who may be prone to complications and may inform the development of interventions to improve the ability of vulnerable older women to undergo surgery and receive chemotherapy.

REFERENCES

1. Tew WP. Ovarian cancer in the older woman. *J Geriatric Oncol.* September 2007;7(5):354-361.
2. Oberaigner W, Minicozzi P, Bielska-Lasota M, et al. Survival for ovarian cancer in Europe: the across-country variation did not shrink in the past decade. *Acta Oncologica.* 2012;51(4):441-453.
3. Edwards BK, Howe HL, Ries LA, et al. Annual report to the nation on the status of cancer, 1973-1999, featuring implications of age and aging on U.S. cancer burden. *Cancer.* 2002;94(10):2766-2792.
4. Yancik R, Ries LA. Cancer in older persons: an international issue in an aging world. *Seminars in Oncology.* 2004;31(2):128-136.
5. Vercelli M, Capocaccia R, Quaglia A, et al. Relative survival in elderly European cancer patients: evidence for health care inequalities. The EUROCARE Working Group. *Crit Rev Oncol Hematol.* 2000;35(3):161-179.
6. Tew WP, Muss HB, Kimmick GG, et al. Breast and ovarian cancer in the older woman. *J Clin Oncol.* Aug 20, 2014;32(24):2553-2561.
7. VanderWalde N, Jagsi R, Dotan E, et al. NCCN guidelines insights: older adult oncology, version 2.2016. *J Natl Compr Canc Netw.* November 2016;14(11):1357-1370.
8. Kanesvaran R, Li H, Koo KN, et al. Analysis of prognostic factors of comprehensive geriatric assessment and development of a clinical scoring system in elderly Asian patients with cancer. *J Clin Oncol.* 2011;29(27):3620-3627.
9. Hurria A, Togawa K, Mohile SG, et al. Predicting chemotherapy toxicity in older adults with cancer: a prospective multicenter study. *J Clin Oncol.* 2011;29(25):3457-3465.
10. Won E, Hurria A, Feng T, et al. CA125 level association with chemotherapy toxicity and functional status in older women with ovarian cancer. *Int J Gynecol Cancer.* July 2013;23(6):1022-1028.
11. Falandry C, Weber B, Savoye AM, et al. Development of a geriatric vulnerability score in elderly patients with advanced ovarian cancer treated with first-line carboplatin: a GINECO prospective trial. *Ann Oncol.* 2013;24(11):2808-2813.
12. Von Gruenigen VE, Huang H, Tew WP, et al. Geriatric assessment and tolerance to chemotherapy in elderly women with ovarian, primary peritoneal or fallopian tube cancer: a Gynecologic Oncology Group study. *Gyn Oncol.* 2014;134(2):439.

13. Hightower RD, Nguyen HN, Averette HE, et al. National survey of ovarian carcinoma. IV: patterns of care and related survival for older patients. *Cancer.* 1994;73(2):377-383.

14. Fairfield KM, Lucas FL, Earle CC, et al. Regional variation in cancer-directed surgery and mortality among women with epithelial ovarian cancer in the Medicare population. *Cancer.* 2010;116(20):4840-4848.

15. Thrall MM, Goff BA, Symons RG, et al. Thirty-day mortality after primary cytoreductive surgery for advanced ovarian cancer in the elderly. *Obstet Gynecol.* 2011;118(3):537-547.

16. Moore KN, Reid MS, Fong DN, et al. Ovarian cancer in the octogenarian: does the paradigm of aggressive cytoreductive surgery and chemotherapy still apply? *Gyn Oncol.* 2008;110(2):133-139.

17. Aletti GD, Eisenhauer EL, Santillan A, et al. Identification of patient groups at highest risk from traditional approach to ovarian cancer treatment. *Gyn Oncol.* 2011;120(1):23-28.

18. Wright AA, Bohlke K, Armstrong DK, et al. Neoadjuvant chemotherapy for newly diagnosed, advanced ovarian cancer: Society of Gynecologic Oncology and American Society of Clinical Oncology Clinical Practice Guidelines. *J Clin Oncol.* 2016;34(28):3460-3473.

19. Hershman D, Jacobson JS, McBride R, et al. Effectiveness of platinum-based chemotherapy among elderly patients with advanced ovarian cancer. *Gyn Oncol.* 2004;94:540.

20. Lin JJ, Egorova N, Franco R, et al. Ovarian cancer treatment and survival trends among women older than 65 years of age in the United States, 1995-2008. *Obstet Gynecol.* 2016;127:81.

21. Tew WP Java J, Chi D, et al. Treatment outcomes for older women with advanced ovarian cancer: results from a phase III clinical treal (GOG182) [abstract]. *J Clin Oncol.* 2010;28(suppl 15). Abstract 5030.

22. Tredan O, Geay JF, Touzet S, et al. Carboplatin/cyclophosphamide or carboplatin/paclitaxel in elderly patients with advanced ovarian cancer? Analysis of two consecutive trials from the Groupe d'Investigateurs Nationaux pour l'Etude des Cancers Ovariens. *Ann Oncol.* 2007;18(2):256-262.

23. Freyer G, Geay JF, Touzet S, et al. Comprehensive geriatric assessment predicts tolerance to chemotherapy and survival in elderly patients with advanced ovarian carcinoma: a GINECO study. *Ann Oncol.* 2005;16(11):1795-1800.

24. Tinquaut F, Freyer G, Chauvin F, et al. Prognostic factors for overall survival in elderly patients with advanced ovarian cancer treated with chemotherapy: results of a pooled analysis of three GINECO phase II trials. *Gyn Oncol.* 2016;143(1):22-26.

25. Pignata S, Breda E, Scambia G, et al. A phase II study of weekly carboplatin and paclitaxel as first-line treatment of elderly patients with advanced ovarian cancer. A Multicentre Italian Trial in Ovarian cancer (MITO-5) study. *Crit Rev Oncol Hematol.* 2008;66:229.

26. Pignata S, Scambia G, Katsaros D, et al. Carboplatin plus paclitaxel once a week versus every 3 weeks in patients with advanced ovarian cancer (MITO-7): a randomised, multicentre, open-label, phase 3 trial. *Lancet Oncol.* 2014;15(4):396-405.

27. Fader AN, von Gruenigen V, Gibbons H, et al. Improved tolerance of primary chemotherapy with reduced-dose carboplatin and paclitaxel in elderly ovarian cancer patients. *Gynecol Oncol.* 2008;109:33.

28. Wright JD, Ananth CV, Tsui J, et al. Comparative effectiveness of upfront treatment strategies in elderly women with ovarian cancer. *Cancer.* 2014;120(8):1246-1254.

29. Vergote I, Trope CG, Amant F, et al. Neoadjuvant chemotherapy or primary surgery in stage IIIC or IV ovarian cancer. *New Engl J Med.* 2010;363(10):943-953.

30. Kehoe S, Hook J, Nankivell M, et al. Chemotherapy or upfront surgery for newly diagnosed advanced ovarian cancer: results from the MRC CHORUS Trial [abstract]. *J Clin Oncol.* 2013;31(suppl). Abstract 5500.

31. van Meurs HS, Tajik P, Hof MH, et al. Which patients benefit most from primary surgery or neoadjuvant chemotherapy in stage IIIC or IV ovarian cancer? An exploratory analysis of the European Organisation for Research and Treatment of Cancer 55971 randomised trial. *Eur J Cancer.* 2013;49(15):3191-3201.

32. Markman M, Bundy BN, Alberts DS, et al. Phase III trial of standard-dose intravenous cisplatin plus paclitaxel versus moderately high-dose carboplatin followed by intravenous paclitaxel and intraperitoneal cisplatin in small-volume stage III ovarian carcinoma: an intergroup study of the Gynecologic Oncology Group, Southwestern Oncology Group, and Eastern Cooperative Oncology Group. *J Clin Oncol.* 2001;19(4):1001-1007.

33. Armstrong DK, Bundy B, Wenzel L, et al. Intraperitoneal cisplatin and paclitaxel in ovarian cancer. *New Engl J Med.* 2006;354(1):34-43.

34. Alberts DS, Liu PY, Hannigan EV, et al. Intraperitoneal cisplatin plus intravenous cyclophosphamide versus intravenous cisplatin plus intravenous cyclophosphamide for stage III ovarian cancer. *New Engl J Med.* 1996;335(26):1950-1955.

35. Tew WP, O'Cearbhaill R, Zhou Q, et al. Intraperitoneal chemotherapy in older women with epithelial ovarian cancer [abstract]. *J Clin Oncol.* 2009;27(15s). Abstract 5541.

36. Cascales-Campos P, Gil J, Gil E, et al. Cytoreduction and HIPEC after neoadjuvant chemotherapy in stage IIIC-IV ovarian cancer: critical analysis in elderly patients. *Eur J Obstet Gynecol Reprod Biol.* 2014;179:88-93.

37. Pfisterer J, Plante M, Vergote I, et al. Gemcitabine plus carboplatin compared with carboplatin in patients with platinum-sensitive recurrent ovarian cancer: an intergroup trial of the AGO-OVAR, the NCIC CTG, and the EORTC GCG. *J Clin Oncol.* 2006;24(29):4699-4707.

38. Pujade-Lauraine E, Wagner U, Aavall-Lundqvist E, et al. Pegylated liposomal doxorubicin and carboplatin compared with paclitaxel and carboplatin for patients with platinum-sensitive ovarian cancer in late relapse. *J Clin Oncol.* 2010;28(20):3323-3329.

39. Pignata S, Ferrandina G, Scarfone G, et al. Poor outcome of elderly patients with platinum-sensitive recurrent ovarian cancer: results from the SOCRATES retrospective study. *Crit Rev Oncol Hematol.* 2009;71(3):233-241.

40. Kurtz JE, Kaminsky MC, Floquet A, et al. Ovarian cancer in elderly patients: carboplatin and pegylated liposomal doxorubicin versus carboplatin and paclitaxel in late relapse: a Gynecologic Cancer Intergroup (GCIG) CALYPSO sub-study. *Ann Oncol.* 2011;22(11):2417-2423.

41. Tew WP, Lichtman SM. Ovarian cancer in older women. *Semin Oncol.* 2008;35(6):582-589.

42. Griffiths RW, Zee YK, Evans S, et al. Outcomes after multiple lines of chemotherapy for platinum-resistant epithelial cancers of the ovary, peritoneum, and fallopian tube. *Int J Gyn Cancer.* 2011;21(1):58-65.

43. Lewin SN, Buttin BM, Powell MA, et al. Resource utilization for ovarian cancer patients at the end of life: how much is too much? *Gyn Oncol.* 2005;99(2):261-266.

44. Kaye SB, Lubinski J, Matulonis U, et al. Phase II, open-label, randomized, multicenter study comparing the efficacy and safety of olaparib, a poly (ADP-ribose) polymerase inhibitor, and pegylated liposomal doxorubicin in patients with BRCA1 or BRCA2 mutations and recurrent ovarian cancer. *J Clin Oncol.* 2012;30(4):372-379.

45. Boyd J, Sonoda Y, Federici MG, et al. Clinicopathologic features of BRCA-linked and sporadic ovarian cancer. *JAMA.* 2000;283(17):2260-2265.
46. Burger RA, Brady MF, Bookman MA, et al. Incorporation of bevacizumab in the primary treatment of ovarian cancer. *New Engl J Med.* 2011;365(26):2473-2483.
47. Insert AP. Highlights of Prescribing Information. 2014.
48. Mohile SG, Hardt M, Tew W, et al. Toxicity of bevacizumab in combination with chemotherapy in older patients. *Oncologist.* 2013;18(4):408-414.
49. Du Bois A, Floquet A, Kim JW, et al. Randomized, double-blind, phase III trial of pazopanib versus placebo in women who have not progressed after first-line chemotherapy for advanced epithelial ovarian, fallopian tube, or primary peritoneal cancer (AEOC): Results of an international intergroup trial (AGO-OVAR16) [abstract]. *J Clin Oncol.* 2013;31(suppl). Abstract LBA5503.
50. Ledermann JA, Perren T, Raja FA, et al. Randomized double-blind phase III trial of cediranib (AZE 2171) in relapsed platinum sensitive ovarian cancer: results of the ICON6 trial. *NCRI Conference*; November 3-6, 2013; Liverpool, UK. LB80.
51. Liu J, Barry WT, Birrer MJ, et al. A randomized phase 2 trial comparing efficacy of the combination of the PARP inhibitor olaparib and the antiangiogenic cediranib against olaparib alone in recurrent platinum-sensitive ovarian cancer. *J Clin Oncol.* 2014;32(5s):LBA5500.
52. Wong H, Tang YF, Yao TJ, et al. The outcomes and safety of single-agent sorafenib in the treatment of elderly patients with advanced hepatocellular carcinoma (HCC). *Oncologist.* 2011;16(12):1721-1728.
53. Gonsalves W, Ganti AK. Targeted anti-cancer therapy in the elderly. *Crit Rev Oncol Hematol.* 2011;78(3):227-242.

Head and Neck Cancer in Older Adults

Ronald J. Maggiore, Noam VanderWalde, and Melissa Crawley

Head and neck cancers (HNCs) usually manifest as squamous cell carcinomas within the paranasal sinuses, nasal cavity, oral cavity, pharynx (nasopharynx, oropharynx, and hypopharynx), and larynx. In 2016, there will be an estimated 61,760 new cases of oral cavity/pharynx and larynx cancers and 13,190 related deaths in the United States (1). Despite the increasing trend of human papilloma virus (HPV)-related cancers (usually oropharynx) in younger patients (2,3), HNC remains primarily a cancer of older adults (median age at diagnosis = 62 years) (4). In addition, the incidence of newly diagnosed HNC among older adults is expected to increase by more than 60% by the year 2030 (5).

Treatment decision making for older HNC patients remains difficult, and "gold-standard" treatments are not well defined. The majority of HNC patients present with locoregionally advanced (LA; stages III and IVA-B) disease, often warranting multimodality therapy such as concurrent chemoradiation (CRT) (6). These treatments often lead to significant acute and late-term toxicities, which can impact treatment adherence, quality of life (QOL), and survival. Thus, older and/or functionally vulnerable patients are often considered poor candidates for multimodality treatment and are subsequently less likely to receive standard-of-care therapy compared to their younger counterparts (7,8). This dichotomy is also evident in radiation therapy (RT) practices for older HNC patients (9).

OLDER ADULTS WITH HNC: LACK OF A ROBUST EVIDENCE BASE

Despite older adults being disproportionately affected by HNC, the evidence base for treatment decision making in older adults with HNC remains insufficient because existing clinical trial data included few adults age 65 years or older (Table 20.1), and older adults remain underrepresented or underaccrued in cancer clinical trials in general (Table 20.2) (22,23). Age-related changes in swallowing and physical function with concomitant rise of comorbidity makes this a vulnerable patient population in light of the inherent intensity of combined modality treatments commonly employed

TABLE 20.1 Inclusion of Older Adults in Representative Seminal HNC Clinical Trials

Trial	Randomization	Number of Patients	Median Age	Results
		Larynx Preservation Studies		
VA Larynx (10)	Definitive sequential chemotherapy (cisplatin + 5-FU) + RT vs. surgery + postoperative RT	322	62 (range 24–79)	OS: no difference Larynx preserved in 64%
RTOG 91-11 (11)	Sequential chemotherapy (cisplatin + 5-FU) + RT vs. concurrent CRT (cisplatin) vs. RT alone	547	59 (range 26–79)	Larynx preservation, LC: better with concurrent chemoradiotherapy
EORTC 24954 (12)	Sequential chemotherapy (cisplatin + 5-FU) + RT vs. alternating chemotherapy + RT	450	55 (range 35–76)	No difference
		Definitive CRT		
GORTEC Oropharynx Calais et al. (13)	RT alone vs. CRT (carboplatin + 5-FU)	226	55 (mean) (range 32–74)	OS, DFS, and LC were all improved with chemotherapy
Intergroup Trial Adelstein et al. (14)	RT alone vs. CRT (bolus cisplatin) vs. split-course RT with bolus cisplatin and infusional 5-FU	295	57 (mean) (range 25–80)	Did not meet accrual: OS was improved with RT and bolus cisplatin
RTOG 97-03 (15)	CRT (daily cisplatin and 5-FU) vs. CRT (daily hydroxyurea with 5-FU (FHX)) vs. CRT (weekly cisplatin and paclitaxel)	241	56 (range 21–83)	Phase II: All 3 regimens feasible
Hellenic COG (16)	RT alone vs. CRT (cisplatin) vs. CRT (carboplatin)	128	57 (range 31–78)	OS improved with concurrent chemo. Cisplatin with best median OS and TTP

(continued)

TABLE 20.1 Inclusion of Older Adults in Representative Seminal HNC Clinical Trials (*continued*)

Trial	Randomization	Number of Patients	Median Age	Results
UKHAN1 Trial (17) (nonsurgery arms)	RT alone vs. CRT (vinblastine + methotrexate + 5-FU or methotrexate alone; VbMF) vs. RT with adjuvant chemo vs. RT with concurrent and adjuvant chemo	713	60 (range 17–84)	Improvement in EFS with RT + concurrent
Bonner et al. Trial (18)	CRT (cetuximab) vs. RT alone	424	57 (range 34–83)	LC and OS improved with cetuximab
Adjuvant CRT				
RTOG 9501 (19)	RT alone vs. CRT (cisplatin)	459	~56 (range 24–80)	LC and DFS improved with chemotherapy
EORTC 22931 (20)	RT alone vs. CRT (cisplatin)	167	54 (no range given)	LC, PFS, and OS improved with chemotherapy
French Lymph Node—Positive Trial Racadot et al. (21)	RT alone vs. CRT (carboplatin)	144	55.5 (mean) (no range given)	No difference
UKHAN1 Trial (surgery arms) (17)	RT alone vs. CRT (VbMF)	253	~58 (range 32–81)	No difference

COG, Cooperative Oncology Group; CRT, chemoradiation; DFS, disease-free survival; EFS, event-free survival; EORTC, European Organization for Research and Treatment of Cancer; 5-FU, 5-fluorouracil; GORTEC, French Head and Neck Cancer Group; HNC, head and neck cancer; LC, local control; OS, overall survival; PFS, progression free survival; RT, radiation therapy; RTOG, Radiation Therapy Oncology Group; TTP, time to progression.

for HNC. For example, advanced age increases the risk of acute RT-related dysphagia in HNC, and baseline dysphagia is an independent risk factor for later RT-related dysphagia (24). In addition, more than 80% of patients with HNC, irrespective of age, develop sarcopenia by the time they complete definitive RT or CRT (25,26). Long-term sequelae from such therapies can have significant impacts on functional outcomes (27).

TABLE 20.2 Select Ongoing Clinical Trials Targeting Older Adults With HNC (as of March 30, 2016)

Study Name	Patients	Outcomes Being Studied
EGESOR: Impact of Comprehensive Geriatric Assessment on Malnutrition, Functional Status and Survival in Elderly Patients With Head and Neck Squamous Cell Carcinomas (HNSCCs): a Randomized Controlled Multicenter Clinical Trial (//clinicaltrials.gov/ct2/show/NCT02025062) (Multi-center, France)	Age: ≥65 y Function: N/A Cancer: Any SCCHN diagnosis	Primary: Composite: OS + loss ≥ 2 ADL points + ≥10% weight loss Secondary: Hospitalization, PFS, HR-QOL (up to 24 mo)
ELAN-RT: Non Inferiority Trial of Standard RT Versus Hypofractionated Split Course in Elderly Vulnerable Patients With Head and Neck Squamous Cell Cancer (GORTEC-ELAN-RT) (//clinicaltrials.gov/ct2/show/NCT01864850) (Multi-center, France)	Age: ≥70 y Function: Baseline GA: "Unfit," ECOG PS 0-1 Cancer: Stages II-IVB SCCHN Treatment: RT alone: Standard: 70 Gy/2 wk vs. Experimental: hypofractionated 55 Gy/7 wk (2.5–3 Gy per fraction per protocol)	Primary: Locoregional control (6 mo) Secondary: OS, PFS, DC, ADL impairment, HR-QOL, safety/toxicity (up to 18 mo)
ELAN-FIT: Phase II Multicenter Trial Evaluating First Line Carboplatin, 5-Fluorouracil and Cetuximab in Patients With Recurrent or Metastatic Head and Neck Squamous Cell Cancer, Aged 70 and Over, Ranked as Fit (No Frailty) by Geriatric Assessment (//clinicaltrials.gov/ct2/show/NCT01864772) (Multi-center, France)	Age: ≥70 y and Cr Cl ≥ 50 (MDRD) Function: Baseline GA: "Fit," ECOG PS 0-1 Cancer: R/M SCCHN except NPC, SNC Treatment: EXTREME (carboplatin/5-FU/cetuximab × six cycles, followed by cetuximab maintenance)	Primary Outcomes: ORR + safety/toxicity (at 1 and 3 mo postchemo) and < 2 point loss in ADLs (at 1-mo postinitial chemo) Secondary: Best ORR, OS, PFS, response duration on maintenance, safety/toxicity maintenance (up to 1 y); HR-QOL, ADL, IADLs up to 1-mo posttreatment

(continued)

TABLE 20.2 Select Ongoing Clinical Trials Targeting Older Adults With HNC (as of March 30, 2016) *(continued)*

Study Name	Patients	Outcomes Being Studied
ELAN-UNFIT: Multicentric Randomized Phase III Trial Comparing Methotrexate and Cetuximab in First-line Treatment of Recurrent and/or Metastatic Squamous Cell Head and Neck Cancer in Elderly Unfit Patients According to Geriatric Evaluation (//clinicaltrials.gov/ct2/show/NCT01884623) (Multi-center, France)	Age: ≥70 y and CrCl > 50 (MDRD) Function: Baseline GA: "Unfit," ECOG PS 0-2 Cancer: R/M SCCHN except NPC, SNC Treatment: Weekly cetuximab vs. weekly methotrexate	Primary Outcomes: ORR + safety/toxicity (at 1 and 3 mo postchemo) and < 2 point loss in ADLs (at 1-mo postinitial chemo) Secondary: Best ORR, OS, PFS, response duration on maintenance, safety/toxicity maintenance (up to 1 y); HR-QOL, ADL, IADLs up to 1-mo posttreatment

ADLs, activities of daily living; CrCl, creatinine clearance; CRT, chemoradiation; DC, distant control; ECOG PS, Eastern Cooperative Oncology Group performance status; GA, geriatric assessment; HNC, head and neck cancer; HNSCCs, head and neck squamous cell carcinomas; HR-QOL, health-related quality of life; IADLs, instrumental activities of daily living; MDRD, modification of diet in renal disease calculation; N/A, not applicable; NPC, nasopharynx cancer; ORR, objective response rate; OS, overall survival; PFS, progression-free survival; R/M, recurrent/metastatic; RT, radiation therapy; SCCHN, squamous cell carcinoma of the head and neck; SNC, sinonasal cancer.

RISK FOR ADVERSE EVENTS: THERAPY-RELATED ISSUES FOR OLDER ADULTS WITH HNC

Localized Disease

Surgery remains the mainstay of treatment for early-stage HNCs. Even among locally advanced cancers of the oral cavity, initial surgical management is often preferred. The evolution of transoral robotic surgery (TORS) has allowed this technology to be implemented to treat select early-stage and LA cases of oropharyngeal cancers, thereby potentially avoiding adjuvant RT/CRT and their associated toxicities. However, for those patients with unresectable primary tumors, or obvious extracapsular extension on imaging, adjuvant CRT will be required after resection, and thus the benefit of TORS over upfront CRT is questionable. For aggressive T4 tumors of the larynx, upfront total laryngectomy may still confer the best long-term disease control (28). Moreover, age may not be as critical as other risk factors for perioperative morbidity, but mortality may still be higher in patients aged 70 years or older (29,30).

Definitive RT for early-stage cancers may represent an alternative to surgery in select patients, particularly those with laryngeal cancers, with good cancer control and likely better voice preservation (31,32). Patients with T1/T2N0 glottic cancers have excellent long-term results from hypofractionated RT alone, often with less morbidity (28). Additionally, patients with T1/T2N0 tonsillar primaries have historically had excellent local control and survival with RT alone (30,31). Although many of these early-stage HNC patients are now being approached with surgery first (32), in older patients who may be poor surgical candidates, RT alone, especially when it can be employed unilaterally, can confer a more optimal risk/benefit balance (33,34).

LA Disease

Organ-preservation approaches utilizing RT and CRT have become preferred in many cases of LA-HNC involving certain sites in order to avoid perioperative morbidity, potentially maintain long-term speech and swallowing function, and reserve surgery as salvage therapy for local recurrences. CRT has been preferred over RT for LA oropharynx cancers as well as larynx cancers, particularly with improved locoregional control and improved laryngectomy-free survival. However, overall survival may not be better and in some cases may be worse with CRT (RTOG 91-11) (35). The incremental survival benefit that chemotherapy confers when combined with concurrent RT is small (6.5%), and becomes less with advancing age, particularly in patients age greater than 70 years (36). Subsequent studies have offered further mixed results on the benefit of the addition of chemotherapy or cetuximab to RT in older adults with LA-HNC (37–39). However, single-institution retrospective studies have shown that select older patients with LA-HNC may still derive benefits from CRT (40,41).

A combined analysis of two large randomized trials (42,43) showed that adjuvant RT or CRT is largely determined by presence of "high-risk" pathologic features (i.e., positive surgical margins, extracapsular extension). It is important to note that older HNC patients were significantly underrepresented in these two trials. Furthermore, we know that the addition of chemotherapy can increase the acute treatment-related toxicities 2- to 3-fold, and long-term small improvements in overall survival must be weighed carefully in more functionally vulnerable/frail patients and/or those with multimorbidity. The benefit of the addition of cetuximab as systemic therapy to adjuvant RT in HNC patients whose cancers have "intermediate-risk" pathologic features (e.g., lymphovascular invasion, perineural invasion) is part of RTOG 0920, which does not exclude older adults based on chronologic age but is limited to those with a performance status of 0 to 1 (44).

Recurrent/Metastatic (R/M) Disease

For most recurrent and all metastatic HNC cases, chemotherapy remains the cornerstone of treatment. Older adults may tolerate combination chemotherapies well but may be at risk for specific toxicities (45). It is important to note the studies showing that virtually all combination chemotherapies can improve response rates and progression-free survival, but not overall survival compared to monotherapies (46). It was not until the EXTREME trial that the addition of cetuximab to platinum/5-fluorouracil showed the addition of an agent to improve overall survival (47). However, the toxicity of a triplet regimen in younger adults coupled with paucity of data in older adults (<20% of patients enrolled were age ≥ 65 years) makes such a regimen unwieldy in common clinical practice for many older or functionally vulnerable younger adults with metastatic HNC. It will be important in the future to evaluate more targeted or immunotherapeutic agents, including PD-1 inhibitors such as pembrolizumab, which has efficacy even in heavily pretreated patients (48), especially in older adults who may not otherwise be suitable candidates for "traditional" systemic therapeutic options.

For select local or locoregional recurrences, surgery with RT or CRT can be considered for salvage on a case-by-case basis. In patients who have local failure after remission, there is an estimated 50% to 60% mortality rate (49). Historically, salvage surgery is the pillar of treatment, with local control rates of 60% to 70%; however, surgery may not be an option for many patients because of disease spread, critical anatomic involvement, and poor QOL (50,51). Re-irradiation with chemotherapy (CRRT) in carefully selected patients still results in poor survival and high rates of major toxicities (52). Two phase II trials evaluating the efficacy of CRRT have been conducted: RTOG 9610 (53) (median age = 62 years) and RTOG 9911 (median age = 60 years) (54). Grade 3 to 5 toxicities with CRRT were 25% to 36% (8%–11% grade 5 = death) with 2-year survival only 15% to 25% (53,54). Standard techniques for RT delivery are limited by dose tolerance limitations of traditional surrounding tissues, with significant risk for late-term toxicities, including cervical fibrosis, osteoradionecrosis, trismus, and carotid hemorrhage (55). However, stereotactic body radiation therapy (SBRT) techniques have been developed in this setting (56) to improve feasibility of re-irradiation and decreases treatment time, which may be appealing for older adults (56).

FUNCTIONAL AND GERO-CENTRIC ISSUES FOR OLDER AND AT-RISK YOUNGER ADULTS WITH HNC

Late-term effects of HNC therapy can have a profound impact on the QOL of survivors irrespective of age, including adverse effects on speech, swallowing, and nutrition (27). Older adults with HNC who received RT or CRT, compared to younger adults, have worse self-reported physical performance measures (57). Age, cochlear RT dose, and use of cisplatin-based CRT increases the risk of ototoxicity, which can persist long term (58). Coupled with the aforementioned prevalence of sarcopenia, malnutrition with attendant short- and long-term risks for aspiration and gastrostomy tube dependence remain critical aspects for ongoing care. However, exercise- and/or nutrition-based intervention studies to mitigate the toxicities of RT/CRT remain sparse even among younger HNC patients (59).

Another approach is to incorporate geriatric assessment (GA) tools, validate them, and utilize predictive findings to tailor HNC therapy intensity and/or supportive care interventions. GAs are only recently being evaluated in the context of older adults with HNC. Pilot data have shown that a GA may not necessarily be as predictive of toxicity in older adults with HNC undergoing RT or CRT, but instrumental activities of daily living impairment may be a predictor (60). Serial geriatric screening (G8 tool) and GAs in older adults with HNC undergoing definitive RT or CRT demonstrate cumulative impairments in several gero-centric domains from baseline to 4 weeks into RT/CRT (61). Long-term objective trajectory data are needed to complement the largely patient-reported outcomes in the geriatric HNC literature. To start to address this knowledge gap, a group of trials evaluating older adults with HNC have commenced in France (62). These includes the "umbrella" trial, EGESOR (//clinicaltrials .gov/ct2/show/NCT02025062), which encompasses all patients aged 65 years or older with HNC undergoing treatment to evaluate a composite outcome of overall survival, weight loss, and loss of ADLs. Within the scope of this study, those aged 70 or over who were selected for definitive RT without chemotherapy will undergo either a hypoactionated course of RT versus standard RT based on GA determining whether they are "unfit" or "fit," respectively, with locoregional control as the primary outcome (ELAN_RT: // clinicaltrials.gov/ct2/show/NCT01864850). In addition, those with metastatic/ recurrent disease will be stratified, based on GA-determined fitness, either to triplet therapy (i.e., EXTREME regimen) (ELAN FIT: //clinicaltrials.gov/ct2/show/ NCT01884623) or monotherapy (cetuximab or methotrexate) (ELAN UNFIT: //clinicaltrials.gov/ct2/show/NCT01884623). These studies will evaluate response rates along with toxicity and loss of ADLs as the primary outcomes. Combined-modality treatments (e.g., CRT) focused on older adults and/or functionally vulnerable patients will require further investigation, particularly with newer systemic agents and treatment paradigms (e.g., immunotherapy, response-adapted treatment) emerging.

TAKE HOME POINTS

1. Older adults represent a significant proportion of HNC patients, particularly nonoropharynx patients.
2. Combined-modality treatments confer significant short- and late-term risks and have a less robust evidence base.
3. Radiation monotherapy may be preferable in select patients with early-stage disease; perhaps also for LA-HNC patients with poor functional status or multimorbidity.
4. Noncancer risks and patient preferences must be taken into account during treatment decision making for R/M HNC, given the morbidity of CRRT or combination chemotherapy.
5. Functional, nutritional, and psychosocial issues stemming from HNC therapy can have late-term morbidity and impact during survivorship irrespective of age.

REFERENCES

1. American Cancer Society. *Cancer Facts and Figures 2016*. Atlanta, GA: American Cancer Society; 2016.
2. Patel SC, Carpenter WR, Tyree S, et al. Increasing incidence of oral tongue squamous cell carcinoma in young white women, age 18 to 44 years. *J Clin Oncol.* 2011;29:1488-1494.
3. Gillison ML, Broutian T, Pickard RK, et al. Prevalence of oral HPV infection in the United States, 2009-2010. *JAMA.* 2012;307:693-703.
4. American Cancer Society. *Cancer Treatment and Survivorship Facts and Figures 2014-2015*. Atlanta, GA: American Cancer Society; 2014.

5. Smith BD, Smith GL, Hurria A, et al. Future of cancer incidence in the United States: burdens upon an aging, changing nation. *J Clin Oncol.* 2009;27:2758-2765.

6. Argiris A, Eng C. Epidemiology, staging, and screening of head and neck cancer. *Cancer Treat Res.* 2003;114:15-60.

7. de Rijke JM, Schouten LJ, Schouten HC, et al. Age-specific differences in the diagnostics and treatment of cancer patients aged 50 years and older in the province of Limburg, the Netherlands. *Ann Oncol.* 1996;7:677-685.

8. Fentiman IS, Tirelli U, Monfardini S, et al. Cancer in the elderly: why so badly treated? *Lancet.* 1990;335:1020-1022.

9. Huang SH, O'Sullivan B, Waldron J, et al. Patterns of care in elderly head-and-neck cancer radiation oncology patients: a single-center cohort study. *Int J Radiat Oncol Biol Phys.* 2011;79:46-51.

10. Department of Veterans Affairs Laryngeal Cancer Study Group. Induction chemotherapy plus radiation compared with surgery plus radiation in patients with advanced laryngeal cancer. *N Engl J Med.* 1991;324:1685-1690.

11. Forastiere AA, Goepfert H, Maor M, et al. Concurrent chemotherapy and radiotherapy for organ preservation in advanced laryngeal cancer. *N Engl J Med.* 2003;349:2091-2098.

12. Lefebvre JL, Rolland F, Tesselaar M, et al. Phase 3 randomized trial of larynx preservation comparing sequential vs alternating chemotherapy and radiotherapy. *J Natl Cancer Inst.* 2009;101:142-152.

13. Calais G, Alfonsi M, Bardet E, et al. Randomized trial of radiation therapy versus concomitant chemotherapy and radiation therapy for advanced-stage oropharynx carcinoma. *J Natl Cancer Inst.* 1999;91:2081-2086.

14. Adelstein DJ, Li Y, Adams GL, et al. An intergroup phase III comparison of standard radiation therapy and two schedules of concurrent chemoradiotherapy in patients with unresectable squamous cell head and neck cancer. *J Clin Oncol.* 2003;21:92-98.

15. Garden AS, Harris J, Vokes EE, et al. Preliminary results of Radiation Therapy Oncology Group 97–03: a randomized phase II trial of concurrent radiation and chemotherapy for advanced squamous cell carcinomas of the head and neck. *J Clin Oncol.* 2004;22:2856-2864.

16. Fountzilas G, Ciuleanu E, Dafni U, et al. Concomitant radiochemotherapy vs radiotherapy alone in patients with head and neck cancer: a Hellenic Cooperative Oncology Group Phase III Study. *Med Oncol.* 2004;21:95-107.

17. Tobias JS, Monson K, Gupta N, et al. Chemoradiotherapy for locally advanced head and neck cancer: 10-year follow-up of the UK Head and Neck (UKHAN1) trial. *Lancet Oncol.* 2010;11:66-74.

18. Bonner JA, Harari PM, Giralt J, et al. Radiotherapy plus cetuximab for squamous-cell carcinoma of the head and neck. *N Engl J Med.* 2006;354:567-578.

19. Cooper JS, Pajak TF, Forastiere AA, et al. Postoperative concurrent radiotherapy and chemotherapy for high-risk squamous-cell carcinoma of the head and neck. *N Engl J Med.* 2004;350:1937-1944.

20. Bernier J, Domenge C, Ozsahin M, et al. Postoperative irradiation with or without concomitant chemotherapy for locally advanced head and neck cancer. *N Engl J Med.* 2004;350:1945-1952.

21. Racadot S, Mercier M, Dussart S, et al. Randomized clinical trial of post-operative radiotherapy versus concomitant carboplatin and radiotherapy for head and neck cancers with lymph node involvement. *Radiother Oncol.* 2008;87:164-172.

22. Talarico L, Chen G, Pazdur R. Enrollment of elderly patients in clinical trials for cancer drug registration: a 7-year experience by the US Food and Drug Administration. *J Clin Oncol.* 2004;22:4626-4631.

23. Hutchins LF, Unger JM, Crowley JJ, et al. Underrepresentation of patients 65 years of age or older in cancer-treatment trials. *N Engl J Med.* 1999;341:2061-2067.

24. Mortensen HR, Overgaard J, Jensen K, et al. Factors associated with acute and late dysphagia in the DAHANCA 6 & 7 randomized trial with accelerated radiotherapy for head and neck cancer. *Acta Oncol.* 2013;52:1535-1542.

25. Chamchod S, Fueller CD, Grossberg AJ, et al. Sarcopenia/cachexia is associated with reduced survival and locoregional control in head and neck cancer patients receiving radiotherapy: results from quantitative imaging analysis of lean body mass. *Oncology* (Williston Park). 2015;29(4 suppl 1):pii:205153.

26. Hasan S, Miranda D, Landau E, et al. Sarcopenia in head-and-neck cancer: a significant problem in patients receiving intensity modulated (IMRT) and image guided radiation (IGRT) as assessed by a validated CT-based assessment tool. *Int J Radiat Oncol Biol Phys.* 2014;88:496-497.

27. Murphy BA, Deng, J. Advances in supportive care for late effects of head and neck cancer. *J Clin Oncol.* 2015;33:3314-3321.

28. Grover S, Swisher-McClure S, Mitra N, et al. Total laryngectomy versus larynx preservation for T4a larynx cancer: patterns of care and survival outcomes. *Int J Radiat Oncol Biol Phys.* 2015;92:594-601.

29. Sanabria A, Carvalho AL, Melo Rl, et al. Predictive factors for complications in elderly patients who underwent head and neck oncologic surgery. *Head Neck.* 2008;30:170-177.

30. Milet PR, Mallet Y, El Bedoui S, et al. Head and neck cancer surgery in the elderly— does age influence the postoperative course? *Oral Oncol.* 2010;46:92-95.

31. Chera BS, Amdur RJ, Morris CG, et al. T1N0 to T2N0 squamous cell carcinoma of the glottic larynx treated with definitive radiotherapy. *Int J Radiat Oncol Biol Phys.* 2010;78:461-466.

32. Aaltonen LM, Rautiainen N, Sellman J, et al. Voice quality after treatment of early vocal cord cancer: a randomized trial comparing laser surgery with radiation therapy. *Int J Radiat Oncol Biol Phys.* 2014;90:255-260.

33. Chronowski GM, Garden AS, Morrison WH, et al. Unilateral radiotherapy for the treatment of tonsil cancer. *Int J Radiat Oncol Biol Phys.* 2012;83:204-209.

34. Kennedy WR, Herman MP, Deraniyagala RL, et al. Ipsilateral radiotherapy for squamous cell carcinoma of the tonsil. *Eur Arch Otorhinolaryngol.* 2016;273(8):2117-2125.

35. Forastiere AA, Zhang Q, Weber RS, et al. Long-term results of RTOG 91-11: a comparison of three nonsurgical treatment strategies to preserve the larynx in patients with locally advanced larynx cancer. *J Clin Oncol.* 2013;31(7):845-852.

36. Pignon JP, Le Maître A, Maillard E, et al. Meta-analysis of chemotherapy in head and neck cancer (MACH-NC): an update of 93 randomised trials and 17,346 patients. *Radiother Oncol.* 2009;92:4-14.

37. VanderWalde NA, Meyer AM, Deal AM, et al. Effectiveness of chemoradiation for head and neck cancer in an older patient population. *Int J Radiat Oncol Biol Phys.* 2014;89:30-37.

38. Amini A, Jones BL, McDermott JD, et al. Survival outcomes with concurrent chemoradiation for elderly patients with locally advanced head and neck cancer according to the National Cancer Data Base. *Cancer.* 2016;122(10):1533-1543.

39. Bonner JA, Harari PM, Giralt J, et al. Radiotherapy plus cetuximab for locoregionally advanced head and neck cancer: 5-year survival data from a phase 3 randomised trial, and relation between cetuximab-induced rash and survival. *Lancet Oncol.* 2010;11:21-28.

40. Maggiore RJ, Curran EK, Witt ME, et al. Survival and selected outcomes of older adults with locally advanced head/neck cancer treated with chemoradiation therapy. *J Geriatr Oncol.* 2013;4:327-333.

41. Michal SA, Adelstein DJ, Rybicki LA, et al. Multi-agent concurrent chemoradiotherapy for locally advanced head and neck squamous cell cancer in the elderly. *Head Neck.* 2011;34:1147-1152.

42. Bernier J, Domenge C, Ozsahin M, et al. Postoperative irradiation with or without concomitant chemotherapy for locally advanced head and neck cancer. *N Engl J Med.* 2004;350:1945-1952.

43. Cooper JS, Pajak TF, Forastiere AA, et al. Postoperative concurrent radiotherapy and chemotherapy for high-risk squamous cell carcinoma of the head and neck. *N Engl J Med* 2004;350:1937-1944.

44. RTOG 0920 Protocol Information. Available at: https://www.rtog.org/ClinicalTrials/ProtocolTable/StudyDetails.aspx?study=0920. Accessed March 12, 2016.

45. Argiris A, Li Y, Murphy BA, et al. Outcome of elderly patients with recurrent or metastatic head and neck cancer treated with cisplatin-based chemotherapy. *J Clin Oncol.* 2004;22:262-268.

46. Price KA, Cohen EE. Current treatment options for metastatic head and neck cancer. *Curr Treat Options Oncol.* 2012;13:35-46.

47. Vermorken JB, Mesia R, Rivera F, et al. Platinum-based chemotherapy plus cetuximab in head and neck cancer. *N Engl J Med.* 2008;359:1116-1127.

48. Seiwert TY, Haddad RI, Gupta S, et al. Antitumor activity and safety of pembrolizumab in patients (pts) with advanced squamous cell carcinoma of the head and neck (SCCHN): preliminary results from the KEYNOTE-012 expansion cohort [abstract]. *J Clin Oncol.* 2015;33(suppl). Abstract LBA6008.

49. Hong WK, Bromer RH, Amato DA, et al. Patterns of relapse in locally advanced head and neck cancer patients who achieved complete remission after combined modality therapy. *Cancer.* 1985;56:1242-1245.

50. Taussky D, Dulguerov P, Allal AS. Salvage surgery after radical accelerated radiotherapy with concomitant boost technique for head and neck carcinomas. *Head Neck.* 2005;27:182-186.

51. Gokhale AS, Lavertu P. Surgical salvage after chemoradiation of head and neck cancer: complications and outcomes. *Curr Oncol Rep.* 2001;3:72-76.

52. Salama JK, Vokes EE. Concurrent chemotherapy and re-irradiation for locoregionally recurrent head and neck cancer. *Semin Oncol.* 2008;35:251-261.

53. Spencer SA, Harris J, Wheeler RH, et al. Final report of RTOG 9610, a multi-institutional trial of reirradiation and chemotherapy for unresectable recurrent squamous cell carcinoma of the head and neck. *Head Neck.* 2008;30:281-288.

54. Langer CJ, Harris J, Horwitz EM, et al. Phase II study of low-dose paclitaxel and cisplatin in combination with split-course concomitant twice-daily reirradiation in recurrent squamous cell carcinoma of the head and neck: results of Radiation Therapy Oncology Group Protocol 9911. *J Clin Oncol.* 2007;25:4800-4805.

55. Heron DE, Ferris RL, Karamouzis M, et al. Stereotactic body radiotherapy for recurrent squamous cell carcinoma of the head and neck: results of a phase I dose-escalation trial. *Int J Radiat Oncol Biol Phys.* 2009;75:1493-1500.

56. Xu KM, Quan K, Clump DA, et al. Stereotactic ablative radiosurgery for locally advanced or recurrent skull base malignancies with prior external beam radiation therapy. *Front Oncol.* 2015;5:65.

57. Van der Schroeff MP, Derks W, Hordijk GJ, et al. The effect of age on survival and quality of life in elderly head and neck cancer patients: a long-term prospective study. *Eur Arch Otorhinolaryngol.* 2007;264:415-422.

58. Theunissen EA, Bosma SC, Zuur CL, et al. Sensorineural hearing loss in patients with head and neck cancer after chemoradiotherapy and radiotherapy: a review of the literature. *Head Neck.* 2015;37:281-292.

59. Capozzi LC, McNeely ML, Lau HY, et al. Patient-reported outcomes, body composition, and nutritional status in patients with head and neck cancer: results from an exploratory randomized controlled exercise trial. *Cancer.* 2016;122(8):1185-1200.

60. VanderWalde NA, Deal AM, Comitz E, et al. Functional age and tolerance to radiotherapy: a prospective study of a comprehensive geriatric assessment [abstract]. *J Clin Oncol.* 2015;33(suppl). Abstract e20534.

61. Pottel L, Lycke M, Boterberg T, et al. G-8 indicates overall and quality-adjusted survival in older head and neck cancer patients treated with curative radiochemotherapy. *BMC Cancer* 2015;15:875-886.

62. Brugel L, Laurent M, Caillet P, et al. Impact of comprehensive geriatric assessment on survival, function, and nutritional status in elderly patients with head and neck cancer: protocol for a multicentre randomised controlled trial (EGéSOR). *BMC Cancer.* 2014;14:427-435.

Pancreatic Cancer

Elizabeth Won

INTRODUCTION

In the United States, more than 48,000 patients are diagnosed with pancreatic cancer annually, and it is the fourth most common cause of cancer death. Pancreatic cancer is a disease occurring in older adults, with a median age of 71 years at diagnosis and highest incidence among patients age 75 to 84 years (1). However, older patients are less likely to be recommended for surgery and less likely to receive chemotherapy compared with younger patients (2). Clearly, patient-related factors such as comorbidities, functional status, and limited social support affect the ability to deliver and tolerate treatment and thus have a direct effect on the survival of older adults. However, there are data that elderly patients have a lower likelihood of being offered treatment based on age alone (3,4). This review evaluates the current knowledge and the remaining challenges in optimal management of elderly patients with pancreatic cancer.

TREATMENT OF EARLY STAGE PANCREATIC CANCER IN OLDER PATIENTS

Surgery for Pancreas Cancer

The only potentially curative approach for pancreatic cancer is surgical resection. Only 15% to 20% of all patients are candidates for pancreatomy or pancreaticoduodenectomy (Whipple procedure), which is a complex, invasive procedure with high rates of morbidity and mortality. Older patients are less likely to undergo surgery. A study examining the Surveillance, Epidemiology, and End Results (SEER) database for treatment of pancreatic cancer between 1983 and 2007 showed that for patients older than 70 years, the odds of surgery being done were 55% less than for younger patients (4). Single institution reports have demonstrated that Whipple surgery can be performed safely in patients aged 80 years and above (5–7), with lower mortality rates seen at high-volume institutions. However, nationally operative mortality (death before hospital discharge) has been shown to increase proportionally with age: 6.7% of patients aged 65 to 69 years, 9.3% of patients aged 70 to 79 years, and 15.5% of patients aged 80 years or older (8). Unfortunately, the 5-year survival for localized pancreatic cancer remains very poor, approximately 29%, and therefore the benefit of surgery must be weighed carefully with the risks (9).

In a study by Tan et al., the authors examined a national database for the presence of geriatric events after surgery in patients over the age of 65 (10). These events included dehydration, delirium, falls, fractures, failure to thrive, and pressure ulcers, which are not commonly reported in the surgical literature. A quarter of all patients undergoing pancreatic cancer surgery experience a geriatric event, with even higher rates seen in those aged 75 years or older. These geriatric events were associated with prolonged hospitalization (odds ratio [OR] 5.97; 95% confidence interval [CI] 5.16–5.80) and higher cost (OR, 4.97; 95% CI 4.58–5.39). This is consistent with the surgical literature reporting higher postoperative complications and longer hospitalizations in older patients (11,12). Furthermore, discharge to an inpatient nursing facility increases from 10.6% to 36.7% when comparing patients aged 65 to 69 to those 80 years and older (8).

There are conflicting data about the overall prognosis after pancreatic surgery, with some studies suggesting decreased overall survival (OS) in older patients (8,13,14). Sho et al. showed median survival of 16.6 months in patients aged 80 years and above compared to 23.2 months in younger patients, with worse disease-specific survival in the older patient group ($P = .013$) (15). Multiple factors likely play a role in the prognosis after surgery, including tumor biology, ability of elderly patients to complete adjuvant chemotherapy, decreased functional reserve, and geriatric syndromes affecting recovery after pancreatic resection.

Preoperative Geriatric Assessment

Comprehensive geriatric assessment (CGA) has the potential to identify those at risk for postoperative complications, functional disability, and cognitive decline and to provide an opportunity to implement interventions and support before, during, and after surgery (16,17). The University of Chicago team prospectively studied the ability of a CGA to predict surgical outcomes in older patients undergoing Whipple surgery (18). A measure of frailty, *self-reported exhaustion*, which would have not been identified on a traditional preoperative evaluation, was predictive of major surgical complications (OR = 4.06; $P = .01$), necessity of intensive care unit (ICU) stay (OR = 4.30; $P = .01$), and length of overall hospital stay ($\beta = 0.27$; $P = .02$).

Postoperative management of elderly surgical patients must be specialized to avoid geriatric events, including delirium, malnutrition, pressure ulcers, falls, infection, functional decline, and polypharmacy. With adequate and collaborative perioperative care between the surgical and geriatric teams, the risk of morbidity and mortality for older patients may be mitigated.

Adjuvant Chemotherapy

Adjuvant chemotherapy has been shown to improve outcomes compared to surgical resection alone in two large phase 3 studies (Table 21.1). There are limited data regarding the number of elderly represented in these trials; however, both studies reported no differences in survival by age in the multivariable analysis. It is important to note that the median age in these trials was 62 and 63 years, respectively, and the median age at the time of diagnosis of pancreatic cancer in the United States is 71 years. Gemcitabine has been the accepted standard adjuvant chemotherapy and should be considered in a fit patient who has recovered from surgery. Significant common toxicities include myelosuppression, fatigue, diarrhea, nausea, decreased appetite, and flu-like symptoms after infusion.

TABLE 21.1 Adjuvant Chemotherapy Trials for Pancreatic Cancer

Study	Regimen	Patient Characteristics	Major Toxicities	Outcomes	Summary
CONKO-001 trial (19)	Adjuvant gemcitabine 1,000 mg/m^2 day 1, 8, 15 of 28-d schedule for six cycles vs. observation	N = 368 Median age 62 y	▪ Hematologic toxicity: -30% any grade -2.4% grade 3/4 ▪ Nonhematologic toxicity: -21% nausea/vomiting -9% diarrhea, edema -4% infection ▪ LFT elevation -20% any grade AST/ALT -0.5% grade 3/4	▪ Median DFS 13.4 vs. 5.7 mo ▪ Median OS 22.8 vs. 20.2 mo 5-y survival 20.7% vs. 10.4%	▪ Tolerable regimen that improves survival ▪ Only 62% of patients were given the full six cycles of treatment with average weekly dose of 700 mg/m^2 ▪ Requires close monitoring for myelosuppresion and neutropenic fever
ESPAC-3 trial (20)	Adjuvant folinic acid 20 mg/m^2 followed by 5-FU 425 mg/m^2 IV given day 1–5 every 28 d for six cycles vs. gemcitabine 1,000 mg/m^2 day 1, 8, 15 of 28-d schedule for six cycles vs. observation	N = 1,088 Median age 63 y	▪ 5-FU arm: significantly higher rates of grade 3/4 stomatitis, diarrhea ▪ Gemcitabine arm: higher rates of 3/4 hematologic toxicity ▪ 14% of 5-FU patients with SAEs compared to 7.5% receiving gemcitabine (P < .001)	▪ Median OS 23.0 mo in 5-FU arm vs. 23.6 mo with gemcitabine	▪ 5-FU arm: 55% received full six cycles; median dose intensity 79% ▪ Gemcitabine arm: 60% received full six cycles, median dose intensity 89% ▪ No significant differences in quality of life scores

5-FU, 5-fluorouracil; ALT, alanine transaminase; AST, aspartate transaminase; DFS, disease-free survival; LFT, liver function tests; OS, overall survival; SAE, serious adverse events.

There are no data on dose modifications to improve tolerability for older patients and potential impacts on efficacy. For older patients, close weekly monitoring of toxicity with a low threshold for dose adjustments is recommended.

Although the benefits of adjuvant chemotherapy are evident, the rates of older patients receiving treatment remain low. A SEER analysis showed that less than half of all patients 65 years or older received adjuvant therapy after surgery (21). Not receiving adjuvant chemotherapy has been shown to be an independent poor prognostic factor in older patients. In a community-based cohort, which included 178 patients aged 70 and above, patients who did not receive adjuvant chemotherapy had significantly worse median OS of 13.1 months versus 21.8 months for treated patients (hazard ratio [HR] 1.89, $P = .002$). In contrast, older patients who did receive adjuvant chemotherapy had similar outcomes to younger patients (21.8 vs. 22.5 months, $P = .576$) (22). Pancreatic cancer remained the cause of death equally in both groups. Efforts to increase the use of adjuvant chemotherapy in older patients may improve overall outcomes; clearly more research is necessary in this area. Postsurgical geriatric assessments may provide data to better stratify older patients who might benefit from adjuvant therapy.

MANAGEMENT OF ADVANCED/METASTATIC DISEASE

Systemic Chemotherapy

More than half of patients have metastatic disease at the time of diagnosis. The prognosis remains dismal, with a 5-year survival rate of 7% (1). Gemcitabine was considered the standard of care for patients with metastatic pancreas cancer. The MPACT phase 3 trial demonstrated the superiority of gemcitabine and nab-paclitaxel compared with gemcitabine monotherapy, OS 8.5 months versus 6.7 months, respectively, $P < .001$ (23). The median age of patients in the study was 63 years, with only 42% of patients 65 years of age or older. FOLFIRINOX chemotherapy was compared to gemcitabine monotherapy in the ACCORD-11 trial, showing an OS of 11.1 months versus 6.8 months, $P < .001$ (24). Treatment-related toxicity for FOLFIRINOX was high, with higher rates of grade 3 or 4 adverse events. This study excluded patients with an Eastern Cooperative Oncology Group (ECOG) score greater than 1 and patients older than 75 years of age. The median age of patients in the study was 61 years, with only 29% of patients between 65 and 75. Although these studies have advanced the treatment options for metastatic pancreatic cancer, the limited representation of older patients in the studies makes it difficult to extrapolate the data to an elderly population.

There are few small, mostly retrospective, studies focused on older patients (Table 21.2). These studies suggest not only that chemotherapy is feasible in elderly patients with pancreatic cancer, but also that those with good functional status can obtain palliative benefit comparable to what is seen in younger patients.

There are data showing that dose and schedule attenuations in the combination chemotherapy regimens can reduce side effects without impacting efficacy. A single-institution study revealed that changing the gemcitabine and nab-paclitaxel regimen from weekly to every other week resulted in a median overall survival (OS) of 11.1 months and median progression-free survival (PFS) of 4.8 months. The attenuated

TABLE 21.2 Elderly-Specific Trials of Advanced Pancreatic Cancer

Authors	Type of Study	Regimen	Definition of Elderly (Age in Years)	Patient Characteristics	Conclusions
Aldoss et al. (25)	Retrospective review of Veterans Affair Central Cancer Registry 1995–2007	Data do not include chemotherapy regimen	≥80	N = 440	■ 83% received no treatment, 12% (n = 52) received chemotherapy ■ In chemotherapy group, median OS was 4.9 mo vs. 1.7 mo without therapy
Locher et al. (26)	Prospective observational study	Gemcitabine	≥70	N = 39, of which 17 had metastatic disease, 22 had locally advanced disease Median age 74, majority had ECOG 2–3 status	■ 23 patients (59%) received 100% of planned dose intensity; 38% required dose reductions ■ 38% grade 3–4 neutropenia ■ ECOG PS improved in 18% during treatment; disease-related symptoms improved in 16% ■ OS 10 mo

(*continued*)

TABLE 21.2 Elderly-Specific Trials of Advanced Pancreatic Cancer (*Continued*)

Authors	Type of Study	Regimen	Definition of Elderly (Age in Years)	Patient Characteristics	Conclusions
Marechal et al. (27)	Retrospective review of patients included in phase 2 and 3 studies	■ Gemcitabine ■ Gemcitabine combination therapy	≥70	N = 99; 42 ≥70 y Over 70% had KPS ≥ 90%	■ Higher rate of neutropenia, anemia, and peripheral neuropathy in older patients ■ No difference in OS or TTP based on age
Vickers et al. (28)	Retrospective analysis of phase 3 study with dichotomy for age	Randomized to gemcitabine plus erlotinib or placebo	≥65	N = 569; 268 ≥65 y	■ Neither age nor comorbidity index was associated with OS ■ Median OS approximately 6 mo in both groups, no difference in age ■ Higher infection rates in combination arm in age ≥ 65 y. No difference in toxicity with age in gemcitabine arm

(continued)

TABLE 21.2 Elderly-Specific Trials of Advanced Pancreatic Cancer (*Continued*)

Authors	Type of Study	Regimen	Definition of Elderly (Age in Years)	Patient Characteristics	Conclusions
Nakai et al. (29)	Retrospective review 2001–2009	▪ Gemcitabine ▪ Gemcitabine + S-1	≥75	*N* = 237; 69 ≥75 y, of which only 59% received chemotherapy	▪ Comorbidity index, but not age, was prognostic
Li et al. (30)	Retrospective review 2005–2013	▪ Gemcitabine (55%) ▪ Gemcitabine combination (33%) ▪ FOLFOX (3%) ▪ FOLFIRINOX (3%)	≥75	Total *N* = 237; Age 75–79, *n* = 114 Age 80–84, *n* = 84 Age ≥85, *n* = 39 197 (83%) received chemotherapy	▪ Entire population, median OS 7 mo ▪ For patients who received chemotherapy, OS 7.9 mo vs. 2.3 mo in no therapy group (*P* < .01) ▪ 56% had grade ≥3 event requiring hospitalization
Alessandretti et al. (31)	Retrospective review	Dose-attenuated FOLFIRINOX	>65	*N* = 21; median age 67 (range 65–79)	▪ Grade 3/4 toxicity in 33% ▪ Approximately 25% required further dose reductions ▪ Median OS 11.8 mo, PFS 6.9 mo

ECOG PS, Eastern Cooperative Oncology Group Performance Status; KPS, Karnofsky Performance Status; OS, overall survival; PFS, progression-free survival; TTP; time to progression.

schedule reduced the rates of grade 3 neurological toxicity significantly (<2% vs. 17% in the MPACT study) (32). The Memorial Sloan Kettering Cancer Center group has been using FOLFIRINOX with a 20% dose reduction compared to the dosages in the ACCORD-11 trial while showing similar efficacy (median OS 12.5 months) and decreased rates of toxicity reported in the original trial (33).

Considering the data available, a potential algorithm for treatment is proposed in Figure 21.1. For elderly patients who are fully functional and candidates for FOLFIRINOX, dose attenuation is recommended. This proposed algorithm is based on ECOG score, which is commonly used by practicing oncologists to assess patients. There is evidence that ECOG score does not correlate with geriatric assessment results and may misrepresent functional status and/or patient vulnerability to chemotherapy toxicity.

Palliation and Supportive Measures

Patients with advanced pancreatic cancer often present with a high symptom burden, so palliative care is a vital part of the management of these patients. In general, elderly patients with cancer pain are undertreated and many underreport their pain symptoms. Untreated pain can result in worsening of quality of life, depressed mood, and deterioration of functional status (34). Oral narcotics can be very effective for cancer pain control; however, caution should be undertaken to avoid polypharmacy toxicity, delirium, and increasing risk of falls. Another treatment option for control of pain is a celiac block, which may decrease the amount of narcotics necessary. Obstruction is a common complication in pancreatic cancer. Biliary stent placement

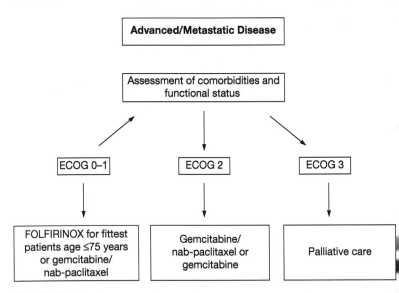

FIGURE 21.1 Choices of chemotherapy regimens for elderly patients with metastatic pancreatic cancer.

ECOG, Eastern Cooperative Oncology Group.

can resolve biliary obstruction in 90% of patients and has been shown to improve quality of life. Duodenal obstructions can be palliated with stents or gastrojejunostomy tubes for comfort. A multidisciplinary approach for addressing the patient's symptoms, concerns, and personal expectations and goals from the time of diagnosis to end of life is recommended in all pancreatic cancer patients.

CONCLUSION

As our patient population ages, oncology research and treatment guidelines must adapt accordingly. Age alone should not be the determinant for the selection of patients for treatment in pancreatic cancer. Older patients who receive treatment have improved outcomes similar to those of younger patients. CGAs may help to better tailor treatment approaches in our older patients and provide an avenue for future research into this malignancy.

TAKE HOME POINTS

1. Pancreas surgery provides the only curative option for localized pancreatic cancer; however, it is an intensive procedure with potentially high rates of complications in older patients.
2. Preoperative geriatric assessment should be considered for older patients who are surgical candidates, with close postsurgical follow-up for cardiopulmonary and geriatric complications.
3. Adjuvant chemotherapy can improve survival outcomes, but requires close monitoring, in the older patient who has recovered sufficiently after surgery.
4. Although systemic chemotherapy has been shown to improve outcomes, advanced pancreatic cancer has a very poor prognosis. Patient goals and preferences should be addressed on an ongoing basis, with supportive measures provided for symptoms.
5. For older patients who receive systemic chemotherapy, dose attenuations and schedule modifications should be considered given the palliative nature of the treatment.

REFERENCES

1. SEER Cancer Statistics Factsheets: Pancreas Cancer. National Cancer Institute. Bethesda, MD. Available at: https://seer.cancer.gov/statfacts/html/pancreas.html. Accessed March 13, 2017.
2. Niederhuber JE, Brennan MF, Menck HR. The National Cancer Database report on pancreatic cancer. *Cancer*. 1995;76:1671-1676.
3. Bouchardy C, Rapiti E, Blagojevic S, et al. Older female cancer patients: importance, causes, and consequences of undertreatment. *J Clin Oncol*. 2007;25:1858-1869.
4. Amin S, Lucas AL, Frucht H. Evidence for treatment and survival disparities by age in pancreatic adenocarcinoma: a population-based analysis. *Pancreas*. 2013;42(2):249-253.

5. Sohn TA, Yeo CJ, Cameron JL, et al. Should pancreaticoduodenectomy be performed in octogenarians? *J Gastrointest Surg.* 1998;2:207-216.

6. Stauffer JA, Grewal MS, Martin JK, et al. Pancreas surgery is safe for octogenarians. *J Am Geriatr Soc.* 2011;59:184-186.

7. Hatzaras I, Schmidt C, Klemanski D, et al. Pancreatic resection in the octogenarian: a safe option for pancreatic malignancy. *J Am Coll Surg.* 2011;212:373-377.

8. Finlayson E, Fan Z, Birkmeyer JD. Outcomes in octogenarians undergoing high-risk cancer operation: a national study. *J Am Coll Surg.* 2007;205:729-734.

9. Howlader N, Noone AM, Krapcho M, et al., eds. *SEER Cancer Statistics Review (CSR), 1975-2013,* Bethesda, MD: National Cancer Institute. Available at: http://seer.cancer.gov/csr/1975_2013. Accessed March 13, 2017.

10. Tan H-J, Saliba D, Kwan L, et al. Burden of geriatric events among older adults undergoing major cancer surgery. *J Clin Oncol.* 2016;34(11):1231-1238. doi:10.1200/JCO.2015.63.4592.

11. Riall TS, Sheffield KM, Kuo YF, et al. Resection benefits older adults with locoregional pancreatic cancer despite greater short-term morbidity and mortality. *J Am Geriatr Soc.* 2011;59:647-654.

12. Brozzetti S, Mazzoni G, Miccini M, et al. Surgical treatment of pancreatic head carcinoma in elderly patients. *Arch Surg.* 2006;141(2):137-142.

13. Makary MA, Winter JM, Cameron JL, et al. Pancreaticoduodenectomy in the very elderly. *J Gastrointest Surg.* 2006;10:347-356.

14. Bathe OF, Levi D, Caldera H, et al. Radical resection of periampullary tumors in the elderly: evaluation of long-term results. *World J Surg.* 2000;24:353-358.

15. Sho M, Murakami Y, Kawai M, et al. Prognosis after surgical treatment for pancreatic cancer in patients aged 80 years or older: a multicenter study. *J Hepatobiliary Pancreat Sci.* 2016;23:188-197.

16. Korc-Gordzicki B, Downey RJ, Sharokni A, et al. Surgical considerations in older adults with cancer. *J Clin Oncol.* 2014;32:2647-2653.

17. PACE Participants, Audisio RA, Pope D, et al. Shall we operate? Preoperative assessment in elderly cancer patients (PACE) can help. A SIOG surgical task force prospective study. *Crit Rev Oncol Hematol.* 2008;65:156-163.

18. Dale W, Hemmerich J, Kamm A, et al. Geriatric assessment improves prediction of surgical outcomes in older adults undergoing pancreaticoduodenectomy: a prospective cohort study. *Ann Surg.* 2014:259:960-965.

19. Oettle H, Neuhaus P, Hochhaus A, et al. Adjuvant chemotherapy with gemcitabine and long-term outcomes among patients with resected pancreatic cancer: the CONKO-001 randomized trial. *JAMA.* 2013;310(14):1473-1481. doi:10.1001/jama.2013.279201.

20. Oettle H, Post S, Neuhaus P, et al. Adjuvant chemotherapy with gemcitabine vs observation in patients undergoing curative-intent resection of pancreatic cancer: a randomized controlled trial. *JAMA.* 2007;297(3):267-277.

21. Davila JA, Chiao EY, Hasche JC, et al. Utilization and determinants of adjuvant therapy among older patients who receive curative surgery for pancreatic cancer. *Pancreas.* 2009;38:e18-e25.

22. Nagrial AM, Chang DK, Nguyen NQ, et al. Adjuvant chemotherapy in elderly patient with pancreatic cancer. *Br J Cancer.* 2014;110:313-319.

23. Von Hoff DD, Ervin T, Arena FP, et al. Increased survival in pancreatic cancer with nab-paclitaxel plus gemcitabine. *N Eng J Med.* 2013;369:1691-1703.

24. Conroy T, Desseigne F, Ychou M, et al. FOLFIRINOX versus gemcitabine for metastatic pancreas cancer. *N Engl J Med.* 2011;364:1817-1825.

25. Aldoss IT, Tashi T, Gonsalves W. Role of chemotherapy in very elderly patients with metastatic pancreatic cancer—a Veterans Affairs Cancer Registry analysis. *J Geriatr Oncol.* 2011;2:209-214.

26. Locher C, Fabre-Guillevin E, Brunetti F, et al. Fixed-dose rate gemcitabine in elderly patients with advanced pancreatic cancer: an observational study. *Crit Rev Oncol Hematol.* 2008;68:172-182.

27. Maréchal R, Demols A, Gay F, et al. Tolerance and efficacy of gemcitabine and gemcitabine-based regimens in elderly patients with advanced pancreatic cancer. *Pancreas.* 2008;36:e16-e21.

28. Vickers MM, Powell ED, Asmis TR, et al. Comorbidity, age and overall survival in patients with advanced pancreatic cancer—results from NCIC CTG PA.3: a phase III trial of gemcitabine plus erlotinib or placebo. *Eur J Cancer.* 2012;48(10):1434-1442.

29. Nakai Y, Isayama H, Sasaki T, et al. Comorbidity, not age, is prognostic in patients with advanced pancreatic cancer receiving gemcitabine-based chemotherapy. *Crit Rev Oncol Hematol.* 2011;78(3):252-259.

30. Li D, Capanu M, Yu KH, et al. Treatment, outcomes, and clinical trial participation in elderly patients with metastatic pancreas cancer. *Clin Colorectal Cancer.* 2015;14:269-276.

31. Alessandretti MB, Moreira RB, Brandao EP, et al. Safety and efficacy of modified dose attenuated FOLFIRINOX chemotherapy in patients over 65 years with advanced pancreatic adenocarcinoma [abstract]. *J Clin Oncol.* 2013.(suppl). Abstract e15176.

32. Krishna K, Blazer MA, Wei L, et al. Modified gemcitabine and nab-paclitaxel in patients with metastatic pancreatic cancer (MPC): a single-institution experience [abstract]. *J Clin Oncol.* 2015;33(suppl 3). Abstract 366.

33. Lowery MA, Yu KH, Adel NG, et al. Activity of front-line FOLFIRINOX (FFX) in stage III/IV pancreatic adenocarcinoma (PC) at Memorial Sloan-Kettering Cancer Center (MSKCC) [abstract]. *J Clin Oncol.* 2012;30(suppl). Abstract 4057.

34. Ferrell BR, Wisdom C, Wenzl C. Quality of life as an outcome variable in the management of cancer pain. *Cancer.* 1989;63:2321-2327.

Bladder and Renal Cancer

Ravindran Kanesvaran

BLADDER CANCER IN THE ELDERLY

Cancer is a disease of aging, and bladder cancer (BC) is a classic example of the interaction between cancer and aging. The median age of diagnosis of BC in the United States from the period 2008 to 2012 was 73 years (1). It is the fifth most commonly diagnosed cancer in the United States, with a predominant majority of patients being elderly (1). The management of BC in the elderly is complicated by their functional status and the numerous other comorbidities that afflict them. Hence, it is important for these patients to get a comprehensive geriatric assessment (CGA) in order to better stratify them into the appropriate treatment group. Numerous CGA-based studies have found it to be an important tool that can not only prognosticate but also predict treatment toxicity and treatment selection (2–4). In general, these patients can then be classified into three categories—the fit patients, the vulnerable patients, or the frail elderly patients (5). In this chapter we review the data pertaining to the numerous treatment modalities that are used for the treatment of BC and renal cell carcinoma (RCC) in the elderly, taking into account their general state of health and their CGA results.

Superficial BC

The recommendation for the fit elderly BC patient will be to undergo a complete transurethral resection of the bladder tumor (TURBT) and intravesical therapy. There are limited data describing the benefit of intravesical therapy in elderly BC patients with nonmuscle invasive disease. A single-institution study that stratified patients into those aged above and below 70 years with superficial BC found that older patients had a higher risk of cancer recurrence in spite of bacillus Calmette-Guerin (BCG) intravesical therapy (6). In another Surveillance, Epidemiology, and End Results (SEER) database study, overall survival (OS) for this group of patients appears to be longer when treated with adjuvant BCG therapy compared to those without it (7). Based on the CGA, frail patients may be limited in terms of the treatment options available for them. Treatment of patients with low-risk disease with TURBT may be appropriate and can be done under regional anesthesia if they are unfit for general anesthesia. Even intermediate and high-risk frail patients can receive intravesical BCG, as it is a low-risk local procedure. However, those patients with a short predicted life expectancy should just be treated expectantly for any symptoms that may arise from the disease.

Muscle Invasive Bladder Cancer

Muscle invasive bladder cancer (MIBC) is defined as cancer that has invaded the muscularis propria of the bladder wall (T2 disease and beyond). Treatment for localized MIBC involves multimodality therapy. Hence, apart from a CGA to assess the fitness of the patient to receive these various treatment modalities, it is also important for these cases to be discussed in a multidisciplinary tumor board setting.

RADICAL CYSTECTOMY

Fit elderly MIBC patients should receive radical cystectomy as part of their treatment if the intent is curative. However, patient selection is important in order to reduce the risk of postoperative morbidity and mortality associated with the surgery. In age-unselected populations, the morbidity and mortality from radical cystectomy from a large number of studies range from 30% to 70% and 0.3% to 7.9% respectively (8). The development of nomograms has helped with predicting 90-day survival and complication rates from this procedure with reasonable accuracy (8,9). Nonetheless, apart from the risk stratification based on nomograms, increasing age by itself seems to predict poorer outcomes and is associated with worse cancer-specific outcomes in patients undergoing radical cystectomy (10). The urinary diversion tends to contribute to the postsurgical complications experienced by elderly patients. Still, older patients who tend to receive ileal conduits seem to report no difference in terms of diversion-related complications, operative mortality, and quality of life (QOL) compared to those who had orthotopic bladder surgery (11). There are a number of surgical techniques that can be used to perform the radical cystectomy, though there is limited data regarding the use of these modalities specific to elderly MIBC patients (1). One meta-analysis looking at laparoscopic versus open radical cystectomy reported lower intraoperative blood loss but longer operative time with laparoscopic surgery (12). In a randomized study in older MIBC patients, robot-assisted radical cystectomy, which is gaining popularity of late, has shown findings of lower blood loss and longer preoperative time, but was found to have similar lengths of stay when compared to the open surgery group (13). In summary, elderly MIBC patients who are fit should receive radical cystectomy as the standard of care after a careful assessment using some of the validated nomograms for postoperative mortality and morbidity. The choice of urinary diversion and surgical method can be made after a discussion with the patient based on the evidence described earlier and the level of expertise available in the particular center.

CHEMOTHERAPY

Chemotherapy plays an integral role in the treatment of MIBC patients. It can be used in the neoadjuvant setting, adjuvant setting, or together with radiotherapy as concurrent chemoradiotherapy (CRT) in MIBC treatment. Cisplatin is a key component of two of the proven chemotherapy combinations used in the treatment of MIBC; together with gemcitabine (GC) or together with methotrexate, vinblastine, and doxorubicin (MVAC). However, due to its significant toxicities, it can only be used for a select group of patients known as cisplatin-eligible MIBC or metastatic BC patients as defined by a consensus group statement published in 2011 (14). The inclusion criteria for cisplatin-eligible patients are based on their performance status, creatinine clearance, degree of hearing loss, degree of peripheral neuropathy and New York Heart Association classification (15). For cisplatin-eligible patients, neoadjuvant chemotherapy with MVAC for treatment of MIBC would be the treatment of choice prior to radical cystectomy based on improvement of OS as reported in a large meta-analysis (16). Unfortunately, trials on adjuvant therapy for MIBC have failed to show a statistically significant OS benefit due to poor accruals (17). Thus, the preferred treatment approach should be with neoadjuvant chemotherapy. As all these data were drawn from all persons enrolled into the studies and were not specific to elderly MIBC patients, these patients should be assessed for their risk of getting grade 3 to 5 chemo-related toxicities based on available chemo-toxicity prediction tools that have been developed (3). A review of how to treat BC in the elderly nicely summarizes the lack of data for elderly patients and how best to extrapolate from available data to treat this group of patients (18).

CHEMORADIOTHERAPY

For select elderly MIBC patients who are unfit for surgery or are keen for a bladder-sparing approach, concurrent CRT may be a suitable option. These patients should have no invasion of adjacent viscera, no nodal involvement, no carcinoma in situ, and no disease near the bladder trigone with hydronephrosis. They should have had maximal TURBT and most importantly be found to be fit enough to tolerate concurrent CRT. Thereafter, these patients should comply with surveillance cystoscopy and, should any recurrence be detected, be prepared for a radical cystectomy. A number of elderly-specific studies have shown promising data, with complete response and disease-free survival rates comparable to patients who had undergone radical cystectomy (19). In a pooled analysis of Radiation Therapy Oncology Group (RTOG) studies, though older patients were less likely to complete CRT compared with younger patients, they reported similar complete response rates, bladder preservation rates, and disease-specific survival rates as their younger counterparts (20). In summary, CRT is a reasonable curative option to consider in elderly cancer patients who desire bladder preservation. Frail MIBC patients are unlikely to be candidates for radical cystectomy or CRT, but they can be offered palliative care for symptom control. RT alone can be considered a reasonable palliative option for these patients, as it may help control symptoms like pain and hematuria and also slow down the growth of the tumor (21).

Metastatic Bladder Cancer

The OS from metastatic bladder cancer (MBC), even with combination chemotherapy, is relatively poor at about 1 year on average (22). The current standard of care for fit MBC patients in the first line would be to use either MVAC or GC chemotherapy. A phase 3 study comparing both these regimens reported comparable survival outcomes with increased toxicities from the use of MVAC (22). Hence, GC has become the treatment of choice in fit cisplatin-eligible elderly MBC patients. For those who are cisplatin-ineligible, carboplatin may be substituted with similar outcomes and lower toxicity when compared to MCV (methotrexate, carboplatin, and vinblastine) chemotherapy (23). In the very near future, immune checkpoint inhibitors may be an important therapeutic option with a tolerable side effect profile that elderly MBC patients can avail themselves of (24).

Frail elderly MBC patients can either be given single-agent GC chemotherapy (25) or offered best supportive care with palliative treatment for symptom relief.

RCC IN THE ELDERLY

RCC is predominantly a disease afflicting the elderly, with a median age of diagnosis of 64 years. It is a heterogenous group of histopathologic subtypes, with clear cell carcinoma being the dominant subtype accounting for more than 75% of all RCCs. About 30% of RCC patients are metastatic at diagnosis, and recurrence rates of those treated for localized disease are as high as 50%. All elderly RCC patients should get a CGA done as well. Currently, the only available treatment guideline specific to the treatment of metastatic renal cell carcinoma (mRCC) in elderly patients is the one developed in 2009 by a SIOG task force (26).

Localized RCC

FIT ELDERLY PATIENT WITH LOCALIZED RCC

In a fit elderly patient, there are a number of options to treat a localized RCC. These options vary depending on the size and site of the tumor. For solitary RCC that is 4 cm or larger, the treatment of choice would be a radical nephrectomy (RN). This can be done safely laparoscopically, with one study showing reduced morbidity in terms of genitourinary complication rate and blood loss in elderly RCC patients compared to laparoscopic partial nephrectomy (PN) or open PN (27). With the rampant use of imaging in the investigation of symptoms in elderly patients, there has been an increase in the detection of small renal masses (<4 cm), of which a substantial number are RCC (28). In fit elderly patients, nephron-sparing surgeries are the treatment of choice for localized small RCCs based on their location. In certain locations, PN may not be possible, necessitating use of RN in those circumstances. There are currently no data to support any form of adjuvant therapy following surgical resection of the RCC (29). Therefore, these patients should be on an active surveillance protocol, although there is currently no consensus on the exact frequency of imaging in the various guidelines (30).

FRAIL ELDERLY PATIENT WITH LOCALIZED RCC

Frail elderly patients with a solitary renal mass may not have many treatment options available to them. For large tumors (≥4 cm), these patients may not be fit for any form of surgery and will be treated expectantly for symptom control with palliative care. However, they may have more options with local ablative therapy if they have small RCCs (<4 cm). The common methods of ablative therapy are radiofrequency ablation (RFA) or cryoablation. A systematic review comparing cryoablation versus PN reported higher rates of tumor progression with cryoablation, but both had similar low rates of distant metastases of less than 2% (31), hence making it a suitable option for the frail elderly patient. Another feasible option for the frail elderly RCC patient would be active surveillance of a small RCC (32).

Metastatic RCC

Since 2005, a number of targeted therapies have been developed that have revolutionized the way we treat elderly mRCC patients. Apart from high-dose interleukin-2, which has shown efficacy in a small group of younger patients, there are no data to support cytokine use in the elderly (33). These mRCC patients should first be stratified into the appropriate prognostic risk group as defined by either the MSKCC or IMDC criteria (34). Table 22.1 shows the various phase 3 clinical trials that have led to the approval of the targeted therapies for use in the different settings in the treatment of mRCC. Data for the elderly can be extrapolated from these phase 3 studies, as about one-third of the patients enrolled in them were over 65 years of age (26). A study comparing patient preference between sunitinib and pazopanib reported that a majority of patients prefer pazopanib due to its better toxicity profile and QOL (44). Although this was not an elderly-specific study, the lower toxicities and better QOL assessment make it a suitable choice for the elderly.

For MSKCC poor risk (PR) patients, temsirolimus—though the drug of choice—has not been shown to increase survival in patients over 65 years of age compared to interferon (IFN) (38). In the second-line setting, there are a number of drugs approved for use (Table 22.1). Recently reported studies indicate that treatment with nivolumab (PD1 inhibitor) or the tyrosine kinase inhibitor cabozantinib may be suitable options for elderly mRCC patients after they were found to have superior efficacy and better tolerability when compared with everolimus (39,40). Although these drugs have shown that they are reasonably well tolerated in the younger population in which they were tested, it is important to note that elderly patients have a multitude of other issues (such as comorbidity, decreased physiological reserve, and polypharmacy) that must be taken into account before they are treated with these drugs.

TAKE HOME POINTS

1. All elderly BC and RCC patients should get a CGA done and have their case discussed in a multidisciplinary tumor board before deciding on the most appropriate treatment for them. If chemotherapy is planned, chemotoxicity prediction tools should be used as well.
2. Fit elderly BC patients should be offered the same treatment options as are offered to younger patients, including surgery, CRT, or palliative chemotherapy depending on the stage of the disease.
3. Frail elderly patients with MBC should be offered expectant management with palliative care. However, with superficial BC, TURBT and intravesical therapy may still be offered in view of their tolerability even in frail elderly patients.
4. Fit elderly patients with RCC should be offered surgery (RN or PN depending on the size and location of the lesion). Patients with mRCC, depending on their risk stratification, should receive targeted therapies just like their younger counterparts.
5. Frail elderly patients with localized RCC may be offered local ablative therapy or active surveillance; mRCC patients can be offered targeted therapies depending on their degree of frailty, concurrent medication use, and predicted life expectancy.

TABLE 22.1 Summary of Selected Phase 3 Trials for Approved Agents With Elderly mRCC Patients Enrolled

Line of Treatment (MSKCC Risk Group)	Phase 3 Trial	Median Age (Years)	Age of Oldest Patient (Years)	PFS (Months)	OS (Months)	Common Toxicities
First (GR)	Sunitinib (35)	62	87	11	26.4	Diarrhea, vomiting, hypertension, PPE, neutropenia, anemia, thrombocytopenia,
First (GR)	Bevacizumab + IFN-α (36)	61	82	8.5	18.3	bleeding, hypertension, and proteinuria.
First (GR)	Pazopanib (37)	59	85	9.2	22.9	Diarrhea, vomiting, hypertension, hair color changes, nausea, anorexia, ALT and AST elevation.
First (PR)	Temsirolimus (38)	58	81	3.8	10.9	Rash, peripheral edema, stomatitis, nausea, hyperglycemia, and hyperlipidemia.
Second	Nivolumab (39)	62	88	4.6	25.0	Fatigue, nausea, pruritis, and diarrhea.
Second	Cabozantinib(40)	63	86	7.4	-	Diarrhea, fatigue, nausea, decreased appetite, and PPE.
Second	Everolimus (41)	61	85	4	14.8	Stomatitis, rash, fatigue, pneumonitis, and diarrhea.
Second	Axitinib (42)	61	82	8.3	20.1	Diarrhea, fatigue, hypertension, and PPE
Second	Sorafenib (43)	58	86	5.5	17.8	Fatigue, diarrhea, nausea, and rash.

ALT, alanine aminotransferase; AST, aspartate aminotransferase; GR, good risk; IFN, interferon; OS, overall survival; PFS, progression-free survival; PPE, palmar-plantar erythrodysesthesia syndrome; PR, poor risk.

REFERENCES

1. Guancial EA, Roussel B, Bergsma DP, et al. Bladder cancer in the elderly patient: challenges and solutions. *Clin Interv Aging.* 2015;10:939-949.
2. Caillet P, Canoui-Poitrine F, Vouriot J, et al. Comprehensive geriatric assessment in the decision-making process in elderly patients with cancer: ELCAPA study. *J Clin Oncol.* 2011;29(27):3636-3642.
3. Hurria A, Togawa K, Mohile SG, et al. Predicting chemotherapy toxicity in older adults with cancer: a prospective multicenter study. *J Clin Oncol.* 2011;29(25):3457-3465.
4. Kanesvaran R, Li H, Koo KN, et al. Analysis of prognostic factors of comprehensive geriatric assessment and development of a clinical scoring system in elderly Asian patients with cancer. *J Clin Oncol.* 2011;29(27):3620-3627.
5. Balducci L, Extermann M. Management of the frail person with advanced cancer. *Crit Rev Oncol Hematol.* 2000;33(2):143-148.
6. Herr HW. Age and outcome of superficial bladder cancer treated with bacille Calmette-Guerin therapy. *Urology.* 2007;70(1):65-68.
7. Spencer BA, McBride RB, Hershman DL, et al. Adjuvant intravesical bacillus Calmette-Guerin therapy and survival among elderly patients with non-muscle-invasive bladder cancer. *J Oncol Pract.* 2013;9(2):92-98.
8. Aziz A, May M, Burger M, et al. Prediction of 90-day mortality after radical cystectomy for bladder cancer in a prospective European multicenter cohort. *Eur Urol.* 2014;66(1):156-163.
9. Isbarn H, Jeldres C, Zini L, et al. A population based assessment of perioperative mortality after cystectomy for bladder cancer. *J Urol.* 2009;182(1):70-77.
10. Nielsen ME, Shariat SF, Karakiewicz PI, et al. Advanced age is associated with poorer bladder cancer-specific survival in patients treated with radical cystectomy. *Eur Urol.* 2007;51(3):699-706; discussion 706-708.
11. Sogni F, Brausi M, Frea B, et al. Morbidity and quality of life in elderly patients receiving ileal conduit or orthotopic neobladder after radical cystectomy for invasive bladder cancer. *Urology.* 2008;71(5):919-923.
12. Tang K, Li H, Xia D, et al. Laparoscopic versus open radical cystectomy in bladder cancer: a systematic review and meta-analysis of comparative studies. *PLOS ONE.* 2014;9(5):e95667.
13. Nix J, Smith A, Kurpad R, et al. Prospective randomized controlled trial of robotic versus open radical cystectomy for bladder cancer: perioperative and pathologic results. *Eur Urol.* 2010;57(2):196-201.
14. Galsky MD, Hahn NM, Rosenberg J, et al. A consensus definition of patients with metastatic urothelial carcinoma who are unfit for cisplatin-based chemotherapy. *Lancet Oncol.* 2011;12(3):211-214.
15. Galsky MD, Chen GJ, Oh WK, et al. Comparative effectiveness of cisplatin-based and carboplatin-based chemotherapy for treatment of advanced urothelial carcinoma. *Ann Oncol.* 2012;23(2):406-410.
16. Advanced Bladder Cancer Meta-analysis Collaboration. Neoadjuvant chemotherapy in invasive bladder cancer: update of a systematic review and meta-analysis of individual patient data advanced bladder cancer (ABC) meta-analysis collaboration. *Eur Urol.* 2005;48(2):202-205; discussion 5-6.
17. Sternberg CN, Skoneczna I, Kerst JM, et al. Immediate versus deferred chemotherapy after radical cystectomy in patients with pT3-pT4 or N+ M0 urothelial carcinoma of the bladder (EORTC 30994): an intergroup, open-label, randomised phase 3 trial. *Lancet Oncol.* 2015;16(1):76-86.

18. Galsky MD. How I treat bladder cancer in elderly patients. *J Geriatr Oncol.* 2015;6(1):1-7.

19. Clayman RH, Galland-Girodet S, Niemierko A, et al. Outcomes of selective bladder preservation in the elderly treated with conservative surgery and chemoradiation. *Int J Radiat Oncol Biol Phys.* 2013;87(2):S83.

20. Mak RH, Hunt D, Shipley WU, et al. Long-term outcomes in patients with muscle-invasive bladder cancer after selective bladder-preserving combined-modality therapy: a pooled analysis of Radiation Therapy Oncology Group protocols 8802, 8903, 9506, 9706, 9906, and 0233. *J Clin Oncol.* 2014;32(34):3801-3809.

21. Kouloulias V, Tolia M, Kolliarakis N, et al. Evaluation of acute toxicity and symptoms palliation in a hypofractionated weekly schedule of external radiotherapy for elderly patients with muscular invasive bladder cancer. *Int Braz J Urol.* 2013;39(1):77-82.

22. von der Maase H, Hansen SW, Roberts JT, et al. Gemcitabine and cisplatin versus methotrexate, vinblastine, doxorubicin, and cisplatin in advanced or metastatic bladder cancer: results of a large, randomized, multinational, multicenter, phase III study. *J Clin Oncol.* 2000;18(17):3068-3077.

23. De Santis M, Bellmunt J, Mead G, et al. Randomized phase II/III trial assessing gemcitabine/carboplatin and methotrexate/carboplatin/vinblastine in patients with advanced urothelial cancer who are unfit for cisplatin-based chemotherapy: EORTC study 30986. *J Clin Oncol.* 2012;30(2):191-199.

24. Powles T, Eder JP, Fine GD, et al. MPDL3280A (anti-PD-L1) treatment leads to clinical activity in metastatic bladder cancer. *Nature.* 2014;515(7528):558-562.

25. Stadler WM, Kuzel T, Roth B, et al. Phase II study of single-agent gemcitabine in previously untreated patients with metastatic urothelial cancer. *J Clin Oncol.* 1997;15(11):3394-3398.

26. Bellmunt J, Negrier S, Escudier B, et al. The medical treatment of metastatic renal cell cancer in the elderly: position paper of a SIOG taskforce. *Crit Rev Oncol Hematol.* 2009;69(1):64-72.

27. Becker A, Ravi P, Roghmann F, et al. Laparoscopic radical nephrectomy vs laparoscopic or open partial nephrectomy for T1 renal cell carcinoma: comparison of complication rates in elderly patients during the initial phase of adoption. *Urology.* 2014;83(6):1285-1291.

28. Sun M, Thuret R, Abdollah F, et al. Age-adjusted incidence, mortality, and survival rates of stage-specific renal cell carcinoma in North America: a trend analysis. *Eur Urol.* 2011;59(1):135-141.

29. Haas NB, Manola J, Uzzo RG, et al. Adjuvant sunitinib or sorafenib for high-risk, non-metastatic renal-cell carcinoma (ECOG-ACRIN E2805): a double-blind, placebo-controlled, randomised, phase 3 trial. *Lancet.* 2016;387(10032):2006-2016.

30. Williamson TJ, Pearson JR, Ischia J, et al. Guideline of guidelines: follow-up after nephrectomy for renal cell carcinoma. *BJU Int.* 2016;117(4):555-562.

31. Klatte T, Grubmuller B, Waldert M, et al. Laparoscopic cryoablation versus partial nephrectomy for the treatment of small renal masses: systematic review and cumulative analysis of observational studies. *Eur Urol.* 2011;60(3):435-443.

32. Borghesi M, Brunocilla E, Volpe A, et al. Active surveillance for clinically localized renal tumors: an updated review of current indications and clinical outcomes. *Int J Urol.* 2015;22(5):432-438.

33. Fyfe GA, Fisher RI, Rosenberg SA, et al. Long-term response data for 255 patients with metastatic renal cell carcinoma treated with high-dose recombinant interleukin-2 therapy. *J Clin Oncol.* 1996;14(8):2410-2411.

34. Heng DY, Xie W, Regan MM, et al. Prognostic factors for overall survival in patients with metastatic renal cell carcinoma treated with vascular endothelial growth factor-targeted agents: results from a large, multicenter study. *J Clin Oncol.* 2009;27(34):5794-5799.

35. Motzer RJ, Hutson TE, Tomczak P, et al. Sunitinib versus interferon alfa in metastatic renal-cell carcinoma. *N Engl J Med.* 2007;356(2):115-124.

36. Rini BI, Halabi S, Rosenberg JE, et al. Phase III trial of bevacizumab plus interferon alfa versus interferon alfa monotherapy in patients with metastatic renal cell carcinoma: final results of CALGB 90206. *J Clin Oncol.* 2010;28(13):2137-2143.

37. Sternberg CN, Davis ID, Mardiak J, et al. Pazopanib in locally advanced or metastatic renal cell carcinoma: results of a randomized phase III trial. *J Clin Oncol.* 2010;28(6):1061-1068.

38. Hudes G, Carducci M, Tomczak P, et al. Temsirolimus, interferon alfa, or both for advanced renal-cell carcinoma. *N Engl J Med.* 2007;356(22):2271-2281.

39. Motzer RJ, Escudier B, McDermott DF, et al. Nivolumab versus everolimus in advanced renal-cell carcinoma. *N Engl J Med.* 2015;373(19):1803-1813.

40. Choueiri TK, Escudier B, Powles T, et al. Cabozantinib versus everolimus in advanced renal-cell carcinoma. *N Engl J Med.* 2015;373(19):1814-1823.

41. Motzer RJ, Escudier B, Oudard S, et al. Efficacy of everolimus in advanced renal cell carcinoma: a double-blind, randomised, placebo-controlled phase III trial. *Lancet.* 2008;372(9637):449-456.

42. Rini BI, Escudier B, Tomczak P, et al. Comparative effectiveness of axitinib versus sorafenib in advanced renal cell carcinoma (AXIS): a randomised phase 3 trial. *Lancet.* 2011;378(9807):1931-1939.

43. Escudier B, Eisen T, Stadler WM, et al. Sorafenib for treatment of renal cell carcinoma: Final efficacy and safety results of the phase III treatment approaches in renal cancer global evaluation trial. *J Clin Oncol.* 2009;27(20):3312-3318.

44. Escudier B, Porta C, Bono P, et al. Randomized, controlled, double-blind, cross-over trial assessing treatment preference for pazopanib versus sunitinib in patients with metastatic renal cell carcinoma: PISCES Study. *J Clin Oncol.* 2014;32(14):1412-1418.

23 Non-Hodgkin Lymphoma and Hodgkin Lymphoma

Colette Owens and Paul A. Hamlin

INTRODUCTION

Lymphomas are a heterogeneous group of malignancies of B, T, and NK lymphocytes that comprise more than 60 complex entities. By the year 2030, the United States is expected to experience an increased incidence of non-Hodgkin lymphoma (NHL) by 67% and Hodgkin lymphoma (HL) by 70% in older adults as a reflection of the aging population. Sixty percent of patients with new diagnoses of NHL are over age 65, with a median of 66 years (1). Given these demographic dynamics, the oncologist is increasingly required to manage complex older lymphoma patients in the context of age-related organ dysfunction and comorbidity.

STAGING AND INITIAL WORKUP

The updated World Health Organization schema classifies lymphomas based on morphologic, immunologic, genetic, and clinical information (2). The diagnosis of lymphoma requires adequate material for histologic, immunohistochemical (IHC), molecular, and cytogenetic analysis, preferably by an excisional biopsy, although a core biopsy is at times sufficient. Additionally, each patient should receive a careful history and physical, with blood work that includes a complete blood count, comprehensive panel, calcium, lactate dehydrogenase (LDH), uric acid, serum electrophoresis, beta-2 microglobulin, and viral testing for hepatitis B and C and HIV, and PET and/or CT chest, abdomen and pelvis. The updated Lugano staging classification of 2014 included the integration of PET scan into the initial staging of flourodeoxyglucose (FDG) avid lymphomas with the use of the Deauville 5-point scale in response assessments, eliminated the A/B designations except for HL, and eliminated routine bone marrow biopsy in diffuse large B cell lymphoma (DLBCL) and HL because of the predictive value of PET scans (3). Those at high risk for central nervous system (CNS) involvement should have a diagnostic lumbar puncture for cytology and flow cytometry.

Clinical prognostic scores are important in understanding prognoses, and help to frame treatment decisions in the older patient. Generally, there is a risk model for each major disease histology, including the International Prognostic Index

(IPI) and Age adjusted International Prognostic Index (aaIPI), Follicular Lymphoma International Prognostic Index (FLIPI) 1 and 2, Mantle cell International Prognostic Index (MIPI), and International Prognostic Score (IPS) (Table 23.1). Age figures prominently in all of these models, with recent analysis suggesting that a more relevant inflection point for worse outcomes among elderly patients is between 70 and 75, rather than 60 years as in earlier reports (4–6,57) (Table 23.2).

TABLE 23.1 Prognostic Models Within Specific Disease Types

Disease Type	Clinical Factors	Survival Estimates
DLBCL **IPI** **aaIPI**	Age >60 Stage III/IV PS >1 LDH > ULN ENS >2 LDH PS >1 Stage III/IV	Low (0–1) 2 y OS 84%, 5 y OS 73% Low-Int (2) 2 y OS, 66% 5 y OS 51% High-Int (3) 2 y OS, 54% 5 y OS 43% High (4–5) 2 y OS, 34% 5 y OS 26% Low (0) 5 y OS 83%, Low-Int (1) 5 y OS 69%, High-Int (2) 5 y OS 46%, High (3) 5 y OS 32%
FL **FLIPI1** **FLIPI2**	Age >60 Stage III/IV Hgb <12g/L LDH > ULN >4 nodal sites Age >60 Hgb <12g/L BM involvement B2M > ULN LN diameter > 6 cm	Low (0–1) 5 y OS 91%, 10 y 71% Int (1–2) 5 y OS 78%, 10 y OS 51% High ≥ 3, 5 y OS 53%, 10 y 36% Low (0) 3 y PFS 91%, 5 y 80% Int (1–2) 3 y PFS 69%, 5 y PFS 51% High (3–5), 3 y PFS 51%, 5 y 19%
Mantle cell lymphoma **MIPI**	Age Ki67 PS LDH compared ULN WBC	Low 5 y OS 81% Int 5 y OS 63% High 5 y OS 35%
Hodgkin lymphoma **IPS**	Age >45 Stage IV Hgb <10.5 g/L Albumin <4 g/dL WBC >15 ALC <600 or less than 8% of total WBC count Male gender	0 factors 5 y FFP 84%, 5 y OS 89% 1 factor 5 y FFP 77%, 5 y OS 90% 2 factors 5 y FFP 67%, 5 y OS 81% 3 factors 5 y FFP 60%, 5 y OS 78% 4 factors 5 y FFP 51%, 5 y OS 61% ≥5 factors 5 y FFP 42%, 5 y OS 56%

ALC, absolute lymphocyte count; B2M, beta-2 microglobulin; DLBCL, diffuse large B cell lymphoma; ENS, extra-nodal sites; FFP, freedom from progression; FL, follicular lymphoma; LN, lymph node; OS, overall survival; PFS, progression-free survival; PS, performance status; ULN, upper limit of normal; WBC, white blood cell.

TABLE 23.2 Representative Therapeutic Options in DLBCL for Older Patients

Regimen	Planned RDI	Median Age (range)	ORR (CR/PR)	EFS	OS	TRM
RCHOP21 (phase III)	100%	69 (60–80)	83% (75%/7%)	57% at 2 y	70% at 2 y	6%
RCHOP21 (retrospective)	70%	76	87% (79%/8%)	57% at 2 y	68% at 3 y	NR
RminiCHOP (phase II)	~50%	83 (80–95)	74% (63%/11%)	47% at 2 y (PFS)	59% at 2 y	8%
DR-COP (phase II)	NA	69 (61–92)	86% (75%/11%)	60% at 3 y	74% at 3 y	5%
Nonanthracycline-Based Treatment						
R-GCVP (phase II)	NA	76 (52–90)	61% (39%/23%)	50% at 2 y (PFS)	56% at 2 y	NR
R-Benda (phase II)	NA	85 (80–95)	69% (54%/15%)	40% at 2 y (PFS)	40% at 2 y	0%
RminiCEOP (phase III)	100%	73 (64–84)	81% (68%/13%)	54% at 2 y	74% at 2 y	6%

CR, complete remission; DLBCL, diffuse large B cell lymphoma; EFS, event free survival; NR, not reported; ORR, overall response rate; OS, overall survival; PFS, progression-free survival; PR, partial remission; RDI, relative dose intensity; TRM, treatment-related mortality.

HISTOLOGIC AND BIOLOGIC RISK FACTORS

Lymphomas can be classified into indolent, aggressive, and very aggressive based on histology and outcomes. Generally, the indolent behaving lymphomas (small lymphocytic lymphoma [SLL], follicular center cell lymphoma [FCL], marginal zone lymphoma [MZL], and Waldenstrom's macroglobulinemia [WM]) now have median survivals of more than a decade, whereas aggressive lymphomas (DLBCL, peripheral T cell lymphoma [PTCL], mantle cell lymphoma [MCL]) are life threatening within months without treatment, and highly aggressive entities (Burkitt lymphoma [BL], high-grade DLBCL) may present with rapid courses that become life threatening within weeks. Beyond these broad clinical generalizations, an increasingly nuanced understanding of biologic factors that influence outcomes is essential.

In DLBCL, the cell of origin by gene expression profiling (GEP) is prognostic for survival, with germinal center (GCB) phenotype having a better outcome than non-GC/activated B cell (ABC) phenotype with CHOP and rituximab cyclophosphamide doxorubicin oncovin (vincristine) prednisone (RCHOP) therapy (7–9). IHC models designed to approximate GEP exist (e.g., the Hans model) and are implemented given their clinical utility and availability, but problems exist with sensitivity and specificity. Ultimately, newer molecular techniques will likely supersede IHC. Additionally, the concurrent presence of immunoglobulin heavy chain translocations with the anti-apoptotic t(14;18) BCL2 and t(8;14) cMYC cellular proliferation signal (or less frequently

BCL6 translocations) have been termed a "double hit biology" (DH). Approximately 10% of patients with DLBCL will have DH biology, which is associated with very aggressive disease behavior, older age at diagnosis, and higher CNS risk. Approximately one-third of DLBCL patients may have protein overexpression of BCL2 or BCL6 and MYC, termed "double expressers," identified with more aggressive behavior as well, but to a more variable degree. In addition, the Epstein–Barr virus (EBV) has also been connected to the inferior outcomes in both elderly DLBCL and HL patients. These patients typically have more advanced disease, involvement of multiple extranodal sites, high risk scores, and inferior progression-free and overall survival (OS).

TREATMENT OF OLDER PATIENTS WITH LYMPHOMA

For lymphoma, the difficulties associated with clinical decision making in older patients are often most evident in the setting of aggressive histologies, such as DLBCL, MCL, and HL; hence, we will focus on these entities. Untreated, these entities will become life limiting. The goal of the medical oncologist is balancing the pursuit of curative intent in DLBCL and HL, or improvement in PFS in MCL, with the risk of morbidity and mortality in older patients. A consideration of actual life expectancy helps contextualize what treatment will mean for the patient, particularly if not treating the lymphoma will decrease life expectancy. Based on data from the Surveillance, Epidemiology, and End Results (SEER) database, 23% of patients over the age of 65 receive no treatment at all, and this proportion increased to 33% in patients over the age of 80 (10). Illustrative of this point, at 80 years old, a person in average health has a predicted life expectancy of about 5 years without a lymphoma diagnosis. Consequently, an aggressive NHL is likely the greatest risk to this patient's life, and treatment should be a consideration in the context of the patient's goals and wishes. When life expectancy is less than 1 year despite the lymphoma diagnosis, palliative efforts are most appropriate. Historically, performance status and clinical judgment have been used by physicians to attempt to identify those patients who are at greatest risk of toxicity (11,12). However, clinician judgment alone is inadequate in identifying all older patients at risk. Efforts have been made to identify those a greatest risk of toxicitiy (13–15). Comprehensive geriatric assessments (CGAs) are better at delineating those most at risk (16). Utilizing a CGA in DLBCL, Tucci et al. demonstrated that a CGA was better at delineating fit versus unfit in comparison to physician judgment, with about 20% potentially misidentified as fit by physicians (7). In practice, those with the highest risk of toxicity should be considered for dose modifications or reduced-intensity treatments; in this context, geriatric assessments are increasingly being established as important adjuncts to decision making (17).

Comorbidity

In NHL patients over the age of 60 years, 60% to 70% have some comorbidity. The number and severity of comorbidity increases with increasing age in lymphoma patients, and the presence of comorbidities is associated with increased treatment-related mortality, treatment-related toxicity, reduced-intensity treatment, and decreased OS (18–20). Comorbidities specifically assessed by indices of risk, such as the Charlson

Comorbidity Index, have also been shown to be an independent adverse prognostic factor in patients over age 65 (21,22). Frailty is a distinct physiologic state separate from comorbidity and independently identifies a population at highest risk for toxicity and mortality. Though there is no standardized definition of *frailty*, it typically is characterized by decreasing physiologic reserves with the inability to adapt to illness or stressors in older patients. It often includes geriatric syndromes, such as falls, incontinence, and delirium, as well as physical symptoms of weakness, slowness, and weight loss. Data from Tucci and the Lymphoma Italian Foundation studies have delineated fit and frail patients, with results indicating the overlap in defining *frail* and the utility of defining these groups when pursuing curative management (7).

DISEASE-SPECIFIC MANAGEMENT

Diffuse Large B Cell Lymphoma

DLBCL, the most common subtype of NHL, is associated with a median age of 70 years and increasing incidence in older patients; it is fatal without treatment. Front-line anthracycline-based chemoimmunotherapy affords OS rates of 60% to 70% (23,24). Choosing which older patients can tolerate curative therapy requires integration of comorbidity, functional status, and disease characteristics.

TREATMENT

RCHOP chemotherapy is the standard of care. However, this anthracycline-based regimen has been associated with a treatment-related mortality of approximately 6% to 12% and risk of cardiotoxicity in older individuals (23,24). Consequently, the decision to pursue an anthracycline-based regimen must include a thorough evaluation of performance status, comorbidity, and organ function with clinician judgment.

Maneuvers to mitigate toxicity—Prephase

The German Non-Hodgkin Lymphoma Study Group implemented a "pre-phase" treatment of 5 to 7 days of prednisone and a 1-mg dose of vincristine prior to the initiation of chemotherapy, resulting in a 50% reduction in cycle 1 and cycle 2 treatment-related mortality in the RICOVER-60 study (24). Other prospective studies have also suggested a clinical benefit of this strategy (25,26).

Early stage

Early stage I/II disease is highly curable; treatment includes combined modality or chemotherapy alone (27,28). In the pre-rituximab era the SWOG 8736 trial established CHOP × 3 followed by involved field radiation therapy (IFRT) as superior to CHOP × eight cycles in both PFS and OS (29). However, long-term follow-up has shown that this difference ultimately disappears after 8 years (29). Rituximab + CHOP × 3 followed by IFRT in the SWOG 0014 trial in patients with one or more risk factors reported good outcomes, with a PFS of 88% at a median follow-up of 5 years (29). It should be noted that the LYSA group compared RCHOP × four or six cycles with or without radiation using an adapted strategy based on IPI and interim PET, and showed that the combined modality was not superior to RCHOP alone (30). The decision to include radiation therapy is made depending on disease location, risk of radiation toxicity, comorbidity, and life expectancy. It should also be considered as a definitive treatment in patients who will not tolerate chemotherapy.

Advanced stage

RCHOP every 21 days for six to eight cycles based on the LNH 9805 study is the standard of care established in patients 60 to 80 years old, with significant improvement in 5-year PFS and OS versus CHOP (31). Other trials have examined a dose dense every 14-day regimen or maintenance rituximab strategies and found no improvement in survival, but these trials did demonstrate the importance of rituximab. Higher rituximab density may improve outcomes in elderly males given more rapid clearance (32).

Dose-adjusted (DA) etoposide prednisone oncovin cyclophosphamide doxorubicin (R-EPOCH) is an infusional regimen that may have improved efficacy in certain subsets of DLBCL, including "double hit" (BCL2, MYC by FISH), GCB, and high proliferative rate tumors (MYC expression, high Ki67), and may be less cardiotoxic due to infusional doxorubicin (33,34). However, early reports of the phase III trial comparing DA-R-EPOCH to RCHOP have not confirmed an advantage (35). Nonetheless, this infusional regimen may be attractive in certain older patients given the decreased association with cardiotoxicity.

Reduced intensity/Nonanthracycline

For patients who are poor candidates for full-dose anthracycline-based treatment, there are several reduced therapy options and nonanthracycline-based regimens that retain curative intent. Typically, patients over the age of 80 or those who are frail, or have multiple comorbidities or geriatric syndromes, are not ideal candidates for full-course RCHOP. Trading some efficacy for reduced toxicity is a reasonable strategy in this scenario. A phase II GELA trial evaluated RminiCHOP (relative dose intensity [RDI] of about 50% compared to RCHOP) in patients over the age of 80 and showed a 2-year PFS and OS of 47% and 59%, respectively (5). Infusional doxorubicin and liposomal doxorubicin (Doxil) may be safer options, with less cardiac toxicity, and can be considered in patients where an anthracycline is not an absolute contraindication, but often a nonanthracycline based regimen is preferable (36). Fields et al. demonstrated that a regimen of R-GCVP (rituximab, gemcitabine, cytoxan, vincristine, and prednisone) had a 2-year PFS and OS of 49.8% and 55.8% (6). Other nonanthracycline regimens include R-CEPP, R-CEOP (etoposide replacing doxorubicin), R-CDOP (liposomal doxorubicin), R-bendamustine, and rituximab, cyclophosphamide, mitoxantrone, oncovin, prednisone (R-CNOP) (4,37).

Salvage therapy with high-dose therapy and autologous stem cell rescue (HDT/ASCR) in elderly

In patients who relapse following RCHOP, chemotherapy alone is generally not curative. Second-line chemotherapy followed by HDT/ASCR is the standard of care. For the majority of older patients, HDT/ASCR is not an option due to comorbidity and treatment-related mortality associated with transplant. In the older patient with relapsed disease, the goals become palliative rather than curative. If a patient is transplant ineligible, second-line regimens include clinical trials, R-CVP,

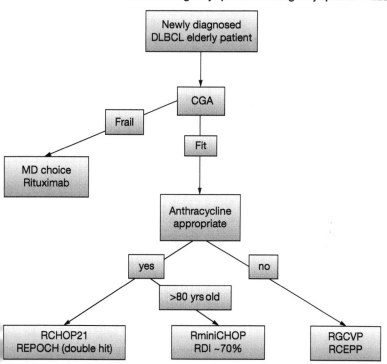

FIGURE 23.1 A suggested clinical algorithm for therapeutic decisions in older DLBCL patients.

DLBCL, diffuse large B cell lymphoma; CGA, comprehensive geriatric assessments; RCEPP, rituximab cyclophosphamide etoposide procarbazine prednisone.

rituximab, gemcitabine, oxaliplatin (R-Gem-Ox), rituximab-bendamustine, CEPP, and rituximab with lenalidomide (Figure 23.1) (4–6,38).

Mantle Cell Lymphoma

MCL is a rare NHL classified as an indolent lymphoma due to its incurability, but with a more aggressive disease behavior and a median survival of 5 to 7 years. The median age of MCL patients is 65, and patients typically present with advanced stage involving lymph nodes, the bone marrow, and gastrointestinal (GI) tract. It has a male predominance of 2:1 and comprises 3% to 10% of NHL in Western countries. A essential feature of MCL is the translocation 11;14, which causes the dysregulation of cell cyclinD1 (rarely D2 or D3). It is characterized by an immunophenotype of CD5(+), CD10(-), CD20(+), CD23(-/+), CD43(+), and Cyclin D1(+) with t(11;14) by FISH. SOX 11 is another marker in MCL that has prognostic significance. The presence of a high Ki67%, p53, or MYC expression tends to portend a more aggressive disease course. These are often seen with the blastic MCL subtype, which tends to behave aggressively and yield worse outcomes.

TREATMENT

In select patients, the initial management of older individuals will include consideration for upfront cytarabine-containing induction, followed by HDT/ASCR or R-HyperCVAD (Course A: cyclophosphamide, vincristine, adriamycin, dexamethasone; Course B: methotrexate, cytarabine) given potential PFS improvements over less intensive chemoimmunotherapy. As these approaches are not curative, most older individuals are not recommended this course of action, because of the associated toxicities. Anthracycline-based induction therapy had been one of the standard treatments in MCL (39). RCHOP plus rituximab maintenance is one treatment strategy with duration of responses over 6 years and OS of 87% (40). However, an anthracycline may not be necessary for the treatment of MCL, particularly in older patients who may not tolerate an anthracycline-based regimen. A nonanthracycline-based strategy of rituximab-bendamustine, based on the StiL trial (subgroup) and the BRIGHT trials, is increasingly being used as the initial treatment in older patients. The STiL trial compared RCHOP to bendamustine rituximab (BR) upfront in indolent lymphomas, and MCL demonstrated an improved PFS with BR (69.5 vs. 31.2 months) with less toxicity and better tolerability (40). Similarly, the BRIGHT trial also demonstrated that BR was noninferior to RCHOP/rituximab cyclophosphamide vincristine prednisone (RCVP) with good tolerability (39). With the majority of patients above 60 years in both these trials, BR is a safe and effective treatment with less toxicity and should be considered in older patients, particularly those with significant comorbidity or requiring a nonanthracycline approach. Maintenance rituximab following BR does not appear to improve outcomes.

Biologic-based regimens are also being explored in older patients, such as lenalidomide and rituximab followed by maintenance, and preliminarily are associated with admirable outcomes: ORR 87 and 2-year OS 97% (41). A bortezomib-based regimen—bortezomib with rituximab, cyclophosphamide, doxorubicin, and prednisone (VR-CAP)—had improved PFS (24.7 vs. 14.4 months) versus RCHOP, but no difference in OS (42).

Relapse

There is no standard of care for relapse/refractory MCL. In the recurrent setting, several agents have recently been approved, including ibrutinib (Bruton's tyrosine kinase inhibitor), lenalidomide (immunomodulatory agent), and bortezomib (proteasome inhibitor). Sequential use of standard chemotherapy is an option as well, depending on the regimen used in the first line. There are also trials that are investigating new combinations of these new agents and chemoimmunotherapy. Other agents with promising activity in MCL include venetoclax, with studies ongoing.

Hodgkin Lymphoma

HL, an entity distinct from NHLs, is the most common lymphoid malignancy in young patients, but possesses a bimodal age distribution with 15% to 35% of patients presenting over the age of 60. Disease biology, comorbidity, functional status, and organ dysfunction can compromise the curability of older HL patients, who often have advanced-stage disease, higher risk scores, EBV positivity, and mixed cellularity histology. Based on retrospective data and population databases, older patients with HL (over age 60) have significantly worse outcomes in comparison to younger patients. Although there have been improvements in overall outcomes, this difference continues to persist in prospective studies. For example, in the E2496 study, the cumulative incidence of death was 30% for older patients and 10% for younger at 5 years (43). CALGB 8251 was a prospective trial reporting outcomes with adriamycin bleomycin vinblastine dacarbazine (ABVD): in older patients (≥60 years) 5-year OS was 31%, versus 63% for those aged 40 to 59, and 79% for those less than 40 years old.

TREATMENT
Early stage disease

The standard approach for early stage disease was established by Bonadonna, employing ABVD x4 cycles followed by IFRT (44). Over the years there has been a drive to limit the amount of treatment, to mitigate toxicity while maintaining efficacy. The NCIC HD6 study reported good outcomes with patients treated with ABVD x4 alone if they achieved a CT complete remission (CR) after two cycles of therapy. In early stage favorable disease, the HD10 German Hodgkin study group (GHSG) evaluated ABVD × 2 followed by IFRT at 20 Gy for patients with no risk factors as defined by GHSG; these patients demonstrated OS of 96.6% to 97.5% (45). The advent of PET imaging technology has also helped to limit treatment in early stage patients. The UK RAPID study evaluated ABVD × 3 followed by interim PET; if the PET was negative (Deauville 1-2), then patients were monitored. PET positive patients received an additional cycle of ABVD followed by IFRT (46). Outcomes at 3-year PFS were 93.8% versus 90.7% and OS 97% versus 99.5% for IFRT versus observation respectively, thereby avoiding radiation in 75% of patients (46). In early stage unfavorable disease, the GHSG HD11 trial established ABVD x4 followed by 30 Gy IFRT as an effective treatment option with a 5-year PFS of 87% (47). A full six cycles of ABVD with or without radiation can also be considered, with 5-year PFS of 81% versus 86% with RT, and a 5-year OS of 90% versus 97% with RT (48). Thus, there are several different potential strategies to employ for older patients for early stage HL that take advantage of reduced exposure to chemotherapy and/or radiation, which can be tailored based on the patient. In older, frail patients, radiation alone may be a consideration if there is a concern for significant chemotherapy toxicity, particularly in the context of a latency period of 8 to 12 days for the radiation-related effects.

Advanced stage

Patients with advanced stage HL can be risk-stratified based on the IPS; older patients frequently have higher IPS scores. ABVD is the standard of care for advanced stage HL (44,48,49). Regimens such as Stanford V and bleomycin etoposide adriamycin cyclophosphamide oncovin procarbazine prednisone (escBEACOPP) (HD9 trial) have been compared with ABVD and in older patients are associated with increased toxicity and no improvement in outcomes. Older patients are more vulnerable to bleomycin toxicity, which can at times be fatal. The RATHL trial employed PET imaging after two cycles to risk-adapt therapy in advanced stage HL patients. PET negative patients (Deauville 1-3) were randomized to ABVD versus AVD for 4 additional cycles. Outcomes were comparable between ABVD and AVD groups, with PFS 85.4% versus 84.4% and OS 97.1% versus 97.4%, indicating that omitting bleomycin decreased pulmonary toxicity without affecting efficacy in interim negative PET2 patients (50,51). Ongoing efforts are incorporating brentuximab vedotin (BV) into treatment paradigms in lieu of bleomycin.

In patients who cannot receive an anthracycline, other regimens—such as chlorambucil, procarbazine, prednisone, vinblastine (ChLVVP); mustard (nitrogen) oncovin procarbazine prednisone (MOPP) and C-MOPP; vinblastine, cyclophosphamide, procarbazine, etoposide, mitoxantrone, bleomycin, prednisolone (VEPEMB); and PVAG—can be considered (52). Single-agent BV is active in older HL patients, but unlikely to be curative alone (53). In advanced stage disease, the role of radiation is unclear, but in those patients with partial responses or bulk, radiation can be considered and may confer an overall benefit.

Relapse

Salvage chemotherapy followed by HDT/ASCR with or without radiation is the standard of care for patients with relapsed disease. This has resulted in cure in greater than 60% of patients. The applicability of transplant, however, must be assessed in the context of the older patient. More recently, BV has shown single-agent activity in relapsed disease posttransplant with ORR of 75% and a CR of 34% and is approved for failure after HDT/ASCT or failure of at least two prior chemotherapy regimens in patients who are not transplant candidates. BV should be considered in older patients with relapsed HL, particularly if they are not candidates for transplant, but with close attention to peripheral neuropathy.

Immunotherapy with PD1 inhibitors (nivolumab, pembrolizumab) has been an exciting area of research with high response rates. In phase I trials with nivolumab in relapse/refractory HL, overall response rates were 87% and CR of 17% (54). Similarly, relapsed/refractory patients treated with pembrolizumab (KEYNOTE-013) showed ORR 66% with 21% CR (55). Nivolumab is now FDA approved for HL. Ongoing trials are investigating the role of antibody drug conjugate (ADC) and immunotherapy in the relapsed and upfront setting and in combination.

Indolent Lymphomas

Indolent lymphomas include follicular Grade 1, 2, 3a and MZL (splenic, nodal, and extranodal), lymphoplasmacytic lymphoma, and WM. Because of their indolent clinical behavior, patients often do not require treatment at diagnosis. There are several options for treatment of indolent lymphomas, and there are specific National Comprehensive Cancer Nerwork/Groupe d'Etude des Lymphomes Folliculaires (NCCN/GELF) criteria that help decide when treatment is indicated. These include cytopenias, organ dysfunction, B symptoms, bulky disease (single mass > 7 cm or 3 or more masses > 3 cm), splenomegaly, and rate of disease progression. If a patient is asymptomatic and does not have the aforementioned criteria, then watchful waiting is appropriate. Importantly, in patients over the age of 70 diagnosed with an indolent lymphoma who undergo watchful waiting, 40% never require treatment.

If treatment is required, there are many options, which include single-agent rituximab, combination chemoimmunotherapy (BR, RCVP, RCHOP), radioimmunotherapy, and newer agents (idelesalib, lenalidomide). Given the many therapeutic options and long disease course, treatment decisions can more easily be matched to patient tolerability. The aforementioned StiL and BRIGHT trials have indicated that in indolent lymphomas, BR is noninferior, or even superior, to RCHOP with less toxicity (39,40). Patients with progressive disease within 24 months of chemoimmunotherapy may have a more aggressive disease course (56).

TAKE HOME POINTS

1. Clinician-designated assessment of performance status has been inadequate in determining those patients who are at highest risk or deciding who is appropriate for curative therapy.
2. CGA and integrated evaluation of disease factors, physical factors, and social and psychological factors in older patients will help to delineate those for whom curative treatment is feasible and those for whom noncurative options are more appropriate.
3. Age alone should not be the determinant of treatment recommendations.
4. In aggressive lymphomas, curative treatments should be considered, with modifications as appropriate where the lymphoma is the greatest risk to a patient's life.
5. In indolent lymphoma, expectant monitoring is frequently appropriate; there are many therapeutic options available to facilitate disease control while balancing toxicity.

REFERENCES

1. Ries LAG, Eisner MP, Kosary CL, et al. eds. *SEER Cancer Statistics Review, 1975-2000.* Bethesda, MD: National Cancer Institute; 2003. Available at: http://seer.cancer.gov/csr/1975_2/1/2010. Accessed February 1, 2016.
2. Swerdllow SH, Campo E, Harris NL. *WHO Classification of Tumours of Haematopoietic and Lymphoid Tissues.* France: IARC Press; 2008.
3. Barrington SF, Mikhaeel G, Kostakoglu L, et al. Role of imaging in the staging and response assessment of lymphoma: consensus of the International Conference on Malignant Lymphomas Imaging Working Group. *J Clin Oncol.* 2014;32(27):3048-3058.
4. Weidmann E, Neumann A, Fauth F, et al. Phase II study of bendamustine in combination with rituximab as first-line treatment in patients 80 years or older with aggressive B-cell lymphomas. *Ann Oncol.* 2011;22(8):1839-1844.
5. Peyrade F, Jardin F, Thieblemon C, et al. Attenuated immunochemotherapy regimen (R-miniCHOP) in elderly patients older than 80 years with diffuse large B-cell lymphoma: a multicentre, single-arm, phase 2 trial. *Lancet Oncol.* 2011;12:460-468.
6. Fields PA, Townsend W, Webb A, et al. De novo treatment of diffuse large B-cell lymphoma with rituximab, cyclophosphamide, vincristine, gemcitabine, and prednisolone in patients with cardiac comorbidity: a United Kingdom National Cancer Research Institute Trial. *J Clin Oncol.* 2014;32:282-287.

7. Tucci A, Martelli M, Rigacci L, et al. Comprehensive geriatric assessment is an essential tool to support treatment decisions in elderly patients with diffuse large B-cell lymphoma: a prospective multicenter evaluation in 173 patients by the Lymphoma Italian Foundation (FIL). *Leuk Lymphoma.* 2015;56(4):921-926.

8. Mareschal S, Lanic H, Ruminy P, et al. The proportion of activated B-cell like subtype among de novo diffuse large B-cell lymphoma increases with age. *Haematologica.* 2011;96(12):1888-1890.

9. Klapper W, Kreuz M, Kohler CW, et al. Patient age at diagnosis is associated with the molecular characteristics of diffuse large B-cell lymphoma. *Blood.* 2012;119: 1882-1887.

10. Hamlin PA, Satram-Hoang S, Reyes C, et al. Treatment patterns and comparative effectiveness in elderly diffuse large B-cell lymphoma patients: a surveillance, epidemiology, and end results-medicare analysis. *Oncologist.* 2014;19(12):1249-1257.

11. Thieblemont C, Grossoeuvre A, Houot R, et al. Non-Hodgkin's lymphoma in very elderly patients over 80 years: a descriptive analysis of clinical presentation and outcome. *Ann Oncol.* 2008;19(4):774-779.

12. Siegel AB, Lachs M, Coleman M, Leonard JP. Lymphoma in elderly patients: novel functional assessment techniques provide better discrimination among patients than traditional performance status measures. *Clin Lymphoma Myeloma.* 2006;7(1):65-69.

13. Wildes TM, Goede V, Hamlin P. Personalizing therapy for older adults with lymphoid malignancies: options and obstacles. *American Society of Clinical Oncology educational book/ASCO. ASCO Meeting.* 2013.

14. Extermann M, Boler I, Reich RR, et al. Predicting the risk of chemotherapy toxicity in older patients: the Chemotherapy Risk Assessment Scale for High-Age Patients (CRASH) score. *Cancer.* 2012;118:3377-3386.

15. Extermann M, Overcash J, Lyman GH, et al. Comorbidity and functional status are independent in older cancer patients. *J Clin Oncol.* 1998;16:1582-1587.

16. Maas HA, Janssen-Heijnen ML, Olde Rikkert MG, Machteld Wymenga AN. Comprehensive geriatric assessment and its clinical impact in oncology. *Eur J Cancer.* 2007;43(15):2161-2169.

17. Balducci L, Extermann M. Management of cancer in the older person: a practical approach. *Oncologist.* 2000;5:224-237.

18. Janssen-Heijnen MLG, van Spronsen DJ, Lemmens VEPP, et al. A population-based study of severity of comorbidity among patients with non-Hodgkin's lymphoma: prognostic impact independent of International Prognostic Index. *Br J Haematol.* 2005;129:597-606.

19. Wieringa A, Boslooper K, Hoogendoorn M, et al. Comorbidity is an independent prognostic factor in patients with advanced-stage diffuse large B-cell lymphoma treated with R-CHOP: a population-based cohort study. *Br J Haematol.* 2014;165(4):489-496.

20. Kobayashi Y, Miura K, Hojo A, et al. Charlson Comorbidity Index is an independent prognostic factor among elderly patients with diffuse large B-cell lymphoma *J Cancer Res Clin Oncol.* 2011;137(7):1079-1084.

21. Charlson ME, Pompei P, Ales KL, et al. A new method of classifying prognostic comorbidity in longitudinal studies: development and validation. *J Chronic Dis.* 1987;40:373-383.

22. Parmelee PA, Thuras PD, Katz IR, Lawton MP. Validation of the Cumulative Illness Rating Scale in a geriatric residential population. *J Am Geriatr Soc.* 1995 43(2):130-137.

23. Delarue R, Tilly H, Mounier N, et al. Dose-dense rituximab-CHOP compared with standard rituximab-CHOP in elderly patients with diffuse large B-cell lymphoma (the LNH03-6B study): a randomised phase 3 trial. *Lancet Oncol.* 2013;14(6):525-533.

24. Pfreundschuh M, Schubert J, Ziepert M, et al. Six versus eight cycles of bi-weekly CHOP-14 with or without rituximab in elderly patients with aggressive CD20+ B-cell lymphomas: a randomised controlled trial (RICOVER-60). *Lancet Oncol.* 2008;9(2):105-116.

25. Peyrade F, Serge B, Delwail V, et al. Pre-phase chemotherapy followed by ofatumumab (ofa) and reduced dose CHOP (ofa-mini-CHOP) for patients over 80 years with diffuse large B-cell lymphoma (DLBCL)–a lymphoma study association (LYSA) prospective phase II study (lnh09-7b). *Blood.* 2014;124(21):3042.

26. Owens CN, Iannotta A, Gerecitano JF, et al. Effect of prednisone and rituximab prephase on early toxicity in older DLBCL patients (pts) receiving RCHOP within a NHL specific comprehensive geriatric assessment (CGA) trial. *ASCO Annual Meeting Proceedings.* 2015;33(15) (suppl).

27. Sehn, LH, Savage, KJ, Hoskins, P, et al. Limited-stage diffuse large B-cell lymphoma (DLBCL) patients with a negative pet scan following three cycles of R-CHOP can be effectively treated with abbreviated chemoimmunotherapy alone. *Blood.* 2007; 110(11):787-787.

28. Miller TP, Dahlberg S, Cassady JR, et al. Chemotherapy alone compared with chemotherapy plus radiotherapy for localized intermediate and high-grade non-Hodgkin's lymphoma. *N Engl J Med.* 1998;339(1):21-26.

29. Persky DO, Unger JM, Spier CM, et al. Phase II study of rituximab plus three cycles of CHOP and involved-field radiotherapy for patients with limited-stage aggressive B-cell lymphoma: Southwest Oncology Group study 0014. *J Clin Oncol.* 2008;26(14):2258-2263.

30. Lamy T, Damaj G, Gyan E, et al. R-CHOP with or without radiotherapy in non-bulky limited-stage diffuse large B cell lymphoma (DLBCL): preliminary results of the prospective randomized phase III 02-03 trial from the Lysa/Goelams Group. *Blood.* 2014;124(21):393-393.

31. Coiffier B, Thieblemont C, Van Den Neste E, et al. Long-term outcome of patients in the LNH-98.5 trial, the first randomized study comparing rituximab-CHOP to standard CHOP chemotherapy in DLBCL patients: a study by the Groupe d'Etudes des Lymphomes de l'Adulte. *Blood.* 2010;116:2040-2045.

32. Pfreundschuh M, Held G, Zeynalova S, et al. Increased rituximab (R) doses eliminate increased risk and improve outcome of elderly male patients with aggressive CD20+ B-cell lymphomas: the SEXIE-R-CHOP-14 trial of the DSHNHL. *Clin Adv Hematol Oncol.* 2014;12(8):8-9.

33. Wilson WH, Grossbard ML, Pittaluga S, et al. Dose-adjusted EPOCH chemotherapy for untreated large B-cell lymphomas: a pharmacodynamic approach with high efficacy. *Blood.* 2002;99:2685-2693.

34. Wilson WH, Dunleavy K, Pittaluga S, et al. Phase II study of dose-adjusted EPOCH and rituximab in untreated diffuse large B-cell lymphoma with analysis of germinal center and post-germinal center biomarkers. *J Clin Oncol.* 2008;26(16): 2717-2724.

35. Wilson W, Sin-Ho J, Pitcher BN, et al. Phase III randomized study of R-CHOP vs DA-EPOCH-R and molecular analysis of untreated diffuse large B cell lymphoma: CALGB/Alliance 50303. In 58th Annual Meeting and Exposition of the American Society of Hematology; December 2-6, 2016; San Diego, CA: ASH. Abstract 469.

36. Hershman DL, McBride RB, Eisenberger A, et al. Doxorubicin, cardiac risk factors, and cardiac toxicity in elderly patients with diffuse B-cell non-Hodgkin's lymphoma. *J Clin Oncol.* 2008;26(19):3159-3165.

37. Merli F, Luminari S, Rossi G, et al. Cyclophosphamide, doxorubicin, vincristine, prednisone and rituximab versus epirubicin, cyclophosphamide, vinblastine, prednisone and rituximab for the initial treatment of elderly "fit" patients with diffuse large B-cell lymphoma: results from the ANZINTER3 trial of the Intergruppo Italiano Linfomi. *Leuk Lymphoma.* 2012;53:581-588.

38. Meguro A, Ozaki K, Sato K, et al. Rituximab plus 70% cyclophosphamide, doxorubicin, vincristine and prednisone for Japanese patients with diffuse large B-cell lymphoma aged 70 years and older. *Leukemia Lymphoma.* 2012;53(1):43-49.

39. Flinn IW, van der Jagt R, Kahl BS, et al. Randomized trial of bendamustine-rituximab or R-CHOP/R-CVP in first-line treatment of indolent NHL or MCL: the BRIGHT study. *Blood.* 2014;123(19):2944-2952.

40. Rummel MJ, Niederle N, Maschmeyer G, et al. Bendamustine plus rituximab versus CHOP plus rituximab as first-line treatment for patients with indolent and mantle-cell lymphomas: an open-label, multicentre, randomised, phase 3 non-inferiority trial. *Lancet.* 2013;381(9873):1203-1210.

41. Ruan J, Martin P, Shah B, Schuster SJ, et al. Lenalidomide plus rituximab as initial treatment for mantle-cell lymphoma. *N Engl J Med.* 2015;373(19):1835-1844.

42. Cavalli F, Rooney B, Pei L, et al. Randomized phase 3 study of rituximab, cyclophosphamide, doxorubicin, and prednisone plus vincristine (R-CHOP) or bortezomib (VR-CAP) in newly diagnosed mantle cell lymphoma (MCL) patients (pts) ineligible for bone marrow transplantation (BMT). *ASCO Annual Meeting Proceedings.* 2014;32(15) (suppl). Abstract 8500.

43. Gordon LI, Hong F, Fisher RI, et al. Randomized phase III trial of ABVD versus Stanford V with or without radiation therapy in locally extensive and advanced-stage Hodgkin lymphoma: an intergroup study coordinated by the Eastern Cooperative Oncology Group (E2496). *J Clin Oncol.* 2013;31(6):684-691.

44. Bonadonna G, Bonfante V, Viviani S, et al. ABVD plus subtotal nodal versus involved-field radiotherapy in early-stage Hodgkin's disease: long-term results. *J Clin Oncol.* 2004;22(14):2835-2841.

45. Engert A, Diehl V, Pluetschow A, et al. Two cycles of ABVD followed by involved field radiotherapy with 20 gray (Gy) is the new standard of care in the treatment of patients with early-stage Hodgkin lymphoma: final analysis of the randomized German Hodgkin Study Group (GHSG) HD10. *Blood.* 2009;114(22):3495-3502.

46. Radford J, Barrington S, Counsell N, et al. Involved field radiotherapy versus no further treatment in patients with clinical stages IA and IIA Hodgkin lymphoma and a "negative" PET scan after 3 cycles ABVD: results of the UK NCRI RAPID trial. *Blood.* 2012;120:547.

47. Eich HT, Diehl V, Görgen H, et al. Intensified chemotherapy and dose-reduced involved-field radiotherapy in patients with early unfavorable Hodgkin's lymphoma: final analysis of the German Hodgkin Study Group HD11 trial. *J Clin Oncol.* 2010;28(27):4199-4206.

48. Straus DJ, Portlock CS, Qin J, et al. Results of a prospective randomized clinical trial of doxorubicin, bleomycin, vinblastine, and dacarbazine (ABVD) followed by radiation therapy (RT) versus ABVD alone for stages I, II, and IIIA nonbulky Hodgkin disease. *Blood.* 2004;104(12):3483-3489.

49. Canellos GP, Anderson JR, Proper KJ, et al. Chemotherapy of advanced Hodgkin's disease with MOPP, ABVD, or MOPP alternating with ABVD. *N Eng J Med.* 1992;27(21):1478-1484.

50. Barrington SF, Kirkwood AA, Franceschetto A, et al. PET-CT for staging and early response: results from the Response-Adapted Therapy in Advanced Hodgkin Lymphoma study. *Blood.* 2016; 127(12):1531-1538.

51. Johnson, PW, et al. Response-adapted therapy based on interim FDG-PET scans in advanced Hodgkin lymphoma: first analysis of the safety of de-escalation and efficacy of escalation in the international RATHL study (CRUK/07/033). *Hematological Oncology.* 2015;33:102-103.

52. Proctor SJ, Wilkinson J, Jones G, et al. Evaluation of treatment outcome in 175 patients with Hodgkin lymphoma aged 60 years or over: the SHIELD study. *Blood.* 2012;119:6005-6015.

53. Forero-Torres A, Holkova B, Goldschmidt J, et al. Phase 2 study of frontline brentuximab vedotin monotherapy in Hodgkin lymphoma patients aged 60 years and older. *Blood.* 2015;126(26):2798-2804.

54. Ansell SM, Lesokhin AM, Borrello I, et al. PD-1 blockade with nivolumab in relapsed or refractory Hodgkin's lymphoma. *N Engl J Med.* 2015;372(4):311-319.

55. Moskowitz CH, Ribrag V, Michot J, et al. PD-1 blockade with the monoclonal antibody pembrolizumab (MK-3475) in patients with classical Hodgkin lymphoma after brentuximab vedotin failure: preliminary results from a phase 1b study (KEYNOTE-013). *Blood.* 2014;124(21):290.

56. Casulo C, Byrtek M, Dawson K, et al. Early relapse of follicular lymphoma after rituximab plus cyclophosphamide, doxorubicin, vincristine, and prednisone defines patients at high risk for death: an analysis from the National LymphoCare Study. *J Clin Oncol.* 2015;33(23):2516-2522.

57. Advani RH, Chen H, Habermann TM, et al. Comparison of conventional prognostic indices in patients older than 60 years with diffuse large B-cell lymphoma treated with R-CHOP in the US Intergroup Study (ECOG 4494, CALGB 9793): consideration of age greater than 70 years in an elderly prognostic index (E-IPI). *Br J Haemato.* 2010;151(2):143-151.

RECOMMENDED READING

Afifi S, Michael A, Azimi M, et al. Vincristine omission, but not dose reduction, is associated with decreased survival in elderly DLBCL patients. *Hematol Oncol.* 2015; 33:212-213.

Böll B, Bredenfeld H, Görgen H, et al. Phase 2 study of PVAG (prednisone, vinblastine, doxorubicin, gemcitabine) in elderly patients with early unfavorable or advanced stage Hodgkin lymphoma. *Blood.* 2011;118(24):6292-6298.

Duggan DB, Petroni GR, Johnson JL, et al. Randomized comparison of ABVD and MOPP/ABV hybrid for the treatment of advanced Hodgkin's disease: report of an intergroup trial. *J Clin Oncol.* 2003;21(4):607-614.

Hainsworth JD, Flinn IW, Spigel DR, et al. Brief-duration rituximab/chemotherapy followed by maintenance rituximab in patients with diffuse large B-cell lymphoma who are poor candidates for R-CHOP chemotherapy: a phase II trial of the Sarah Cannon Oncology Research Consortium. *Clin Lymphoma Myeloma Leuk.* 2010; 10(1):44-50.

Hamlin PA, Zelenetz AD, Kewalramani T, et al. Age-adjusted International Prognostic Index predicts autologous stem cell transplantation outcome for patients with relapsed or primary refractory diffuse large B-cell lymphoma. *Blood.* 2003;102(6):1989-1996.

Harris NL, Jaffe ES, Stein H, et al. A revised European-American classification of lymphoid neoplasms: a proposal from the International Lymphoma Study Group. *Blood.* 1994;84:1361-1392.

Hermine O, Hoster E, Walewski J, et al. Alternating courses of 3xCHOP and 3xDHAP plus rituximab followed by a high dose ARA-C containing myeloablative regimen and autologous stem cell transplantation (ASCT) increases overall survival when compared to 6 courses of CHOP plus rituximab followed by myeloablative radiochemotherapy and ASCT in mantle cell lymphoma: final analysis of the MCL younger trial of the European Mantle Cell Lymphoma Network [abstract]. *Blood.* 2012;120(21):151.

Hurria A, Togawa K, Mohile SG, et al. Predicting chemotherapy toxicity in older adults with cancer: a prospective multicenter study. *J Clin Oncol.* 2011;29:3457-3465.

Kluin-Nelemans JC, Hoster E, Walewski J. R-CHOP versus R-FC followed by maintenance with rituximab versus interferon-alfa: outcome of the first randomized trial for elderly patients with mantle cell lymphoma. *Blood.* 2011;118(suppl 1).

Lenz G, Dreyling M, Hoster E, et al. Immunochemotherapy with rituximab and cyclophosphamide, doxorubicin, vincristine, and prednisone significantly improves response and time to treatment failure, but not long-term outcome in patients with previously untreated mantle cell lymphoma: results of a prospective randomized trial of the German Low Grade Lymphoma Study Group (GLSG). *J Clin Oncol.* 2005;23(9):1984-1992.

Merli F, Luminari S, Rossi G, et al. Outcome of frail elderly patients with diffuse large B-cell lymphoma prospectively identified by comprehensive geriatric assessment: results from a study of the Fondazione Italiana Linfomi. *Leuk Lymphoma.* 2014;55:38-43.

Moskowitz CH, Nademanee A, Masszi T, et al. Brentuximab vedotin as consolidation therapy after autologous stem-cell transplantation in patients with Hodgkin's lymphoma at risk of relapse or progression (AETHERA): a randomised, double-blind, placebo-controlled, phase 3 trial. *Lancet.* 2015;385(9980):1853-1862.

Shipp MA, Harrington DP, Anderson JR, et al. A predictive model for aggressive non-Hodgkin's lymphoma. *N Engl J Med.* 1993;329(14):987-994.

Tucci A, Ferrari S, Bottelli C, et al. A comprehensive geriatric assessment is more effective than clinical judgment to identify elderly diffuse large cell lymphoma patients who benefit from aggressive therapy. *Cancer.* 2009;115:4547-4553.

Vose JM, Armitage JO, Weisenburger DD, et al. The importance of age in survival of patients treated with chemotherapy for aggressive non-Hodgkin's lymphoma. *J Clin Oncol.* 1988;6:1838-1844.

24 Acute Myeloid Leukemia and Myelodysplastic Syndrome

Li-Wen Huang and Arati V. Rao

ACUTE MYELOID LEUKEMIA

Introduction

Acute myeloid leukemia (AML) comprises 77% of newly diagnosed acute leukemias, with a median age at diagnosis of 67 years. In 2015, 20,830 patients were diagnosed with AML, and unfortunately, more than half of them died from their disease (1). *Elderly patients*, defined as age greater than or equal to 60 years in the AML literature, have lower complete remission (CR) rates and higher relapse risk compared to their younger counterparts when treated with induction chemotherapy (2). Poor outcomes in older AML patients result from a combination of age-related factors in disease biology and patient characteristics.

Biology of AML in the Elderly

AML in elderly patients tend to have a more aggressive biology (Table 24.1), including a higher incidence of secondary AML. Older patients exhibit more unfavorable cytogenetic abnormalities (−7, 7q−, −5, 5q−, abnormalities of 11q, 17p, inv3, complex) and less favorable cytogenetics (t [8;21], t [15;17], t [16;16], inv16) compared to younger patients (2,3). Older patients also have increased expression of proteins involved in intrinsic resistance to chemotherapeutic agents, such as the multidrug resistance 1 gene (MDR1) (4). In a large study of more than 900 older patients with newly diagnosed AML treated with induction chemotherapy, the 5-year overall survival (OS) was about 10%, and multivariate analyses revealed that karyotype, age, nucleophosmin 1 (NPM1) mutation status, white blood cell count, lactate dehydrogenase, and CD34 expression were independent prognostic factors for OS. Based on the multivariate Cox model, an additive risk score was developed to distinguish four prognostic groups: favorable risk, good intermediate risk, adverse intermediate risk, and high risk. The corresponding 3-year OS rates were 39.5%, 30%, 10.6%, and 3.3%, respectively (5).

Patient Characteristics and Role of Geriatric Assessments

Disease biology does not account for the entirety of age-related differences in outcome, as older patients with favorable disease still do worse than their younger

TABLE 24.1 Characteristics of AML in Elderly Versus Younger Patients

Characteristic	Elderly AML	Younger AML
Epidemiology		
Incidence (per 100,000)	18.3	1.9
5-y relative survival (%)	5.8	44
Response to treatment (%)		
CR	43	59
TRM	20	8
Disease characteristics		
MDR1 expression (%)	71	35
Favorable cytogenetics (%)		
t (8:21)	2	8
inv 16	1	4
t (15:17)	4	12
Unfavorable cytogenetics (%)		
−7 or del (7q)	4–8	2–4
−5 or del (5q)	5–7	1–2
Complex	13	6

AML, acute myeloid leukemia; CR, complete remission; del, deletion; inv, inversion; MDR1, multidrug resistance 1; t, translocation; TRM, treatment-related mortality.

Source: Adapted from Refs. (1–4).

counterparts (6). Older AML patients have more comorbidities and age-related renal and hepatic dysfunction that impact their ability to metabolize chemotherapeutic agents and withstand intensive therapy. Other factors, such as functional status, cognition, and social support, also affect treatment tolerance. Several prognostic models have been proposed to predict outcomes for older patients treated with induction chemotherapy (7–9). These models tend to rely on age and Eastern Cooperative Oncology Group (ECOG) performance status (PS) to predict treatment tolerance.

However, compared to younger patients with the same PS, patients older than 65 have higher treatment-related mortality (TRM) after induction chemotherapy, and the difference is more pronounced with worse PS (TRM 13% in older vs. 5% in younger patients with PS 0, 16% vs. 4% for PS 1, 35% vs. 9% for PS 2, 60% vs. 21% for PS 3) (6), suggesting that PS alone does not adequately assess patient characteristics that affect outcome. Higher comorbidity burden has been shown to be associated with lower CR rates, increased TRM, and lower OS after induction chemotherapy (10).

Comprehensive geriatric assessments (CGAs) evaluating cognitive function, physical function, psychological state, and comorbid disease can be a valuable tool to help evaluate the complex host characteristics of older AML patients. In one study, patients aged 60 years or older with newly diagnosed AML and planned intensive chemotherapy underwent pretreatment CGA that included evaluation of cognition, depression, distress, physical function (self-reported and objectively measured), and comorbidity. Objective physical function was assessed using the Short Physical Performance Battery (timed 4-m walk, chair stands, standing balance) and grip strength. After adjusting for age, gender, ECOG PS, cytogenetic risk group, underlying myelodysplastic syndrome (MDS), and hemoglobin, it was noted that impaired cognition (score <77 on the 100-point Modified Mini Mental State Exam) and impaired objective physical function were associated with worse OS in the elderly AML patient (11).

Treatment

Optimal management of elders with AML is controversial due to the heterogeneity of this population, as well as high morbidity and mortality (Table 24.2). If left untreated, a patient with AML has a median survival of less than 2 months; with treatment, median survival is historically less than 1 year but has been improving in recent years (6). In general, older patients are less likely to achieve CR, more likely to relapse, and have a higher induction mortality rate (12).

Standard induction therapy for AML is intensive chemotherapy with traditional 7+3 chemotherapy (cytarabine for seven days and an anthracycline such as daunorubicin or idarubicin, or anthracenedione mitoxantrone for three days). Studies comparing intensive therapy to supportive and palliative care have shown that intensive

TABLE 24.2 Treatment Considerations for Older Patients With AML

Patient Characteristics	Disease Biology	Treatment Considerations

Frail
  ECOG PS ≥3
  HCT-CI >2
  Any ADL
  Impairment
	Favorable	Lower-intensity therapy. Consider intensive therapy if poor PS but no end-stage comorbidity, if risk/benefits consistent with goals of care.

	Intermediate or unfavorable	Best supportive care with palliative care consultation vs. lower-intensity therapy.

Vulnerable
  ECOG PS 0–2
  HCT-CI ≤2
  CGA risk factors
	Favorable	Intensive therapy.

	Intermediate or unfavorable	Lower-intensity therapy vs. intensive therapy if risk/benefits consistent with goals of care.

Fit
  ECOG PS 0–1
  HCT-CI <1
  No CGA risk factors
	Favorable	Intensive therapy should be offered.

	Intermediate or unfavorable	Intensive therapy with RIC HSCT if risk/benefits consistent with goals of care vs. lower-intensity therapies.

ADL, activities of daily living; AML, acute myeloid leukemia; CGA, comprehensive geriatric assessment (risk factors include impairments in cognitive function and physical performance); ECOG PS, Eastern Cooperative Oncology Group performance status; HCT-CI, hematopoietic cell transplantation comorbidity index; RIC HSCT, reduced-intensity conditioning hematopoietic stem cell transplantation.

therapy improves OS without increasing hospitalization days, decreasing quality of life (QOL), or decreasing functional status in carefully selected patients (13,14). Postremission consolidative chemotherapy with high-dose cytarabine (HiDAC) is controversial in elderly patients, and there are as yet no definitive prospective studies. There is no evidence defining optimal duration or intensity of consolidation, although there is a clear association between dose intensity and increased toxicity, especially cerebellar toxicity and myelosuppression (15).

For patients with poor PS or comorbidities who are thought to be poor candidates for intensive therapy, lower-intensity therapy with hypomethylating agents such as azacitidine and decitabine are increasingly utilized. In one large retrospective single-institution study, epigenetic therapy utilizing hypomethylating agents was associated with survival rates similar to those achieved with intensive chemotherapy in older patients with newly diagnosed AML. Although these agents have been shown to be efficacious, with CR rates of 20% to 25%, there have been no prospective randomized trials comparing lower-intensity therapy to intensive induction therapy (16–18).

Because elderly patients are traditionally considered poor candidates for allogeneic hematopoietic stem cell transplantation (HSCT), the development of reduced-intensity conditioning (RIC) regimens has challenged conventions regarding age and HSCT. Clinical trials have demonstrated that allogeneic HSCT following RIC is feasible and may benefit appropriately selected patients, though the treatments did not translate into longer OS (19,20).

MYELODYSPLASTIC SYNDROMES

Introduction

MDS is a disease of the elderly characterized by ineffective hematopoiesis and cytopenias. Among 21,000 patients diagnosed with MDS every year, over 70% are 70 years of age or older (1). MDS encompasses a spectrum of clinical disorders ranging from indolent to very aggressive disease that can progress to AML.

Disease Biology

Given the heterogeneity of MDS, risk stratification schemes have been proposed to help inform treatment decision making. The revised International Prognostic Scoring System-Revised (IPSS-R) incorporates cytogenetic abnormalities, percentage of marrow blasts, and number and severity of cytopenias to divide patients into five risk categories. Very low-risk patients have median OS of 8.8 years and median time to 25% AML evolution of 14.5 years, compared to very high-risk patients with median OS 0.8 years and median time to 25% AML evolution 0.7 years (21). Red blood cell transfusion need has also been shown to be an IPSS-independent risk factor in patients with MDS. A new prognostic model (DIPSS plus) has been established; this model includes red blood cell transfusion need as one of eight risk factors along with age greater than 65 years, hemoglobin less than 10 g/dL, leukocyte count greater than 25×10^9/L, circulating blasts greater than or equal to 1%, constitutional symptoms, platelet count less than 100×10^9/L, and unfavorable karyotype (22).

Patient Characteristics

Beyond assessing disease risk, selection of the optimal treatment strategy for MDS requires a careful assessment of the risk of proposed interventions. As in AML, PS does not adequately capture factors that may affect life expectancy and ability to tolerate treatment. Studies have demonstrated a clear association between increased comorbidities and worse survival, independent of age and disease risk (23,24). One prospective study utilizing CGA in MDS and AML patients found that ADL impairments and high fatigue ratings were independently associated with survival (25). Larger prospective studies to validate prognostic factors and predict treatment response for specific MDS therapies are needed.

Treatment

Treatment strategies for MDS should be adapted to risk (Table 24.3). In general, the goal is to minimize morbidity in lower-risk patients and to alter the natural history of disease in high-risk patients. Supportive care, such as transfusions, hematopoietic growth factors, and antibiotics, to control symptoms of cytopenias remains the primary therapy for patients who have lower-risk MDS or are frail and poor candidates for cytoreductive therapy.

Hypomethylating agents such as azacitidine and decitabine are the primary treatment for most patients and have been shown to improve survival, QOL, and time to progression to AML (15,26,27). For patients with the 5q minus syndrome, a favorable MDS subtype, the immunomodulatory agent lenalidomide has been shown to reverse

TABLE 24.3 Treatment Considerations for Older Patients With MDS

Disease Characteristics (IPSS-R)	Patient Characteristics	Treatment Considerations
Very low, low-risk Asymptomatic	Any	Observation
Very low, low, Intermediate-risk Symptomatic	Any	Hematopoietic growth factors Lenalidomide for 5q deletion
	Good PS Minimal comorbidity (HCT-CI ≤1)	Hypomethylating agents
Intermediate, high, very high risk	Poor PS Major comorbidity (HCT-CI >1)	Supportive care vs. hypomethylating agent
	Good PS Minimal comorbidity (HCT-CI ≤1)	Hypomethylating agents Consider RIC HSCT for excellent PS, if consistent with goals of care

HCT-CI, Hematopoietic Cell Transplantation Comorbidity Index; IPSS-R, revised International Prognostic Scoring System; MDS, myelodysplastic syndrome; PS, performance status; RIC HSCT, reduced-intensity conditioning hematopoietic stem cell transplantation.

cytogenetic abnormalities and reduce red blood cell transfusion requirements (28). Lenalidomide may also benefit patients with low-risk MDS without the 5q deletion and may be considered for such patients who are transfusion dependent (29). The only curative therapy for MDS is an allogeneic HSCT, and HSCT with RIC is increasingly considered for older adults with good functional status and minimal comorbidities. One large study has demonstrated that RIC HSCT improves survival and QOL for higher-risk MDS patients, but in patients with low IPSS scores, survival and QOL are better with nontransplant measures than with RIC HSCT (30).

TAKE HOME POINTS

1. Older patients with AML have worse outcomes than younger patients, as a result of more aggressive disease biology and age-related changes in host characteristics.
2. MDS is a heterogeneous disease of the elderly that comprises a spectrum of clinical behaviors from indolent disease to rapidly progressive disease that can progress to AML.
3. Age and PS do not adequately capture the complexities of the older patient; CGA should be used to evaluate factors that predict treatment tolerance and response.
4. For both AML and MDS, treatment decision making requires an individualized assessment of risk posed by the disease, risks and benefits of proposed interventions, and patient goals of care to determine a treatment that provides meaningful benefit without unacceptable toxicity.
5. In general, fit older patients with high-risk disease should be offered intensive therapy, whereas frail older patients may benefit more from lower-intensity therapy or supportive care.

REFERENCES

1. Howlader N, Noone AM, Krapcho M, et al., eds. *SEER Cancer Statistics Review, 1975-2012.* Bethesda, MD: National Cancer Institute; 2015. Available at: http://seer.cancer.gov/csr/1975_2012. Accessed March 12, 2016.
2. Grimwade D, Walker H, Harrison G, et al. The predictive value of hierarchical cytogenetic classification in older adults with acute myeloid leukemia (AML): analysis of 1065 patients entered into the United Kingdom Medical Research Council AML11 trial. *Blood.* 2001;98:1312-1320.
3. Grimwade D, Walker H, Oliver F, et al. The importance of diagnostic cytogenetics on outcome in AML: analysis of 1,612 patients entered into the MRC AML 10 trial. The Medical Research Council Adult and Children's Leukaemia Working Parties. *Blood.* 1998;92:2322-2333.
4. Leith CP, Kopecky KJ, Chen IM, et al. Frequency and clinical significance of the expression of the multidrug resistance proteins MDR1/P-glycoprotein, MRP1, and LRP in acute myeloid leukemia: a Southwest Oncology Group Study. *Blood.* 1999;94:1086-1099.

5. Rollig C, Thiede C, Gramatzki M, et al. A novel prognostic model in elderly patients with acute myeloid leukemia: results of 909 patients entered into the prospective AML96 trial. *Blood.* 2010;116:971-978.

6. Appelbaum FR, Gundacker H, Head DR, et al. Age and acute myeloid leukemia. *Blood.* 2006;107:3481-3485.

7. Kantarjian H, Ravandi F, O'Brien S, et al. Intensive chemotherapy does not benefit most older patients (age 70 years or older) with acute myeloid leukemia. *Blood.* 2010;116:4422-4429.

8. Krug U, Rollig C, Koschmieder A, et al. Complete remission and early death after intensive chemotherapy in patients aged 60 years or older with acute myeloid leukaemia: a web-based application for prediction of outcomes. *Lancet.* 2010;376:2000-2008.

9. Rollig C, Thiede C, Gramatzki M, et al. A novel prognostic model in elderly patients with acute myeloid leukemia: results of 909 patients entered into the prospective AML96 trial. *Blood.* 2010;116:971-978.

10. Giles FJ, Borthakur G, Ravandi F, et al. The haematopoietic cell transplantation comorbidity index score is predictive of early death and survival in patients over 60 years of age receiving induction therapy for acute myeloid leukaemia. *Br J Haematol.* 2007;136:624-627.

11. Klepin HD, Geiger AM, Tooze JA, et al. Geriatric assessment predicts survival for older adults receiving induction chemotherapy for acute myelogenous leukemia. *Blood.* 2013;121:4287-4294.

12. Klepin HD. Myelodysplastic syndromes and acute myeloid leukemia in the elderly. *Clin Geriatr Med.* 2016;32(1):155-173.

13. Meyers CA, Albitar M, Estey E. Cognitive impairment, fatigue, and cytokine levels in patients with acute myelogenous leukemia or myelodysplastic syndrome. *Cancer.* 2005;104:788-793.

14. Lowenberg B, Zittoun R, Kerkhofs H, et al. On the value of intensive remission induction chemotherapy in elderly patients of 65+ years with acute myeloid leukemia: a randomized phase III study of the European Organization for Research and Treatment of Cancer Leukemia Group. *J Clin Oncol.* 1989;7:1268-1274.

15. Mayer RJ, Davis RB, Schiffer CA, et al. Intensive postremission chemotherapy in adults with acute myeloid leukemia. Cancer and Leukemia Group B. *N Engl J Med.* 1994;331:896-903.

16. Fenaux P, Mufti GJ, Hellstrom-Lindberg E, et al. Azacitidine prolongs overall survival compared with conventional care regimens in elderly patients with low bone marrow blast count acute myeloid leukemia. *J Clin Oncol.* 2010;28:562-569.

17. Kantarjian HM, Thomas XG, Dmoszynska A, et al. Multicenter, randomized, open-label, phase III trial of decitabine versus patient choice, with physician advice, of either supportive care or low-dose cytarabine for the treatment of older patients with newly diagnosed acute myeloid leukemia. *J Clin Oncol.* 2012;30:2670-2677.

18. Dombret H, Seymour JF, Butrym A, et al. International phase 3 study of azacitidine vs conventional care regimens in older patients with newly diagnosed AML with >30% blasts. *Blood.* 2015;126:291-299.

19. Archimbaud E, Jehn U, Thomas X, et al. Multicenter randomized phase II trial of idarubicin vs mitoxantrone, combined with VP-16 and cytarabine for induction/consolidation therapy, followed by a feasibility study of autologous peripheral blood stem cell transplantation in elderly patients with acute myeloid leukemia. *Leukemia.* 1999;13:843-849.

20. Bertz H, Potthoff K, Finke J. Allogeneic stem-cell transplantation from related and unrelated donors in older patients with myeloid leukemia. *J Clin Oncol.* 2003;21:1480-1484.

21. Greenberg PL, Tuechler H, Schanz J, et al. Revised International Prognostic Scoring System for myelodysplastic syndromes. *Blood.* 2012;120:2454-2465.

22. Gangat N, Caramazza D, Vaidya R, et al. DIPSS plus: a refined Dynamic International Prognostic Scoring System for primary myelofibrosis that incorporates prognostic information from karyotype, platelet count, and transfusion status. *J Clin Oncol.* 2011;29:392-397.

23. Della Porta MG, Malcovati L, Strupp C, et al. Risk stratification based on both disease status and extra-hematologic comorbidities in patients with myelodysplastic syndrome. *Haematologica.* 2011;96:441-449.

24. Naqvi K, Garcia-Manero G, Sardesai S, et al. Association of comorbidities with overall survival in myelodysplastic syndrome: development of a prognostic model. *J Clin Oncol.* 2011;29:2240-2246.

25. Deschler B, Ihorst G, Platzbecker U, et al. Parameters detected by geriatric and quality of life assessment in 195 older patients with myelodysplastic syndromes and acute myeloid leukemia are highly predictive for outcome. *Haematologica.* 2013;98:208-216.

26. Silverman LR, Demakos EP, Peterson BL, et al. Randomized controlled trial of azacitidine in patients with the myelodysplastic syndrome: a study of the Cancer and Leukemia Group B. *J Clin Oncol.* 2002;20:2429-2440.

27. Kornblith AB, Herndon JE, Silverman LR, et al. Impact of azacytidine on the quality of life of patients with myelodysplastic syndrome treated in a randomized phase III trial: a Cancer and Leukemia Group B study. *J Clin Oncol.* 2002;20:2441-2452.

28. List A, Dewald G, Bennett J, et al. Lenalidomide in the myelodysplastic syndrome with chromosome 5q deletion. *N Engl J Med.* 2006;355:1456-1465.

29. Sibon D, Cannas G, Baracco F, et al. Lenalidomide in lower-risk myelodysplastic syndromes with karyotypes other than deletion 5q and refractory to erythropoiesis stimulating agents. *Br J Haematol.* 2012;156:619-625.

30. Koreth J, Pidala J, Perez WS, et al. Role of reduced-intensity conditioning allogeneic hematopoietic stem-cell transplantation in older patients with de novo myelodysplastic syndromes: an international collaborative decision analysis. *J Clin Oncol.* 2013;31:2662-2670.

Hematopoietic Cell Transplantation for Older Patients

Sergio Giralt

INTRODUCTION

In 1974, Thomas et al. published their seminal paper of the use of high-dose chemoradiotherapy followed by the infusion of related human leucocyte antigen (HLA) compatible bone marrow in 100 patients with refractory acute leukemia (1). This paper demonstrated that high-dose chemoradiotherapy followed by an HLA-identical bone marrow transplant could result in long-term disease control in a fraction of patients with refractory acute leukemia.

Initially it was felt that most of the curative potential of this strategy was derived from the steep dose–response curve of alkylating agents and radiotherapy and tumor cell response in human tumors. Doubling the dose of alkylating agents increases tumor cell kill by a log or more, and increasing the dose of alkylating agents by 5- to 10-fold overcomes the resistance of tumor cells against lower doses. Thus, over the next 20 years, high-dose chemoradiotherapy followed by either autologous or allogeneic hematopoietic cell transplant (HCT) was extensively explored in a variety of hematologic and nonhematologic malignancies (2).

However, due to the toxic side effects of high-dose chemoradiotherapy and the intensive supportive care required during the period of intense myelosuppression after the conditioning regimen, allogeneic and autologous HCT was initially limited to younger patients with few if any comorbidities (1,2).

In 1997, the first reports of reduced-intensity conditioning (RIC) regimens appeared in the literature, with subsequent reports demonstrating that RIC regimens can be delivered to older patients or patients with comorbidities and achieve acceptable toxicities and outcomes (3–5). With the advent of RIC regimens and with improvements in supportive care, the average age of an HCT recipient for both autologous or allogeneic has increased significantly, as depicted in Figure 25.1, and is now considered standard of care for most patients over the age of 65; many transplant centers no longer have an age limit for the procedure (6). In this chapter, we summarize the rationale for exploring HCT in older patients, current indications and results, and future directions.

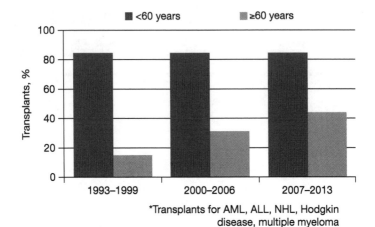

Trends in Autologous Transplants by
Recipient Age*

*Transplants for AML, ALL, NHL, Hodgkin
disease, multiple myeloma

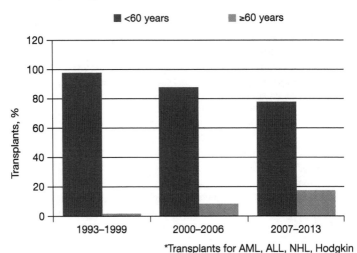

Trends in Allogeneic Transplants by
Recipient Age*

*Transplants for AML, ALL, NHL, Hodgkin
disease, multiple myeloma

FIGURE 25.1 Trends in age of HCT recipients as reported to the Center for International Blood and Marrow Research.

ALL, acute lymphoblastic leukemia; AML, acute myeloid leukemia; NHL, non-hodgkin lymphoma; HCT, hematopoietic cell transplantation.

RATIONALE FOR EXPLORING HCT IN OLDER PATIENTS

Table 25.1 summarizes the incidence and prevalence of the most common blood cancers in the United States today, as well as the median age of onset and the role of HCT in the treatment of the disease. For many blood cancers, HCT represents the only curative approach or the approach with the best chance of long-term disease control. Nevertheless, most of the patients who can benefit from this procedure are either older or medically debilitated.

TABLE 25.1 Most Common Hematologic Malignancies With Median Age of Onset, Incidence, Prevalence, and Role of Hematopoietic Cell Transplantation

Diagnosis	Median Age at Onset	Incidence per Year	Role of HCT
AML	63	10,500	Allogeneic HCT as consolidation of high-risk CR1 patients. Allogeneic HCT as salvage therapy for patients with advanced disease
Acute lymphoblastic leukemia	12	6,950	Allogeneic HCT as consolidation of high-risk CR1 patients. Allogeneic HCT as salvage therapy for patients with advanced disease
MDS	70	16,000 estimate	Allogeneic HCT only curative therapy
Chronic lymphocytic leukemia	70	16,000	Allogeneic HCT only curative therapy
Chronic myeloid leukemia	64	6,000	Allogeneic HCT as salvage therapy for patients who have failed tyrosine kinase inhibitors
Non-Hodgkin lymphoma	66	72,000	Autologous HCT as consolidation of chemosensitive relapse of DLBCL, follicular lymphoma. Consolidation of high-risk CR1 patients (mantle cell lymphoma, double hit lymphoma, high IPI scores). Allogeneic HCT as salvage for patients who relapse after autologous HCT
Multiple myeloma	73	18,000	Autologous HCT as consolidation of an initial remission considered standard of care Allogeneic HCT as salvage for patients who relapse after autologous HCT

AML, acute myeloid leukemia; CR1, complete remission 1; DLBCL, diffuse large B cell lymphoma; HCT, hematopoietic cell transplant; MDS, myelodysplastic syndromes.

Source: Adapted from Refs. (6,7).

BASICS OF HEMATOPOIETIC CELL TRANSPLANTATION (8)

Hematopoietic cell transplantation is a complex procedure. The patient receives a combination of chemical and physical agents to eliminate a malignant disorder or a poorly functioning bone marrow, supported by reinfusion of hematopoietic stem cells (HSCs) from the patient or a third party (related or unrelated). As with solid organ transplantation, HCT candidates should meet a set of organ function and psychosocial criteria that may vary from transplant center to transplant center, but are aimed at determining the risk-benefit ratio of HCT versus other treatment approaches. Figure 25.2 depicts the different components and phases of the HCT procedure.

Depending on the source of stem cells, HCT can be categorized as either autologous (HSCs are obtained from patient) or allogeneic (HSCs are obtained from a third party). HSCs can be obtained from the marrow cavity or can be mobilized in large quantities into the peripheral blood using medications such as filgrastim or plerixafor and collected through apheresis techniques.

The conditioning regimen is the combination of agents given to eliminate malignant cells exploiting the dose response phenomena that most cancer cells exhibit and in the setting of HCT suppress the host immune system to allow engraftment of donor cells. Conditioning regimen intensity has been classified according to their myelosuppressive effects into myeloablative, reduced intensity, and nonmyeloablative.

Myeloablative conditioning regimens were long considered necessary for engraftment of allografts, but their considerable extramedullary toxicity typically limited their use to patients under the age of 60 years who had a good performance status and no comorbidities. RIC regimens use lower doses of busulfan, melphalan, cyclophosphamide, or Total Body Irradiation (TBI) (typically 2 Gy) often in combination with fludarabine are the ones most commonly used in older patients and in patients with comorbidities. These regimens rely more heavily on immunologic (GVL) effects to induce tumor regression and contain lower doses of drugs with cytoreductive activity. Graft-versus-host disease (GVHD) and infections remain the major causes of nonrelapse mortality (NRM).

Successful HCT requires that the patient tolerate the side effects of the conditioning regimen, so that the HSCs proliferate and mature adequately; the patient must also tolerate the treatment and prevention of infectious complications that can occur during the severely immuno compromised state of such patients during the first months after HCT. The HCT procedure can be divided into five phases:

Phase 1: Chemotherapy phase
Phase 2: Cytopenic phase
Phase 3: Early recovery phase
Phase 4: Early convalescence phase
Phase 5: Late convalescence

HCT is associated with a variety of complications that are summarized in Table 25.2

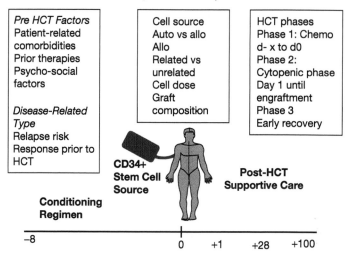

FIGURE 25.2 Components of the hematopoietic cell transplantation (HCT) procedure.

CURRENT STATUS OF HEMATOPOIETIC CELL TRANSPLANTATION IN OLDER PATIENTS

Reflecting the age distribution of different blood cancers in North America, the most common indications for HCT in patients over the age of 60 are myeloma for autografting and acute myeloid leukemia (AML) for allografting (7,9) (Table 25.3). Nevertheless, only a minority of older patients are actually undergoing HCT for a variety of hematologic malignancies that could clinically benefit them (7).

The magnitude of underutilization of HCT is probably most dramatic in myeloma, a malignant disorder of plasma cells in which randomized trials have demonstrated a significant benefit for high-dose therapy, mortality rates are extremely low, and advancing age does not significantly affect outcome (10). Costa et al. utilizing Surveillance, Epidemiology, and End Results (SEER) data and CIBMTR data demonstrated that patients over the age of 65 had less than a 25% likelihood of receiving an autologous HCT; likewise, African Americans have a 50% less likelihood of undergoing the procedure (10). Physician referral bias probably plays a role in this disparity as to who receives an allograft, as shown by the results of a survey conducted by Pidala et al., and most likely also plays a role in referrals for autografting (11,12).

The factors that influence utilization of HCT among medically fit older patients with hematologic malignancies are not well understood. El-Jawahari et al. reported on 127 patients with advanced myelodysplastic syndromes (MDSs) and examined the effects of age, gender, cytogenetics, International Prognostic Scoring System (IPSS) category, performance status, distance from HCT center, and baseline patient-reported quality of life (QOL) on the likelihood of receiving an allogeneic HCT with RIC

TABLE 25.2 Post–Hematopoietic Cell Transplantation Complications

Complication	Incidence	Implications for Older Patient
Myelosuppression	Universal with exception of truly nonablative regimens	Prolonged myelosuppression increases risks of life-threatening infections; thus, strategies that may accelerate neutrophil recovery in older patients could be beneficial
Mucositis	50%–70% in ablative regimens 30%–50% in RIC regimens <10% in truly nonablative regimens	Severe mucositis may require opioid analgesia for pain control, which is less well-tolerated in older patients. Risk of aspiration from severe mucositis may be more frequent in older patients. One of the major benefits of RIC is reduction in the risk of severe mucositis.
Infections	>50% of patients will have some infectious complication. Most common is neutropenic fever, gram positive sepsis, or CMV reactivation in the context of allogeneic HCT	For older patients, the ability to recover from infectious complications may be affected by prior comorbid states and ability to tolerate anti-infective therapies such as foscarnet or amphotericin B.
Gastrointestinal toxicities	Loss of appetite almost universal Severe nausea and emesis rare with current antiemetic regimens Severe diarrhea uncommon with RIC regimens (seen more frequently with melphalan)	As with other toxicities, gastrointestinal toxicities can be more common and more severe in older patients. Essential to maintain good hydration and adequate electrolyte replacements; nutritional intervention may have to be considered earlier
Pulmonary toxicities	Pneumonitis Diffuse alveolar hemorrhage Idiopathic pneumonia syndrome occurs in 5%–10% of patients	Patients with pre-HCT pulmonary comorbidities are at higher risk for pulmonary toxicities
Hepatic toxicities	SOS/VOD rare with RIC, but can still occur in high-risk patients	Similar risk factors as with younger patients
Cardiac toxicities	Arrythmias Congestive heart failure	Atrial fibrillation common occurrence after high-dose melphalan
GVHD	Rash Diarrhea Hyperbilirubinemia Severe immunodeficiency	High-dose steroids poorly tolerated in older patients. Age a predictor of poor outcome in patients with grade 2–4 GVHD

(continued)

TABLE 25.2 Post–Hematopoietic Cell Transplantation Complications (*continued*)

Complication	Incidence	Implications for Older Patient
Graft failure	Rare	Rare but more common with older donors

CMV, cytomegalovirus; GVHD, graft-versus-host disease; HCT, hematopoietic cell transplant; RIC, reduced-intensity conditioning; SOS, sinusoidal obstructive syndrome; VOD, veno-occlusive disease.

Source: Adapted from Ref. (8). Wiedewult M, Giralt S. *Clinical Hematopoietic Cell Transplantation American Society of Hematology Self-Assessment Program 6th Edition*. Washington, DC: American Society of Hematology.

TABLE 25.3 Most Common Indications for HCT in North America

Indication	Type of HCT	Approximate Numbers of HCTs Performed in North America in 2012	Relevance for Older Patient
Myeloma	Auto	6,000	Median age at onset 70 y of age. Older individuals benefit from aggressive treatment as much as younger patients
Diffuse large cell lymphoma	Auto	3,000	Data for autografts in older patients show similar outcomes to younger patients
AML	Allo	3,000	Disease affects older individuals who also have the worse prognosis with chemo. Most comparative analysis has shown benefit for allografting early in the course of the disease
Myelodysplasia	Allo	1,300	Rapidly growing indication because disease affects primarily older individuals, no other curative therapy exists, and HCT is now covered by insurance

AML, acute myeloid leukemia; HCT, hematopoietic cell transplant.

Source: Adapted from Ref. (9). Pasquini MC, Zhu X. Current uses and outcomes of hematopoietic stem cell transplantation: CIBMTR Summary Slides, 2015. Available at: http://www.cibmtr.org.

conditioning. A total of 44 patients (35%) had undergone RIC HCT. In multivariable analyses, younger age and higher IPSS (intermediate-2/high) predicted a higher likelihood of receiving a RIC HCT (13).

Mitchell et al. showed that advancing age was a predictor of *not* receiving an HCT for patients with leukemia or lymphoma and that receipt of an HCT was associated with a longer survival (14). Other causes for not proceeding to HCT have been reviewed by Majhail et al. (7).

OUTCOMES OF AUTOLOGOUS HEMATOPOIETIC CELL TRANSPLANTATION IN OLDER PATIENTS

Autologous HCT is being more frequently performed in patients over the age of 60, with improvements in NRM and overall outcomes (7,15,16). Table 25.4 summarizes the largest series of autologous transplants for older patients (age 60 or above) (17–24). Most series are heavily weighted with patients who have either myeloma or diffuse large B cell lymphoma (DLBCL), and median age was less than 65. The common themes are that NRM was routinely less than 5% and although retrospective when compared to outcomes of younger patients, the results were either comparable or only slightly inferior.

TABLE 25.4 Outcomes of Autologous Transplant for Lymphoma and Myeloma in Patients Over the Age of 60

Reference	N (Median Age)	Diagnosis	Outcomes Compared With Younger Group	Comments
(17)	463 (63)	DLBCL	NRM at 1 y 4.4% vs. 2.8% PFS at 3 y 51% vs. 62% OS at 3 y 60% vs. 70%	EBMT Registry analysis. More CR1 patients in younger group
(18)	93 (66)	DLBCL	NRM at 1 y 5%, 4% vs. 2.2% PFS at 4 y 38% vs. 42%	Single-institution data over 8-y period.
(19)	202 (65)	DLBCL (37%) MCL (34%)	NRM at 1 y 4% PFS/OS at 3 y 60%	Single institution, no comparison to younger group. HCT-CI not predictive of outcome
(20)	99 (68)	DLBCL (53%)	NRM at 3 y 8% OS at 3 y 61%	Single institution, 16% actuarial risk of MDS.
(21)	79 (67)	MCL	NRM at 1 y 3.8% PFS at 5 y 29% OS at 5 y 61%	EBMT Registry. Elderly patients more likely to have failed two lines of treatment
(22)	484 (64)	DLBCL	NRM at 1 y 5.9% PFS at 3 y 40.6% OS at 3 y 49.6%	Japanese National Registry shows no difference in outcomes in patients 60–65 or over 70 y of age
(23)	15 (64)	Hodgkin	PFS at 3y 73% OS at 3 y 88% No toxic deaths	Single institution. No difference in outcomes between older and younger patients

DLBCL, diffuse large B cell lymphoma; EBMT, European bone marrow transplant; HCT, hematopoietic cell transplant; MCL, mantle cell lymphoma; MDS, myelodysplastic syndromes; NRM, non relapse mortality; OS, overall survival; PFS, progression-free survival.

Source: Adapted from Refs. (17–23).

The number of autografts for older patients with myeloma has also increased dramatically in the last 10 years. Using data from the European Bone Marrow Transplant (EBMT) Registry, Auner et al. reported that in the period from 1991 to 1996 a total of 381 patients with myeloma underwent autografting in Europe versus 6,518 in the 5-year period of 2006 through 2010. Even more dramatic is the increased activity in patients over the age of 70, of which only two were reported to the EBMT from 1991 to 1996 in contrast to 2,617 from 2006 to 2010 (15). The largest registry analyses regarding outcomes of older patients with myeloma are summarized in Table 25.4, and support the results of single-center retrospective studies comparing HCT outcomes between older and younger patients. Of the eight studies reviewed, three suggested inferior but acceptable outcomes for older patients undergoing HCT when compared to younger patients, with NRM rates of 2% to 18%. Notably, many of the patients over the age of 65 received melphalan 200 mg/m^2 without worse outcomes than younger patients (24–26).

OUTCOMES OF ALLOGENEIC HEMATOPOIETIC CELL TRANSPLANTATION IN OLDER PATIENTS

As with autologous HCT, the use of allogeneic HCT for patients over the age of 60 has also increased dramatically over the last 10 years. In the United States alone, the use of allografting for MDS has more than doubled since 2009, after the Center for Medicare & Medicaid Services approved coverage for allografting for MDS while evidence is being gathered to make a final determination (27). Table 25.5 summarizes the largest series of allografting in older patients with primarily AML or MDS (28–33).

TABLE 25.5 Representative Studies of Allogeneic HCT for Older Patients With Hematologic Malignancies

Reference	N (Median Age in Years)	Diagnosis HCT Type	OS/NRM/RR	Comments
(29)	757 (60)	AML Allogeneic All donors	50–54: 48% at 3 y 55–59: 45% 60–64: 38% >65: 37%	In multivariate analyses, age not important for outcome. Disease status, HCT-CI, and KPS were
(30)	142 (66)	All heme malignancies Allogeneic unrelated donors	OS at 2 y 50% EFS at 2 y 43% NRM at 2 y 23%	Outcomes for older and younger patients were similar
(31)	97 (64)	AML All donor types	OS at 5 y 35% EFS at 5 y 32% NRM at 5 y 18%	On multivariate analysis, allogeneic HCT associated with better outcomes

(continued)

TABLE 25.5 Representative Studies of Allogeneic HCT for Older Patients With Hematologic Malignancies (*continued*)

Reference	N (Median Age in Years)	Diagnosis HCT Type	OS/NRM/RR	Comments
(32)	79 (58)	AML/MDS	CR1: 1 y NRM 19% OS/EFS 71/68% at 2 y All patients: 1 y NRM 20% OS/EFS:46%/44% at 2 y	Fludarabine/ busulfan 12.8 mg/kg well-tolerated ablative regimen Age not a major predictor of outcome
(33)	126 (62) 55 (67)	AML/MDS	60–64 years OS at 2 y 34% EFS at 2 y 31% NRM at 2 y 32% >65 y OS at 2 y 36% EFS at 2 y 34% NRM at 2y 34%	Cytogenetic risk category and performance status *not* age-important predictors of treatment outcome
(34)	114 (65)	AML CR1	NRM: OS/EFS 48%/42% at 2 y	Prospective trial with fludarabine/ busulfan and ATG

AML, acute myeloid leukemia; ATG, antithymocyte globulin; EFS, event-free survival; HCT, hematopoietic cell transplant; MDS, myelodysplastic syndromes; NRM, non relapse mortality; OS, overall survival; RR, relapse rate.

Rashidi et al. performed a meta-analysis of all published articles regarding HCT for AML patients greater than 60 years old. A total of 13 studies (749 patients) were identified. The pooled estimates and 95% confidence intervals (CI) for relapse-free survival (RFS) at 2 and 3 years were 44% (95% CI, 33%–55%), and 35% (95% CI, 26%–45%), respectively. Similarly, for overall survival (OS) the results were 45% (95% CI, 35%–54%), and 38% (95% CI, 29%–48%), respectively. Some of the most representative studies are summarized in Table 25.5 (34).

COMPARATIVE OUTCOMES TO NONTRANSPLANT THERAPIES

Versluis et al. analyzed treatment outcomes of four successive prospective HOVON-SAKK trials for AML trials. Among 1,155 patients aged 60 years and older, 640 obtained a complete remission after induction chemotherapy. Postremission therapy consisted of allogeneic HSCT following RIC (n = 97), gemtuzumab ozogamicin (n = 110), chemotherapy (n = 44), autologous HSCT (n = 23), or no further treatment (n = 366). For patients who received an allogeneic HCT, 5-year OS was 35% compared to 21% for those who received no additional postremission therapy, and 26% for patients who received either additional chemotherapy or autologous HSCT.

Allogeneic HCT was the postremission therapy associated with the best outcomes, particularly in patients with intermediate-risk or adverse-risk disease (30).

Devine et al. performed a prospective multicenter phase 2 study to assess the efficacy of RCT HSCT for patients between the ages of 60 and 74 years with AML in first complete remission. A total of 114 patients with a median age of 65 years were included; most patients received cells from matched unrelated donors. Disease-free survival and OS at 2 years after transplantation were 42% and 48%, respectively, for the entire group. NRM at 2 years was 15% (95% CI, 8%–21%). The relapse rate at 2 years was 44% (33).

Farag et al., utilizing data from the CIBMTR and Cancer and Leukemia Group B (CALGB), compared treatment outcomes of 94 patients with AML in CR1 between 60 and 70 years of age with the outcomes of patients treated with induction and postremission chemotherapy on CALGB protocols who had at least a 4-month remission. The median age for HCT recipients was slightly lower than that of the chemotherapy patients (median age, 63 years vs. 65 years); otherwise there were no significant differences between the groups. Allogeneic HCT was associated with significantly lower risk of relapse (32% vs. 81% at 3 years; $P < .001$), higher NRM (36% vs. 4% at 3 years; $P < .001$), and longer leukemia-free survival (32% vs. 15% at 3 years; $P = .001$) with a trend to OS improvement for HCT recipients (37% vs. 25% at 3 years; $P = .08$) (35).

CONCLUSION

The use of autologous and allogeneic HCT in patients over the age of 60 has dramatically increased over the last decade. Although results are comparable to those achieved in younger patient populations, there still is a significant risk of morbidity and disease recurrence. Age is no longer considered an absolute barrier to using HCT, but few patients over the age of 80 are undergoing this procedure.

Moving forward, further prospective trials exploring relapse reduction strategies with post-HCT therapies that incorporate targeted agents or immune therapeutics will be essential to improve the rates of disease control, as further dose escalation of the conditioning regimen is unlikely to improve outcomes without increasing toxicities. Likewise, a concerted effort is underway to design and implement studies on ways to reduce morbidity and mortality through novel strategies such as cytokine blockade or graft engineering.

TAKE HOME POINTS

1. High-dose therapy with curative intent is feasible in older patients with hematologic malignancies.
2. The regimens, GVHD prophylaxis, and supportive care measures must be tailored to patient and comorbidities.
3. There is a huge knowledge gap regarding long-term follow-up and survivorship issues regarding older patients who have undergone HCTs.
4. A multidisciplinary approach is needed to optimize outcomes.
5. Disease recurrence remains the most important cause of treatment failure in this patient population.

REFERENCES

1. Thomas ED, Storb R, Clift RA, et al. Bone-marrow transplantation. *N Engl J Med.* 1975;292:832-843, 895.

2. Appelbaum F. Hematopoietic-cell transplantation at 50. *N Engl J Med.* 2007;357:1472-1475.

3. Giralt S, Estey E, Albitar M, et al. Engraftment of allogeneic hematopoietic progenitor cells with purine analog-containing chemotherapy: harnessing graft-versus-leukemia without myeloablative therapy. *Blood.* 1997;89:4531-4536.

4. Slavin S, Nagler A, Naparstak E, et al. Nonmyeloablative stem cell transplantation and cell therapy as an alternative to conventional bone marrow transplantation with lethal cytoreduction for the treatment of malignant and nonmalignant hematologic diseases. *Blood.* 1998;91:756-763.

5. McSweeney PA, Niederwieser D, Shizuru JA, et al. Hematopoietic cell transplantation in older patients with hematologic malignancies: replacing high-dose cytotoxic therapy with graft-versus-tumor effects. *Blood.* 2001;97:3390-3400.

6. Majhail NS, Farnia SH, Carpenter PA, et al. Indications for autologous and allogeneic hematopoietic cell transplantation: guidelines from the American Society for Blood and Marrow Transplantation. *Biol Blood Marrow Transplant.* November 2015;21(11):1863-1869. doi:10.1016/j.bbmt.2015.07.032.

7. Majhail NS, Omondi NA, Denzen E, et al. Access to hematopoietic cell transplantation in the United States. *Biol Blood Marrow Transplant.* 2010;16:1070-1075.

8. Wiedewult M, Giralt S. *Clinical Hematopoietic Cell Transplantation American Society of Hematology Self-Assessment Program 6th Edition.* Washington, DC:American Society of Hematology.

9. Pasquini MC, Zhu X. Current uses and outcomes of hematopoietic stem cell transplantation: CIBMTR summary slides, 2015. Available at: http://www.cibmtr.org Accessed June 1, 2016.

10. Costa LJ, Xing-Huang J, Hari PN. Disparities in utilization of autologous hematopoietic cell transplantation for treatment of multiple myeloma. *Biol Blood Marrow Transplant.* 2015;21:701-706.

11. Pidala J, Craig BM, Lee SJ, et al. Practice variation in physician referral for allogeneic hematopoietic cell transplantation. *Bone Marrow Transplant.* January 2013;48(1) 63-67. doi:10.1038/bmt.2012.95.

12. Majhail N, Jagasia M. Referral to transplant center for hematopoietic cell transplantation. *Hematol Oncol Clin North Am.* 2014;28:1201.

13. El-Jawahri A, Kim HT, Steensma DP, et al. Does quality of life impact the decision to pursue stem cell transplantation for elderly patients with advanced MDS? *Bone MarrowTransplant.* 2016;51:1121-1126. doi:10.1038/bmt.2016.40.

14. Mitchell JM, Conklin EA. Factors affecting receipt of expensive cancer treatments and mortality: evidence from stem cell transplantation for leukemia and lymphoma. *Health Serv Res.* February 2015;50(1):197-216. doi:10.1111/1475-6773.12208.

15. Auner HW, Szydlo R, Hoek J, et al. Trends in autologous hematopoietic cell transplantation for multiple myeloma in Europe: increased use and improved outcomes in elderly patients in recent years. *Bone Marrow Transplant.* 2015;50:209-215.

16. McCarthy PL Jr, Hahn T, Hassebroek A, et al. Trends in use of and survival after autologous hematopoietic cell transplantation in North America, 1995-2005: significant improvement in survival for lymphoma and myeloma during a period of increasing recipient age. *Biol Blood Marrow Transplant.* 2013;19:1116-1123.

17. Jantunen E, Canals C, Rambaldi A, et al. Autologous stem cell transplantation in elderly patients (≥60 years) with diffuse large B-cell lymphoma: an analysis based on data in the European Blood and Marrow Transplantation registry. *Haematologica.* 2008;93:1837-1842.

18. Buadi FK, Micallef IN, Ansell SM, et al. Autologous hematopoietic stem cell transplantation for older patients with relapsed non-Hodgkin's lymphoma. *Bone Marrow Transplant.* 2006;1017-1022.

19. Dahi PB, Tamari R, Devlin SM, et al. Favorable outcomes in elderly patients undergoing high-dose therapy and autologous stem cell transplantation for non-Hodgkin lymphoma. *Biol Blood Marrow Transplant.* December 2014;20(12):2004-2009. doi:10.1016/j.bbmt.2014.08.019.

20. Hosing C, Saliba RM, Okoroji GJ, et al. High-dose chemotherapy and autologous hematopoietic progenitor cell transplantation for nonHodgkin's lymphoma in patients >65 years of age. *Ann Oncol.* 2008;19:1166-1171.

21. Jantunen E, Canals C, Attal M, et al. Autologous stem-cell transplantation in patients with mantle cell lymphoma beyond 65 years of age: a study from the European Group for Blood and Marrow Transplantation (EBMT). *Ann Oncol.* 2012;23:166-171.

22. Chihara D, Izutsu K, Kondo E, et al. High-dose chemotherapy with autologous stem cell transplantation for elderly patients with relapsed/refractory diffuse large B cell lymphoma: a nationwide retrospective study. *Biol Blood Marrow Transplant.* 2014;20:684-689.

23. Puig N, Pintilie M, Seshadri T, et al. High-dose chemotherapy and auto-SCT in elderly patients with Hodgkin's lymphoma. *Bone Marrow Transplant.* 2011;46:1399-1344.

24. Sharma M, Zhang MJ, Zhong X, et al. Older patients with myeloma derive similar benefit from autologous transplantation. *Biol Blood Marrow Transplant.* 2014;20:1796-1803.

25. Auner HW, Garderet L, Kroger N. Autologous hematopoietic cell transplantation in elderly patients with multiple myeloma. *Br J Haematol.* 2015;171;453-462.

26. Shah N, Callander N, Ganguly S, et al. Hematopoietic stem cell transplantation for multiple myeloma: guidelines from the American Society for Blood and Marrow Transplantation. *Biol Blood Marrow Transplant.* 2015;21:1155-1166.

27. Giralt SA, Horowitz M, Weisdorf D, Cutler C. Review of stem-cell transplantation for myelodysplastic syndromes in older patients in the context of the Decision Memo for Allogeneic Hematopoietic Stem Cell Transplantation for Myelodysplastic Syndrome emanating from the Centers for Medicare and Medicaid Services. *J Clin Oncol.* February 10, 2011;29(5):566-572. doi:10.1200/JCO.2010.32.1919.

28. Aoki J, Kanamori H, Tanaka M1, et al. Impact of age on outcomes of allogeneic hematopoietic stem cell transplantation with reduced intensity conditioning in elderly patients with acute myeloid leukemia. *Am J Hematol.* March 2016;91(3):302-307. doi:10.1002/ajh.24270.

29. El Cheikh J, Sfumato P, Sobh M, et al. Allogeneic hematopoietic stem cell transplantation after reduced-intensity conditioning regimen for elderly patients (60 years and older) with hematological malignancies using unrelated donors: a retrospective study from the French Society for Stem Cell Transplantation (SFGM-TC). *Haematologica.* 2016;101:e262-e265. doi:10.3324/haematol.2015.139345.

30. Versluis J, Hazenberg CL, Passweg JR, et al. Post-remission treatment with allogeneic stem cell transplantation in patients aged 60 years and older with acute myeloid leukaemia: a time-dependent analysis. *Lancet Haematol.* October 2015;2(10): e427-e436. doi:10.1016/S2352-3026(15)00148-9.

31. Alatrash G, de Lima M, Hamerschlak N, et al. Myeloablative reduced-toxicity i.v. busulfan-fludarabine and allogeneic hematopoietic stem cell transplant for patients with acute myeloid leukemia or myelodysplastic syndrome in the sixth through eighth decades of life. *Biol Blood Marrow Transplant.* October 2011;17(10):1490-1496. doi:10.1016/j.bbmt.2011.02.007.

32. McClune BL, Weisdorf DJ, Pedersen TL, et al. Effect of age on outcome of reduced-intensity hematopoietic cell transplantation for older patients with acute myeloid leukemia in first complete remission or with myelodysplastic syndrome. *J Clin Oncol.* 2010;28(11):1878-1887.

33. Devine SM, Owzar K, Blum W, et al. Phase II study of allogeneic transplantation for older patients with acute myeloid leukemia if first complete remission using a reduced intensity conditioning regimen: results from Cancer and Leukemia Group B 100103 (Alliance for Clinical Trials in Oncology/Blood and Marrow Transplant Clinical Trial Network 0502). *J Clin Oncol.* 2015:10:4167-4175.

34. Rashidi A, Ebadi M, Coldtz GA, DiPersio JF. Outcomes of allogeneic stem cell transplantation in elderly patients with acute myeloid leukemia: a systematic review and meta-analysis. *Biol Blood Marrow Transplant.* January 2016;22(1):119-124. doi:10.1016/j.bbmt.2015.08.029.

35. Farag SS, Maharry K, Zhang M-J, et al. Comparison of reduced-intensity hematopoietic cell transplantation with chemotherapy in patients aged 60-70 years with acute myeloid leukemia in first remission. *Biol Blood Marrow Transplant.* 2011;17:1796-1803.

V

Communication With the Older Cancer Patient

26 INTERPRET: A Model for the Cross-Linguistic Medical Interview in the Geriatrics Oncology Setting

Francesca Gany, Xiaoxiao Huang, and Javier Gonzalez

INTRODUCTION

The immigrant population in the United States is growing rapidly. There are now more than 41 million foreign-born individuals—more than 13.1% of the population—residing in the United States (1,2). More than 350 languages and dialects are spoken within the United States. The portion of the population that is limited English proficient (LEP) is growing. LEP individuals do not speak English as their primary language and have a limited ability to read, speak, write, or understand English (3). According to the 2014 American Community Survey, approximately 25 million people in the United States reported that they speak English less than "very well" or are LEP, and among them 15% were over age 65 (2).

Effective communication between provider and patient is among the most important elements in establishing a correct diagnosis and proper treatment plan (4,5). Communication is the most important factor in the accuracy and completeness of historical data obtained, in treatment adherence, in the relationship between doctor and patient, in satisfaction, and in efficiency of encounters (6–8). In language-discordant medical interviews, the diagnostic and therapeutic power of the medical interview is often compromised (9; Gany F, Gonzalez C, Prakash K, et al. manuscript in preparation). Physicians may order unnecessary, hazardous, or expensive diagnostic tests or, alternatively, may be less likely to order needed tests (10). Language barriers undermine the patient's ability to receive and understand health information and to engage in important and often complex conversations that, in geriatric oncology, involve key processes, such as treatment planning or end-of-life decision making.

This chapter examines the medical interview with the LEP patient in the geriatric oncology setting, and offers solutions for maximizing the exchange of information and the building of the therapeutic alliance.

INTERPRET AND THE MEDICAL INTERVIEW

A unique framework, INTERPRET, provides guidelines and skills for selecting an interpreter and conducting a language-discordant medical encounter. INTERPRET guides the selection of the medical interpreter and provides the tools to work with the LEP patient and his or her family and/or caregiver through that interpreter. INTERPRET addresses several issues: identifying the need for interpretation, selecting the appropriate interpreter, stating expectations and guidelines, presenting and processing information, checking for understanding, and providing exit instructions.

Moreover, this chapter addresses the role of caregivers and family members in the language-discordant encounter. Caregivers and family members may be prominent and active participants in the geriatric oncology encounter and could help provide and recall patient information, assist with adherence, and potentially participate in shared decision making. They may also be bilingual.

I: Identify the need for an interpreter.
N: Narrow the choice of an interpreter.
T: Tell expectations.
E: Engage the patient directly.
R: Reduce—length, speed, jargon, volume.
P: Process information.
R: Repeat the key information.
E: Exit instructions must be made clear and provided in writing.
T: Therapeutic encounter more readily achieved.

I—Identify the Need for an Interpreter

An *interpreter* is a person who translates orally. This is often confused with a *translator*, a person who produces a rendering from one language to another in writing. In a bilingual medical interview, an interpreter, rather than a translator, is needed to produce a meaningful encounter (11). Even if the patient seems to speak sufficient English, an interpreter may be needed. The medical interview is far more demanding linguistically than ordinary conversation. Clients can express themselves more freely and often feel better understood in their native languages (12).

A provider who speaks a little bit of the patient's language should still get an interpreter. Even if the provider claims to be fluent in a language other than English, an interpreter may nevertheless be needed. False fluency is prevalent among health care providers (13). *False fluency* is the illusion that one's level of understanding, speaking, reading, or writing a language is sufficient to render effective communication with a member of that language group (13).

At times the need for an interpreter will be obvious. At more ambiguous times, to identify the patient's interpreting need, the following question can be asked: "If there is a translator available free of charge to you, would you be interested in this for your encounter?"[1] It is critical that this be done before the beginning of the medical interview.

N—Narrow the Choice of an Interpreter

Two types of medical interpreters have historically been called upon: ad hoc interpreters and trained professional interpreters. Whenever possible, use a trained medical interpreter.

TRAINED MEDICAL INTERPRETERS

A medical interpreter should be fully bilingual and should undergo extensive training in at least six areas, including specialized terminology (medical and colloquial), an interpreter code of ethics, the role of the interpreter, memory and shadowing skills, self-critique, and linguistic and cultural competency. In the absence of on-site interpreters, many facilities depend on remote interpreting, which may have the additional effect of reducing the visibility of a third party in the medical encounter. Whichever type of remote system the facility uses, the provider must assure the patient that all conversations are confidential.

AD HOC "INTERPRETERS"

Ad hoc "interpreters" have included family members and caregivers, "innocent bystanders" awaiting their own appointments, or untrained bilingual hospital employees. In spite of good intentions, they frequently make linguistic and semantic errors or inject their own opinions. Because they are untrained, they tend to filter, screen, omit, add, or subtract information. They may be unfamiliar with medical terminology. In one observational study, 23% to 52% of words and phrases were incorrectly interpreted by ad hoc, or nonprofessional, "interpreters" (13).

SPECIAL CONSIDERATIONS WHEN WORKING WITH FAMILY AND CAREGIVERS

Family members are probably, in most circumstances, the worst "ad hoc" choice. If a family member or caregiver is insistent upon being present and/or the situation merits their presence and intervention and the patient agrees, she or he can be included—ideally in a noninterpreting role. Although it may not be best clinically, it is important to recognize that patients do have the right to choose someone familiar to them, as long as they know that a facility-provided interpreter is an option (14). The physical exam may provide an opportunity to speak with the patient through a facility-trained interpreter to ensure that the patient does not have any additional items to discuss. This is especially important if domestic abuse is suspected.

T—Tell Expectations

Before meeting the patient, the health care provider should tell the interpreter his or her expectations for the medical interview. This should include the role to be played by the interpreter and the overall plan for conducting the interview. A trained interpreter

---

[1] Although the word *translator* is not technically correct, the majority of lay people use the word *translator* in place of *interpreter*.

may, at that point, indicate his or her own expectations. The provider should ensure an understanding of confidentiality. "Everything we talk about here must remain within these walls" or "What is said during the course of the interview must be kept confidential. Only the patient may give permission for information to be shared with anyone else."

It is imperative to quickly divulge to the parties involved what the specific goals of the conversation will be and to assess the interpreter's understanding and ability to render, in the target language, difficult and/or culture-bound concepts embedded in the American biomedical health care system that may not always have equivalents. Some examples of such culture-bound concepts include hospice care, psycho-oncology, support groups, nurse practitioner, health care proxy, do not resuscitate (DNR), shared decision making, and even confidentiality, to name a few. Evidence exists that many geriatric patients in the oncology setting do not fully participate in the shared decision-making process or benefit from the range of palliative services available to them, because of lack of understanding (15).

SPECIAL CONSIDERATIONS WHEN WORKING WITH FAMILY AND CAREGIVERS

In the geriatric oncology setting, telling expectations is all the more important considering the cognitive and functional aspects of the patient's health, possibly made more complex by the cultural differences in the role of the family member/caregiver. It is therefore crucial for the health care provider to involve all the players in the conversation and to set clear expectations and boundaries. Special circumstances requiring additional attention may include delivering bad news; shared decision making; communicating with an angry patient; discussing pain management; discussing prognosis; transitioning into palliative care; discussing death, dying, and end-of-life goals of care; and explaining complex tests or assessment evaluations that may require cultural and linguistic nuance (e.g., using proverbs in a mental health status test).

E—Engage the Patient Directly

The medical interview is the core clinical interaction between the patient and the clinician. It is, therefore, of the utmost importance that the provider be fully engaged in what the patient is saying, and have access to the emotional content associated with the interview.

The beginning of the encounter is a particularly important time of the interview. Patients often remember best the first things that occur, referred to as the "primacy effect" (4). There are several steps that can be taken by the provider, in collaboration with the medical interpreter, to engage the patient. First, the provider should introduce himself or herself and explain what the interpreter will do. This reduces the patient's anxiety, and confirms that the provider and the patient will be forming the primary bond, encouraging the establishment of a therapeutic alliance.

The physical arrangement of the medical interview can also facilitate engagement. To minimize the distraction of the presence of an interpreter, the provider should sit or stand directly in front of the patient and the interpreter should sit or stand either outside the patient's direct line of vision, behind the patient, or be remotely located. In addition, the provider should look at the patient, not at the interpreter. Special considerations should be taken in the geriatric oncology setting given mobility, audio, visual, and other spatial challenges and limitations.

Appropriate language use also engages the patient. Therefore, the provider should avoid using the third person form of address, using only the first or second. Do not say, "Ask him how he feels." Instead ask, "How do you feel?" Saying "I" and "you" establishes direct communication and fosters a relationship between the provider and the patient, not between the interpreter and the patient. This will help render the interpreter "invisible."

SPECIAL CONSIDERATIONS WHEN WORKING WITH FAMILY AND CAREGIVERS

The health care provider should use caution to ensure that information originates from the patient and not from the family member or caregiver. As much as possible, the patient should corroborate whatever information has been provided by other parties and should be as active an agent of his or her health as any other patient would normally be.

The patient-centered model of care practiced in the United Sates may not be easily understood by geriatric patients or their caregivers who were born abroad. The interpreter in these situations could step out of this role to volunteer information that may facilitate a more seamless cross-cultural exchange.

R—Reduce—Length, Speed, Jargon, Volume

Patients have varying literacy levels, whether engaged in language-concordant or -discordant encounters. Try to assess the patient's level of education and literacy and tailor your comments accordingly. Be aware, though, that just because the patient does not speak English does not mean that she or he is poorly educated or linguistically unsophisticated in her or his own language. This also applies to the family member/caregiver. Whatever the patients' literacy level is, most patients understand their providers better when information is delivered without the use of jargon. Therefore, providers should use simple, elementary terms and language as much as possible. The use of jargon may impede the interpreting process and overwhelm the patient (12).

P—Process Information

The provider should process the patient's information without asking the interpreter for his or her own "interpretation". The provider should ask for clarification directly from the patient. If a provider relies on the interpreter to make sense of what the patient said, she or he may miss out on critical diagnostic information.

It is also important to consider nonverbal communication. Nonverbal communication includes all of the conscious and unconscious unspoken gestures, behaviors, and actions that express thoughts, feelings, and information (16). It is critical to assess congruence in verbal and nonverbal behavior. A patient whose words and actions do not match may indicate patient distress and the need for the provider to explore feelings that are not being expressed directly. It is also important to recognize that the meanings attached to nonverbal communication are not universal. For example, a lack of eye contact should not be assumed to be disrespectful. Rather, in some cultures, making eye contact is considered disrespectful (17,18). Nodding should not be assumed to be an indicator of affirmation. Often it may be a sign of respect rather than agreement (18).

R—Repeat the Key Information

What transpired during the medical interview should be thoroughly reviewed. The patient should be asked for his or her understanding and summary. While asking a patient to go over what was talked about is a good technique for all interviews, it takes on added importance in an interpreted interview. This serves as a "back-translation" for the medical provider.

SPECIAL CONSIDERATIONS WHEN WORKING WITH FAMILY AND CAREGIVERS

In this setting, it may be necessary to enlist the caregiver in this endeavor, for example, when a patient is cognitively impaired. The caregiver should be subject to the same standards in terms of his or her understanding as the patient would be, and special caution should be taken when prescribing, giving safety instructions, and so forth.

Moreover, asking the patient and the caregiver whether there is anything that has been omitted gives the patient, the caregiver, and the provider a final opportunity to bring up concerns. If the provider simply asks, "Do you understand?" the patient will tend to say, "Yes," whether or not she or he actually does.

E—Exit Instructions Need to be Made Clear and Provided in Writing

Persons best remember the first things and last things that occur (4). Appropriate closure can, therefore, add power to the interview. This is very important for the LEP patient, who usually receives less information about the treatment plan (19). As a result, these patients are less likely to keep subsequent appointments and are more likely to make emergency room visits than are patients who have same-language encounters (20). It may be particularly critical for geriatric patients with cognitive deficits.

Providing adequate written follow-up information is essential. Providers should speak with their patients about dosing and write down instructions; if possible, the interpreter should immediately provide a written translation, including possible side effects. For accuracy, the provider should ask the patient or caregiver to repeat the dosing information or, if literate, to read back what the interpreter has written. Providers should not neglect the writing of instructions just because the patient is not literate in English. Written instructions can then be used by family members not present at the medical interview.

Formally closing the interview is one of the most critical parts of the medical encounter. A handshake or other gesture may be appropriate depending on the patient's age, gender, cultural background, and the level of intimacy established during the interview. Alternatively, choosing to walk the patient back to the waiting room may have an important meaning for the patient. Regardless of the particular gesture chosen to end the interview, the physician should aim to close the interview in an energetic and positive manner (21).

T—Therapeutic Encounter More Readily Achieved

The therapeutic process begins with the patient's decision to seek help. The provider's contribution to this process begins with the first interview with the patient and continues with all subsequent encounters. The ability of the provider to attentively listen to the patient has great therapeutic value in itself (22). The challenges in forging a successful therapeutic encounter are amplified by the presence of a language barrier. Because of the language barrier, the provider may feel very distant from the patient, with the provider hearing WHAT is being said, at times incompletely, and perhaps not perceiving HOW it is being said, all of which set up a greater chance of misdiagnosis (12,23) and a treatment plan that is not tailored to the particular patient and may thus fail. In addition, it may be more difficult to convey trust in the presence of an interpreter. When the sense of trust, openness, and respect needed to establish this therapeutic relationship does not exist, it can impair the other functions of the interview (24).

In summary, if the INTERPRET model is successfully followed, the therapeutic relationship should be more easily attained by the end of the interview. The patient and provider are more likely to leave the medical interview with a sense of mutual understanding, agreement, and respect. As the United States becomes more heterogeneous, the need for medical interpreters will only increase. The adequate training of interpreters and providers ensures that the medical interview is a therapeutic encounter. Mastery of the medical interview and effective utilization of interpreters should, therefore, become a core clinical skill, and should be incorporated into medical, nursing, and physician assistant school curricula and continuing medical education.

TAKE HOME POINTS

1. Effective communication between a provider and patient is among the most important elements in establishing a correct diagnosis and proper treatment plan.
2. In language-discordant medical interviews, the diagnostic and therapeutic power of the medical interview is often compromised.
3. The INTERPRET framework provides guidelines and skills for selecting an interpreter and conducting a language-discordant medical encounter.

REFERENCES

1. Lopez MH, Passel J, Rohal M. U.S. Foreign-Born Population Trends. *Modern Immigration Wave Brings 59 Million to US, Driving Population Growth and Change Through 2065*. Washington, DC. Pew Research Center; 2015:65-69; chap 5. Available at: http://www.pewhispanic.org/files/2015/09/2015-09-28_modern-immigration-wave_REPORT.pdf. Accessed April 14, 2017.
2. U.S. Census. *2014 American Community Survey 5-Year Estimates*. Available at: https://www.census.gov/programs-surveys/acs/news/data-releases/2014/release.html. Accessed March 18, 2016.
3. LEP.gov. Commonly asked questions and answers regarding limited English proficient (LEP) individuals. 2011. Available at: http://www.lep.gov/faqs/faqs.html#OneQ1.
4. Lipkin M, Frankel RM, Beckman HB, et al. Performing the medical interview. In: Lipkin M Jr, Putnam SM, Lazare A, eds. *The Medical Interview: Clinical Care, Education, and Research*. New York, NY: Springer-Verlag; 1995:65-82.
5. Hornberger JC, Gibson CD Jr, Wood W, et al. Eliminating language barriers for non-English-speaking patients. *Medical Care*. 1996;34(8), 845–856.

6. Hampers LD, Cha S, Gutglass DJ, et al. Language barriers and resource utilization in a pediatric emergency department. *Pediatrics.* 1999;103:1253-1256.

7. Baker D, Parker R, Williams M, et al. Use and effectiveness of interpreters in an emergency department. *JAMA.* 1996;275:783-788.

8. Andrulis D, Goodman N, Pryor C. *What a Difference an Interpreter Can Make: Health Care Experiences with Limited English Proficiency.* Waltham, MA: The Access Project, Brandeis; 2002.

9. Flores G, Abreu M, Olivar MA, Kastner B. Access barriers to health care for Latino children. *Arch Pediatr Adolesc Med.* 1988;152(11):111-125.

10. Woloshin S, Bickell N, Schwartz L, et al. Language barriers in medicine in the United States. *JAMA.* 1995;273(9):724-728.

11. Massachusetts Medical Interpreters Association. *NCIHC National Standards of Practice.* 1996. Available at: http://www.imiaweb.org/standards/ncihcstandards.asp.

12. Granski JM, Carrillo D. The use of bilingual, bicultural paraprofessionals in mental health services: issues for hiring, training and supervision. *Community Ment Health J.* 1997;33(1):51-60.

13. Flores G, Laws B, Mayo SJ, et al. Errors in medical interpretation and their potential clinical consequences in pediatric encounters. *Pediatrics.* 2002;111(1):6-14.

14. Office of Civil Rights. Guidance Memorandum: Title VI (2000).

15. Hurria A, Dale W, Mooney M, et al. Designing therapeutic clinical trials for older and frail adults with cancer: U13 conference recommendations. *J Clin Oncol.* 2014;32:2587-2594.

16. Lindberg JB, Hunter ML, Kruszewski AZ. *Introduction to Person-Centered Nursing.* London: JB Lippincott; 1983.

17. Duranti A. Language and bodies in social space: Samoan ceremonial greetings. *Am Anthropol.* 1992;94(3):657-691.

18. Ohta AS. The foreign language learner in Japanese society: successful learners of Japanese respond to Miller's "law of inverse returns." *J Assoc Teach JPN.* 1993;27(2):205-228.

19. Shapiro J, Saltzer E. Cross-cultural aspects of physician-patient communication patterns. *Urban Health.* 1981;10:10-15.

20. Manson A. Language concordance as a determinant of patient compliance and emergency room visits in patients with asthma. *Med Care.* 1988;26:1119-1128.

21. Lazare A, Putnam S, Lipkin M. Three functions of the medical interview. In: Lipkin M, Putnam S, Lazare A, eds. *The Medical Interview.* New York, NY: Springer; 1995:3-19.

22. Novack D. Therapeutic aspects of the clinical encounter. In: Lipkin M, Putnam S, Lazare A, eds. *The Medical Interview.* New York, NY: Springer Press; 1995.

23. Marcos L. Effects of interpreters on the evaluation of psychopathology in non-English speaking patients. *Am J Psychiat.* 1979;136:171-174.

24. Cohen-Cole SA. The language problem: integration of psychosocial variables in medical care. *Psychosomatics.* 1983;24:52-60.

27

Communication With Cognitively Impaired Older Adults and Their Families

Rebecca Saracino, Christian J. Nelson, and Andrew J. Roth

Cancer steadily increases in prevalence as people age (1). Simultaneously, communication difficulties become compounded when older adult patients must deal with multiple deficits including sensory losses and physical frailty (2). These issues can become extremely challenging when older patients have cognitive deficits and begin losing or have lost aspects of their autonomy and independence. These challenges arise across the cancer experience (Table 27.1), and affect not only the patient, but also informal caregivers, clinicians, and treatment team members (2). The challenge for oncology staff is to know how to communicate appropriately with patients across circumstances. Benefits of improved communication also include enhancement of trust, improvement in the accuracy of information and understanding, and a decrease in the frequency of mistakes (4). Unfortunately, little research has been done in the area of communicating with elderly cancer patients who have cognitive deficits. Thus, this chapter reviews the existing communication literature from the

TABLE 27.1 Critical Time Points to Consider Patients' Capacity

- Soon after diagnosis and when there is a need to make treatment decisions, including the complex choice of whether to treat or not treat the cancer, depending on the overall health and multiple medical comorbidities of the patient and likely life expectancy
- Informed consent issues for medical procedures
- Dealing with health care proxies, especially when there is no other family or supportive family member around
- Dealing with issues of independent living
- When dementia is present at diagnosis or arises in the midst of chronic treatment for cancer
- In dealing with confusion or delirium in the general ward setting

Source: From Ref. (3). Roth A, Nelson, C. Issues for cognitively impaired elderly patients. In Kissane D, Bultz B, Butow P, Finlay I, eds. *Handbook of Communication in Oncology and Palliative Care*. New York, NY: Oxford University Press; 2010:547-556.

field of geriatric psychiatry and cognitive disorders, and attempts to provide practical solutions for common problems that arise in the oncology setting.

COMMUNICATION SKILLS

Dialogues between physicians and elderly patients are often marked by ineffective communication, as a result of characteristics of the physician and/or patient and circumstances that can make these encounters particularly challenging. Patients of all ages report significant levels of unmet needs, particularly in the following realms of communication: information provision, psychosocial support, and response to emotional cues (5). These issues are particularly relevant to older patients, and attending to these unmet needs is crucial for optimal care. For example, research has demonstrated that the communication process in initial consultations may influence a patient's psychological health and adherence over time. Patient satisfaction is consistently related to provider behavior (6). Clinicians, therefore, may benefit from improving communication with older patients during medical visits. The most effective method for learning communication skills is observation of ideal and effective communication strategies, followed by rehearsing the skills in role-play, receiving immediate feedback on performance to permit modification, and then repeating the practice (7). In this way, the trainee has the opportunity to hone his or her own communication patterns without negative experiences. This positive experiential process has been recognized as the central component in successful acquisition of communication skills.

Working with multiple clinical staff and maintaining appropriate communication among these staff members may be specifically important in working with cognitively impaired elderly patients. For example, in an inpatient service, there is a need for accurate information to be handed on from one shift to another and from one specialty to another, as staff cannot rely on the cognitively impaired patients to give accurate information. The problems of evaluating changes and monitoring responses to various treatments are heightened if each of the health care professionals does not have the same understanding of the patient's needs. Some professionals may not realize that patient input may be misleading. Direct verbal communication as well as accurate and clear charting are imperative.

WORKING WITH FAMILY MEMBERS

The views of family members, their interpretations of medical issues, and how much they are allowed to participate in helping patients make decisions are also important concerns. Often, cognitive changes are not static, though they may be stable for some time depending on the cause and trajectory of the illness and other factors; it is important for a clinician to distinguish reversible from irreversible changes in cognition, as these can significantly affect treatment decisions and prognoses. Relatives or caregivers bring their subjective biases to the situation, which may or may not be relevant to the patient's primary needs. Therefore, decisions about who is an appropriate supplementary historian while protecting patient confidentiality is an important consideration. The relatives or caregivers may only see the patient at selected times or may be overwhelmed and frustrated with caregiver burden. As a result, it is important to be able to elicit accurate information from the patient's perspective as well as that of the relative or caregiver. Consider seeing patients alone first, in order to understand their perception of the situation and if there is anything they want to disclose to you without the caregiver or relative in the room. There are times that this need is not perceived until you have met with the family member and reviewed the situation. It may also be important to maintain structure and limits during the consult, attempting to remain neutral while listening to and considering all perspectives and concerns. There are also times when a family member may be domineering and push a specific course of treatment or management; in such instances, it is important to continue to use your clinical judgment and perhaps request consultations from other services such as a patient representatives or social worker to help understand and better manage the situation. There can also be gains by teaching caregivers of those with cognitive deficits how to communicate better with their loved ones (8) (Table 27.2).

TABLE 27.2 Skills to Help Communicate With Cognitively Impaired Older Adults

Issues	Skills
Informed treatment decisions	■ Giving written information that is easy to understand and grade-level appropriate for the audience ■ Using simple phrases ■ Taking breaks in conversation to clarify understanding ■ Having patient paraphrase understanding ■ Joint meeting with treatment team
Working with family members	■ Consider meeting with the patient alone ■ Maintain limits and structure during consult ■ Act as advocate for the patient with aggressive family members ■ Consult from patient representative and social work ■ Suggest ways family members or caregivers can communicate more effectively with the patient
Loss of independence	■ Multidisciplinary approach to assess cognitive, emotional, and physical deficits ■ Consider DMV evaluation for question of driving capacity ■ Discuss alternatives for activities, additional supports, and resources

DMV, Department of Motor Vehicles.

LOSS OF INDEPENDENCE

Another prominent issue that often arises when dealing with cognitively impaired elderly patients is loss of independence. A glaring example of this is the decision to take away driving privileges when a patient becomes too frail or impaired by cognitive changes. Usually, a multidisciplinary approach with inclusion of family is helpful in resolving these situations, including discussion of loss of autonomy and its consequences. At times, a work-up for cognitive problems including Mini-Mental Status Exam (MMSE) (9) or other brief screen, a formal neuropsychological evaluation, and occupational therapy evaluation may help clarify the deficits and determine what constraints are necessary. In the specific example of driving, an evaluation by the Department of Motor Vehicles may provide supplementary information to make this decision. As patients lose their independence, it is important to discuss new ways of maintaining activities, such as arranging alternate transportation.

ETHICAL ISSUES/CAPACITY

Ethical questions about treatment options also commonly arise. For instance, ethics enters into the appropriateness of suggesting surgical treatment for a newly diagnosed lung cancer in a patient with dementia, or deciding to embark on a rigorous chemotherapy regimen in a patient who has a good performance status but also slight cognitive problems that may be the harbinger of Alzheimer's disease. When cognitive deficits are so clear and severe that it has been deemed by a physician, and understood by family, that the patient does not have decisional capacity, direction to a health care proxy is fairly straightforward. Unfortunately, the ambiguous and perhaps unstable nature of the cognitive problems often complicates this process.

The assessment of capacity entails a process to determine if a patient is able to give informed consent, or to refuse a procedure or course of action related to medical care that might be critical to survival. Questions related to capacity are more common when a patient refuses recommendations compared to when a patient is agreeable. A capacity evaluation can be challenging in older patients with mild to severe cognitive deficits or psychiatric syndromes such as depression, delirium, or dementia; however, cognitive impairment does not rule out capacity. Psychiatric consultation is requested in more challenging situations when there are mild to moderate deficits in cognitive processes or decision-making abilities. Assessment of capacity takes into account whether a patient understands pertinent medical issues and recommended treatment, the pros and cons of accepting or refusing the recommendations, and the ability to state a preference. Capacity to understand and participate in decision making usually encompasses a particular situation and decision ("Should I have another MRI to determine further progression of my disease?") rather than a person's global and general ability to make decisions.

A patient needs to understand the benefits of the recommendation, the potential risks of the recommendation, and the consequences of refusing the recommendation. A mental status examination, as well as a brief cognitive exam, is helpful. Corroborative data about baseline mental status or end-of-life directives from family or friends can be helpful. Obtaining and documenting discussion with and attestation from the health care proxy and family are important when a patient has limited capacity.

If an individual is deemed to have sufficient capacity, it is important to ensure that informed consent is obtained before moving ahead with treatment. Informed consent is often not considered until a patient refuses care. Especially when patients or family members have sensory deficits, it is important to take the time to explain the information in language that the patient can understand, and then check with the patient, or have the patient paraphrase your discussion to ensure that the patient understands the information. Patients should be able to clarify the need for the treatment, the side effects or complications from the treatment, and the risks of refusing the treatment (10). When considering capacity, the more life-threatening the nature of the disease and treatment proposed, the higher the standard for the patient to understand the need for the treatment, potential side effects and complications, and risks of refusal. Some basic suggestions for navigating informed consent in this situation include providing written information that is easy to understand and written at a grade level appropriate for the audience, using simple phrases, and taking frequent breaks in the conversation to clarify (e.g., have the patient paraphrase) the plan. Psychiatrists can assist in evaluations for capacity to make treatment decisions with cognitively impaired patients, including understanding appreciation and judgmental capacity in reasoning about a choice. They can also assist with identifying the role of surrogate decision makers in this setting. Recognizing when powers of attorney, health care proxies, or court-appointed guardians are necessary and which hospital resources are available to assist in these measures will relieve the tension surrounding very stressful situations. Including family members when capacity is questioned is also recommended (11).

CONCLUSION

Interventions aimed at improving physician interactions with older patients have yet to be widely explored. In fact, there is a remarkable dearth of geriatric communication training programs in the oncology setting, despite the fact that cancer occurs primarily in the elderly. Attention given to enhancing clinician-patient communication skills with elderly cancer patients and their families could optimize the health care delivered to older patients, and improve the sensitivity and effectiveness of cancer clinicians in communicating with elderly patients.

TAKE HOME POINTS

1. The most effective method for learning communication skills is observation of ideal communication strategies, followed by rehearsal of the skills in role-play, and receipt of immediate feedback on performance.
2. Creating a team-based approach to communicating with an older patient about complicated treatment options is imperative.
3. Staff should be educated about the components of frailty and comorbidities that interfere with effective communication.
4. When navigating informed consent with potentially cognitively impaired older patients, include written information that is easy to understand, use simple phrases, and take frequent breaks in the conversation to clarify the plan.

REFERENCES

1. Siegel RL, Miller KD, Jemel A. Cancer statistics, 2016. *CA Cancer J Clin.* 2016; 66:7-30. doi:10.3322/caac.21332.
2. Amalraj S, Starkweather C, Nguyen C. Health literacy, communication, and treatment decision-making in older cancer patients. *Oncology.* 2009;23(4):369.
3. Roth A, Nelson, C. Issues for cognitively impaired elderly patients. In Kissane D, Bultz B, Butow P, Finlay I, eds. *Handbook of Communication in Oncology and Palliative Care.* New York, NY: Oxford University Press; 2010:547-556.
4. Arora NK, Street RL, Epstein RM, Butow PN. Facilitating patient-centered cancer communication: a road map. *Patient Educ Couns.* 2009;77(3):319-321.
5. Thompson TL, Robinson JD, Beisecker AE. The older patient-physician interaction. In: Nussbaum JF, Coupland J, eds. *Handbook of Communication and Aging Research.* Mahwah, NJ: Lawrence Erlbaum; 2004:451-477.
6. Song L, Bensen JT, Zimmer C, et al. Patient-health care provider communication among patients with newly diagnosed prostate cancer: findings from a population-based survey. *Patient Educ Couns.* 2013;91:79-84.
7. Bylund CL. Communication skills training for healthcare providers. In: *The International Encyclopedia of Interpersonal Communication.* Hoboken, NJ: John Wiley & Sons; 2015. doi:10.1002/9781118540190.
8. Smith ER, Broughton M, Baker MS, et al. Memory and communication support in dementia: research-based strategies for caregivers. *Int Psychogeriatr.* 2011;23:256-263. doi:10.1017/S1041610210001845.
9. Folstein MF, Folstein SE, McHugh PR. "Mini-mental state": a practical method for grading the cognitive state of patients for the clinician. *J Psychiatr Res.* 1975;12(3):189-198.
10. Appelbaum PS. Assessment of patients' competence to consent to treatment. *N Engl J Med.* 2007;357(18):1834-1840.
11. Fields LM, Calvert JD. Informed consent procedures with cognitively impaired patients: a review of ethics and best practices. *Psychiatry Clin Neurosci.* 2015;69(8):462-471.

VI The Nursing Home Patient With Cancer

28 Levels of Residential Care in the Elderly and the Role of Cancer Screening

Miriam B. Rodin

The logic of cancer screening makes certain assumptions about the population to be screened, and the clinician needs to understand how well individual patients fit those assumptions. This chapter describes the spectrum of residential settings specialized for the elderly ranging from the fit to the frail, and explains the terminology that is often confusing to nongeriatricians. Correctly identifying the level of support that is offered in each residential type will help clinicians to understand the role of cancer screening in each residential population.

SPECTRUM OF RESIDENTIAL OPTIONS FOR OLDER ADULTS

We tend to use the words *nursing home* and *long-term care* interchangeably, but in fact the latter is defined in regulatory language and health finance systems and the former is not. *Long-term care* is a catchall for a spectrum of medical, rehabilitative, and personal care services given outside of hospitals. With the explosion of the aging population, there is a panoply of residential facilities and housing developments targeted at older adults sorted along a broad spectrum of functional status from "healthy aging" tennis players to bedridden dementia patients. Specifically, although everyone uses the term, there is no such thing as a nursing home. Where people live is a clue to their performance status.

Table 28.1 shows the spectrum of residential options targeted to older adults. "Home" is included here because a substantial amount of postacute and chronic care is delivered in people's own homes. Home-based care depends heavily on the unpaid care given by family members, often an aging spouse, supplemented by paid caregivers and visiting health professionals (1). If there is a need for assistance but no available caregiver, the rest of the residential options come into play.

There are two basic levels of assistance. The first is for instrumental activities of daily living (IADLs). IADLs are the higher-level functions that include managing money, cleaning the house, going shopping, preparing meals, and so forth. For elderly who do not need any assistance with these, there are "retirement" or "active senior living" communities that are usually downsized private homes or apartments linked to sports, fitness, and recreational centers. There is assistance with groundskeeping, common area, and outdoor maintenance. IADL assistance provides for

TABLE 28.1 Typology and Characteristics of Residential Options for the Elderly and Disabled, Population Screening Considerations

Residential Type	Level of Assistance Required/ Impairments	Who Pays?	Medical Provider	Other Staffing, Providers
Retirement community	None–mild	Private funds for residence; Medicare, and supplemental and private for medical	Office-based PCP	Home maintenance, private-pay CG
Senior citizen housing (low income)	None–moderate	Private funds for residence (i.e., social security); Medicare and supplemental	Office-based PCP, home health as needed	Building services, home health services up to 2–3× week
Independent living $+	Mild	Private funds	PCP office-based	Activities, transportation, dining, housekeeping
ALF $+	Moderate	Private funds	PCP office-based	Activities, meals, transportation, health aides, RN day time, medication management
LTAC*, ** $	Moderate to severe of indeterminate duration	Medicare, Medicaid, private medical, VA	Staff physicians	Hospital-level staffing (5:1), urban areas only
Acute rehabilitation*, ** $	Moderate to severe, expected improvement	Medicare, Medicaid, private medical, VA	Staff physiatrists	Hospital-level staffing (5:1), urban areas only
Subacute skilled nursing (SNF) *, ** $	Mild to severe, expected improvement, specified skilled RN needs associated with acute illness	Medicare, Medicaid, VA, 100 days	Weekly-monthly physician/ APN visits	RN, LPN, CNA (10-20:1) OT/PT/SLP
Subacute rehabilitation (SNF)*, ** $	Mild to severe, specified functional decline associated with acute illness, expected improvement	Medicare, Medicaid, VA, 100 days	Weekly-monthly physician/ APN visits	RN, LPN, CNA (10-20:1) OT/PT/SLP

(continued)

TABLE 28.1 Typology and Characteristics of Residential Options for the Elderly and Disabled, Population Screening Considerations (*continued*)

Residential Type	Level of Assistance Required/ Impairments	Who Pays?	Medical Provider	Other Staffing, Providers
+Home care/ Day care/PACE	Mild to moderate, no expected improvement	Public aid, Medicaid, VA	Home visiting MD, RN; as required at center, office-based	Home health aide, bathing, social work, etc.
LTCF * $ +	Moderate to severe with expected decline, includes "memory care"	Medicaid or private, VA	Q 60 days PCP or APN	Same building as SNF
Congregate; foster care * model *, ** $	Mild-severe	Dual eligible, private pay, VA, family	Office-based PCP	Case management, varies by state
Facility Key:	*Facility subject to state licensing, inspections, Medicare/ Medicaid regulations, including scheduled assessments (MDS 3.0)	**Requiring qualifying hospital stays, ICD-10 diagnosis	$ Many are for-profit, corporate chain providers	+ Some with religious affiliation or beneficent endowments

ALF, assisted living facility; APN, advanced practice nurse; CG, caregiver; CNA, certified nursing assistant; LPN, licensed practical nurse; LTAC, long-term acute care; LTCF, long-term care facility; OT, occupational therapy; PACE, Program of All-Inclusive Care for the Elderly; PCP, primary care provider; PT, physical therapy; SNF, skilled nursing facility; SLP, speech and language pathology; VA, Veterans Administration.

individual task-based limitations and it allows people to remain safely at home alone. For example, help with housekeeping is often provided by family members. Housekeeping "chore workers" may be provided by the State Departments on Aging at reduced cost. Senior "call-a ride" services substitute for family when elderly give up driving.

For those who are able to pay privately, "independent living" assumes or anticipates some higher-level instrumental dependence such as need for transportation. "Assisted living" assumes more IADL dependence and assisted living facilities (ALFs) usually advertise their planned recreational activities and dining facilities for elderly who no longer shop and prepare their own meals but are able to socialize (2). ALFs generally also assume mobility problems. The prevalence of walking aids, should there ever be a survey, increases from home to independent to assisted living to residential care. ALFs frequently provide medication supervision. Senior residences, independent living, and ALFs are neither defined nor regulated as health care facilities. Medicare does not pay for them (3).

The next level of assistance is for activities of daily living (ADLs). ADLs are the basic self-care activities of eating, bathing, transferring, toileting, taking medications, and making telephone calls that become difficult due to physical illness, disability, and sensory or cognitive decline. An elder's ability to stay home depends on having a family member or other caregiver there daily. Day care can substitute for home assistance if a working caregiver is there at night. We are often concerned about the safety of ADL-dependent elders who insist on staying home alone. Expressing this concern often elicits an emphatic, "I'm not going into a nursing home." Some home-based services, such as the VA HBHC (hospital-based home care) and PACE (Program of All-inclusive Care for the Elderly) are specifically designed as nursing home diversionary programs (2). They are targeted to elderly who are homebound and are nursing home appropriate in order to prevent nursing home placement.

The structure or building that is the "nursing home" has two different populations. The basic distinction is whether the stay is a continuation of an acute hospital episode or not, as set out in Medicare Part A. Postacute care is further divided into long-term acute care (LTAC) and subacute care. Additional terms include inpatient rehabilitation and intermediate or stepdown or transitional care. Eligibility for each level is defined by Medicare and supervised by the states with respect to documented functional status and immediate medical history (4). LTAC supplies hospital—indeed, intensive care unit (ICU) level—care indefinitely. Acute (inpatient) rehabilitation hospitals (levels 1–2) provide high-intensity rehabilitation. Skilled nursing facilities (SNFs) and subacute rehabilitation facilities are classified by levels 3 through 7 rehab and three levels of intensity of nursing documented by standardized assessments of the Minimum Data Set (MDS) 3.0 (1).

Medicare Part A was enacted with the original Medicare legislation in 1965. When hospitals were tasked with prospective payment (diagnosis-related groups or DRGs) in the early 1980s, complex patients were discharged to community care facilities that were unprepared to provide the complexity of care these patients required. Historically, they were residences for the elderly who were poor or frail and had no family to care for them. It soon became clear that the situation was unacceptable. The OBRA 1987 regulations specified that structured functional assessments be performed on all residents to find out what and how much care was going to be needed to return Medicare beneficiaries to their homes. In other words, Medicare pays only for short-term care that assumes return to prior level of function.

As shown in Table 28.1, postacute care facilities are covered by private funds, long-term care insurance, Medicare, Medicaid, and VA third-party payers with the expectation that health and performance will improve. When people have either returned to their previous state of health and function or when they plateau, they are discharged or they stay for indefinite residential care, long-term care. Medicare does not pay for that. Medicaid pays for long-term residential care once people have "spent down" their remaining private assets.

The Medicare Part A–skilled nursing and rehabilitation services are given at home or in subacute facilities and are limited to 100 days per diagnosis per year. Medicare Part A (Med A) will pay 100% of 20 days in a SNF but only charges above the per diem room and board of an additional 80 days of postacute care for a qualifying diagnosis after a qualifying inpatient stay of 3 calendar days. Thus, a patient in subacute care can probably pursue screening after discharge. While they are Med A, the facility has to pay for screenings, and many will not.

WHO LIVES IN THE "NURSING HOME"?

About 1.4 million Americans live in "nursing homes" (5). The majority, 79.1% of long-term acute, postacute, and subacute admissions, came from hospitals (5). The distinctions are how the services are paid for, the specific nursing tasks, and volume of rehabilitation. However, all of these services are located in the same physical structure. The long-term care facility (LTCF) is the same building as the subacute rehab and SNF. In 2016, 33.2% of LTCF residents were there under Medicare A subacute coverage (3). Another source reported that 12.5% of LTCF residents on Medicare A generated 25% of the income for these facilities (2). About one-third of patients admitted to Med A SNF will go home within 30 days, another one-third will go home within 6 months, and one-third will remain as LTCF "custodial care" residents (5). LTCF deaths are concentrated in the first 6 months after admission. Overall, in the first year after "placement," 50% to 60% of the elderly will die (4–7).

In other words, although we all know what a nursing home is, the real issue is **functional status**. The vast majority of elderly live at home and receive the bulk of their care from family members (3). Unpaid family caregivers provide an estimated $385 billion in home care that very likely could never be provided by a social welfare or fee-for-service system (8). Living in a facility that is not one's home where care is not provided by one's family suggests significant functional dependence.

Functional status has been shown to predict trajectories of further decline in community-living elderly (9). Having used the Medicare A benefit for SNF at all predicts further decline for up to half of beneficiaries (10). There are several validated predictive tools for mortality in hospitalized and nursing home residents (11–13). Dementia is an independent risk factor that confers high risk both for nursing home placement and for 4-year mortality (14–18).

THE LOGIC OF CANCER SCREENING

Physicians who practice in SNFs and LTCFs are aware of the debility of the population and the many reasons to avoid facility-wide policies in favor of cancer screening. Such policies have largely disappeared. The clear majority of LTCF residents, greater than 90%, are unlikely to benefit from cancer screening due to foreshortened life expectancy due to age, comorbidity, and frailty. Many will lack the cognitive capacity to participate in shared decision making about screening or about the treatment of a malignancy if it is found.

The Cancer in the Elderly working groups have been proactive in urging careful functional screening of elderly cancer patients. Levels of functional impairment that may be subtle in the clinic (19) still have been shown to predict excess toxicity with chemotherapy (20). For that reason alone, residence in a LTCF should prompt a careful assessment of decisional capacity and likelihood of benefit during the best estimate of remaining life expectancy.

Primary care physicians are under pressure to provide "quality" care and meaningful use of electronic health records (EHR). Normal use of EHR in the clinic triggers algorithms requiring responses in real time. Nursing homes rarely have EHR capacity, and residents are generally seen every month or two by an assigned physician or advanced practice nurse. Some elderly continue to see their office-based primary care providers, where they are exposed to guideline-driven care. Table 28.2 summarizes current United States Preventive Services Task Force (USPSTF) (21–27) and American Cancer Society (ACS) (28–30) cancer screening guidelines. Specifically, guidelines are addressed to adults "at average risk" for cancer, but they provide little guidance on application to special populations (31). The American Geriatrics Society and the American College of Physicians, through the Choosing Wisely campaign, have addressed the value of cancer screening in the elderly, specifically advising on how to individualize assessments of burden and benefit conveyed by screening (31). Table 28.2 shows that the guidelines recommend reserving screening for breast cancer, colon cancer, and prostate cancer, all of which have their peak incidence in the elderly, for those with at least a 10-year estimated life expectancy. There are no recommendations for ovarian cancer screening, and elderly women are exempted from cervical cancer screening. Lung cancer screening has relatively recently achieved validation for high-risk individuals up to age 80, with no qualification for life expectancy. Prostate cancer screening is discouraged by the USPSTF (21–27). The ACS guideline on prostate cancer screening does not address older age (28).

TABLE 28.2 Current ACS and USPSTF Adult Screening Guidelines for Breast, Cervical, Uterine/Ovarian, Colorectal, Prostate, and Lung Cancer

Site	Source and Date	Population	Test	Age Range (Y)	Frequency (Y)	Other Considerations
Breast	ACS 2015	Women age ≥20 y	Mammography	40–74 or older if RLE 10 y	Annually	No recommendation for BSE, annual CBE
	USPSTF 2002			40–74 or older if RLE 10 y	1–2 years	No recommendation

(continued)

TABLE 28.2 Current ACS and USPSTF Adult Screening Guidelines for Breast, Cervical, Uterine/Ovarian, Colorectal, Prostate, and Lung Cancer (*continued*)

Site	Source and Date	Population	Test	Age Range (Y)	Frequency (Y)	Other Considerations
Cervical	ACS 2015	Women age 21–65	Pap smear	21–29 30–65 30–65	Q 3 y Q 5 y if done with HPV or q 3 y if Pap only and no HPV	Age >65 and ≥ 3 consecutive negative Pap tests or ≥ 2 negative Pap+HPV in the last 10 and most recent <5 y ago, may cease screening. Total hysterectomy for nonmalignant condition, no further screening
	USPSTF 2012		HPV DNA test		Q 5 y	
Endometrial/ ovarian	None					High-risk known genetic carriers
Colorectal	ACS 2008 with 2016 pending	Men and women aged ≥50 y	Colonoscopy		Q 10 y	ACS also endorses stool chemical, DNA; flexsig, barium x-ray and CT colonography with qualifications
	USPSTF 2008	Men and women ages ≥50 y	Any of the ACS methods as described	50–75		
Prostate	ACS 2001	Men aged ≥50	DRE and PSA	≥50-NUL	None stated	Men with at least a 10 y life expectancy should be provided individualized counseling and shared decision making
	USPSTF	No recommendation (2016)				
Lung	ACS 2013	Current and former smokers	Low-dose spiral CT	55–74	≥30 pack-years; ≤15 y abstention from smoking	In good health not otherwise defined
	USPSTF 2013			55–80		No medical contraindication

BSE, breast self-exam; CBE, clinical breast exam; HPV DNA, human papillomavirus DNA; NUL, no upper limit; RLE, remaining life expectancy.

Mammography and colon cancer screening have been specifically studied to provide reference estimates to individualize screening decisions for the elderly (32–36). There are population-based estimates of survival (33,34) that show about 25% of elderly beyond the age of 75 do not have a 10-year remaining life expectancy. They are mostly the elderly with multiple comorbidities and functional deficits severe enough to require assistance. This describes the long-term care population.

IS THERE A ROLE FOR CANCER SCREENING IN NURSING HOMES?

The question, "Should nursing home residents be screened for cancer?" can be answered briefly. With few exceptions, cancer screening will not benefit people who live in nursing homes. However, this depends on the examiner's understanding of what a nursing home is and who lives there. This chapter has presented current population descriptive data showing how the LTC "nursing home" population differs from the average risk population assumed by the screening models. There are some possible circumstances in which cancer screening might be appropriate care for an LTCF resident. The average age of LTC residents is in the mid-80s. About 16% of LTCF residents are under age 65 and another 18% are under age 75 (2,5). The younger group includes adults with developmental disabilities or severe physical disabilities such as brain injuries, quadriplegia, and degenerative diseases. Some are chronically mentally ill adults who may eventually transition to community care. If they are otherwise healthy and able to participate in decision making, the standard population screening recommendations should apply. In particular, mentally ill and disabled women are often at high risk for sexual abuse and have had substandard well woman care. In this case Pap smears and mammograms should be ordered. Heavy smoking is prevalent in this population. Low-dose CT screening for lung cancer and colon cancer screening might be appropriate for patients who can participate in decision making.

Aside from intentional screening, LTCF residents experience frequent hospitalizations during which blood testing and imaging may find an incidental early stage malignancy. Colonoscopy for rectal bleeding, CT to rule out pulmonary embolism (PE), and a prostate-specific antigen (PSA) test ordered by an intern all can find an early stage malignancy. In this event, oncologists are consulted for advice on management. Here, the best way to proceed is to follow the principles of geriatric oncology, weighing the benefit and risk of treating an asymptomatic tumor in a frail elder (19,20). Thinking about the individual patient, if you would not be able to treat it curatively, and then prospectively, it does not seem reasonable to screen for it.

Few elderly residents of "nursing homes" would benefit from cancer screening because of reduced life expectancy, comorbidities that limit treatment options for screen-detected cancers, and inability to participate in informed decision making. Physicians caring for elderly should be familiar with prognostic tools to assist in screening and treatment decision making. Should an oncologist be faced with a screen-detected or incidental early stage malignancy in an elderly person, and a functional assessment reveals dependencies in motor and cognitive function, the web site www.ePrognosis.org is a repository of scales for estimating survival in a range of elderly populations.

TAKE HOME POINTS

1. The jargon around senior citizen housing and residential care is confusing and physicians should be careful to understand exactly how much assistance a patient requires.
2. Cancer screening should be reserved for elderly with estimated remaining life expectancy long enough to benefit from early detection.
3. Few elderly who reside in LTC can satisfy that requirement due to functional dependency, cognitive impairment, and comorbidity.
4. Some younger adult residents in LTC due to developmental, physical, or mental health disability should be provided with recommended screening.
5. The standardized geriatric assessment tools provided by the Cancer in the Elderly working groups should be completed for any elderly person prior to screening, just as would be recommended prior to treatment if a malignancy were detected.

REFERENCES

1. https://dhhs.cms.gov/statistics. Accessed February 4, 2016.
2. https://www.longtermcarelink.net/eldercare/nursing_home.htm.
3. National Health Policy Forum. The basics: national spending for long-term services and supports. 2014. Available at: www.ahpf.org/library/the-basics/Basics_LTSS_03_27_14.pdf. Accessed January 2016.
4. MedPAC. Skilled Nursing Facility Services, chap 8 pp.181–210.
5. The Henry J. Kaiser Family Foundation. Number of nursing facility residents. 2011. Available at: http://kff.org/other/state-indicator/number-of-nursing-facility-residents/. Accessed January 2015.
6. Congressional Budget Office. Rising demand for long-term services and supports for elderly people. 2013. Available at: https://www.cbo.gov/sites/default/files/113th Congress 201302014/reports/44363-ltc.pdf. Accessed January 2016.
7. Rodin MB. Cancer patients admitted to nursing homes: what do we know? *J Am Med Dir Assoc.* 2008:9(3):149-156. doi:10.1016/jamda.2007.
8. http://caregiveraction.org/resources/caregiver-statistics.
9. Guralnik JM, Simonsick EM, Ferrucci L, et al. A short physical performance battery assessing lower extremity function: association with self-reported disability and prediction of mortality and nursing home admission. *J Gerontol.* 1994;49(2):M85-M94. doi:10.1093/geronj/49.2.M85.
10. Buurman BM, Han L, Murphy TE, et al. Trajectories of disability among older persons before and after a hospitalization leading to a skilled nursing facility admission. *J Am Med Dir Assoc.* 2016;17:225-231.
11. Carey EC, Covinsky KE, Lui LY, et al. Prediction of mortality in community-living frail elderly people with long-term care needs. *J Am Geriatr Soc.* 2008;56:68-75.
12. Lee SJ, Lindquist K, Segal MR, Covinsky KE. Development and validation of a prognostic index for 4-year mortality in older adults. *JAMA.* 2006;295(7):801-808.

13. Hjalltadotrir I, Hallberg IR, Ekwall AK, Nyberg P. Predicting mortality of residents at admission to nursing home: a longitudinal cohort study. *BMC Health Serv Res.* 2011;11:86.

14. Seger W, Sittaro N-A, Lohse R, Rabb J. Vergleich von pflegeverlauf und sterblichkert von pflegebedurftigen mit und ohne medizinische rehabilitation [A comparison of care history and mortality of people in need of personal care with or without medical rehabilitation]. *Z Gerontol Geriatr.* 2013;46:756-768. doi:10.1007/s00391-013-05219.

15. Cereda E, Pedrolli C, Zagami A, et al. Alzheimer's disease and mortality in traditional long term care facilities. *Arch Gerontol Geriatr.* 2013;56:437-441.

16. Mitchell SL, Miller SG, Teno JM, et al. Prediction of 6-month survival of nursing home residents with advanced dementia using ADEPT vs hospice eligibility guidelines. *JAMA.* 2010;304(17):1929-1935.

17. Tom SE, Hubbard RA, Crane PK, et al. Characterization of dementia and Alzheimer's disease in an older population: updated incidence and life expectancy with and without dementia. *Am J Publ Health.* 2015;105(2):408-413.

18. Alzheimer's Association. Alzheimer's Association report: 2015 Alzheimer's disease facts and figures. *Alzheimers Dement.* 2015;11:332-384.

19. Jolly TA, Deal AM, Nyrop KA, et al. Geriatric assessment-identified deficits in older cancer patients with normal performance status. *Oncologist.* 2015;20(4):379-385. doi:10.1634/theoncologist.2014-0247.

20. Hurria A, Naylor M, Cohen HJ. Improving the quality of cancer care in an aging population: recommendations from an IOM report. *JAMA.* 2013;310:1795-1796.

21. https://www.uspreventiveservicestaskforce.org/Page/Document/UpdateSummaryFinal/cervical-cancer-screening. Released March 2012. Accessed January 2016.

22. https://www.uspreventiveservicestaskforce.org/Page/Document/Recommendation StatementFinal/lung-cancer-screening. Released December 2013. Accessed January 2016.

23. https://www.uspreventiveservicestaskforce.org/Page/Document/UpdateSummaryFinal/breast-cancer-screening1. Released January 2016. Accessed January 2016.

24. https://www.uspreventiveservicestaskforce.org/Page/Document/UpdateSummaryFinal/colorectal-cancer-screening2. Released June 2016. Accessed June 2016.

25. https://www.uspreventiveservicestaskforce.org/Page/Document/UpdateSummaryFinal/ovarian-cancer-screening. Released September 2012. Accessed January 2016.

26. https://www.uspreventiveservicestaskforce.org/Page/Document/UpdateSummaryFinal/prostate-cancer-screening. Released May 2012. Accessed 2016.

27. http://www.uspreventiveservicestaskforce.org/Page/Document/.

28. http://www.cancer.org/healthy/findcancerearly/cancerscreeningguidelines/american-cancer-society-guidelines-for-the-early-detection-of-cancer.

29. Smith RA, Manassaram-Baptiste D, Brooks D, et al. Cancer screening in the United States, 2015: a review of current American Cancer Society guidelines and current issues in cancer screening. *CA Cancer J Clin.* 2015;65:30-54.

30. Oeffinger KC, Fontham EH, Etzioni R, et al. Breast cancer screening for women at average risk: 2015 guideline update from the American Cancer Society. *JAMA.* 2015;314(15):1599-1614. doi:10.1001/jama.2015.12783.1.

31. http://geriatricscareonline.org/SubscribeContents/choosing-wiselyreg-five-things-physicians-and-patients-should-question-an-initiative-of-the-abim-foundation/CL015.

32. Mehta KM, Fung KZ, Kistler CE, et al. Impact of cognitive impairment on screening mammography use in older US women. *Am J Pub Health.* 2010;100:1917-1923.

33. Breslau ES, Sheinfeld-Gorin S, Edwards HM, et al. An individualized approach to cancer screening decisions in older adults: a multilevel framework. *J Gen Intern Med.* 2016;31(5):539-547. doi:10.1007/s11606-016-3629-y.

34. Lee SJ, Boscardin WJ, Stijacic-Cenzer I, et al. Time lag to benefit after screening for breast and colorectal cancer: a meta-analysis of survival data from the United States, Sweden, United Kingdom and Denmark. *BMJ.* 2013;345:e8441. doi:10.1136/bmj .e8441.

35. Walter LC, Covinsky KE. Cancer screening in elderly patients: a framework for individualized decision-making. *JAMA.* 2001;285(21):2750-2756.

36. Walter LC, Schonberg MA. Screening mammography in older women: a review. *JAMA.* 2014;311(13):1336-1347. doi:10.1001/jama.2014.2834.

VII

Models of Care: Survivorship

Models of Shared Care

Kristine Swartz, Andrew Chapman, and Patrick Doggett

INTRODUCTION

A population shift is underway in the United States as the number of people over the age of 65 continues to grow. This influx of new patients, coupled with longer life expectancies, places new challenges on clinicians. One hazard of a longer life span is an increased risk of a cancer diagnosis (1). Cancer presents a significant source of morbidity and mortality for older patients. It is estimated that 70% of cancer deaths occur in patients older than 65 (2). As a result, significant resources are spent on the care of these patients. In 2004, the 5-year cost to Medicare for oncological care of patients older than 65 was approximately $21.1 billion (3). The rates of cancer diagnoses and the associated costs are only expected to increase in the next 20 years due to this demographic shift.

GERIATRIC CANCER CARE

The Challenge of Geriatric Cancer Care

Although it is clear that the incidence of cancer increases with advanced age and that there is a high cost associated with delivering this care, the treatment of older cancer patients is complicated by a number of factors. Older patients have more comorbidities and suffer from geriatric syndromes such as dementia, frailty, or falls which can complicate treatment (1–3). Additionally, oncologic clinical trials often have not included geriatric patients (1). As a result, oncologists lack a strong body of age-appropriate evidence-based research to guide treatment decisions. Finally, older patients can face ageism when being evaluated for cancer care (3). Fit older patients with limited comorbidities may be denied first-line, and often the most appropriate, cancer care because of their age alone. Conversely, frail, older patients may be offered overly aggressive treatment leading to additional morbidity. These factors underscore the need for an individualized, geriatric-focused approach to cancer care.

The Comprehensive Geriatric Assessment

In 2005, based on systematic review, the International Society of Geriatric Oncology (SIOG) recommended that all geriatric oncology patients undergo a comprehensive geriatric assessment (CGA) (4). This standard assessment evaluates the patient in the following domains: functional status, comorbidities, cognition, polypharmacy, psychological status, social supports, and geriatric syndromes (5). These assessments require a number of different assessment tools and often the input of a multidisciplinary team of health care providers. The compiled information provides insight into the global health of the patient and allows for a classification of the patient as fit, vulnerable, or frail (6). When used in the oncological setting, the CGA identifies patients with unrecognized health problems (7). Additionally, when the CGA guides treatment, research has shown improved patient function and reduced hospitalizations (4,8). While emphasizing the importance of the CGA, no one tool or assessment approach is endorsed by SIOG. Please refer to Chapter 13 for more details on CGA.

Dedicated Geriatric Oncology Clinics

There is a recognized impending shortage of health care providers trained in geriatric principles. There are currently around 7,500 practicing geriatricians in this country. The number needed is expected to double in the next 30 years to meet the care needs of the aging population (9). The number of oncologists formally trained in geriatric principles is infinitely smaller. In an effort to improve cancer care for older patients, there has been an emergence of specialized geriatric oncology clinics (10). The field of geriatric oncology strives to combine geriatric and oncology principles and perform research to better understand how to best care for older cancer patients. As this is an emerging field, there is no standardization for how these clinics are structured. With the expected shortage, exploring different models of care is necessary to provide improved cancer care for older adults.

Five of the more common geriatric oncology models of care are the shared care model, the consultative clinic model, the geriatric oncologist as primary provider, the screen and refer model, and the geriatrics-driven and embedded consultative model (1–3,11).

MODELS OF GERIATRIC CANCER CARE

Shared Care Model

The shared care model involves a partnership between the patient's geriatrician and oncologist (2). Depending on the status of the patient's cancer, either provider can serve as the primary medical decision maker. Often the primary care provider (PCP) makes the initial cancer diagnosis and refers the patient to the oncologist. The oncologist will develop the treatment plan and oversee the patient's care during this period. Care decisions after treatment often return to the PCP. This model requires strong communication and cooperation between the patient's providers. It has the benefit of allowing the patient to maintain his or her PCP while also gaining the expertise of the oncologist. Sharing care roles also reduces the level of responsibility placed on the individual provider (Table 29.1).

TABLE 29.1 Models of Care

Models of Geriatric Oncologic Care	Description
Shared Care Model	Medical management divided between PCP and oncologist. Role of primary medical decision maker shifts depending on stage of cancer care.
Screen and Refer Model	Uses validated screening tools to perform CGA. Patients referred to specialist if they have care needs exceeding resources oncologist can offer.
Oncologist as Primary Provider Model	Comprehensive care provided by physicians who are dual trained in geriatrics and oncology.
Multidisciplinary Consultative Model	Community oncologists refer patients to undergo a multidisciplinary CGA. Recommendations for care relayed to patient's primary oncologist.
Geriatrics-Driven and Embedded Consultative Model	Oncology clinics have an embedded geriatrician who can perform a CGA and/or can be consulted with ongoing geriatric care questions.

CGA, comprehensive geriatric assessment; PCP, primary care provider.

Screen and Refer Model

This model employs validated screening tools to initially assess patients (3). These tools assess patients in the various domains typically addressed in a CGA. Based on the results, the oncologist can determine if the practice has the ability to meet the patient's needs. If those needs cannot be met, patients are then referred to community providers—ideally trained geriatric health care providers—who can offer the needed support. This model has the benefit of allowing providers the opportunity to perform a basic geriatric assessment without needing to convene a multidisciplinary team to perform the assessment. This model is limited by the time required to conduct these screening assessments (12). Additionally, it requires that providers and social workers have a strong knowledge of and partnership with community resources and providers to ensure timely referral.

Geriatric Oncologist as Primary Provider Model

This model utilizes physicians who have dual training both in geriatrics and oncology to serve both as the patient's PCP and oncologist (3,11). The model has the benefit of being able to provide the patient with continuity of care and the ease of having to coordinate with only one provider. This model is limited by the small number of oncologists who have dual training. Additionally, the providers who serve in these roles often have limitations on their patient panels, because they remain the PCP and it requires significant time to manage all aspects of their patients' care.

Multidisciplinary Consultative Model

In this model, oncologists may refer their patients to undergo a comprehensive evaluation prior to starting or during their cancer therapy. These assessments can include input from a geriatrician, an oncologist, a pharmacist, a social worker, physical therapist or occupational therapist, and other disciplines (3,11). At the end of the assessment, the patient departs with treatment recommendations from the multidisciplinary team. The benefit of this program is that it allows patients to maintain their outpatient oncologist. This system also allows for large number of patients to be assessed prior to treatment. This model is limited because the patient's contact with these resources tends to occur only just prior to starting treatment. It is less common for patients to have follow-up visits with this team, making this model less responsive to potential treatment issues that might arise. This model also uses a significant amount of time and resources that usually require larger institutional support to maintain.

Geriatrics-Driven and Embedded Consultative Model

In this model, geriatricians who are either employed by the oncology clinic or employed by the same parent institution are used to perform CGAs (3,11). Additionally, in some locations these geriatricians are also asked to address nononcological issues that may develop during the patient's treatment. By having the geriatrician embedded in the clinic, there is the benefit of improved care coordination and collaboration. However, like other consultative models, there is the potential that patients only have contact with a geriatrician at the outset of their care.

CONCLUSION

As the population ages, there will be an increasing need to develop effective strategies for caring for older cancer patients. Shared care models provide geriatric cancer patients a comprehensive approach to their oncological care (13). Each model attempts to incorporate geriatric principles into the management of the patient. Although these models aim to improve care, more research is needed to determine if these models improve cancer outcomes and if one specific model is superior.

TAKE HOME POINTS

1. Older patients account for the majority of cancer-related deaths.
2. Care of geriatric oncology patients accounts for significant costs in the health care system, and that cost is expected to continue to grow.
3. A CGA is recommended for all geriatric oncology patients.
4. Geriatric oncology clinics around the country have developed various models of care which are tailored to the resources available to the home institution.
5. There is a need for continued research to determine what models improve cancer outcomes for patients.

REFERENCES

1. Terret C, Zulian GB, Naiem A, Albrand G. Multidisciplinary approach to the geriatric oncology patient. *J Clin Oncol.* 2007;25(14):1876-1881.
2. Cohen HJ. A model for the shared care of elderly patients with cancer. *J Am Geriatr Soc.* 2009;57(suppl 2):s300-s302.
3. Dale W, Chow S, Sajid S. Socioeconomic considerations and shared-care models of cancer care for older adults. *Clin Geriatr Med.* 2016;32(1):35-44.
4. Extermann M, Aapro M, Bernabei R, et al. Use of comprehensive geriatric assessment in older cancer patients: recommendations from the task force on CGA of the International Society of Geriatric Oncology (SIOG). *Crit Rev Oncol Hematol.* 2005;55(3):241-252.
5. Rodin MB, Mohile SG. A practical approach to geriatric assessment in oncology. *J Clin Oncol.* 2007;25(14):1936-1944.
6. Hurria A, Gupta S, Zauderer M, et al. Developing a cancer-specific geriatric assessment. *Cancer.* 2005;104(9):1998-2005.
7. Horgan AM, Leighl NB, Coate L, et al. Impact and feasibility of a comprehensive geriatric assessment in the oncology setting: a pilot study. *Am J Clin Oncol.* 2012;35(4):322-328.
8. Hurria A, Togawa K, Mohile SG, et al. Predicting chemotherapy toxicity in older adults with cancer: a prospective multicenter study. *J Clin Oncol.* 2011;29(25):3457-3465.
9. AGS Advocacy and Public Policy. Available at: http://www.americangeriatrics.org/advocacy_public_policy/gwps/gwps_faqs/id:3188. Accessed September 30, 2016.
10. McNeil C. Geriatric oncology clinics on the rise. *J Natl Cancer Inst.* 2013; 105(9):585-586.
11. Magnuson A, Dale W, Mohile S. Models of care in geriatric oncology. *Curr Geriatr Rep.* 2014;3(3):182-189.
12. Williams GR, Deal AM, Jolly TA, et al. Feasibility of geriatric assessment in community oncology clinics. *J Geriatr Oncol.* 2014;5(3):245-251.
13. Hamaker ME, Vos AG, Smorenburg CH, et al. The value of geriatric assessments in predicting treatment tolerance and all-cause mortality in older patients with cancer. *Oncologist.* 2012;17(11):1439-1449.

Survivorship Care for Older Adults With Cancer: The Role of Primary Care Physicians and Utility of Care Plans as a Communication Tool

Keith M. Bellizzi and Bonnie E. Gould Rothberg

INTRODUCTION

The converging trends of an aging population, increased cancer incidence as a function of age, and advances in medicine and supportive care for cancer have resulted in a growing population of cancer survivors aged 65 years and above (1). The U.S. Census Bureau predicts a doubling of adults 65 years or above between 2000 and 2030 (2) such that, among the projected 18 million cancer survivors in 2022, more than 75% will be individuals of age 65 years and above (3–5).

This burgeoning of geriatric cancer survivors has several implications for the delivery of appropriate survivorship care. First, the number of oncology office visits required by survivors is projected to surpass the available oncologic workforce (6). Consequently, the traditional model of oncologists providing survivorship care after completion of active therapy should be reconsidered to potentially include collaboration with primary care physicians. Second, the cornerstones of survivorship care, developed based on the extensively curated experiences of adult survivors of childhood-onset cancers (7) and proactive groups of middle-aged breast cancer survivors (8,9), should be adjusted to accommodate the needs of the geriatric population. The four pillars of survivorship care (Table 30.1) (10) must be integrated with care for preexisting comorbid medical conditions (e.g., cardiovascular disease, arthritis, diabetes, chronic obstructive pulmonary disease, and depression) typically present among older patients.

SURVIVORSHIP CARE PLAN (SCP) COMPONENTS AND RATIONALE

National organizations, including the Institute of Medicine, American Society of Clinical Oncology (ASCO), and LiveStrong, have recognized the importance of integrated, coordinated posttreatment survivorship care for the general adult cancer population to advocate for use of an SCP (Table 30.2) (11) that provides a treatment summary and follow-up care plan (12). Most recently, the American College of Surgeon's Commission on Cancer (CoC) has mandated that, in order to receive CoC accreditation, hospitals must provide each patient an SCP after completion of active therapy. Although an SCP is a helpful document, emphasis should be placed on patient engagement and not simply the transfer of information (11). Yet, none of these recommendations specifically address contextualizing SCPs to older adults. Moreover, with the transition of survivorship care to a multidisciplinary setting beyond the

TABLE 30.1 Pillars of Survivorship Care

1. Surveillance for recurrence and secondary cancers

2. Encouragement of beneficial lifestyle choices

3. Management of long-term systemic therapy sequelae

4. Addressing of psychosocial burdens associated with a cancer diagnosis

Source: Adapted from Ref. (10). Westfall MY, Overholser L, Zittleman L, Westfall JM. Cancer survivorship for primary care: annotated bibliography. *J Cancer Policy.* 2015;4(1):7-12.

TABLE 30.2 Treatment Summary and Follow-Up Care Plan Elements

Treatment Summary Elements	**SCP Elements**
Diagnostic tests and results	Surveillance for recurrence or new cancer
Tumor characteristics (e.g., site, stage and grade, hormone receptor status, marker information)	Assessment and treatment or referral for persistent effects, including psychosocial and economic as well as physical issues
Dates of treatment initiation and completion	Evaluation of risk for and prevention of late effects (e.g., second cancers, cardiac problems, thyroid disorders, osteoporosis) and health promotion (lifestyle interventions: diet, weight control, physical activity, sunscreen use, alcohol control, smoking cessation)
Type of treatment, indicators of treatment response, and toxicities experienced during treatment	Coordination of care (e.g., frequency of visits, tests to be performed, who performs tests)
Psychosocial, nutritional, and other supportive services provided	
Contact information for treating institutions and health care providers	

SCP, survivorship care plan.

Source: Ref. (11). Rowland JH, Bellizzi KM. Cancer survivorship issues: life after treatment and implications for an aging population. *J Clin Oncol.* 2014;32(24):2662-2668.

survivor/oncologist dyad, the SCP is now viewed as the essential tool for care coordination among patients and all of their providers (13). Here, we summarize how to best leverage the SCP to ameliorate problems in and enhance geriatric survivorship care, both by addressing specific elements of the SCP itself and by considering how SCPs optimize transitioning patients to nononcologist-driven survivorship care.

SURVIVOR-CENTERED MEDICAL HOMES AND THE PRIMARY CARE PHYSICIAN

The need for survivorship care first arose among childhood cancer survivors due to achieving long-term remissions and cures (14,15). Transitioning young adults from pediatric specialty care to adult care specialty clinics that cater to the "adult survivor of childhood cancers (ASCCs)" population are now commonplace at tertiary (16) and community (17) centers that treat pediatric cancers. These centers provide a patient-centered medical home (18) that ensures survivorship care according to Children's Oncology Group guidelines (19). Care is often led by a physician, frequently an internist or a family practitioner with survivorship care expertise (7,16), who coordinates care among a team of oncology nurse practitioners, social workers, psychologists, and a network of consulting physicians. While additional integration with community primary care providers (PCPs) to manage noncancer-related comorbidities has been attempted by some programs (e.g., 17), a survey of community-based internists indicated that only 5.5% would feel comfortable caring for ASCCs independently, whereas 84% would prefer to collaborate with a designated specialized long-term follow-up clinic (20). A substantial portion of this discomfort stems from the scarcity of ASCCs in general primary care practice. Whereas 48% of PCPs will have not treated an ASCC in the previous 5 years, only 24% will have cared for 3 or more in a similar time frame (20), a fact reinforcing models that favor cancer center-affiliated survivorship clinics.

In contrast, for "adult survivors of adult-onset cancers" (ASAOCs), the optimal model for delivering survivorship care is still uncertain (21,22). Although targeted survivorship/long-term follow-up clinics affiliated with cancer centers are implemented by some (23), these are atypical. Within the United States (24,25), United Kingdom (25,26), Europe (27), Australia (28), and Canada (29,30), the preferred models for survivorship care delivery among ASAOCs are either a complete transition to PCPs for all follow-up care or for a shared-care model between PCP and oncologist. With shared care, the oncologist typically provides consultation to support integration of the four pillars of survivorship care into routine primary care (31). Most PCPs and oncologists alike do not favor "specialized survivorship clinics" (32) for ASAOCs. The expectation is that the growing prevalence of ASAOCs, in contrast to pediatric cancer survivors (enumerated at only 350,000 across the entire United States (33)), should ensure that most PCPs will regularly encounter survivors in their practice, thereby creating familiarity with those patients' needs. Among 509 surveyed British Columbia PCPs, all had at least one breast cancer survivor in their practice, with 61% caring for 10 or more breast cancer survivors (34). Under a "cancer survivor-centered medical home," consolidating care into a single local setting eliminates travel to outside regional/tertiary cancer centers for routine and urgent primary care. Moreover, a systematic review evaluating the effectiveness of survivorship care delivered by oncology specialists versus generalists among both breast and colorectal cancer survivors identified no significant differences in terms of psychological morbidity, quality of life, comorbid sequelae such as poor functional status at the time of recurrence, recurrence, or overall survival (35,36).

This equilibrium has not yet been realized. In several studies, less than half of PCPs would be willing to be the sole providers for ASAOCs, with most preferring a shared-care model with specialists (32,37–39). Among those willing to assume a complete transition of care, the median preferred time of transfer was 2.5 to 3 years after completion of active management, with the additional reassurance that there would be expedited access to both diagnostic investigations and the referring oncologist in the event of suspected recurrence (40). Between 50% and 75% of PCPs reported having inadequate training on the provision of appropriate survivorship care (41–43), with the highest level of comfort reported in screening for new and recurrent malignancies, addressing anxiety/depression, and advocating for healthful lifestyle modifications (32,34,37,44). By contrast, PCPs reported least confidence in managing treatment-related side effects including cardiac, bone, and among breast cancer survivors, lymphedema (34,37), as well as fatigue and distress (34,44). In this context, PCPs were more likely to engage in defensive medicine and prescribe unnecessary tests (43). To address this apparent educational gap, the ASCO and American Cancer Society (ACS) have published guidelines on the appropriate care for survivors of common adult-onset cancers (45,46) and has created a core curriculum for cancer survivorship education (47). The American College of Physicians devoted a chapter of its monthly "In the Clinic" Continuing Medical Education (CME) series to the care of the adult cancer survivor (48), and has included a chapter on survivorship issues in the "Oncology" section of its Medical Knowledge and Self-Assessment board preparation program (49). Finally, Baylor University has launched an internal medicine residency program located at MD Anderson to train internists on the specific needs of adult cancer survivors (50).

Several studies have revealed that the per-visit time required to deliver guideline-appropriate survivorship care exceeds what is allotted in a typical PCP visit (41,51), a concern that would only be magnified among geriatric cancer survivors where yet additional time is required to integrate survivorship care with ongoing medical comorbidities. PCPs have also expressed feeling marginalized from their patients with cancer and then struggle to reestablish the same therapeutic alliance once active treatment has been completed. In this regard, patients corroborated these sentiments by valuing their oncologist for increased expertise and comfort with cancer-related medicine and access to active care following recurrence (41,52–55), as well as the intense doctor-patient bond formed with their oncologist (7,41) prompting a desire to maintain indefinite active ties with their oncologist following completion of active therapy. This latter concern may be less relevant among geriatric cancer survivors, as their comorbid medical conditions may require concurrent PCP visits while undergoing active cancer therapy.

THE SCP AS A COMMUNICATION TOOL BETWEEN THE PATIENT, THE PCP, AND THE ONCOLOGY SPECIALIST

As survivors who receive coordinated shared care from both oncologists *and* PCPs fare better than those who receive exclusive care from either (39), a successful "cancer survivor medical home" requires the efficient meshing of oncologist and PCP with each contributing, at the appropriate time, to survivorship care. Yet, each of PCPs, oncologists, and patients cite inefficient information sharing and care coordination as major gaps in obtaining quality survivorship care (56–58). PCPs cited that their patients undergoing active chemotherapy were less likely to schedule face-to-face primary care visits, and also noted the preferential management of medical comorbidities by the treating oncologist. Among those patients comanaged by their PCPs and oncologists, physician communication was only sporadic, with visit progress notes and diagnostic test results from both PCPs and oncologists inconsistently shared. Moreover, both groups frequently relied on the patient as the intermediary for care coordination, which, especially among older patients with decreased health literacy, increases the risk of misinformation and compromise in transitions of care (56).

The SCP, by both listing the components included in active disease management and outlining potential late effects and guidelines for posttreatment surveillance, is poised as a living document that can facilitate communication between providers as well as with the patient. Qualitative research studies have indicated that while SCPs increased PCP preparedness and confidence in providing survivorship care (59), most PCPs preferred receiving more abbreviated documents (60,61). A large randomized trial of 12 gynecologic oncology medical centers found that 82% of responding PCPs stated they would appreciate an organized SCP and, for those having received an SCP, its receipt enhanced the rate and quality of personal contact with the treating oncologist (61). Moreover, patients who received SCPs were more likely to schedule and adhere to PCP visits in the year following the transition (62), increasing the likelihood of survivorship guideline adherence. Yet, among the 123 participating PCPs where patients received SCPs, only 33% reported having seen the SCP, despite that one was documented as sent under study protocol (61). This highlights a potential administrative pitfall: despite the preparation and dispatch of an SCP, there is the risk of it being buried in the medical record before the PCP can view and integrate its contents. To the best of our knowledge, research describing the use of an SCP as a living document with shared responsibility for periodic and timely updates provided by both PCPs and oncologists is lacking.

Provision of SCPs to older patients adds complexity, largely in the context of coordinating management of medical comorbidities with routine survivorship care. While adequate formal research addressing this integration is largely lacking within the oncologic context, clinical pearls can be derived from other branches of internal medicine. Table 30.3 presents anticipated pitfalls in provision of survivorship care to older adults and remedies that have been suggested to address these gaps (63–66).

TABLE 30.3 Special Considerations for the SCP in the Older Adult Cancer Patient

Pitfall	Remedy
1. Older adults require integration of care among multiple medical subspecialists in addition to the PCP and the oncologist.	■ Inclusion of all health conditions and a geriatric assessment into the SCP. ■ Provision of the care plan to all treating specialists, not just the PCP, as is recommended by the CoC.
2. Polypharmacy among older adults may confound assignment of symptoms to oncology- vs nononcology-related conditions.	■ Involvement of a pharmacist in the care planning process to ensure a comprehensive medication reconciliation that highlights potential adverse effects and drug–drug interactions.
3. Older adults are more likely dependent on family or third-party caregivers to assist with IADLs.	■ Involvement of caregivers during SCP dissemination may increase compliance with care plan recommendations.
4. Family caregivers, especially older spouses, may have their own health conditions to manage, which adds to the already high level of psychological distress observed among caregivers of cancer patients.	■ Appropriate family support should be identified at the outset and periodically adjusted to accommodate the changing needs of the patient and family.
5. Cultural and racial heterogeneity among older cancer survivors.	■ Provision of culturally competent SCPs that address differences in values, beliefs, and goals of different groups.
6. Poor health literacy and physical impairments among older adults.	■ Larger font size may be required to accommodate increasing presbyopia. ■ Readability must match level of health literacy. ■ Provision of a hard copy to those patients uncomfortable with electronic media.

CoC, Commission on Cancer; IADLs, instrumental activities of daily living; PCP, primary care provider; SCP, survivorship care plan.

Source: Adapted from Refs. (63–66).

CONCLUSION

Our capacity to care for the growing population of older adults with cancer will require a paradigm shift in how care is delivered. In this chapter, we explored different models of care, including oncologist-driven and nononcologist-driven, and evidence regarding their utility in geriatric cancer populations. Finally, we introduce the importance of adapting SCPs to not only meet the unique issues of an older population, but also to act as a potentially critical communication tool to be disseminated among all medical specialists, including PCPs, who are providing care to an older adult with a history of cancer.

TAKE HOME POINTS

1. Older patients constitute an increasingly larger proportion of cancer survivors; by 2022, an estimated 75% of all survivors will be 65 years old or more.
2. The four pillars of cancer survivorship care include surveillance for recurrences or secondary cancers, encouragement of beneficial lifestyle choices, management of long-term sequelae from systemic therapy, and addressing of cancer-related psychosocial distress.
3. Compared with individuals under the age of 65, the care of older cancer survivors requires coordination of survivorship care with management of comorbid chronic conditions.
4. Survivorship care of the older adult may best be delivered in the local community and driven by the PCP in consultation with the medical oncologist.
5. Communication between PCP and oncologist must be fluid, and SCPs can serve as the living document that facilitates ongoing dialogue among the patient-PCP-oncologist triad.
6. Within the scope of survivorship care of older adults, special attention should be directed toward:
   –Polypharmacy
   –Correct attribution of symptoms as cancer or other related
   –Addressing caregiver burden when the primary caregiver is similarly burdened with multiple medical comorbidities

REFERENCES

1. Parry C, Kent EE, Mariotto AB, et al. Cancer survivors: a booming population. *Cancer Epidemiol Biomarkers Prev.* 2011;20(10):1996-2005.
2. Vincent GK, Velkoff VA. *The Next Four Decades: The Older Population in the United States 2010 to 2050.* U.S. Census Bureau Report P25-1138; 2010.
3. Howlander N, Noone AM, Krapcho M, et al. *SEER Cancer Statistics Review, 1975-2009* (Vintage 2009 Populations). Bethesda, MD: National Cancer Institute; 2012.
4. Rowland JH, Bellizzi KM. Cancer survivors and survivorship research: a reflection on today's successes and tomorrow's challenges. *Hematol Oncol Clin North Am.* 2008;22(2):181-200.
5. de Moor JS, Mariotto AB, Parry C, et al. Cancer survivors in the United States: prevalence across the survivorship trajectory and implications for care. *Cancer Epidemiol Biomarkers Prev.* 2013;22(4):561-570.
6. Erikson C, Salsberg E, Forte G, et al. Future supply and demand for oncologists. *J Oncol Pract.* 2007;3(2):79-86.
7. Oeffinger KC, McCabe MS. Models for delivering survivorship care. *J Clin Oncol.* 2006;24(32):5117-5124.
8. Miller R. Implementing a survivorship care plan for patients with breast cancer. *Clin J Oncol Nurs.* 2008;12(3):479-487.
9. Hewitt M, Greenfield S, Stovall E, eds. 2006. *From Cancer Patient to Cancer Survivor: Lost in Transition.* Washington, DC: National Academies Press; 2006.

10. Westfall MY, Overholser L, Zittleman L, Westfall JM. Cancer survivorship for primary care: annotated bibliography. *J Cancer Policy.* 2015;4(1):7-12.
11. Rowland JH, Bellizzi KM. Cancer survivorship issues: life after treatment and implications for an aging population. *J Clin Oncol.* 2014;32(24):2662-2668.
12. Stricker CT, O'Brien M. Implementing the Commission on Cancer standards for survivorship care plans. *Clin J Oncol Nurs.* 2014;18(suppl):15-22.
13. Mayer DK, Birken SA, Chen RC. Avoiding implementation errors in cancer survivorship care plan effectiveness studies. *J Clin Oncol.* 2015;33(31):3528-3530.
14. Oeffinger KC, Hudson MM. Long-term complications following childhood and adolescent cancer: foundations for providing risk-based health care for survivors. *CA Cancer J Clin.* 2004;54(4):208-236.
15. Friedman DL, Meadows AT. Late effects of childhood cancer therapy. *Pediatr Clin North Am.* 2002;49:1083-1106.
16. Overholser LS, Moss KM, Kilbourn K, et al. Development of a primary care-based clinic to support adults with a history of childhood cancer: the TACTIC clinic. *J Pediatr Nurs.* 2015;30(5):724-731.
17. McClellan W, Fulbright JM, Doolittle GC, et al. A collaborative step-wise process to implementing an innovative clinic for adult survivors of childhood cancer. *J Pediatr Nurs.* 2015;30(5):e147-e155.
18. Stange KC, Nutting PA, Miller WA, et al. Defining and measuring the patient-centered medical home. *J Gen Med.* 2010;25(6):601-612.
19. Oeffinger KC, Hudson MM, Landier W. Survivorship: childhood cancer survivors *Prim Care.* 2009;36(4):743-780.
20. Suh E, Daugherty CK, Wroblewski K, et al. General internists' preferences and knowledge about the care of adult survivors of childhood cancer. *Ann Int Med.* 2014;160(1):11-17.
21. Halpern MT, Viswanathan M, Evans TS, et al. Models of cancer survivorship care: overview and summary of current evidence. *J Oncol Pract.* 2015;11(1):e19-e27.
22. Virgo KS, Lerro CC, Klabunde CN, et al. Reply to U. Tirelli et al. *J Clin Oncol.* 2014;32(3):258.
23. Tirelli U, Spina M, Augello AF, et al. Is it better to transfer long-term cancer survivors to general practitioners or develop clinics for long-term survivors within cancer centers? *J Clin Oncol.* 2014;32(3):257.
24. Corcoran S, Dunne M, McCabe MS. The role of advanced practice nurses in cancer survivorship care. *Semin Oncol Nurs.* 2015;31(4):338-347.
25. Jefford M, Rowland J, Grunfeld E, et al. Implementing improved post-treatment care for cancer survivors in England with reflections from Australia, Canada and the USA *Br J Cancer.* 2013;108(1):14-20.
26. Rubin G, Berendsen A, Crawford SM, et al. The expanding role of primary care in cancer control. *Lancet Oncol.* 2015;16(9):1231-1272.
27. Khan NF, Ward A, Watson E, et al. Long-term survivors of adult cancers and uptake of primary health services: a systematic review. *Eur J Cancer.* 2008;44(2) 195-204.
28. Jefford M, Kinnane N, Howell P, et al. Implementing novel models of posttreatment care for cancer survivors: enablers, challenges and recommendations. *Asia Pac J Clin Oncol.* 2015;11(4):319-327.
29. Grant M, De Rossi S, Sussman J. Supporting models to transition breast cancer survivors to primary care: formative evaluation of a Cancer Care Ontario initiative *J Oncol Pract.* 2015;11(3):e288-e295
30. Sisler JJ, Brown JB, Stewart M. Family physicians' roles in cancer care: survey of patients on a provincial cancer registry. *Can Fam Physician.* 2004;50(6):889-896.

31. Oeffinger KC, Argenbright KE, Levitt GA, et al. Models of cancer survivorship health care: moving forward. *Am Soc Clin Oncol Educ Book.* 2014;205-213.

32. Cheung WY, Aziz N, Noone AM, et al. Physician preferences and attitudes regarding different models of cancer survivorship care: a comparison of primary care providers and oncologists. *J Cancer Surviv.* 2013;7(3):343-354.

33. Mariotto AB, Rowland JH, Yabroff KR, et al. Long-term survivors of childhood cancers in the United States. *Cancer Epidemiol Biomarkers Prev.* 2009;18(4):1033-1040.

34. Smith SL, Wai ES, Alexander C, Singh-Carlson S. Caring for survivors of breast cancer: perspective of the primary care physician. *Curr Oncol.* 2011;18(5):e218-e226.

35. Lewis RA, Neal RD, Williams NH, et al. Follow-up of cancer in primary care versus secondary care: systematic review. *Br J Gen Pract.* 2009;59(564):e234-e247.

36. Grunfeld E, Levine MN, Julian JJ, et al. Randomized trial of long-term follow-up for early-stage breast cancer: a comparison of family physician versus specialist care. *J Clin Oncol.* 2006;24(6):848-855.

37. Walter FM, Usher-Smith JA, Yadlapalli S, Watson E. Caring for people living with and beyond cancer: an online survey of GPs in England. *Br J Gen Pract.* 2015;65(640):e761-e768.

38. Roorda C, Berendsen AJ, Haverkamp M, et al. Discharge of breast cancer patients to primary care at the end of hospital follow-up: a cross-sectional survey. *Eur J Cancer.* 2013;49(8);1836-1844.

39. Klabunde CN, Han PKJ, Earle CC, et al. Physician roles in the cancer-related follow-up care of cancer survivors. *Fam Med.* 2013;45(7):463-474.

40. Del Giudice ME, Grunfeld E, Harvey BJ, et al. Primary care physicians' views of routine follow-up care of cancer survivors. *J Clin Oncol.* 2009;27(20):3338-3345.

41. Kantsiper M, McDonald EL, Geller G, et al. Transitioning to breast cancer survivorship: perspectives of patients, cancer specialists and primary care providers. *J Gen Intern Med.* 2009;24(suppl 2):S459-S466.

42. Bober SL, Recklitis CJ, Campbell EG, et al. Caring for cancer survivors. *Cancer.* 2009;115(suppl):4409-4418.

43. Virgo KS, Lerro CC, Klabunde CN, et al. Barriers to breast and colorectal cancer survivorship care: perceptions of primary care physicians and medical oncologists in the United States. *J Clin Oncol.* 2013;31(18):2322-2336.

44. Luctar-Flude M, Aiken A, McColl MA, et al. Are primary care providers implementing evidence-based care for breast cancer survivors? *Can Fam Physician.* 2015;61(11):978-984.

45. Runowicz CD, Leach CR, Henry NL, et al. American Cancer Society/American Society of Clinical Oncology breast cancer survivorship care guideline. *J Clin Oncol.* 2016;34(6):611-635.

46. El-Shami K, Oeffinger KC, Erb NL, et al. American Cancer Society colorectal cancer survivorship care guidelines. *CA Cancer J Clin.* 2015;65(6):428-455.

47. Shapiro CL, Jacobsen PB, Henderson T, et al. ASCO core curriculum for cancer survivorship education. *J Oncol Pract.* 2016;12(2):e108-e117.

48. Jacobs LA, Vaughn DJ. Care of the adult cancer survivor. *Ann Int Med.* 2013;158(11):ITC6/1-ITC6/16.

49. Voorhees PM. Effects of cancer therapy and survivorship. In: Mason BA, Block CC, Hartner L, et al., eds. *ACP MKSAP 17: Hematology and Oncology.* Philadelphia, PA: American College of Physicians; 2015:118-122.

50. Internal medicine residency program. Available at: https://www.mdanderson.org/education-and-research/education-and-training/schools-and-programs/graduate-medical-education/residency-and-fellowship-programs/baylor-college-of-medicine/md-anderson-internal-medicine-residency-program.html. Accessed April 9, 2016.

51. Van Dipten C, Olde Hartman TC, Biermans MCJ, Assenfeldt WJJ. Substitution scenario in follow-up of chronic cancer patients in primary care: prevalence, disease duration and estimated extra consultation time. *Fam Pract.* 2016;33(1):4-9.

52. Lewis RA, Neal RD, Hendry M, et al. Patients' and healthcare professionals' views of cancer follow-up: systematic review. *Br J Gen Pract.* 2009;59(564):e248-e259.

53. Bender JL, Wiljer D, Sawka AM, et al. Thyroid cancer survivors' perceptions of survivorship care follow-up options: a cross-sectional, mixed methods study. *Support Care Cancer.* 2016;24(5):2007-2015.

54. Hudson SV, Miller SM, Hemler J, et al. Adult cancer survivors discuss follow-up in primary care: 'Not what I want, but maybe what I need.' *Ann Fam Med.* 2012;10(5):418-427.

55. Nyarko E, Metz JM, Nguyen GT, et al. Cancer survivors' perspectives on delivery of survivorship care by primary care physicians: an internet-based survey. *BMC Fam Pract.* 2015;16(1):143.

56. DiCicco-Bloom B, Cunningham RS. The experience of information sharing among primary care clinicians with cancer survivors and their oncologists. *J Cancer Surviv.* 2013;7(1):124-130.

57. Hewitt ME, Bamundo A, Day R, Harvey C. Perspectives on post-treatment cancer care: qualitative research with survivors, nurses, and physicians. *J Clin Oncol.* 2007;25(16):2270-2273.

58. Taplin SH, Rodgers AB. Toward improving the quality of cancer care: addressing the interfaces of primary and oncology-related subspecialty care. *J Natl Cancer Inst Monogr.* 2010;2010(40):3-10.

59. Mor Shalom M, Hahn EE, Casillas J, Ganz PA. Do survivorship care plans make a difference? A primary care provider perspective. *J Oncol Pract.* 2011;7(5):314-318.

60. Mayer DK, Gerstel A, Leak AN, Smith SK. Patient and provider preferences for survivorship care plans. *J Oncol Pract.* 2012;8(4):e80-e86.

61. Ezendam NPM, Nicolaije KAH, Kruitwagen RF, et al. Survivorship care plans to inform the primary care physician: results from the ROGY care pragmatic cluster randomized controlled trial. *J Cancer Surviv.* 2014;8(4):595-602.

62. Nicolaije KAH, Ezendam NPM, Vos MC, et al. Impact of an automatically generated cancer survivorship care plan on patient-reported outcomes in routine clinical practice: longitudinal outcomes of a pragmatic, cluster randomized trial. *J Clin Oncol.* 2015;33(31):3550-3559.

63. Leach CR, Weaver KE, Aziz NM, et al. The complex health profile of long-term cancer survivors: prevalence and predictors of comorbid conditions. *J Cancer Surviv.* 2014;9:239-251.

64. Nightingale G, Hajjar E, Swartz K, et al. Evaluation of a pharmacist-led medication assessment used to identify prevalence of and associations with polypharmacy and potentially inappropriate medication use among ambulatory senior adults with cancer. *J Clin Oncol.* 2015;33(13):1453-1459.

65. Farrell B, Shamji S, Monahan A, French Merkley V. Reducing polypharmacy in the elderly: cases to help you "rock the boat." *Can Pharm J (Ott).* 2013;146(5):243-244.

66. Ji J, Zoller B, Sundquist K, Sundquist J. Increased risks of coronary heart disease and stroke among spousal caregivers of cancer patients. *Circulation.* 2012;125:1742-1747.

VIII

Palliative Care

31 Treatment of Cancer Pain in the Elderly

Koshy Alexander and Paul Glare

INTRODUCTION

Pain is a common problem in older cancer patients, estimated to affect 80% of those with advanced disease (1). Although there is evidence for some age-related decline in pain sensitivity, older patients are more vulnerable to severe, persistent pain, and less tolerant of it (2). Pain in the elderly is often undertreated (3), which not only causes treatable discomfort but leads to the development of other symptoms that impair quality of life, such as depression, anxiety, isolation, sleep disturbances, loss of appetite, and impaired functional capacity (4). Identification and optimal management of pain thus become a priority in these patients.

The principles of cancer pain management in the elderly are similar to those used with younger patients, with opioids being the mainstay. However, age-related physiologic changes, comorbidities, and polypharmacy should be taken into account. Narcotic abuse in the elderly is an emerging problem (5).

CLASSIFICATION OF CANCER PAIN

The prevalence of pain varies widely depending upon the type of cancer, from 85% in those with primary bone tumors to only 5% in those with leukemias (6). Cancer pain is not a uniform entity with a single effective treatment, and not all cancer pain is due to the tumor. There are several ways to classify cancer pain (Table 31.1). It is helpful to do so as this may direct the optimal treatment approach. Most cancer pain is chronic, but it can be acute. Unlike most chronic nonmalignant pain, chronic cancer pain worsens as disease progresses. It is also associated with pain flares called *breakthrough pain* (BTP). BTP is associated with both pain-related functional impairment and psychological distress (7).

ASSESSMENT

Optimal pain management in the elderly starts with the assessment. In addition to presence and intensity, characteristics such as quality, temporal features, and aggravating and alleviating factors help identify the etiology. An assessment of pain behaviors,

TABLE 31.1 Classification of Pain in Cancer

Basis	Type		Examples
Etiology	Tumor related		Tumor invasion and spread
	Treatment related		Chemotherapy-induced neuropathy
	Cancer-related debility		Myofascial pain, constipation
	Cancer-unrelated comorbidity		Osteoarthritis, osteoporotic fractures
Duration	Acute	Diagnostic procedures	Bone marrow biopsy
		Therapeutic interventions	Postsurgical, postradiation mucositis
		Cancer-related complications	Pulmonary embolism
	Chronic	Flares/breakthrough pain	
		1. Incident pain	Movement-related bone pain
		2. End of dose failure	Pain at the end of dosing interval of medication
		Sustained	Tumor related
Pathophysiology	Nociceptive 1. Somatic 2. Visceral	Noxious stimulus with intact nervous system	Bone pain, organ-specific pains
	Neuropathic	No noxious stimulus, but damaged nerves	Peripheral neuropathy
	Idiopathic	No noxious stimulus and intact nervous system	Pain where no cause can be identified

pain-related morbidity, coping style, and response to prior treatments should be included (8). Social, cultural, and economic factors may play a key role in adherence to the pain management regimen charted out. Comprehensive evaluation includes a physical examination, review of imaging, and other data, with the objective of confirming the pain etiology suggested by the history, along with medication reconciliation.

Cancer pain evaluation is challenging in older patients when there are concomitant comorbidities, cognitive impairment, frailty, or impaired communication (including mechanical ventilation) (9). Patients with mild to moderate dementia may still be able to report pain, but the ability to self-report pain decreases as dementia progresses (10). Observing specific pain behaviors is advocated in this situation (11). Pain scales should be used in the elderly (Table 31.2).

MANAGEMENT

Cancer pain management shares features with the treatment of nonmalignant pain. Analgesic drugs form the cornerstone of cancer pain management. The World Health Organization's (WHO) three-step analgesic ladder provides an algorithm for using analgesics, with the addition of adjuvant agents when there is a neuropathic component (Table 31.3). There is controversy about the need for the second step, as low doses of strong opioids work as well as weak opioids. In practice, many patients prefer to try weak opioids before escalating to strong opioids. Treatment plans should incorporate nonpharmacologic interventions. These aim to treat the affective, cognitive, behavioral, and sociocultural dimensions of cancer pain. Barriers to pain control include inadequate patient and physician education (3).

Pharmacologic Therapies

NONOPIOID ANALGESICS

Acetaminophen is preferred in older cancer patients, as they are at higher risk of the side effects associated with nonsteroidal anti-inflammatory drugs (NSAIDs). Patients should be counseled not to consume more than 3,000 mg of acetaminophen per day due to potential liver toxicity. If NSAIDs are used, it should only be for short intervals (16), as NSAID-associated side effects (e.g., gastrointestinal bleeding,

TABLE 31.2 A Few Validated Pain Assessment Tools in the Elderly Population

Pain Assessment Checklist for Seniors with Limited Ability to Communicate (PACSLAC) (12)

Pain Assessment in Advanced Dementia (PAINAD) (13)

Rotterdam Elderly Pain Observation Scale (REPOS) (14)

Checklist of Nonverbal Pain Indicators (CNPI) (15)

TABLE 31.3 WHO Analgesic Ladder

Step	Recommendations	Suggested Medications
Step 1—mild pain	Nonopioid ± adjuvant	Acetaminophen, NSAIDs Gabapentin, pregabalin
Step 2—moderate pain	Weak opioid ± nonopioid ± adjuvant	Hydrocodone, tramadol; buprenorphine patch Acetaminophen, NSAIDs Gabapentin, pregabalin
Step 3—severe pain	Strong opioid ± nonopioid ± adjuvant	Morphine, oxycodone, hydromorphone, fentanyl, methadone Acetaminophen, NSAIDs Gabapentin, pregabalin

NSAIDs, nonsteroidal anti-inflammatory drugs; WHO, World Health Organization.

renal toxicity, myocardial infarction, and stroke) are dose and time dependent. A gastro-protective medication such as a proton pump inhibitor should be prescribed alongside (17). Cyclo-oxygenase-2 (COX-2) selective inhibitors may increase the risk of thrombotic cardiovascular adverse reactions and do not protect from renal failure. In essence, NSAIDs and COX-2 inhibitors can provoke severe toxicity reactions such as gastrointestinal bleeding, platelet dysfunction, and renal failure (18). Absolute contraindications to the use of NSAIDs include chronic kidney disease, active peptic ulcer disease, and heart failure.

OPIOIDS

Commonly prescribed weak opioids include codeine, hydrocodone, tramadol, and tapentadol. Propoxyphene is no longer available. Meperidine is not recommended for cancer pain. Strong opioids and their key clinical pharmacologic characteristics are shown in Table 31.4. When initiating therapy with a strong opioid, it is typically recommended to commence an immediate release (IR) formulation administered around the clock. In the literature, morphine is usually posited as the opioid of first choice in treating cancer pain (19), although there is little evidence to support this choice (20). Low starting doses should be considered in the frail elderly and opioid-naïve patients, with additional pro re nata (PRN) dosing. The starting dose is titrated in 50% to 100% increments every 12 to 24 hours until pain is controlled. Once control is achieved, the IR formulation should be converted to a sustained-release formulation. In this conversion, the total 24-hour period dose of opioid should remain intact; the amount per dose will depend on the frequency of administration called for by the

TABLE 31.4 Opioid Medications in Older Patients

Drug	Equian-algesic PO Dose (mg)	PO Start-ing Dose in Elderly (mg)	Equian-algesic IV Dose (mg)	IV Start-ing Dose in Elderly (mg)	Half-life (hrs)	Duration of Action (hrs)	Cautions
Morphine	30	2.5–7.5	10	1.25–2.5	1.5–3	3–7	Renal failure
Oxycodone	20	2.5	-	-	2–4	3–6	Patients with abuse potential
Hydromor-phone	7.5	0.5–1	1.5	0.2	2–3	2–5	Renal failure
Fentanyl*	-	-	0.1	12.5–25 mcg	3–4	1–2	-

IV, intravenous; PO, by mouth.

*Fentanyl is 75–100 times more potent than morphine. In practical terms, 25 mcg/hr fentanyl (transdermal or IV) is approximately equivalent to 1 mg/hr IV morphine.

particular formulation. Rescue doses of IR formulation should be prescribed for the treatment of BTP, calculated at 10% to 15% of the total daily dose and scheduled based on the half-life of the IR medication (21).

Respiratory depression is rarely seen when cancer pain is managed this way. The main opioid-related adverse effects include constipation, sedation, confusion, and nausea. All patients prescribed opioids should be started on a prophylactic bowel regimen that includes a laxative (22), unless the patient has preexisting diarrhea. The development of sedation, confusion, or hallucinations is usually managed with dose reduction or opioid rotation. Other less common opioid-associated adverse effects seen in the older cancer patient include dry mouth, pruritus, urinary retention, and neurotoxicity (myoclonus, hallucinations).

In about 25% of patients, it may be necessary to switch opioids due to the development of dose-limiting adverse effects. When considering opioid rotation, the differences in potency among opioid drugs and the considerable interpatient variability in response to opioids should be taken into account. The estimate of relative potency among opioids has been codified in equianalgesic dose tables (Table 31.3). To reduce the risk of unintentional overdose, a reduction typically of 25% to 50% in the equianalgesic dose should be made (23). In the unlikely event that clinically serious respiratory depression (respiratory rate <8 bpm) were to occur, naloxone may have to be administered, depending on the clinical situation. At Memorial Sloan Kettering Cancer Center (MSKCC), we give dilute naloxone, unless the patient is coding. Paradoxically, patients who are the most tolerant to opioids need the least dose of naloxone. We dilute the contents of one ampule (0.4 mg naloxone in 1 mL normal saline [NS]) into 9 mL NS, and 1 mL of this dilute solution given via intravenous piggyback (IVPB) over 4 to 5 minutes until the respiratory rate improves. The half-life of naloxone is very short and it wears off in minutes, so this treatment may have to be repeated.

Although most cancer pain is managed with oral/transdermal opioids, the intravenous (IV) route will be needed in patients admitted with a pain crisis. A pain/palliative care consult should be called. Patient-controlled analgesia (PCA) can provide the medication as a continuous infusion at a basal rate, with additional demand doses that can be utilized if needed, with lockout periods that are set to prevent overdosing. Options for an unresponsive pain crisis, depending on the overall clinical situation, include IV Toradol, IV Tylenol, dexamethasone, and ketamine. This may even be a case for terminal sedation.

ADJUVANT MEDICATIONS

It remains controversial whether some types of pain are less responsive to opioids than others. Co-analgesics such as anticonvulsants, antidepressants, corticosteroids, and muscle relaxants are well integrated into cancer pain-management strategies. Anticonvulsants and antidepressants are often given in addition to opioids when neuropathic pain is not fully controlled, and may be tried as first-line options for the treatment of pure neuropathic cancer pain.

Gabapentin and pregabalin are safer antiepileptics than older agents such as carbamazepine. They should be renally dosed and escalated slowly, watching for sedation and dizziness. Serotonin–norepinephrine reuptake inhibiting antidepressants (duloxetine (24), venlafaxine (25)) have also been shown to be effective for neuropathic pain. They are better tolerated by the elderly than the tricyclic antidepressants, which have potential for significant anticholinergic side effects and cognitive changes.

Other Interventions

Some patients may continue to have pain that is not relieved by medications or may develop intolerable side effects. In such cases, other management options can be considered.

Radiation Therapy: This reduces pain by shrinking the tumor. A single dose of radiation may be effective for some people. Stereotactic radiosurgery may offer better pain control with fewer treatment toxicities than external beam radiation (26).

Nerve Blocks: Nerve blocks may be helpful depending on the site of the cancer and pain. Celiac and other plexus blocks have about a 75% chance of success (27).

Surgery: When a tumor is pressing on nerves or other body parts, operations to remove all or part of the tumor can relieve pain.

Nonpharmacologic Therapies

Nonpharmacologic therapies are generally classified as physical, cognitive, behavioral, and other complementary methods. Meditation, progressive relaxation, aromatherapy, biofeedback, therapeutic touch, transcutaneous electrical nerve stimulation (TENS), hypnosis, music therapy, acupressure, and cold–hot treatments are noninvasive methods that may have a role in managing cancer pain (28).

CONCLUSION

Good cancer pain management can be challenging in the older patient, but is most likely to be achieved with a multidisciplinary approach using a combination of nonpharmacologic and pharmacologic interventions. After initiation of treatment, patients should be reassessed frequently until the distressing symptom is controlled, while watching for medication side effects. There should be a low threshold for referring difficult-to-manage cases to a pain specialist or palliative care team.

TAKE HOME POINTS

1. Cancer pain is not a uniform entity with a single effective treatment.
2. Acetaminophen is the preferred nonopioid analgesic in older cancer patients.
3. Start opioids at low doses in the frail elderly and opioid-naïve patients.
4. All patients prescribed opioids should be started on a prophylactic bowel regimen.
5. Anticonvulsants and antidepressants may be tried as first-line options for the treatment of pure neuropathic cancer pain.

REFERENCES

1. Rao A, Cohen HJ. Symptom management in the elderly cancer patient: fatigue, pain, and depression. *J Natl Cancer Inst Monogr.* 2004;(32):150-157.
2. Gibson S. Older people's pain. *Pain Clin Updates.* 2006;14(3):1-4.
3. Janjan N. Improving cancer pain control with NCCN guideline-based analgesic administration: a patient-centered outcome. *J Natl Compr Canc Netw.* 2014;12(9):1243-1249.
4. Cabezon-Gutierrez L, Gómez-Pavón J, Pérez-Cajaraville J, et al. Update on oncological pain in the elderly [in Spanish]. *Rev Esp Geriatr Gerontol.* 2015;50(6):289-297.
5. Culberson JW, Ziska M. Prescription drug misuse/abuse in the elderly. *Geriatrics.* 2008;63(9):22-31.
6. Daut RL, Cleeland CS. The prevalence and severity of pain in cancer. *Cancer.* 1982;50(9):1913-1918.
7. Portenoy RK, Payne D, Jacobsen P. Breakthrough pain: characteristics and impact in patients with cancer pain. *Pain.* 1999;81(1-2):129-134.
8. Malec M, Shega JW. Pain management in the elderly. *Med Clin North Am.* 2015;99(2):337-350.
9. Tracy B, Sean Morrison R. Pain management in older adults. *Clin Ther.* 2013;35(11):1659-1668.
10. Herr K, Coyne PJ, Key T, et al. Pain assessment in the nonverbal patient: position statement with clinical practice recommendations. *Pain Manag Nurs.* 2006;7(2):44-52.
11. Gregory J. The complexity of pain assessment in older people. *Nurs Older People.* 2015;27(8):16-21.
12. Fuchs-Lacelle S, Hadjistavropoulos T. Development and preliminary validation of the Pain Assessment Checklist for Seniors with Limited Ability to Communicate (PACSLAC). *Pain Manag Nurs.* 2004;5(1):37-49.
13. Warden V, Hurley AC, Volicer L. Development and psychometric evaluation of the Pain Assessment in Advanced Dementia (PAINAD) scale. *J Am Med Dir Assoc.* 2003;4(1):9-15.
14. van Herk R, van Dijk M, Tibboel D, et al. The Rotterdam Elderly Pain Observation Scale (REPOS): a new behavioral pain scale for non-communicative adults and cognitively impaired elderly persons. *J Pain Manag.* 2009;1(4):367-378.
15. Feldt KS. The checklist of nonverbal pain indicators (CNPI). *Pain Manag Nurs.* 2000;1(1):13-21.
16. Ferrell B, Argoff CE, Epplin J, et al. Pharmacological management of persistent pain in older persons. *J Am Geriatr Soc.* 2009;57:1331-1346.
17. Medlock S, Eslami S, Askari M, et al. Co-prescription of gastroprotective agents and their efficacy in elderly patients taking nonsteroidal anti-inflammatory drugs: a systematic review of observational studies. *Clin Gastroenterol Hepatol.* 2013;11(10):1259-1269.e10.
18. Ripamonti CI, Bandieri E, Roila F. Management of cancer pain: ESMO clinical practice guidelines. *Ann Oncol.* 2011;22(suppl 6):vi69-vi77.
19. Hanks GW, Conno F, Cherny N, et al. Morphine and alternative opioids in cancer pain: the EAPC recommendations. *Br J Cancer.* 2001;84(5):587-593.
20. Caraceni A, Pigni A, Brunelli C. Is oral morphine still the first choice opioid for moderate to severe cancer pain? A systematic review within the European Palliative Care Research Collaborative guidelines project. *Palliat Med.* 2011;25(5):402-409.
21. Makris UE, Abrams RC, Gurland B, Reid MC. Management of persistent pain in the older patient: a clinical review. *JAMA.* 2014;312(8):825-836.

22. Hawley PH, Byeon JJ. A comparison of sennosides-based bowel protocols with and without docusate in hospitalized patients with cancer. *J Palliat Med.* 2008;11(4):575-581.

23. Nalamachu SR. Opioid rotation in clinical practice. *Adv Ther.* 2012;29(10):849-63.

24. Lunn MP, Hughes RA, Wiffen PJ. Duloxetine for treating painful neuropathy, chronic pain or fibromyalgia. *Cochrane Database Syst Rev.* 2014;1:Cd007115.

25. Saarto T, Wiffen PJ. Antidepressants for neuropathic pain. *Cochrane Database Syst Rev.* 2007:(4):Cd005454.

26. Sohn S, Chung CK, Sohn MJ, et al. Stereotactic radiosurgery compared with external radiation therapy as a primary treatment in spine metastasis from renal cell carcinoma: a multicenter, matched-pair study. *J Neurooncol.* 2014;119(1):121-128.

27. Smith TJ, Saiki CB.Cancer pain management. *Mayo Clin Proc.* 2015;90(10): 1428-1439.

28. Singh P, Chaturvedi A. Complementary and alternative medicine in cancer pain management: a systematic review. *Indian J Palliat Care.* 2015;21(1):105-115.

32   Palliation of Nonpain Symptoms

Katherine Wang and Emily Chai

INTRODUCTION

A geriatric patient with cancer may experience symptoms—attributable to malignancy itself or to side effects of treatment—that significantly impact quality of life. Palliative care places priority on eliciting symptoms and offering relief with treatments in line with the patient's overall goals. This chapter addresses some of the most common cancer- and treatment-related symptoms including fatigue, anorexia, constipation, nausea and vomiting, and wound odor.

Symptom management is challenging in the older oncology patient. First, symptomatology associated with preexisting comorbidities increases the complexity of managing cancer- and treatment-related symptoms. Cognitive impairment or acute delirium may also adversely impact a patient's ability to reliably report symptoms. Finally, both polypharmacy and age-related alterations in pharmacokinetics and pharmacodynamics complicate the selection and titration of medications for symptom relief (1).

Adhering to the following core principles of geriatrics will ensure safe and effective management of older oncology patients:

1. Incorporate functional assessment into routine practice. Functional ability is both a key indicator of overall health and an important patient-centered outcome, and can help guide selection of appropriate treatments.
2. Be aware that iatrogenesis, or the unintended effects of medical therapies, is common and often preventable.
3. Start at lower doses when considering medications for symptom relief. Be alert for the potential need to escalate rapidly, depending on the response.
4. Integrate the patient's goals, values, and priorities into decisions about treatment options. Recognize that the risks and benefits of treatment in a geriatric patient may differ from those in a younger patient.
5. Use validated symptom assessment tools such as the Edmonton Symptom Assessment Scale (ESAS) and the Memorial Symptom Assessment Scale (MSAS) to screen for and track symptoms over time (2,3).

FATIGUE

Cancer-related fatigue, present in up to 90% of cancer patients, is common, disabling, undertreated, and inversely related with quality of life (4,5). The National Comprehensive Cancer Network defines *cancer-related fatigue* as a "distressing, persistent, subjective sense of physical, emotional, and/or cognitive tiredness or exhaustion related to cancer or cancer treatment that is not proportional to recent activity and that significantly interferes with usual functioning" (6).

The pathophysiology of cancer-related fatigue is poorly understood but may relate to proinflammatory cytokines, dysfunction of the hypothalamic–pituitary–adrenal axis, or serotonin dysregulation (7,8). Fatigue in geriatric cancer patients may be multifactorial: (a) primary fatigue that is due to the cancer and/or therapy or (b) secondary fatigue that is linked to concurrent syndromes or illnesses (e.g., anemia, fever), medications, insomnia, or depression.

Assessment

Clinicians should screen for fatigue using single-item scale (e.g., "I get tired for no reason") or other tools such as the ESAS, Functional Assessment for Chronic Illness Therapy Fatigue (FACIT-Fatigue), or Brief Fatigue Inventory (9–12). A single-item scale is rapid and validated, but we recommend the ESAS for longitudinal symptom assessment. A thorough workup of secondary causes of fatigue includes labs such as complete blood count (CBC)/iron studies, thyroid-stimulating hormone (TSH), basic chemistry, hepatic function panel, and vitamin B_{12} levels.

Treatment

Consider treating secondary causes of fatigue if consistent with patient's goals. This might include erythropoietin or transfusion for anemia, antidepressants for mood disorders, reducing or rotating medications in the case of polypharmacy, or hormone substitution in the case of hypothyroidism or hypogonadism.

If the aforementioned strategy involves therapies deemed too burdensome for the patient, then focus on treating the symptoms of fatigue. Nonpharmacologic strategies to reduce symptoms of fatigue include education and expectation-setting, exercise, and therapy (cognitive behavioral therapy, individual or group psychotherapy) (13,14). Acupuncture may have some benefit (15). Pharmacologic therapies that have mixed data to support their use are listed in Table 32.1.

TABLE 32.1 Pharmacologic Therapy for Cancer-Related Fatigue

Agent	Evidence	Dosing	Side Effects
Methylphenidate	More effective than placebo in several trials, but not linked with improved quality of life or reduced depression (16,17)	Start at 5 mg daily, titrate to 40 mg daily Dosed in morning and at noon	Loss of appetite, slurred speech, nervousness, cardiac symptoms Avoid in glaucoma, cardiac arrhythmias

(continued)

TABLE 32.1 Pharmacologic Therapy for Cancer-Related Fatigue (*continued*)

Agent	Evidence	Dosing	Side Effects
Modafinil	No benefit over placebo in meta-analysis (16)	Start at 50–100 mg once or twice daily Dosed in morning and at noon	Stomach upset, headache, dizziness, rhinitis, cardiac arrhythmias
Megestrol acetate	Improves appetite, increases activity, and contributes to overall well-being	Start at lowest dose of 160 mg daily, up to 800 mg daily	Hypertension, weight gain, hot flashes, mood swings, GI upset, risk of thromboembolic events
Corticosteroids	Better than placebo at short-term improvements (2 wk) in fatigue and quality of life (18)	Prednisone 7.5–10 mg daily Dexamethasone 1–4 mg daily Methylprednisolone 30 mg daily	Insomnia, mood swings, infection, hyperglycemia
Ginseng	Some benefit seen in small RCT, but requires further study (19)		Many drug interactions including warfarin, aspirin

GI, gastrointestinal; RCT, randomized controlled trials.

ANOREXIA AND CACHEXIA

Anorexia (the loss of appetite) and cachexia (involuntary weight loss associated with decreased muscle mass and adipose tissue) are reported in up to 80% of patients with cancer and cause significant distress for patients and their families (20). Due in part to the hypermetabolic and hypercatabolic state of malignancy, cancer cachexia is a complex syndrome with variable diagnostic criteria that is not fully understood or easily treatable. It often signals advancement of the underlying malignancy and portends a poor prognosis (21,22). Older adults are particularly at risk for anorexia given the higher likelihood of polypharmacy, chronic comorbidities (e.g., chronic kidney disease [CKD], heart failure, chronic obstructive pulmonary disease [COPD]), and age-related changes in taste and smell that may reduce appetite.

Assessment

Clinicians must consider secondary causes of impaired food intake such as nausea, vomiting, constipation, xerostomia, mucositis, candidiasis, hypothyroidism, or hyperthyroidism. Thorough workup should include depression screening and labs such as TSH.

Treatment

If anorexia and cachexia are the result of advanced underlying malignancy, then no therapies have been shown to extend life. Adjusting expectations and providing education will reinforce for patients and families the significance of these symptoms as indicative of the severity of underlying illness. Nonpharmacologic therapies should be encouraged, such as offering favorite foods via small, frequent meals, giving assistance with eating if needed, and reducing polypharmacy.

Pharmacologic therapy has limited proven benefit (18). The two most extensively studied treatments—progestins and corticosteroids—are shown to improve appetite and weight but not to extend life. There is also limited benefit for long-term quality of life (23). If a trial is desired, megestrol acetate is given at the lowest starting dose (160 mg daily). Side effects include edema and increased thromboembolic risk. Of corticosteroids, dexamethasone 2–20 mg daily or prednisone 20–40 mg daily have been studied; given short-lived benefit and high toxicity, we do not recommend steroids if life expectancy is on the order of months to years. Dronabinol and other synthetic cannabinoids, while helpful in stimulating appetite in patients with AIDS, have not demonstrated benefit for cancer-related anorexia and cachexia and are not routinely recommended (24).

CONSTIPATION

Constipation is a common, frustrating complaint among older adults; cancer and related therapies (notably, opioids) increase the likelihood of developing constipation. A cascade of secondary symptoms may result, including anorexia, nausea, vomiting, abdominal pain, delirium, urinary retention or incontinence, and overflow fecal incontinence. The definition of constipation may include decreased frequency or symptoms such as straining, requiring self-disimpaction, or incomplete evacuation.

Assessment

Clinicians should evaluate for reversible secondary causes of constipation: dehydration, decreased dietary fiber, or medications. Consider eliminating common medications that may cause constipation such as antacids, anticholinergics, antidepressants (especially tricyclics), antihistamines, beta-blockers and calcium channel blockers, calcium supplements, diuretics, iron, levodopa, ondansetron, and opioids. Pay particular attention to bowel sounds on abdominal exam. Rectal exam will allow the clinician to assess for fecal impaction, masses, strictures, or rectoceles. If there is concern for bowel obstruction, consider abdominal plain film. Lab work may include CBC, electrolytes, calcium, phosphorus, magnesium, and TSH.

Treatment

Selection of pharmacologic agents depends on side effect profile, route of delivery, and patient preference; there are no widely accepted evidence-based guidelines for the treatment of constipation (25). However, in particular for patients on chronic opiates, a daily bowel regimen is essential for preventing constipation. Table 32.2 outlines various oral and rectal options (27). Dosing does not need to be adjusted for geriatric patients. Fiber and bulk-forming laxatives (e.g., psyllium) should only be used if the patient is mobile and has adequate water intake. There is limited evidence for nonpharmacologic therapies such as massage, exercise, or biofeedback in the management of constipation.

TABLE 32.2 Pharmacologic Therapy for Constipation

	Class	Examples	Advantages	Disadvantages
Oral	Stool softener/ lubricant	Docusate	May be synergistic when used with stimulant	Ineffective as single agent Requires frequent dosing
	Osmotic	Polyethylene glycol, lactulose, magnesium citrate, milk of magnesia	Increases water retention in intestinal lumen	Can cause distention, diarrhea, electrolyte abnormalities Need to be able to ingest large amounts of fluid
	Stimulant	Senna, bisacodyl, cascara, castor oil	Effective for opioid-induced constipation Stimulates peristalsis	Can cause cramping and diarrhea Avoid in bowel obstruction
	Opioid antagonist	Naloxegol	Targeted therapy	Expensive
Rectal	Lubricant suppository	Glycerin	Softens stools, some stimulant properties	None
	Stimulant suppository	Bisacodyl	May be more convenient/rapid than oral laxatives	Can cause cramping/diarrhea
	Enemas	Warm tap water, soapsuds, mineral oil, docusate "mini-enema"	Stimulates defecation reflex from lumen distention	May be irritant to mucosal membrane Soapsuds may cause cramping
		Sodium phosphate (Fleet)		Do not use in geriatric patients, can precipitate electrolyte abnormalities
Other	Opioid antagonist	Methylnaltrexone (26) SQ 0.15 mg/kg every other day	Opioid-induced constipation only Selective peripheral mu-opioid receptor antagonist Up to 80% responded 4 hrs after first dose	Expensive Limited data, focused on those with limited prognoses Thus far only compared with placebo, not first line therapy

SQ, subcutaneous.

NAUSEA AND VOMITING

Nausea and vomiting are common and distressing complaints for older adults with cancer that may lead to anorexia, weight loss, dehydration, and electrolyte abnormalities. Nausea and vomiting may exist in the context of chemotherapy (iatrogenic due to treatment itself or due to anticipatory nausea), or as a result of malignancy itself. Uremia, gastroparesis, metabolic disorders, increased intracranial pressure, medications, and liver capsular stretch are also known to cause nausea and vomiting. The vomiting center receives inputs from four sites, each with associated neurotransmitters (see Figure 32.1) (28). Rational and effective therapy thus depends on identifying the etiology of the vomiting and targeting the appropriate neurotransmitters.

Assessment

A thorough history (duration, frequency, severity, and timing) and exam (for sequelae that should be treated, such as dehydration, or for potentially treatable etiologies, such as gastroparesis or obstruction) are essential. Imaging and procedures may be helpful to assess for or rule out conditions such as obstruction, gastric outlet obstruction, or peptic ulcer.

Treatment

The etiology of nausea and vomiting is often multifactorial and therefore may require a combination of agents for control. See Table 32.3 for recommended pharmacologic therapy, based on presumed etiology. We recommend against the use of scopolamine patch in geriatric patients given the high potential for delirium due to anticholinergic effect. Adjunctive nonpharmacologic therapy might include acupuncture (particular benefit has been seen postoperatively and after chemotherapy) and relaxation/meditation.

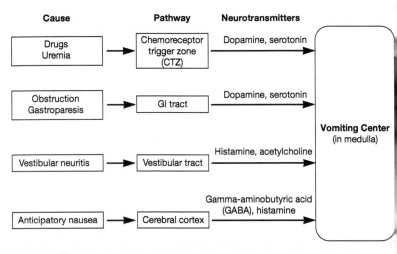

FIGURE 32.1 Neurotransmitters implicated in emetogenic pathways.

TABLE 32.3 Pharmacologic Therapy for Nausea and Vomiting

Class	Example	Mechanism	Side Effects
Antidopaminergic	Metoclopramide, prochlorperazine, promethazine, haloperidol	Block pathways from GI tract and CTZ	Extrapyramidal effects sedation Do not use in bowel obstruction
Serotonin receptor antagonists	Ondansetron granisetron	Block pathways occurring through vagal stimulation, serotonin (5-HT3) receptors in GI tract and CTZ Indicated in chemotherapy-induced nausea	Constipation, headache
Antihistamines	Diphenhydramine, hydroxyzine, meclizine	Uncertain mechanism	Sedation, constipation, delirium, dry mouth
Benzodiazepines	Lorazepam, diazepam, oxazepam	Block pathways via cerebral cortex Indicated in anticipatory nausea	Sedation, delirium, falls/fractures
Cannabinoids	Dronabinol	Uncertain mechanism Indicated with failure of conventional therapies	Tachycardia, hypotension, muscle relaxation, dizziness, depression, paranoia
Corticosteroids	Dexamethasone, methylprednisolone, prednisone	May help via inflammatory mediators, reduce edema Indicated if concurrent bone pain/anorexia	Insomnia, hypertension, weight gain, infection, osteoporosis, lower extremity edema

CTZ, chemoreceptor trigger zone; GI, gastrointestinal.

Source: Adapted from Ref. (28). CAPC: Symptom Management Courses, Nausea and Vomiting [online]. New York: Center to Advance Palliative Care (CAPC); March 29, 2016. Available at: https://www.capc.org/providers/courses/.

WOUND ODOR

Malignant wounds occur when cancerous cells (from a primary lesion or metastasis to the skin) invade the epithelium, thereby interrupting vascularity and causing necrosis to the area. Bacteria colonizing these lesions are prone to releasing odor, causing distress for patients and caregivers and leading to embarrassment, stigma, and social isolation.

Assessment

Evaluate for signs of infection such as pain, purulence, erythema, or surrounding warmth. These findings are not necessarily diagnostic of acute infection and need to be evaluated within the particular clinical context. Similarly, odor may result from byproducts of anaerobic and gram-negative organisms simply colonizing the wound (29).

Treatment

Malignant wounds may not be curable; therefore, treatment options are guided by patients' goals. If appropriate, palliative radiation therapy may be considered; if there is concern for active infection, then systemic treatment may be initiated (e.g., metronidazole 500 mg PO or IV 3–4 times daily). Often, however, palliative treatment involves managing the wound bed and odor with local therapy. Some evidence-based strategies are listed in Table 32.4 (30).

TABLE 32.4 Strategies for Managing Malignant Wounds

Addressing Wound Bed

Debridement of necrotic tissue	Enzymatic or surgical
Absorbent hydrocolloid dressings	Use dressings to control exudate Avoid wet-to-dry dressings as can cause pain/bleeding
Topical metronidazole	Available as gel or tablets (crush and sprinkle over wound) Use 1–2 times daily for up to 2 wk; may be repeated
Silver sulfadiazine or silver-impregnated dressings	Antimicrobial effect
Cadexomer iodine	Available as ointment, powder, impregnated bandages Studied mostly in diabetic and venous stasis ulcers Can cause stinging when applied
Yogurt or buttermilk	Apply for 15 min after wound is cleaned May lower wound pH and thereby control proliferation
Honey	Can be bactericidal

Masking or Absorbing Odor

Scented candle, essential oil, coffee beans, vanilla, cider vinegar	Use with caution as competing scent may be poorly tolerated
Activated charcoal, kitty litter	Place on tray under the bed
Baking soda	May be applied between dressing layers to absorb odor

CONCLUSION

In older cancer patients, cancer and cancer treatment-related symptom management can be very complex. Older adults frequently have preexisting chronic conditions and inability to report symptoms timely and accurately when cognition is impaired. The use of symptom assessment tools can be very helpful and should be included in the evaluation of the patient. There are multiple modalities to help these patients have less distressing symptoms and better quality of life.

TAKE HOME POINTS

1. Consider patient goals and values when weighing risks and benefits of treatments.
2. Employ validated symptom assessment tools when applicable.
3. Assess for the underlying etiology of symptoms to help guide targeted therapy.
4. Recognize that the burden/benefit ratio for treatments is different in an older population.
5. Utilize multiple modalities (including interventional radiology, radiation oncology, and massage) for palliation of cancer and treatment-related symptoms.

REFERENCES

1. Leipzig RM. Geriatric pharmacology and drug prescribing for older adults. In: Soriano RP, Fernandez HM, Cassel CK, Leipzig RM, eds. *Fundamentals of Geriatric Medicine: A Case-Based Approach.* New York, NY: Springer; 2007:39-55.
2. Bruera E, Kuehn N, Miller MJ, et al. The Edmonton Symptom Assessment System (ESAS): a simple method for the assessment of palliative care patients. *J Palliat Care.* 1991;7(2):6-9.
3. Portenoy RK, Thaler HT, Kornblith AB, et al. The Memorial Symptom Assessment Scale: an instrument for the evaluation of symptom prevalence, characteristics and distress. *Eur J Cancer.* 1994;30:1326-1336.
4. Prue G, Rankin J, Allen J, et al. Cancer-related fatigue: a critical appraisal. *Eur J Cancer.* 2006;42(7):846-863.
5. Gupta D, Lis CG, Grutsch JF. The relationship between cancer-related fatigue and patient satisfaction with quality of life in cancer. *J Pain Symptom Manage.* 2007;34(1):40-47.
6. Piper BF, Cella D. Cancer-related fatigue: definitions and clinical subtypes. *J Natl Compr Canc Netw.* 2010;8(8):958-966.
7. Bower JE, Ganz PA, Irwin MR, et al. Cytokine genetic variations and fatigue among patients with breast cancer. *J Clin Oncol.* 2013;31(13):1656-1661.
8. Morrow GR, Andrews PL, Hickok JT, et al. Fatigue associated with cancer and its treatment. *Support Care Cancer.* 2002;10(5):389-398.
9. Kirsh KL, Passik S, Holtsclaw E, et al. I get tired for no reason: a single item screening for cancer-related fatigue. *J Pain Symptom Manage.* 2001;22(5):931-937.
10. Cella D, Lai J-S, Chang CH, et al. Fatigue in cancer patients compared with fatigue in the general United States population. *Cancer.* 2002; 94:528-538.
11. Mendoza TR, Wang XS, Cleeland CS, et al. The rapid assessment of fatigue severity in cancer patients: use of the Brief Fatigue Inventory. *Cancer.* 1999;85(5):1186-1196.

12. Reddy S, Bruera E, Pace E, et al. Clinically important improvement in the intensity of fatigue in patients with advanced cancer. *J Palliat Med.* 2007;10(5):1068-1075.

13. Payne C, Wiffen PJ, Martin S. Interventions for fatigue and weight loss in adults with advanced progressive illness. *Cochrane Database Syst Rev.* 2012;1:CD008427.

14. Mock V. Evidence-based treatment of cancer-related fatigue. *J Natl Cancer Inst Monogr.* 2004;32:112-118.

15. Molassiotis A, Bardy J, Finnegan-John J, et al. Acupuncture for cancer-related fatigue in patients with breast cancer: a pragmatic randomized controlled trial. *J Clin Oncol.* 30(36):4470-4476.

16. Qu D, Zhang Z, Yu X, et al. Psychotropic drugs for the management of cancer-related fatigue: a systematic review and meta-analysis. *Eur J Cancer Care.* 2016;25:970-979.

17. Minton O, Richardson A, Sharpe M, et al. Drug therapy for the management of cancer-related fatigue. *Cochrane Database Syst Rev.* 2010;7:CD006704.

18. Yennurajalingam S, Frisbee-Hume S, Palmer JL, et al. Reduction of cancer-related fatigue with dexamethasone: a double-blind, randomized, placebo-controlled trial in patients with advanced cancer. *J Clin Oncol.* 2013;31(25):3076-3082.

19. Yennurajalingam S, Reddy A, Tannir NM, et al. High-dose Asian ginseng (Panax ginseng) for cancer-related fatigue: a preliminary report. *Integr Cancer Ther.* 2015;14(5):419-427.

20. Wallengren O, Lundholm K, Bosaeus I. Diagnostic criteria of cancer cachexia relation to quality of life, exercise capacity and survival in unselected palliative care patients. *Support Care Cancer.* 2013;21(6):1569-1577.

21. Dewys WD, Begg C, Lavin PT, et al. Prognostic effect of weight loss prior to chemotherapy in cancer patients. *Am J Med.* 1980;69(4):491-497.

22. Martin L, Birdsell L, Macdonald N, et al. Cancer cachexia in the age of obesity: skeletal muscle depletion is a powerful prognostic factor, independent of body mass index. *J Clin Oncol.* 2013;31(12):1539-1547.

23. Yavuzsen T, Davis MP, Walsh D, et al. Systematic review of the treatment of cancer-associated anorexia and weight loss. *J Clin Oncol.* 2005; 23(33):8500-8511.

24. Jatoi A, Windschitl HE, Loprinzi CL, et al. Dronabinol versus megestrol acetate versus combination therapy for cancer-associated anorexia: a North Central Cancer Treatment Group study. *J Clin Oncol.* 2002;20(2):567-573.

25. Candy B, Jones L, Larkin PJ, et al. Laxatives for the management of constipation in people receiving palliative care. *Cochrane Database Syst Rev.* 2015;5:CD003448.

26. Bull J, Wellman CV, Israel RJ, et al. Fixed-dose subcutaneous methylnaltrexone in patients with advanced illness and opioid-induced constipation: results of a randomized, placebo-controlled study and open-label extension. *J Palliat Med.* 2015;18(7):593-600.

27. Chai E, Meier D, Morris J, eds. Table 45.2 Constipation: pharmacologic treatment guidelines. *Palliative Care.* Oxford: Oxford University Press; 2014:239-243.

28. CAPC. Symptom Management Courses, Nausea and Vomiting [online]. New York: Center to Advance Palliative Care (CAPC); March 29, 2016. Available at: https://www.capc.org/providers/courses/.

29. PCNOW. Fast Fact #218 Managing wound odor [online]. March 29, 2016. Available at: http://www.mypcnow.org/#!blank/jigxu.

30. O'Brien C. Malignant wounds: managing odour. *Can Fam Physician.* March 2012; 58(3):272-274.

Advance Care Planning

Anca Dinescu

DEFINITION AND RELEVANCE

Advance care planning (ACP) is defined as the process in which individuals discuss and anticipate how their condition or poor health may affect them in the future and, if they wish, negotiate their preferences for future care plans (1,2). ACP may encompass clinical, emotional, cultural, spiritual, and legal aspects. ACP invites ongoing conversation with the elderly oncologic patient about treatment preferences in the event of worsening illness, even if death is not imminent. ACP also helps providers continue to "hear the patient's voice" even after the patient has lost capacity to articulate his or her health care preferences.

The Elderly Oncology Patient

ACP for the geriatric patient afflicted by cancer is specially challenging.

- There is greater variability in functional and cognitive status, with a tendency toward increased dependence on family for the execution of the agreed-upon plan of care (i.e., hospital discharge, the logistics of going through chemotherapy, hemodialysis, etc.).
- There is higher prevalence of sensory impairments that may affect the quality of the ACP discussion.
- The presence of multiple health providers involved in care, due to multiple medical conditions, makes the dissemination and integration of the ACP into the plan of care more difficult.
- There is a lack of available health care decision-making surrogates and high prevalence of guardians secondary to few or absent family members in this age group.
- There is a relative lack of evidence indicating whether a certain medical procedure/ treatment would be clearly beneficial for the elderly patient, as many randomized controlled trials exclude older adults.

IMPORTANCE, MYTH, AND BARRIERS

Most practitioners agree that discussing ACP with their patients is important. In addition, data show that patients are interested in engaging in ACP discussions with their providers (2). Nonetheless, these conversations are perceived as uncomfortable and challenging.

Myth of Possible Harm

In the past, practitioners expressed concern that discussing ACP with the patient might create anxiety or depression and induce a loss of hope. Subsequent studies have not supported these beliefs (3–7). Most report that patients and families desire open and realistic dialogue about therapeutic options and prognosis. *ACP discussions should be guided by the universal rule of informed consent and the patient's desire for information* (2). The role of the practitioner is to ask patients about their wish to know information, and to offer the framework and opportunity for ACP.

Barriers

On the provider side, lack of time, lack of formal training, and ultimately lack of knowledge about what should be included in ACP add to the lack of communication and procedural skills to routinely address ACP. Physicians also may feel insecure about the legal implications of ACP documentation and how to interpret preexisting documents. Providers' fear of stirring up difficult emotions (8,9) or straining the patient-provider relationship (10) is met at times by patient and family ambivalence and reticence about discussing ACP (11). Lack of reliable prognostication models and lack of data to compare treatment efficacies in elderly represent disease-specific barriers. *System barriers* include lack of clear standardization of ACP content, confusion among multiple forms of ACP documentation, still-difficult electronic medical records (EMR) repositories for ACP documents, and poor of reimbursement of clinician time (12). The recent change in Medicare payment incorporates reimbursement for ACP in the "Welcome to Medicare" visit in an attempt to rectify this last barrier, but does not cover any ongoing or future discussions. The generalization of EMR addressed the ease of retrieval of completed ACP as compared to a paper chart, but the lack of a designated place inside the EMR still makes it difficult to retrieve advance care plans that are embedded in the progress notes.

THE COMPONENTS OF ACP

There is no standardization of what is expected to be covered during ACP discussions or how to approach the ACP discussion by any professional or quality entity. There are, however, expert opinion and best practices, in the form of checklists or conversation guides.

Making capacity assessment a first step in ACP with the elderly patient is necessary, as cognitive impairment is common and widely unrecognized or underappreciated. Moreover, some types of cancers and cancer treatments are highly associated with worsening cognitive impairment that might impede capacity in some patients. Capacity is a clinical determination, available to every practitioner. Capacity encompasses one's ability to comprehend the presented information; to weigh proposed benefits, risks, and alternatives; to make a decision; to integrate personal preferences and to consistently communicate that decision.

ACP discussions may include the following topics:

1. *Identification of a surrogate decision maker*. Documenting a health care agent or proxy (HCP) or the next of kin (NOK) is a key component of ACP so that in

the event of loss of capacity to make health care decisions, a proxy voice may be easily identified.

2. *Life-long values* and preferences for health care are a frequently overlooked and underrated part of the ACP. The description of values and preferences may guide future unanticipated decisions in the event the patients are too ill to speak for themselves.

3. Understanding what is important to the patients, what makes them happy, what worries them, what guides their decisions in life, what they enjoy doing and who their support is will help practitioners and surrogates to honor the patients' preferences even when they lack capacity to communicate these preferences. *The Magic Questions* (13) is a simple approach to eliciting patients' values (see Table 33.1).

4. Identification of *patient preferences for the traditional areas of concern* in medical care. The words *areas of concern* refer to three big categories of interventions:

   - *Complex therapies* such as dialysis, chemotherapy, extensive surgeries, and so on.
   - *Life-supporting treatments* that have been addressed in past judicial/legal proceedings and are sanctioned by law in some states (intravenous [IV] hydration and nutrition, code status).
   - Interventions and issues that often arise in advanced and serious illness (e.g., prolonged respiratory support, artificial feeding, rehospitalizations, transition to nursing home, and hospice).

Patient preferences in these areas of concern are shaped not only by medical knowledge, but also by social, spiritual, and cultural beliefs and practices. For example, the discussion regarding the use of artificial nutrition for an elderly patient with advanced neurocognitive impairment or end-stage cancer should include an exploration of the cultural, spiritual, and practical beliefs of the patient and/or family in addition to medical citation of risks and benefits.

SYSTEMATIC APPROACH TO ACP

Approach—Overarching Principles

■ ACP is a two-way street. Practitioners should elicit information about patient preferences, but they should also provide education about health care systems, levels of care (long-term care, hospice), the importance of a HCP, and so on as part of the ACP.

TABLE 33.1 Magic Questions Script for Eliciting Lifelong Values During ACP

It helps me to be a better doctor for you when I know about you as a person.

1. Tell me about yourself (your loved one).
2. What makes you (or your loved one) happy these days?
3. What worries you (or your loved one) for the future?

ACP, advance care planning.

- The code status or the better-known part of it, the DNR (do not resuscitate) order, does not and should not represent the main focus of ACP. At times practitioners restrict the conversation about care preferences to this potentially life-saving procedure used in case of cardiac arrest. No study to date has identified code status or DNR as the center of patient interest about medical care. As outlined earlier, data show that patients are interested in discussing with their provider a plan that would rather realistically incorporate lifelong values and preferences. Moreover, patient normal and anticipated death should not be confounded with an unexpected cardiac arrest; a code procedure at that time is generally regarded as poor-quality care and an undignified death. ACP is a stepwise process that unfolds over time.
- Early initiation of ACP discussion after serious illness diagnosis is associated with better overall outcomes, without harmful effects, and potential cost saving.
- ACP may not be finalized in a single visit. ACP can be refined over time as the patient interacts with the medical system or life-changing experiences occur.

Timing

Discussing ACP outside the setting of a serious illness has little evidence of relevance in most of the cases (12,14,15). There is no current evidence-based agreement, but rather expert recommendations, on the "perfect time" to start ACP (1):

1. **Early after diagnosis of a serious illness such as cancer**
   This approach tends to occur mainly in the outpatient setting. It takes into consideration the patient's psychological state and comfort level, and emphasizes the benefits of rational, timely planning as opposed to planning in a time of crisis. It also allows for meaningful inclusion of the surrogate in the ACP.
2. **Following a trigger event (such a hospitalization, recurrence, relapse, etc.)**
   ACP usually occurs in the inpatient setting, recognizing that a significant transition has occurred and focusing on identifying a specific plan needed in the moment. It allows little psychological adjustment time, it reflects the patient's voice less well and it is executed many times by the surrogate.

Who Should Do It?

There are various expert opinions regarding who is the most qualified practitioner to discuss ACP.

- Discussing ACP with the *primary care physician* in the setting of a cancer diagnosis takes advantage of the familiarity of a longstanding relationship between patient and practitioner, but might suffer from lack of expert information about cancer trajectory, prognosis, treatment options, and their implications for overall patient quality of life.
- ACP performed by the *oncologist* carries the benefit of specialist information but might lack the longstanding relationship. Nonetheless, some patients battle cancer for a long time, so the oncologist may develop a very close relationship with the patient.

■ Discussing ACP with *palliative care or geriatrics specialists* carries the benefit of these experts' ability to explore medical and nonmedical issues and also their expertise in level of care, services at the end of life, and eventual transition to hospice. The palliative care/geriatrics specialist might lack the familiarity of the long relationship with the patient.

Existing data suggest that optimal care occurs when one practitioner will assume the primary responsibility for addressing, documenting, and communicating the ACP discussions and conclusions to the rest of the team (16). Best outcomes are also dependent on that practitioner having the most training to conduct sensitive, effective discussions in the of end-of-life area (7).

Documenting ACP

See Table 33.2 for documentation options.

TABLE 33.2 Types of Advanced Care Planning

Advance Directive Document	Description	Advantages	Disadvantages
Living Will	The oldest form to document patient preferences Usually drafted by a lawyer	Serves as basic documentation of patient preference Is portable Represents "patient voice" Can be updated	Documents "standard" procedures only (i.e., intubation, code status, feeding tube, etc.) without the larger, expert-guided, comprehensive discussion Usually groups together decisions about property and money with medical decisions, undercutting the importance of medical decisions May not be available Requires interpretation; is not actionable immediately
Out-of-hospital DNR orders	State-specific document that states patient code status/DNR outside the hospital	Serves as documentation of the desired approach in case of cardiac arrest at home or in the ambulance Are portable	Extremely limited perspective on actual patient preferences in the setting of serious illness

(continued)

TABLE 33.2 Types of Advanced Care Planning (*continued*)

Advance Directive Document	Description	Advantages	Disadvantages
Orders for Life-Supporting Therapies	A state- or county-dependent set of orders designed to document patient preferences for medical interventions at the end of life (different names from state to state: POLST, MOLST)	There are actual actionable medical orders They are completed by medical providers, after a broader discussion with the patient about medical intervention at the end of life Represent "patient voice" Are portable Can be updated	Need to be approved by state/county legislature and then adopted by hospitals via policy Do not provide insight about other common concerns in the setting of serious illness (e.g., nursing home, rehospitalization)

DNR, do-not-resuscitate; MOLST, medical orders for life-sustaining treatment; POLST, physician orders for life-sustaining treatment.

TAKE HOME POINTS

1. ACP is a stepwise process that unfolds over time and can be refined and updated.
2. The educational aspect of ACP is crucial and frequently overlooked by practitioners.
3. ACP discussion should start early.
4. Selecting one practitioner with the best set of communication skills and ability to conduct effective discussions about the end of life is crucial.
5. Capacity assessment should be the first step in discussing ACP with the elderly patient.
6. A complete ACP discussion should address the following: identification of surrogate, elicitation of life long values, and preferences for frequent areas of concern at the end of life.
7. Code status or obtaining a DNR should not be the main focus of ACP.

REFERENCES

1. Lund S, Richardson A, May C. Barriers to advance care planning at the end of life: an explanatory systematic review of implementation studies. *PLOS ONE*.2015;10(2):e0116629. Open Access February 13, 2015.
2. Parry R, Land V, Seymour J. How to communicate with patients about future illness progression and end of life: a systematic review. *BMJ Support Palliat Care* 2014;4:331-341.

3. Bernacki RE, Block S. Communication about serious illness care goals: a review and synthesis of best practices. *JAMA Intern Med.* December 2014;174(12):1994-2003. doi:10.1001/jamainternmed.2014.5271.

4. Mack JW, Cronin A, Taback N, et al. End-of-life care discussions among patients with advanced cancer: a cohort study. *Ann Intern Med.* 2012;156(3):204-210.

5. Detering KM. The impact of advance care planning on end of life care in elderly patients: randomised controlled trial. *BMJ.* 2010;340:C1345.

6. Emanuele J. Talking with terminally ill patients and their caregivers about death, dying, and bereavement: is it stressful? Is it helpful? *Arch Intern Med.* 2014;164(18):1999-2004.

7. Clayton JM. Sustaining hope when communicating with terminally ill patients and their families: a systematic review. *Psychooncology.* 2008;17(7):641-659.

8. Keating NL. Physician factors associated with discussions about end-of-life care. *Cancer.* 2010;116(4):998-1006.

9. Jones L. Advance care planning in advanced cancer: can it be achieved? An exploratory randomized patient preference trial of a care planning discussion. *Palliat Support Care.* 2011;9(1):3-13.

10. Yeh JC. May 2014, American Society of Clinical Oncology. Available at: JOP .ascopubs.org. Accessed February 2016.

11. Almack K. After you: conversations between patients and healthcare professionals in planning for end of life care. *BMC Palliat Care.* 2012;11:15.

12. Lum HD. Advance care planning in the elderly *Med Clin North Am.* 2015;99:391-403.

13. http://www.cherp.research.va.gov/promise/PROMISESummer2013Newsletter.pdf. Accessed February 2016.

14. Schneiderman LJ. Effects of offering advance directives on medical treatments and costs. *Ann Intern Med.* 1992;117(7):599-606.

15. Silveira MJ. Advance directives and outcomes of surrogate decision making before death. *N Engl J Med.* 2010;362(13):1211-1218.

16. Back AL. Abandonment at the end of life from patient, caregiver, nurse, and physician perspectives: loss of continuity and lack of closure. *Arch Intern Med.* 2009;169(5):474-479.

IX   Integrative Medicine

34   Exercise for the Older Adult

Donna J. Wilson

In our present-day society, people are growing older and living longer. It is expected that by the year 2030, 70 million Americans will be over the age of 65. Despite research that has demonstrated the importance of physical activity for maintaining good health, only a small percentage of older adults exercise. Muscular strength and endurance, balance, flexibility, bone density, and (most importantly) cardiovascular and pulmonary functions all begin to steadily decline after age 65. Alarmingly, rates of obesity in this age group also continue to rise (1). It has been demonstrated that the overweight cancer survivor has poor physical function; thus, symptoms from treatment are more severe (2). As the inability to perform activities of daily living (ADLs) increases, illness becomes a predominant theme in the lives of this population (3).

Sarcopenia, an age-related condition, causes loss of skeletal muscle mass and muscle atrophy. Eventually, it can lead to lifelong physical problems. As early as the age of 50, muscle mass begins to decrease by 0.5% to 1% each year, and accelerates significantly with each passing decade (4).

The decrease in muscular strength and mobility has potentially profound implications as overall weakness sets in and one gradually becomes more susceptible to falls and fractures. Aging combined with cancer treatment often hastens the decline in physical function and performance. Studies have shown that exercise can enhance physical function, alleviate the side effects of treatment, and improve the overall quality of life in the older adult with cancer (5,6), but not enough is being done to motivate this population to exercise. This must become a priority of health professionals. Practitioners need to get the message out to older adults with cancer that the benefits of exercise can help them maintain their quality of life. And the best news of all: it is never too late to start exercising.

As with every age group, a patient's exercise level can vary from individual to individual. It is also important to remember that medical conditions common in the older adult (arthritis, diabetes, heart disease, pulmonary insufficiency, muscular atrophy, neuromuscular dysfunction, orthopedic limitations, and cerebral atrophy) may limit exercise performance. To ensure safety, the practitioner must review patients' medical history and test their functional capacity. The 6-minute walk test is a simple and practical measure of functional capacity (7). The patient is asked to walk for 6 minutes (at a natural pace) and the distance walked is measured. Prior to beginning the test, heart rate (HR), oxygen saturation, level of perceived exertion, and/or dyspnea (shortness of breath) index are measured and recorded. During the walk, the patient's oxygen saturation and HR are monitored. While walking, the patient rates the level of dyspnea on a scale from 0 to 10 (0 = none and 10 = severe). This is called the *dyspnea index scale*. At the end of the walk, measurements are recorded again (Table 34.1). This test is done at baseline, during treatment, and after treatment to evaluate exercise response. The distance walked is correlated to the patient's physical functioning in daily living. The importance of the 6-minute walk test is twofold. It demonstrates a patient's improvement in stamina, endurance, and strength, and it can be used as a motivational tool to encourage compliance (8,9).

There are numerous mental and physical health benefits of exercise for the older adult with cancer (10). First, it is more important than ever for overall health and longevity. Exercise and physical activity can decrease fatigue; boost energy; improve flexibility, mobility, and balance; build muscular strength; decrease anxiety; and improve some depressive disorders. Physical activity can also sharpen patients' cognitive function and enable them to sustain their independence (11) (Table 34.2).

People who exercise also have lowered risk of several chronic conditions, including Alzheimer disease, diabetes, obesity, heart disease, osteoporosis, and lowers the risk for several cancers. Before setting up a program for the older adult, a practitioner should refer to the American College of Sports Medicine (ACSM) and American Cancer Society (ACS) for guidelines. A 2010 ASCM roundtable developed the exercise guidelines for cancer survivors from research studies that were done on the safety and efficacy of exercise for this population (10,12,13). All of the research demonstrated that when it comes to exercise, the benefits outweigh the risks. A program for older adults

TABLE 34.1 6-Minute Walk Test

1. Equipment—stopwatch, oximeter, worksheet to record laps, chair
2. Walking area 100-ft segments of straight unimpeded hallway
3. Prior to test, record: HR, RR, oxygen saturation, dyspnea index
4. Patients walks as far as possible for 6 min
5. At the end of 6 min, record: HR, RR, oxygen saturation, dyspnea index, distance walked

HR, heart rate; RR, respiration rate.

TABLE 34.2 Mental and Physical Health Benefits of Exercise for the Older Person With Cancer

1. Decrease fatigue
2. Boost energy
3. Build muscular strength
4. Decrease anxiety
5. Improve some depressive disorders
6. Sharpen cognitive function
7. Enable maintenance of patient's independence

with cancer should include (a) cardiorespiratory aerobic conditioning, (b) resistance exercises to build muscular strength and endurance, and (c) flexibility training and neuromotor regimen to improve posture, gait, and balance. The exercise program should take into consideration whether the patient is still in treatment and his or her level of physical activity.

CARDIO-RESPIRATORY CONDITIONING

The ACSM and ACS recommendations for the older adult advise beginning aerobic exercise at a low to moderate intensity 150 minutes a week (20–30 minutes 3–5 times a week). It is acceptable to do one long session and multiple shorter sessions. Aerobic exercises include swimming, walking, riding a stationary bike, low-impact dance, and seated-chair aerobics (with a warmup/cooldown). To optimize adherence and decrease injury risk, aerobic activity should start slowly and gradually progress in time, frequency, and intensity. Inform patients that all activity is beneficial, even if one starts with only 5-minute intervals, two times a day. Instruct patients to use a perceived exertion scale from 0 to 10 to monitor their activity level. On a 10-point scale, 0 to 1 is sitting and 9 to 10 is working as hard as they can (meaning unable to talk, and a sign to stop and rest). Moderate activity is a range from 5 to 6. During moderate activity, patients will breathe harder and their hearts will beat faster, but they can still talk. Vigorous activity is 7 to 8 on the scale; at this level, the patient can only speak in one-word answers. At the 7 to 8 range, have patients slow down and/or stop and let them catch their breath. The United States Department of Health and Human Services physical activity guidelines suggest that the older adult should follow the adult guidelines. The types of activities should focus on aerobics, muscle strengthening, and balance. The type of aerobic activity should be moderate intensity, meaning the patient can still talk, for 150 minutes each week. Muscle strengthening is suggested two times a week and balance three times a week. If this is not possible due to a chronic condition (like cancer), older adults should try to avoid inactivity and be as physically active as their abilities allow (14).

RESISTANCE STRENGTH TRAINING

A general reduction in muscle mass occurs in the normal aging process. This process is accelerated during cancer treatment due to atrophy from disuse. This can have life-changing repercussions, because muscular strength loss often leads to poor mobility and an increase in falls.

Resistance training utilizes concentric and eccentric movements, which are preferred over isometric exercises. Isometric exercises may increase blood pressure and therefore are not always appropriate for the older adult.

Strengthening exercises should focus on the muscle groups that are necessary to perform ADLs. Exercises for the lower body will help improve strength, endurance, and balance. This means patients can get up out of a chair, walk more easily, and climb stairs with less difficulty. Exercises for the upper body will strengthen muscles so one may lift and carry packages. Movements to strengthen the hands and fingers will enable one to open doors, dress without help (button, zip, and snap), and prepare meals.

Exercise intensity is progressive resistance for strength development. There are many ways to strengthen muscles by using dumbbell weights, resistance bands, yoga, or strenuous gardening. In resistance exercises, one pushes against one's own weight to increase strength (e.g., squats and wall push-ups). Muscular endurance can be measured as the number of repetitions of a certain weight. When one can perform three sets of 10 repetitions comfortably, the weight can be increased. It is important to adhere to proper form and progress through the exercises slowly.

Exercise speed entails slow lifting and is safer and more effective than fast movements. A slower training speed involves less momentum and places significantly less stress on joints. It takes about 2 seconds to lift a weight and 4 seconds to lower it while utilizing the full range of joint movement. Increasing repetitions and dumbbell weight should always be a gradual progression.

After training two to three times per week, older adults will experience excellent strength gains and (sometimes) a modest increase in muscle size. The benefits of resistance training include stronger muscles, improved balance, increased stamina and bone density, and reduced blood pressure. Thus, exercise can reduce the incidence and severity of falls.

Most of the research on strength training for cancer patients has been done after cancer treatment, and has reported positive results (15). This evidence supports strength training for all cancer survivors, especially patients with breast and prostate cancers (16). Research has demonstrated that breast cancer patients with lymphedema reduced their symptoms through strength training (17). Resistance training is also encouraged for prostate cancer survivors. These men receive androgen deprivation therapy (to lower testosterone levels) which is associated with a decrease in muscle mass and muscle strength (18). Patients with head and neck cancer may develop shoulder dysfunction that can be addressed through strength training (19).

BALANCE, FLEXIBILITY, AND POSTURE

Balance, a physical performance variable, often declines in the older adult. Multiple factors contribute to poor balance, such as visual disturbances, cognitive impairment, muscular weakness in the legs (especially the quadriceps), limited joint range of motion, limited limb function, and peripheral neuropathy. Programs that include flexibility and strengthening exercises (tai chi, chair aerobics, dancing, walking) have been shown to improve balance.

But why is flexibility lost as we grow older? This is due to connective tissue stiffening and a decrease in mobility. The muscles shorten and contract, the connective tissue weakens, joints stiffen, and range of motion is limited. These effect changes in posture, balance, and gait that are often observed in the older adult and further complicated by a cancer diagnosis.

To prevent muscular imbalances that can lead to falls, this patient population needs to perform stretching exercises regularly to prevent declines in flexibility and range of motion. One of the keys to exercise is maintaining proper form and progressing slowly.

Adherence

Exercise adherence for the older adult with cancer is a subject without easy answers. Many older adults are sedentary. A diagnosis of cancer in someone who is already inactive can further erode that person's motivation to exercise. A study involving a 12-month exercise program followed noncancer-patient sedentary women aged 60 to 85. Results of this study showed that the best predictors of adherence were participant improvements in muscular strength, reasoning ability, and decreased depression (20).

Exercise is safe during and after treatment for the older cancer survivor. Some of the benefits are improvements in aerobic fitness, muscular strength, energy level, and quality of life.

So, how do we "inspire" older adults who often express little interest in physical activity (Table 34.3)? First, we need to understand that many older adults have no past experience with exercise. Also, family members do not always encourage them to pursue it. Some older adults are afraid of injuring themselves or fear that their medical conditions make them poor candidates for exercise programs. Others simply do not know where to go to exercise and lack the transportation options to get there. The Agency on Healthcare Research and Quality (AHRQ) provides several solutions to these stumbling blocks. AHRQ suggests providing exercise education, identifying the available local resources, offering a range of activities, and building a network of social support; doctor recommendations are also influential (21). Because older patients often respect their doctors' advice and have regular contact with them, physicians can play a pivotal role in the initiation and maintenance of exercise behavior within this population. An exercise prescription for an older adult at the time of a cancer diagnosis can include the following easy home program:

Home Exercise Program

10 to 20 minutes daily walking program
Arm circles for flexibility—5 circles each arm
Chair squats for lower body strengthening—5 repetitions

TABLE 34.3 Strategies to Improve Adherence to Exercise in the Older Adult

Exercise education

Identification of local resources

Offering a range of activities

Health professionals provide an exercise prescription and follow-up

Have patient chart his or her progress and bring chart to next office visit

Suggest: walking with a buddy or while listening to music, or get a personal trainer

Designing a Program

When designing an exercise program for older cancer survivors, use visceral language to describe the class. For instance, "Keep Moving." At the initial patient visit, identify treatment-related problems, the activity level prior to cancer treatment, and posttreatment impediments (like balance). Then, set goals and make it fun. To keep the patient motivated, try to thread the new activity into part of his or her usual routine. Start slowly and organize the program around treatment days (if treatment is still ongoing). Keep a log to record progress and patterns of exercise related to treatments. Track patients' progress for biofeedback and note how exercise affects their overall state of health (mind, body, and spirit). Encourage each individual to work at his or her own pace and stay within the comfort zone.

Designing a class format will vary depending on the group, the environment, and the goals of the program. The class should have a ballet bar for balance, chairs, weights or dumbbells, and/or elastic bands. The class can begin with participants sitting in chairs doing breathing exercises and warm-up static and mobilization stretches. This is followed by 10 to 15 minutes of walking aerobics using music and movement patterns. Afterwards, participants return to their chairs for major muscle strengthening. Observe each participant's posture and make sure everyone is using proper breathing methods (contracting abdominal muscles with each exhalation). Breathing exercises are coordinated with each exercise. Breathing out is performed each time a weight is lifted. Make sure that no one is holding the breath when lifting weights. Encourage participants to demonstrate proper form and body alignment throughout all aspects of the exercise program (weight training, joint range of motion, and stretching movements). Keep the intensity low to moderate and continuously monitor that each participant is exercising in a safe and deliberate manner.

CONCLUSION

Although the exercise prescription and goals may vary depending on the cancer diagnosis and treatment side effects, most physical activity is safe and effective for cancer survivors. The psychological and physical benefits of exercise for cancer survivors can decrease fatigue, pain, anxiety/depression, and improve flexibility, muscular and bone strength, and overall quality of life. The benefits of exercise are outstanding: it combats chronic illness, weight management, promotes better sleep, improves sex life, and boosts energy. It is time for all health professionals to prescribe exercise as part of the patient's treatment plan. This will motivate patient's to move thus improve their quality of life. There is extensive research demonstrating the benefits of physical activity. The benefits outweigh the risk. *Exercise is medicine.*

TAKE HOME POINTS

1. Physical activity is safe and beneficial for the older cancer survivor.
2. Avoiding inactivity will maintain independence.
3. Exercise can inhibit or delay the risk of recurrence.

REFERENCES

1. Ligibel JA, Alfano CM, Courneya KS, et al. American Society of Oncology position statement on obesity and cancer. *J Clin Oncol.* 2014;32(31):3568-3574.
2. Kenzik KM, Morey MC, Cohen HJ, et al. Symptoms, weight loss, and physical function in a lifestyle intervention study of older cancer survivors. *J Geriatr Oncol.* 2015;6(6):424-432.
3. Vermeulen J, Neyens JC, van Rossum E, et al. Predicting ADL disability in community-dwelling elderly people using physical frailty indicators: a systematic review. *BMC Geriatr.* 2011;11:33.
4. American College of Sports Medicine, Chodzko-Zajko WJ, Proctor DN, et al. American College of Sports Medicine Position Stand: Exercise and physical activity for older adults. *Med Sci Sports Exerc.* July 2009;41(7):1510-1530.
5. Drouin J. Exercise in older individuals with cancer. *Top Geriatr Rehabil.* 2004;20(2): 81-97.
6. Morey MC, Snyder DC, Sloane R, et al. Effects of home-based diet and exercise on functional outcomes among older, overweight long-term cancer survivors: RENEW: a randomized controlled trial. *JAMA.* 2009;301:1883-1891.
7. ATS Committee on Proficiency Standards for Clinical Pulmonary Function Laboratories. ATS statement: guidelines for the six-minute walk test. *Am J Respir Crit Care Med.* 2002;166(1):111-117.
8. Wilson DJ. Preoperative pulmonary rehabilitation. *Semin Cardiothoracic Vascular Anesth.* 1997;1(3):208-214.
9. Jones LW, Eves ND, Mackey JR, et al. Safety and feasibility of cardiopulmonary exercise testing in patients with advanced cancer. *Lung Cancer.* 2007;55(2):225-232.
10. Schmitz KH, Courneya KS, Matthews C, et al. American College of Sports Medicine roundtable on exercise guidelines for cancer survivors. *Med Sci Sports Exerc.* 2010;42(7):1409-1426.
11. Smith PJ, Blumenthal JA, Hoffman BM, et al. Aerobic exercise and neurocognitive performance: a meta-analytic review of randomized controlled trials. *Psychosom Med.* 2010;72(3):239-252.
12. Irwin ML, ed. *ACSM'S Guide to Exercise and Cancer Survivorship.* American College of Sports Medicine; 2012.
13. Garber CE, Blissmer B, Deschenes MR, et al. Quantity and quality of exercise for developing and maintaining cardiorespiratory, musculoskeletal, and neuromotor fitness in apparently healthy adults: guidance for prescribing exercise. *Med Sci Sports Exerc.* 2011;48(7):1334-1359.
14. U.S. Department of Health and Human Services. *Physical Activity Guidelines for Americans.* Washington, DC: U.S. Department of Health and Human Resources; 2008.
15. De Backer JC, Schep G, Backx FJ, et al. Resistance training in cancer survivors: a systematic review. *Int J Sports Med.* 2009;30(10):703-712.
16. Courneya KS, Segal RJ, Reid RD, et al. Three independent factors predicted adherence in a randomized controlled trial of resistance exercise training among prostate cancer survivors. *J Clin Epidemiol.* June 2004;57(6):571-579.
17. Schmitz KH, Ahmed RL, Troxel A, et al. Weight lifting in women with breast-cancer-related lymphedema. *N Engl J Med.* 2009;361(7):664-673.
18. Galvao DA, Taaffe DR, Spry N, et al. Combined resistance and aerobic exercise program reverses muscle loss in men undergoing androgen suppression therapy for prostate cancer without bone metastases: a randomized controlled trial. *J Clin Oncol.* 2010;28(2):340-347.

19. McNeely ML, Parliament MB, Seikaly H, et al. Effects of exercise on upper extremity pain and dysfunction in head and neck cancer survivors: a randomized controlled trial. *Cancer.* 2008;113(1):214-222.

20. Williams P, Lord SR. Predictors of adherence to a structured exercise program for older women. *Psychol Aging.* 1995;10(4):617-624.

21. Belza B, Walwick J, Shiu-Thornton S, et al. Older adult perspectives on physical activity and exercise: voices from multiple cultures. *Prev Chronic Dis.* 2004;1(4):1-12.

Acupuncture in Geriatric Cancer Care

Theresa Affuso, Jonathan Siman, and Gary Deng

Acupuncture, the most utilized modality of Chinese medicine, evolved and developed over thousands of years. This ancient medicine believed that a vital energy ("qi" in Chinese) flows throughout the body along channels that are called *meridians*. An interruption or obstruction of the body's energy makes one vulnerable to illness. In acupuncture, needles are inserted at specific points along the meridians to regulate the flow of this energy and to produce a therapeutic effect. The application of heat or (in present day) electrical stimulation may be added to the treatment to strengthen its effects (1).

Although the concepts of qi and meridians are inconsistent with our current understanding of human anatomy and physiology, research supports the clinical effects of acupuncture. Recent neuroscience research suggests that it works by modulating the nervous system. Therefore, qi and the meridians may be viewed as metaphors to explain the clinical responses observed by Chinese medicine practitioners during acupuncture treatments (2).

HOW IS ACUPUNCTURE CURRENTLY USED?

Historically, acupuncture was used to prevent and treat many aliments, but it is only in the last few decades that its efficacy has been evaluated with rigorous scientific research methodology. Through these studies and clinical trials, acupuncture's physiologic effects, mechanisms of action, and clinical effectiveness for specific indications have now been documented. Able to induce objective, measurable neurophysiologic changes in animals and humans, acupuncture has been shown in randomized controlled clinical trials to be efficacious for pain, nausea, and vomiting and many other symptoms (3–6). Today, it is perhaps the most accepted modality of Chinese medicine in Western countries, due in large part to this growing body of research.

During the last decade, acupuncture has become increasingly integrated into mainstream cancer care in the United States. Most major comprehensive cancer care centers and many community hospitals have an integrative medicine component that includes acupuncture treatment as a supportive care modality. It is not, however, used as a treatment for disease.

WHAT IS THE EVIDENCE FOR ACUPUNCTURE IN THE CARE OF CANCER PATIENTS?

As yet, there is no evidence that acupuncture has direct effects against cancer, and it should not be used in efforts to treat disease. However, clinical research shows that acupuncture can reduce many physical and emotional symptoms commonly experienced by cancer patients and thereby improve their quality of life. Some of the symptoms benefited by acupuncture include pain, chemotherapy-induced nausea and vomiting (CINV), chemotherapy-induced neuropathy, hot flashes, and xerostomia.

Because **pain** is a common complaint in patients, it is the most thoroughly studied indication for acupuncture. Strong evidence substantiates its use as a supportive treatment for headache, lower back pain, and arthritic pain. Acupuncture is also effective against cancer pain. A randomized placebo controlled trial treated patients experiencing pain (despite stable medication) with auricular acupuncture for 1 month. Pain intensity decreased by 36% at 2 months from baseline in the treatment group, while little pain reduction was seen in the control groups. These results are especially interesting because many of the study patients had neuropathic pain which rarely responds to conventional treatment (7–9). Breast cancer patients taking aromatase inhibitors often experience joint pain. A randomized controlled trial evaluated auricular and full body acupuncture treatment for aromatase inhibitor induced arthralgia in breast cancer patients. Fifty-one postmenopausal women were randomized to receive true or sham acupuncture twice weekly for 6 weeks. Pain severity and pain-related functional interference were significantly reduced by true versus sham acupuncture (10).

CINV is another extensively studied indication for acupuncture. In one investigation, 104 breast cancer patients receiving highly emetogenic chemotherapy were randomized to receive electroacupuncture once daily for 5 days, sham acupuncture, or pharmacotherapy alone. Electroacupuncture significantly reduced the number of episodes of emesis when compared with pharmacology only. In another study, however, the combination of acupuncture and pharmaceuticals commonly used for standard prevention of nausea and vomiting yielded mixed results (11–15).

Several systematic reviews strongly recommend acupuncture for CINV. Diverse acupuncture regimens were employed in the trials included in those reviews, ranging from once daily on the day after chemotherapy to electrical stimulation every 2 hour for 5 days (16,17).

Clinical trials have also shown acupuncture to be effective in the pediatric oncology setting (18,19). Acupressure wristbands, sometimes called sea-bands and commercially available, are placed over and apply constant pressure to the PC6 acupuncture point. This is one of the points in acupuncture shown to reduce nausea. In a randomized controlled trial of 739 patients, applying acupressure to this point on the day of chemotherapy significantly reduced nausea in patients wearing wristbands compared to those with no band controls (20).

Breast or prostate cancer patients undergoing treatment with hormonal therapy may develop severe **hot flashes**. The standard treatment, estrogen or androgen supplementation, is contraindicated in patients with cancer. While several uncontrolled studies suggest that acupuncture may reduce hot flashes in patients with breast or prostate cancer (21–23), some controlled studies have shown mixed results (24,25).

Radiation therapy to the head and neck can damage the salivary glands and consequently cause persistent **dry mouth or xerostomia** in head and neck cancer patients. In a randomized controlled trial of patients who experienced head and neck dysfunction following neck dissection, 58 patients received acupuncture for 4 weeks or usual standard of care (physical therapy, analgesia, or anti-inflammatory drugs). Acupuncture greatly improved the xerostomia and the pain and function of neck and shoulder muscles. The possible neuronal matrix involved was explored in a mechanistic study that used functional MRI (fMRI). In this randomized controlled trial, acupuncture was associated with bilateral activation of the insula and adjacent operculum, changes not seen with the sham acupuncture point. Also, the true acupuncture induced greater saliva production than the sham acupuncture. It may be argued that a trial course of acupuncture (once or twice a week for 4 weeks) is worthwhile in patients with severe dry mouth who fail to respond to other treatments (26–28).

In particular, two studies assessing **gastrointestinal motility** after colorectal surgery and the **prevention of deep vein thrombosis** (DVTs) in elderly patients after gastrointestinal tumor surgery have shown promising results.

A total of 165 patients, about to undergo laparoscopic surgery for colorectal cancer, participated in a study to determine if electroacupuncture could reduce the duration of postoperative ileus and reduce hospital stay. Patients were randomly assigned into three groups. One group received electroacupuncture, one group received sham acupuncture, and one group received usual standard of care. Treatment was once daily from postoperative for four days. Findings: the group that received electroacupuncture had a shorter duration of postoperative ileus and hospital stay after surgery. No such findings were found with the groups receiving sham acupuncture and the usual standard of care (29).

A total of 120 patients, at least 60 years of age and undergoing malignant gastrointestinal tumor surgery, participated in a study to determine if electroacupuncture could reduce the incidence of DVTs. The patients were randomly divided into three groups: one group received the usual standard of care, one group wore compression stockings, and one group received electroacupuncture stimulation. Hemorrheologic parameters were measured and compared before and after surgery. Findings: the group that received the electrical acupoint stimulation showed a significant difference in blood viscosity and blood flow. By speeding up the blood flow in patients' lower limbs, electroacupuncture stimulation shows a great potential to prevent the incidence of symptomless postoperative DVTs in elderly patients (30).

Although some geriatric patients are included in clinical trials, there are few studies that concentrate solely on geriatric oncology patients who are receiving acupuncture. However, acupuncture studies on the general geriatric population have shown positive results. Some of these studies investigated acupuncture's effect on joint pain, gait disturbance, and Alzheimer disease (31–33).

Acupuncture studies on the general population have shown that it decreases **constipation, insomnia, anxiety, tinnitus, and nocturia** (34–38). These symptoms are common complaints of the geriatric patient, and acupuncture may provide a safe option to pharmaceuticals for relief in these areas.

WHAT ARE THE POTENTIAL RISKS OF ACUPUNCTURE?

Acupuncture is generally safe when it is performed by qualified practitioners. During treatment, the patient may feel a light needle pricking sensation and then a sensation of heaviness or soreness at the needle insertion site. The needles are retained for approximately 30 minutes and then removed. There is usually no visible sign of skin penetration, and bleeding (if any) is minor (39).

Patients should be advised to receive acupuncture treatment from practitioners who are professionally trained, properly credentialed, and experienced in treating cancer patients. The practitioners should exercise clean needle techniques and universal precautions.

GUIDELINES, PRECAUTIONS, AND PROFESSIONAL REQUIREMENTS

Given that cancer patients undergoing active treatment may be prone to infection or bleeding, and that cancer or cancer treatment may distort anatomical structures, special safety precautions related to acupuncture are required. Acupuncture should not be performed on patients with absolute neutrophil counts less than 500/µL, platelets less than 20,000/µL, INR greater than 4.0, new-onset cardiac arrhythmia, or mental status changes. Patients with recent stem cell or organ transplantation need to obtain their physician's approval before acupuncture is performed. For geriatric patients with comorbidities, the same guidelines and precautions would be followed.

Licensed acupuncturists have masters' degrees in acupuncture or acupuncture and Oriental medicine. Their training involves 3 to 4 years of rigorous coursework and more than 3,000 hours of study. The majority of physicians who perform acupuncture are certified acupuncturists with approximately 300 hours of training (40).

CONCLUSION

In general, clinical trials should attempt to include more of the geriatric population. Many studies have shown the efficacy of using acupuncture to reduce the side effects of cancer treatment (pain, CINV, chemotherapy-induced neuropathy, hot flashes, and xerostomia). It is now time for trials to focus on the geriatric oncology population and what benefits these patients may derive from acupuncture for symptom control during cancer treatment to health maintenance afterwards.

TAKE HOME POINTS

1. Studies have shown acupuncture to be a safe and effective modality for treating many of the side effects of cancer treatment.
2. Physicians should encourage their geriatric cancer patients to try acupuncture for symptom control.
3. More funding should be allotted for clinical trials that actively seek geriatric cancer patients to be included in acupuncture and oncology studies.

REFERENCES

1. Deng G, Cassileth BR. Acupuncture in cancer care. *Oncology (Williston Park)*. July 2011;25(suppl 7 Nurse Ed):21-23, 30-31.
2. Longhurst JC. Defining meridians: a modern basis of understanding. *J Acupunct Meridian Stud*. 2010;3(2):67-74.
3. Kaptchuk TJ. Acupuncture: theory, efficacy and practice. *Ann Intern Med*. 2002;136(5):374-383.
4. Han JS. Acupuncture and endorphins. *Neurosci Lett*. 2004;361(1-3):258-261.
5. NIH Consensus Conference. Acupuncture. *JAMA*. 1998;280(17):1518-1524.
6. O 'Regan D, Filshie J. Acupuncture and cancer. *Auton Neurosci*. 2010;157(1-2):96-100.
7. Paley CA, Johnson MI, Tashani OA, et al. Acupuncture for cancer pain in adults. *Cochrane Database Syst Rev*. 2011;(1):CD007753.
8. Hopkins Hollis AS. Acupuncture as a treatment modality for the management of cancer pain: the state of the science. *Oncol Nurs Forum*. 2010;37(5):E344-E348.
9. Cassileth BR, Keefe FJ. Integrative and behavioral approaches to the treatment of cancer-related neuropathic pain. *Oncologist*. 2010;15(suppl 2):19-23.
10. Alimi D, Rubino C, Pichard-Leandri E, et al. Analgesic effect of auricular acupuncture for cancer pain: a randomized, blinded, controlled trial. *J Clin Oncol*. 2003;21(22):4120-4126.
11. Ezzo JM, Richardson MA, Vickers A, et al. Acupuncture-point stimulation for chemotherapy-induced nausea or vomiting. *Cochrane Database Syst Rev*. 2006;(2): CD002285.
12. Lee A, Done ML. Stimulation of the wrist acupuncture point P6 for preventing postoperative nausea and vomiting. *Cochrane Database Syst Rev*. 2004;(3):CD003281.
13. Shen J, Wenger N, Glaspy J, et al. Electroacupuncture for control of myeloablative chemotherapy-induced emesis: a randomized controlled trial. *JAMA*. 2000;284(21): 2755-2761.
14. Josefson A, Kreuter M. Acupuncture to reduce nausea during chemotherapy treatment of rheumatic diseases. *Rheumatology (Oxford)*. 2003;42(10):1149-1154.
15. Streitberger K, Friedrich-Rust M, Bardenheuer H, et al. Effect of acupuncture compared with placebo-acupuncture at P6 as additional antiemetic prophylaxis in high-dose chemotherapy and autologous peripheral blood stem cell transplantation: a randomized controlled single-blind trial. *Clin Cancer Res*. 2003;9(7):2538-2544.
16. Ernst E. Acupuncture: what does the most reliable evidence tell us? *J Pain Symptom Manage*. 2004;37(4):709-714.
17. Naeim A, Dy SM, Lorenz KA, et al. Evidence-based recommendations for cancer nausea and vomiting. *J Clin Oncol*. 2008;26(23):3903-3910.
18. Gottschling S, Reindl TK, Meyer S, et al. Acupuncture to alleviate chemotherapy-induced nausea and vomiting in pediatric oncology—a randomized multicenter crossover pilot trial. *Klin Padiatr*. 2008;220(6):365-370.
19. Gardani G, Cerrone R, Biella C, et al. A progress study of 100 cancer patients treated by acupressure for chemotherapy-induced vomiting after failure with the pharmacological approach. *Minerva Med*. 2007;98(6):665-668.
20. Roscoe JA, Morrow GR, Hickok JT, et al. The efficacy of acupressure and acu-stimulation wrist bands for the relief of chemotherapy-induced nausea and vomiting: a University of Rochester Cancer Center Community Clinical Oncology Program multicenter study. *J Pain Symptom Manage*. 2003;26(2):731-742.
21. Harding C, Harris A, Chadwick D. Auricular acupuncture: a novel treatment for vasomotor symptoms associated with luteinizing-hormone releasing hormone agonist treatment for prostate cancer. *BJU Int*. 2009;103(2):186-190.

22. Dong H, Ludicke F, Comte I, et al. An exploratory pilot study of acupuncture on the quality of life and reproductive hormone secretion in menopausal women. *J Altern Complement Med.* 2001;7(6):651-658.

23. Porzio G, Trapasso T, Martelli S, et al. Acupuncture in the treatment of menopause-related symptoms in women taking tamoxifen. *Tumori.* 2002;88(2):128-130.

24. Carpenter JS, Neal JG. Other complementary and alternative modalities: acupuncture, magnets, reflexology and homeopathy. *Am J Med.* 2005;118(suppl 12B):109-117.

25. Lee MS, Shin BC, Ernst E. Acupuncture for treating menopausal hot flushes: a systematic review. *Climacteric.* 2009;12(1):17-25.

26. Pfister DG, Cassileth BR, Deng GE, et al. Acupuncture for pain and dysfunction after neck dissection: results of a randomized controlled trial. *J Clin Oncol.* 2010;28 (15):2565-2570.

27. Deng G, Hou BL, Holodny Al, et al. Functional magnetic resonance imaging (fMRI) changes and saliva production associated with acupuncture at point LI-2: a randomized controlled study. *BMC Complement Altern Med.* 2008;8:37.

28. OSullivan EM, Higginson IJ. Clinical effectiveness and safety of acupuncture in the treatment of irradiation-induced xerostomia in patients with head and neck cancer: a systematic review. *Acupunct Med.* 2010;28(4):191-199.

29. Ng SS, Leung WW, Mak TW, et al. Electroacupuncture reduces the duration of postoperative ileus after laparoscopic surgery for colorectal cancer. *Gastroenterology.* February 2013;144(2):307-313.

30. Hou LL, Yao LW, Niu QM, et al. Preventive effect of electrical acupoint stimulation on lower limb thrombosis: a prospective study of elderly patents after malignant gastrointestinal tumor surgery. *Cancer Nurs.* March-April 2013;36(2):139-44.

31. Çevik C, Anil A, İşeri S. Effective chronic low back and knee pain treatment with acupuncture in geriatric patients. *J Back Musculoskeletal Rehabil.* 2015;28(3):517-520.

32. Fukuda S, Kuriyama N, Egawa M. Acupuncture for gait disturbance in Parkinson's disease: immediate effects of acupuncture treatment *J Am Geriatric Soc.* October 2015;63(10):2189-2190.

33. Liang P, Wang Z, Qian T, Li K. Acupuncture stimulation of Liver 3 and LI 4 modulates the default mode network activity in Alzheimer's disease. *Am J Alzheimers Dis Other Demen.* December 2014;29(8):739-748.

34. Liu J, Zhou W, Lv H, et al. Law of the meridian abnormality based on the effectiveness of electroacupuncture for severe functional constipation. *Zhongguo Zhen Jiu.* August 2015;35(8):785-790.

35. Zhao K. Acupuncture for the treatment of insomnia. *Int Rev Neurobiol.* 2013;111:217-234.

36. Sakatani K, Fujii M, Takemura N, Hirayama T. Effects of acupuncture on anxiety levels and prefrontal cortex activity measured by near infrared spectroscopy: a pilot study. *Adv Exp Med Biol.* 2016;876:297-302.

37. Laureano MR, Onishi ET, Bressan RA, et al. The effectiveness of acupuncture as a treatment for tinnitus: a randomized controlled trial using 99mTc-ECD SPECT. *Eur Radiol.* January 8, 2016;26(9):3234-3242.

38. Yuan Z, He C, Yan S, et al. Acupuncture for overactive bladder in female adults: a randomized controlled trial. *World J Urol.* September 2015; 33(9):1303-1308.

39. Melchart D, Weidenhammer W, Streng A, et al. Prospective investigation of adverse effects of acupuncture in 97,733 patients. *Arch Intern Med.* 2004;164(1):104-105.

40. Lu C, He W, Zhao YK. Introduction and analysis in acupuncture education and qualification examination system in U.S.A. *Zhongguo Zhen Jiu,* December 2013;33(12): 1131-1134.

Complementary Therapies and Integrative Medicine

Gary Deng

Complementary therapies, though not historically part of mainstream Western medicine, are increasingly used together with usual clinical care to reduce symptoms and improve quality of life (QoL). Many complementary therapies take a holistic approach to health. Applying this holistic approach and a judicious selection of complementary therapies to usual care is called *integrative medicine*, or *integrative oncology* when applied to cancer care. By optimizing their nutrition, physical activity, stress management, circadian rhythms, and physical and psychological environment, patients can improve their QoL, build resilience, minimize interruption of treatment, and thus improve survival. In the geriatric population, complementary therapies become especially important. Geriatric patients are often on many medications for multiple comorbidities. These medications, combined with impaired drug metabolism in geriatric patients, lead to increased adverse events, such as cognitive impairment, falls and fractures, and increased hospital stays. As a result, nonpharmacologic interventions should be considered when effective and available. In 2015, the Joint Commission, the largest accreditation body for health care organizations in the United States, clarified the importance of using nonpharmacologic strategies such as relaxation therapy, massage, and acupuncture in pain management (1). Complementary therapies also address modifiable risk factors such as hypertension, obesity, stress, inactivity, and poor sleep quality that are associated with other chronic diseases in addition to cancer. Clinical practice guidelines (2,3) have rated the levels of evidence for the most frequently used therapies, but the science on optimizing their use continues to evolve. This chapter provides a brief overview of the practical applications of complementary therapies in elderly cancer patients to improve QoL, activities of daily living, cognition, sleep, and psychological profiles, and to reduce functional decline and disability.

Tai chi and *qigong* are gentle and fluid mind–body movement therapies that have been widely studied in elderly and frail populations. They are associated with reductions in chronic disease risk factors such as blood pressure, body mass index (BMI), and stress (4,5), as well as improved balance (6,7), sleep (8) and physical functioning (5,9), and reduced fall risk (6). These practices are particularly suitable due to their lower energy cost and slow movement patterns (10). In a randomized controlled trial of senior cancer survivors with physical limitations, tai chi significantly lowered systolic blood pressure and area-under-the-curve cortisol (11).

Yoga incorporates specific postures and movements with coordinated breathing. When adapted for elderly populations, gentle and restorative poses are emphasized. Among older cancer survivors, it reduced fatigue and global side effect burden (scores comprising pain, fatigue, nausea, sleep problems, depression, dyspnea, memory loss, and concentration difficulties) (12), and improved sleep quality while reducing sleep medication use (13). Knowledgeable, attentive instructors should ensure that postures risky for patients with limitations are avoided.

Mindfulness meditation refers to a style of meditation that emphasizes attention on the present moment with an open and accepting attitude. It has been studied substantially in cancer populations and shown to reduce chronic pain, depression, and anxiety while improving skills such as self-regulation (14), but few of these studies have been done in elderly survivors. A randomized trial in patients 75 years of age and above suggests its utility for chronic insomnia, depression, and anxiety (15). Other types of mind–body therapy with similar demonstrated efficacy include *stress management, relaxation training*, and *hypnosis* (16).

Music therapy takes several forms, such as passive listening to reduce procedural anxiety, or active patient participation with guidance from a trained therapist. In the latter case, goals may include enhanced self-expression, relaxation, or engagement with others. Music therapy improves well-being (17) and sleep quality (18), and reduces pain and anxiety (19,20) in a variety of populations, including critical care patients. It may also reduce respiratory rate, systolic blood pressure, and the use of sedatives and analgesics (21). Moreover, this modality may resonate with patients seeking connection with cultures, traditions, or memories that are uniquely important to them, providing a profound shift in an experience of well-being.

Massage and other touch therapies have demonstrated immediate benefits among patients with advanced cancers, including reduced pain and improved respiratory rate, range of motion, and mood (22,23). Reflexology, a type of therapy that focuses on massage of the feet, may be especially useful among frail patients, and may decrease dyspnea (24), pain, and anxiety while reducing postoperative opioid use (25). In addition, massage as well as passive music therapy may better suit patients with greater illness burden than therapies requiring more active participation.

Acupuncture, discussed in Chapter 35, is beneficial for chronic pain (26,27), chemotherapy-induced nausea and vomiting (28), radiation-induced xerostomia (29,30), fatigue, and sleep disturbance (31). Preliminary data also suggest benefits for neuropathic pain (32) and hot flashes (33). Though generally safe when performed by therapists trained in working with cancer patients, caution should be exercised in the setting of anticoagulant therapies, pacemakers, and conditions such as thrombocytopenia.

Other chapters in this text discuss *nutrition* and *exercise* (Chapter 34), but here we provide a brief synopsis from an integrative oncology perspective. There is a high prevalence of suboptimal health behaviors among older, long-term survivors who are interested in lifestyle modification (34), and the positive effects of physical activity and a healthy diet in this population are well established. A Mediterranean-style diet may improve cognitive function and psychological well-being in older adults (35), and the incorporation of whole foods while reducing the amounts of processed foods and sugars to the extent possible is encouraged. At the same time, the desire to seek a safe and natural cure may lead to inappropriate or unmonitored use of dietary supplements or botanicals. In addition to clinical supplementation where needed, patients should be screened for unsupervised dietary supplement use, which is associated with higher mortality (36) and has the potential for herb–drug interactions including reduced efficacy of cancer therapies. *AboutHerbs.com* is a free and comprehensive database produced by our institution that describes supplements popular among cancer survivors and their possible herb–drug interactions.

Exercise for older cancer survivors should be individualized to optimize participation, safety, and efficacy (37). A supervisory approach can also instill self-efficacy and behavioral processes for change that translate into continued successful home-based practice (38). Data from 641 breast, prostate, and colorectal cancer survivors age 65 years and above suggest that even light-intensity activities may reduce rates of physical function decline in those who are unable to participate in moderate-level intensity activities (39).

Integrative oncology takes a patient-centered, proactive, and holistic approach to cancer care, and its use of complementary modalities produces both sidestream and downstream benefits. For example, impaired swallowing caused by xerostomia may increase anxiety and fear, causing a subsequent avoidance of oral intake that leads to malnutrition, isolation, and depression (40). Unresolved nausea and vomiting can aggravate cachexia, lethargy, and weakness and cause emotional distress (28). The use of acupuncture to treat such symptoms can thus have a significant impact on the patient trajectory. Likewise, structured movement therapies may positively modify the strongest predictors of improved physical functioning, BMI and self-efficacy, in older overweight or obese cancer survivors (41). With respect to emotional and mental symptoms, even though more than 4 in 10 elderly cancer patients experience them, only a fraction report a desire for formal psychological help (42). Here too, complementary therapies may offer practical, effective, and safe approaches, which may also reduce the need for medications.

As the number of older cancer survivors increases, more patients will likely experience long-lasting negative effects that require multimodal supportive care. Oncologists should engage patients in a dialogue about their supportive care needs and guide them through active referral to evidence-based integrative therapies that address these symptoms (see Table 36.1). An increasing number of cancer centers and hospitals have made integrative medicine programs available to patients. In addition, because symptom etiologies are often multifactorial, patients may need to employ several strategies, and their needs may shift over time, thereby requiring monitoring and reassessment. Hence, complementary therapies and integrative medicine are dynamic components of successful cancer care, and should be a fundamental component of palliative care and survivorship toolkits.

TABLE 36.1 Evidence-Based Complementary Therapies Appropriate for Geriatric Oncology Patients

Modality	Symptoms or Conditions That Can Be Addressed	
Tai chi and qigong (4–11)	■ Balance ■ Body mass index ■ Fall risk ■ Fear of falling ■ Gait	■ Hypertension ■ Physical activity ■ Self-awareness ■ Sleep ■ Stress
Yoga (adapted to address limitations/comorbidities such as osteoporosis) (12,13)	■ Anxiety ■ Concentration ■ Depression ■ Dyspnea ■ Fatigue	■ Memory loss ■ Pain ■ Reduced sedative use ■ Self-awareness ■ Sleep problems
Mindfulness meditation, stress management, relaxation training, hypnosis (14–16)	■ Anxiety ■ Chronic symptoms ■ Depression ■ Emotional self-regulation	■ Insomnia ■ Pain ■ Self-awareness
Music therapy (17–21)	■ Anxiety ■ Cognition ■ Distress ■ Isolation ■ Pain	■ Procedural anxiety ■ Reduced sedative/analgesic use ■ Respiratory rate ■ Sleep disturbance ■ Systolic blood pressure
Massage (22–25)	■ Anxiety ■ Circulation ■ Dyspnea ■ Mood	■ Pain ■ Range of motion ■ Reduced medication use ■ Respiratory rate
Acupuncture (26–33) Contraindications may include anticoagulant therapies, pacemakers, and conditions such as thrombocytopenia	■ Chemotherapy-induced nausea/vomiting ■ Chronic pain ■ Fatigue	■ Hot flashes ■ Neuropathic pain ■ Radiotherapy-induced xerostomia ■ Sleep disturbance
Exercise (34,37–39)	Optimize with a supervisory approach and goals of increasing performance status, developing a safe home-based practice, and encouraging even light-intensity exercise where possible.	
Nutrition (35,36)	■ Encourage whole foods; reduce processed foods and avoid excessive amount of sugars and trans fats where possible ■ Treat poor nutritional status ■ Screen for unsupervised use of dietary supplements and botanicals that may produce adverse effects or reduce treatment efficacy (see *AboutHerbs.com*)	

TAKE HOME POINTS

1. With earlier detection and better treatments, the number of cancer survivors has increased significantly, and more patients will likely experience long-lasting negative effects that require multimodal supportive care that includes complementary therapies.

2. The Joint Commission and several cancer clinical practice guidelines underscore the importance of using nonpharmacologic strategies, including complementary therapies such as relaxation therapy, massage, and acupuncture, for symptom management.

3. Evidence-based complementary therapies in the geriatric population help to address polypharmacy, poor performance and nutritional status, psychological disturbances, treatment-related symptoms, and other comorbidities.

4. Oncologists should engage patients in a dialogue about their supportive care needs and guide them through active referral to appropriate complementary therapies to ensure safety, efficacy, and continuity of care. Geriatricians should build a panel of trusted complementary therapists to whom they can refer patients.

5. Because symptom etiologies are often multifactorial, integrative supportive care needs may be multimodal and shift over time, thereby requiring monitoring and reassessment.

REFERENCES

1. The Joint Commission. Clarification of the pain management standard: clarification to standard PC.01.02.07. *Jt Comm Perspect.* 2014;34(11):11.

2. Deng GE, Rausch SM, Jones LW, et al. Complementary therapies and integrative medicine in lung cancer: diagnosis and management of lung cancer, 3rd ed: American College of Chest Physicians evidence-based clinical practice guidelines. *Chest.* 2013;143(suppl 5):e420S-e436S.

3. Greenlee H, Balneaves LG, Carlson LE, et al. Clinical practice guidelines on the use of integrative therapies as supportive care in patients treated for breast cancer. *J Natl Cancer Inst Monogr.* 2014;2014(50):346-358.

4. Sun J, Buys N. Community-based mind-body meditative Tai Chi program and its effects on improvement of blood pressure, weight, renal function, serum lipoprotein, and quality of life in Chinese adults with hypertension. *Am J Cardiol.* 2015;116(7):1076-1081.

5. Jahnke RA, Larkey LK, Rogers C. Dissemination and benefits of a replicable Tai Chi and Qigong program for older adults. *Geriatr Nurs.* 2010;31(4):272-280.

6. Li F, Harmer P, Fitzgerald K, et al. Tai chi and postural stability in patients with Parkinson's disease. *N Engl J Med.* 2012;366(6):511-519.

7. Yang Y, Verkuilen JV, Rosengren KS, et al. Effect of combined Taiji and Qigong training on balance mechanisms: a randomized controlled trial of older adults. *Med Sci Monit.* 2007;13(8):Cr339-Cr348.

8. Li F, Fisher KJ, Harmer P, et al. Tai chi and self-rated quality of sleep and daytime sleepiness in older adults: a randomized controlled trial. *J Am Geriatr Soc.* 2004;52(6):892-900.

9. Manor B, Lough M, Gagnon MM, et al. Functional benefits of tai chi training in senior housing facilities. *J Am Geriatr Soc.* 2014;62(8):1484-1489.

10. Winters-Stone K. Tai Ji Quan for the aging cancer survivor: mitigating the accelerated development of disability, falls, and cardiovascular disease from cancer treatment. *J Sport Health Sci.* 2014;3(1):52-57.

11. Campo RA, Light KC, O'Connor K, et al. Blood pressure, salivary cortisol, and inflammatory cytokine outcomes in senior female cancer survivors enrolled in a tai chi chih randomized controlled trial. *J Cancer Surviv.* 2015;9(1):115-125.

12. Sprod LK, Fernandez ID, Janelsins MC, et al. Effects of yoga on cancer-related fatigue and global side-effect burden in older cancer survivors. *J Geriatr Oncol.* 2015;6(1):8-14.

13. Mustian KM, Sprod LK, Janelsins M, et al. Multicenter, randomized controlled trial of yoga for sleep quality among cancer survivors. *J Clin Oncol.* 2013;31(26):3233-3241.

14. Gotink RA, Chu P, Busschbach JJ, et al. Standardised mindfulness-based interventions in healthcare: an overview of systematic reviews and meta-analyses of RCTs. *PLOS ONE.* 2015;10(4):e0124344.

15. Zhang JX, Liu XH, Xie XH, et al. Mindfulness-based stress reduction for chronic insomnia in adults older than 75 years: a randomized, controlled, single-blind clinical trial. *Explore (NY).* 2015;11(3):180-185.

16. Sheinfeld Gorin S, Krebs P, Badr H, et al. Meta-analysis of psychosocial interventions to reduce pain in patients with cancer. *J Clin Oncol.* 2012;30(5):539-547.

17. Chang YS, Chu H, Yang CY, et al. The efficacy of music therapy for people with dementia: a meta-analysis of randomised controlled trials. *J Clin Nurs.* 2015;24(23-24):3425-3440.

18. Jespersen KV, Koenig J, Jennum P, Vuust P. Music for insomnia in adults. *Cochrane Database Syst Rev.* 2015;8:Cd010459.

19. Kim Y, Evangelista LS, Park YG. Anxiolytic effects of music interventions in patients receiving in-center hemodialysis: a systematic review and meta-analysis. *Nephrol Nurs J.* 2015;42(4):339-347; quiz 348.

20. Hole J, Hirsch M, Ball E, Meads C. Music as an aid for postoperative recovery in adults: a systematic review and meta-analysis. *Lancet.* 2015;386(10004):1659-1671.

21. Bradt J, Dileo C. Music interventions for mechanically ventilated patients. *Cochrane Database Syst Rev.* 2014;12:Cd006902.

22. Kutner JS, Smith MC, Corbin L, et al. Massage therapy versus simple touch to improve pain and mood in patients with advanced cancer: a randomized trial. *Ann Intern Med.* 2008;149(6):369-379.

23. Field T. Knee osteoarthritis pain in the elderly can be reduced by massage therapy, yoga and tai chi: a review. *Complement Ther Clin Pract.* 2016;22:87-92.

24. Wyatt G, Sikorskii A, Rahbar MH, et al. Health-related quality-of-life outcomes: reflexology trial with patients with advanced-stage breast cancer. *Oncol Nurs Forum.* 2012;39(6):568-577.

25. Tsay SL, Chen HL, Chen SC, et al. Effects of reflexotherapy on acute postoperative pain and anxiety among patients with digestive cancer. *Cancer Nurs.* 2008;31(2):109-115.

26. Vickers AJ, Cronin AM, Maschino AC, et al. Acupuncture for chronic pain: individual patient data meta-analysis. *Arch Intern Med.* 2012;172(19):1444-1453.

27. Vickers AJ, Linde K. Acupuncture for chronic pain. *JAMA.* 2014;311(9):955-956.

28. Ezzo J, Vickers A, Richardson MA, et al. Acupuncture-point stimulation for chemotherapy-induced nausea and vomiting. *J Clin Oncol.* 2005;23(28):7188-7198.

29. Simcock R, Fallowfield L, Monson K, et al. ARIX: a randomised trial of acupuncture v. oral care sessions in patients with chronic xerostomia following treatment of head and neck cancer. *Ann Oncol.* 2013;24(3):776-783.

30. Pfister DG, Cassileth BR, Deng GE, et al. Acupuncture for pain and dysfunction after neck dissection: results of a randomized controlled trial. *J Clin Oncol.* 2010;28(15):2565-2570.

31. Tao WW, Jiang H, Tao XM, et al. Effects of acupuncture, tuina, tai chi, qigong, and traditional Chinese medicine five element music therapy on symptom management and quality of life for cancer patients: a meta-analysis. *J Pain Symptom Manage.* February 12, 2016;51(4):728-747. doi:10.1016/j.jpainsymman.2015.11.027.

32. Pachman DR, Watson JC, Loprinzi CL. Therapeutic strategies for cancer treatment related peripheral neuropathies. *Curr Treat Options Oncol.* 2014;15(4):567-580.

33. Frisk JW, Hammar ML, Ingvar M, et al. How long do the effects of acupuncture on hot flashes persist in cancer patients? *Support Care Cancer.* 2014;22(5):1409-1415.

34. Mosher CE, Sloane R, Morey MC, et al. Associations between lifestyle factors and quality of life among older long-term breast, prostate, and colorectal cancer survivors. *Cancer.* 2009;115(17):4001-4009.

35. Knight A, Bryan J, Wilson C, et al. A randomised controlled intervention trial evaluating the efficacy of a Mediterranean dietary pattern on cognitive function and psychological well-being in healthy older adults: the MedLey study. *BMC Geriatr.* 2015; 5:55.

36. Inoue-Choi M, Greenlee H, Oppeneer SJ, Robien K. The association between postdiagnosis dietary supplement use and total mortality differs by diet quality among older female cancer survivors. *Cancer Epidemiol Biomarkers Prev.* 2014;23(5):865-875.

37. Klepin HD, Mohile SG, Mihalko S. Exercise for older cancer patients: feasible and helpful? *Interdiscip Top Gerontol.* 2013;38:146-157.

38. Loprinzi PD, Cardinal BJ, Si Q, et al. Theory-based predictors of follow-up exercise behavior after a supervised exercise intervention in older breast cancer survivors. *Support Care Cancer.* 2012;20(10):2511-2521.

39. Blair CK, Morey MC, Desmond RA, et al. Light-intensity activity attenuates functional decline in older cancer survivors. *Med Sci Sports Exerc.* 2014; 46(7):1375-1383.

40. Vesey S. Dysphagia and quality of life. *Br J Community Nurs.* 2013; (suppl):S14-S19.

41. Morey MC, Blair CK, Sloane R, et al. Group trajectory analysis helps to identify older cancer survivors who benefit from distance-based lifestyle interventions. *Cancer.* 2015;121(24):4433-4440.

42. Dubruille S, Libert Y, Merckaert I, et al. The prevalence and implications of elderly inpatients' desire for a formal psychological help at the start of cancer treatment. *Psychooncology.* 2015;24(3):294-301.

Index